T0074568

Romantic Metasubjectivity through Schelling and Jung

Romantic Metasubjectivity through Schelling and Jung: Rethinking the Romantic Subject explores the remarkable intellectual isomorphism between the philosophy of Friedrich Schelling and Carl Jung's analytical psychology in order to offer a crucial and original corrective to the "reflection theory" of subjectivity.

Arguing that the reflection theory of the subject does not do justice to the full compass of Romantic thinking about the human being, *Romantic Metasubjectivity* sees human identity as neither discursive aftereffect nor centred around a self-transparent "I" but rather as constellated around the centripetal force of what Novalis calls "The Self of one's self." The author begins with a unique reading of Schelling's early *Naturphilosophie* as primal site rather than Freudian scene, thinking this site through his *Philosophical Inquiries Into the Nature of Human Freedom* to *The Ages of the World*. Reading Jungian metapsychology and its core concepts as therapeutic amplifications of Schelling, the author articulates an intellectual counter-transference in which Schelling and Jung contemporise each other. The book then demonstrates how Romantic metasubjectivity operates in the libidinal matrix of Romantic poetry through readings of William Wordsworth's *The Prelude* and Percy Shelley's *Prometheus Unbound*. The book concludes with a discussion of the hit TV series *Breaking Bad* as a "case study" of the challenges Romantic metasubjectivity raises for fundamental ethical dilemmas which confront us in the twenty-first century.

Romantic Metasubjectivity is a highly original work of scholarship and will appeal to students and scholars in German Idealism, Romanticism, philosophy, psychoanalysis, theory, Jung studies, and those with an interest in contemporary theories of the subject.

Gord Barentsen received his Ph.D. in English from Western University, London, Canada. His areas of research are Romantic philosophy and literature, psychoanalysis, philosophy, and theory, and he is a founding member of the North American Schelling Society. He currently resides in the suburbs of Melbourne, Australia.

Philosophy & Psychoanalysis book series
Jon Mills
Series editor

Philosophy & Psychoanalysis is dedicated to current developments and cutting-edge research in the philosophical sciences, phenomenology, hermeneutics, existentialism, logic, semiotics, cultural studies, social criticism, and the humanities that engage and enrich psychoanalytic thought through philosophical rigor. With the philosophical turn in psychoanalysis comes a new era of theoretical research that revisits past paradigms while invigorating new approaches to theoretical, historical, contemporary, and applied psychoanalysis. No subject or discipline is immune from psychoanalytic reflection within a philosophical context including psychology, sociology, anthropology, politics, the arts, religion, science, culture, physics, and the nature of morality. Philosophical approaches to psychoanalysis may stimulate new areas of knowledge that have conceptual and applied value beyond the consulting room reflective of greater society at large. In the spirit of pluralism, *Philosophy & Psychoanalysis* is open to any theoretical school in philosophy and psychoanalysis that offers novel, scholarly, and important insights in the way we come to understand our world.

Titles in this series:

Humanizing Evil
Psychoanalytic, philosophical and clinical perspectives
Edited by Ronald C Naso and Jon Mills

Inventing God
Psychology of belief and the rise of secular spirituality
Jon Mills

Jung's Ethics
Moral psychology and his cure of souls
Dan Merkur, Edited by Jon Mills

Temporality and Shame
Perspectives from psychoanalysis and philosophy
Edited by Ladson Hinton and Hessel Willemsen

Progress in Psychoanalysis
Envisioning the future of the profession
Edited by Steven D. Axelrod, Ronald C. Naso and Larry M. Rosenberg

Lacan on Psychosis
From theory to praxis
Edited by Jon Mills and David L. Downing

Ethics and Attachment
How we make moral judgments
Aner Govrin

Jung and Philosophy
Edited by Jon Mills

Innovations in Psychoanalysis:
Originality, development, progress
Edited by Aner Govrin and Jon Mills

Holism
Possibilities and problems
Edited by Christian McMillan, Roderick Main and David Henderson

Romantic Metasubjectivity through Schelling and Jung

Rethinking the Romantic Subject

Gord Barentsen

Routledge
Taylor & Francis Group

LONDON AND NEW YORK

First published 2020
by Routledge
2 Park Square, Milton Park, Abingdon, Oxon OX14 4RN

and by Routledge
52 Vanderbilt Avenue, New York, NY 10017

Routledge is an imprint of the Taylor & Francis Group, an informa business

British Library Cataloguing-in-Publication Data
A catalogue record for this book is available from the British Library

Library of Congress Cataloging-in-Publication Data
A catalog record has been requested for this book

ISBN: 978-0-367-43929-3 (hbk)
ISBN: 978-0-367-43928-6 (pbk)
ISBN: 978-1-003-00652-7 (ebk)

Typeset in Times New Roman
by Nova Techset Private Limited, Bengaluru & Chennai, India

Contents

Acknowledgements

I begin as Schelling and Jung both have done – by returning to the past. At York University, I thank Ian Balfour for stoking a strong enthusiasm for Romanticism many moons ago. Ted Goossen's honesty and encouragement at an early stage helped build my momentum toward graduate school (even though I didn't specialise in Asian religions and learn Sanskrit). At Western University, first and foremost, I must thank my supervisors Joel Faflak and Tilottama Rajan – scholars, colleagues, and friends who demonstrated to me time and again integrity, understanding, and seemingly infinite patience – sometimes in the face of the very worst from others. Their generosity and shared sense of intellectual adventure put them in a class of their own. Steven Bruhm and Kim Solga also deserve mention as two enthusiastic and talented lecturers who helped me develop personally and professionally. Colleagues Jeff King and Christopher Bundock provided me with guidance and friendship during arduous periods of writing. I also express my gratitude to the Ontario Ministry of Training, Colleges, and Universities, which awarded me two Ontario Graduate Scholarships, and to the Faculty of Arts and Humanities for awarding me a Mary Routledge Fellowship.

Other scholars and writers deserve mention for their generosity. Iain Hamilton Grant provided me with a copy of his unpublished translation of Schelling's *On The World Soul*; Jung's grandson Andreas Jung lent me his personal copy of Jung's *Bibliothek-Katalog* for my research; and Joan Steigerwald made her draft work on degeneration available to me. Joe Hughes and Justin Clemens gave me a very warm welcome in Melbourne, Australia, for which I am also deeply grateful.

On the family side of things, I am deeply grateful for the support of my brother David Barentsen; this book is also dedicated to Willem (Bill) and Corre Barentsen, as well as my parents Nona and Stan, all four of whom understood the value of a good education and would have been proud. In Australia, Seven reminded me at all the right times – and as only a feline can – of the importance of nonhuman communication. And last, but absolutely farthest from least…this is for my wife Carolyn, whose understanding, encouragement, patience, and love are the closest of anything in this world to the unconditioned.

Was man nicht erfliegen kann, muß man erhinken.

List of abbreviations

Full information for abbreviated works can be found in the Bibliography.

AF: Schlegel, *Athenaeum Fragments* (in *Philosophical Fragments* [1798–1800])
Ages: Schelling, *Ages of the World* (1815)
Beyond: Freud, *Beyond the Pleasure Principle* (1920)
CF: Schlegel, *Critical Fragments* (in *Philosophical Fragments* [1798–1800])
DR: Deleuze, *Difference and Repetition* (1968)
FO: Schelling, *First Outline of a System of the Philosophy of Nature* (1799)
Freedom: Schelling, *Philosophical Investigations into the Essence of Human Freedom* (1809)
GPP: Schelling, *The Grounding of Positive Philosophy: The Berlin Lectures* (1841)
HCI: Schelling, *Historical-Critical Introduction to the Philosophy of Mythology* (1842)
Ideas: Schlegel, *Ideas* (in *Philosophical Fragments* [1798–1800])
Notes: Novalis, *Notes for a Romantic Encyclopedia* (1798–1799)
"NPS":   Schelling, "On the Nature of Philosophy as Science" (1821)
STI: Schelling, *System of Transcendental Idealism* (1800)
Symbols: Jung, *Symbols of Transformation* (1911–1912/1952)

Introduction
A word to the "Why"s

There is a poetry whose essence is the relation between ideal and real, and which should therefore, following philosophical language, be called transcendental poetry. [...] [T]his poetry should describe itself, and be always and everywhere poetry and the poetry of poetry. (Schlegel, *Athenaeum Fragment* #238; my trans.)

The highest task of education is [...] to be at the same time the Self of one's self. Accordingly, the less strange is our lack of full understanding and feeling for others. (Novalis, *Miscellaneous Remarks* #28; my trans.)

This book develops *Romantic metasubjectivity* as a model of identity more faithful to the full compass of Romantic thinking about the nature of the human being than what currently prevails in criticism. This body of Romantic criticism tends to be dominated on the one hand by psychoanalysis, from which it cherry-picks some concepts and ignores others; on the other hand, it often takes up both deconstruction and poststructuralist theory to articulate the Romantic subject as either a linguistic phenomenon or simply a locus of difference without a unified "I." One prime example of this paradigm is the Lacanian mirror-stage whereby the child "self-alienates," identifying with an image of itself "seemingly predestined" to "primordially" inaugurate its membership in the Symbolic order ("The Mirror Stage" 76). But this does not account for *how* the child recognises the image as its own so as to *self*-alienate. How does one *not* know oneself unless one "has oneself" on some level as a basis of comparison? One cannot self-alienate without a prior acquaintance with *something* as "self" before the event of alienation. In contrast, Romantic metasubjectivity conceives human identity as neither an after-effect of discourse or the movements of difference, nor as an essentialised "I" that is or can be made fully present to itself. That is, Romantic metasubjectivity points directly to the logical impossibility of the *merely* discursive construction of selfhood while offering a more sophisticated alternative to this model.

Romantic metasubjectivity is predicated on what I call the silent intellectual partnership between the philosophy of Friedrich Schelling (1775–1854) and the analytical psychology of Carl Gustav Jung (1875–1961).[1] Jung likely understood Schelling mostly second-hand from Eduard von Hartmann's *Philosophy of the Unconscious* (1869), which profoundly influenced many psychologists in the late nineteenth and early twentieth centuries (Jung, *Memories* 101). However, Jung's *Bibliothek-Katalog*, a list of his library contents at the time of his death in 1961, indicates that Jung owned two later volumes of Schelling's *Sämmtliche Werke* on the Philosophy of Mythology (1856–1857) and the *Treatise on the Deities of Samothrace* (1815), which points to an interest in Schelling's later thinking on mythology (whose specific connections with analytical psychology merit an independent study). Irrespective of Jung's scant first-hand knowledge of Schelling, the remarkable detail with which Schellingian philosophy and analytical psychology articulate the same dynamics suggests that their affinities are arguably far more significant than the oft-repeated connections to Kant, Nietzsche, and Schopenhauer which constitute much orthodox Jungian intellectual history (indeed, that Jung did *not* see Schelling as particularly influential in his own work lends weight to what Jung might have called a shared archetypal constellation of thought). Thus, I conceive this silent partnership as an intellectual countertransference between metaphysics and metapsychology wherein one often addresses the blindness of the other; to use a Schellingian phrase I will explore below, Schelling and Jung are questioning and answering beings to each other. In this sense, Romantic metasubjectivity takes up Henri Ellenberger's compelling but uncorroborated position that "Romantic philosophy and the Philosophy of Nature" are among Jung's most important intellectual sources, as well as Werner Leibbrand's provocative but hitherto largely unexplored argument that "Jung's system cannot be conceived without Schelling's philosophy" (qtd. in Ellenberger 728).

It is an irony of intellectual history that both Schelling (who was often seen as little more than a footnote in a history of German Idealism venerating Fichte and Hegel) and Jung (who for many years remained in the shadow of Freud) ultimately have more to tell us about Romanticism's thinking on the human being than their counterparts. Ironic, too, that both Schelling and Jung suffered from the slings and arrows of political (mis) fortune which favoured their intellectual foils. Hegel's 1818 appointment to the University of Berlin sidelined Schelling's thought, cementing Hegelian philosophy in Prussia until at least 1841 (Beiser, *Hegel* 307ff), when Schelling was finally called in to fill in the chair left vacant by Hegel's death in 1831 (although Schelling's lectures made far less of an impact than his predecessor's). Jung fared worse: all too successfully smeared by Freud's inner circle and variously accused of mysticism, anti-Semitism, and Nazism, after his "defection" from psychoanalysis circa 1912 a tradition of intellectual ostracism began which would see his works shunned (if not slandered) by Derrida, Roudinesco, and many others in the *Tel Quel* years after World War Two.[2] Ironically, those who claimed to be sensitive to the nuances of language and close reading of theoretical works served an oppressive intellectual politics which prevented them from applying the same balanced scrutiny to Jung, whose thought has been largely denied the sensitive, intelligent engagement which psychoanalysis has enjoyed for decades.[3] And when David Simpson writes that "the psychoanalytic model is both a symptom of and a solution to the dramas of subjectivity and self-consciousness that figure so prominently in Romantic writing" (19), he is referring to the critical hegemony of psychoanalysis in Romantic criticism which has persisted largely unchallenged until relatively recently. Such a momentous partnership between Schelling and Jung is bound to raise some eyebrows and pose some important first questions, which are the focus of this Introduction: why focus on Romanticism as the territory for this model of human identity? Why is Schelling such an important precursor? And why is Jung so crucial to developing its specifically psychological valency?

Why Romanticism?

German Romanticism's emergence from, and challenges to, German Idealism in the late eighteenth and early nineteenth centuries form a rich and complicated intellectual history; significant debate exists over the exact nature of their relationship, and particularly over the significance of philosophies of subjectivity at different points in Romanticism's development. Nevertheless, it can be argued as a general principle of Romanticism that, contrary to Idealism's foundationalist desire for first principles, subjectivity was considered "a derivative phenomenon that only becomes accessible to itself under a condition or presupposition [...] beyond its control. [...] [S]elf-consciousness manifests an identity that it cannot represent as such" (Frank, "What Is Early German Romanticism?" 18, 19). Andrew Bowie expands on this crucial distinction:

> The division that can be made between Idealist and Romantic thinking depends upon the extent to which each thinks it possible to restore unity to what the modern world increasingly separates. In the main the Idealist response to the divisions in modernity is to seek new philosophical foundations on the basis of the Cartesian and Kantian conception of the founding role of self-consciousness. For Idealism, what philosophy can analyse in the activity of consciousness is a higher form of the intelligibility present in nature, so that the task of philosophy is to show how our thinking is the key to the inherent intelligibility of things. The essence of the Romantic response, on the other hand, is a realization that, while it must play a vital role in a modern conception of philosophy, the activity of consciousness is never fully transparent to itself. It can therefore never be finally incorporated into a philosophical system, because what we can consciously know of ourselves does not exhaust what we are. (*Aesthetics and Subjectivity* 63)

As Tilottama Rajan puts it, Idealism "denotes a specifically philosophical movement committed to dialectical totalisation, identity, and system" where Romanticism is "the larger literary-cum-philosophical context within which Idealism emerges as no more than an 'idea' continually put under erasure by the exposure of Spirit to its body" ("Introduction" 14 n. 9). Of course, beyond this fundamental difference there are nuanced differences within Romanticism: for example, Rajan points out the ways in which German Romantic thought puts English Romantic thinking and poetry under theoretical analysis to "[reveal] a far greater uneasiness about the limits of poetic Idealism than might appear from the theoretical statements of the [English] poets themselves" (*Dark Interpreter* 28–29). Reading the breadth of Schelling's and Jung's thinking discerns a liminality between these two paradigms which makes them neither "Idealist" nor "Romantic" thinkers; to do justice to the multivalence of these complicated thinkers, one must read the different Idealist or Romantic *intensities* existing at different moments in their oeuvres. Idealism and Romanticism are not in place but in *play* (Lacoue-Labarthe and Nancy 122) through a constitutive tension between system and freedom, between the desire for a circle of knowledge which gives us definitive insight into ourselves and the world and the experience of that which system cannot contain. This said, my focus gravitates toward the specifically Romantic dimensions of Schelling and Jung's oeuvres as forces which unwork, often decisively, the idealist drive to systemic completion which is undoubtedly present in both.

This tension between system and freedom informs the Romantic genre of the fragment and the idea of the Romantic encyclopedia as embodiments of "[a Romantic-]encyclopedic *thinking*" which, contrary to traditional encyclopedias which are "circles of knowledge," "discovers that thought cannot be exhausted in a single discipline or form of thought" (Rajan, "Philosophy as Encyclopedia" 6) and "a perception about the disseminative interconnectedness and incompleteness of knowledge" (Rajan, "The Encyclopedia" 336). In this sense, Schlegel's *Philosophical Fragments* (1798–1800) is a text that emphasises its own incompletion as a manifestation of "the radical atotality of writing," a collection of "erratic pieces" "structurally linked with the whole or totality of which it would have been, or of which it has been, a part[,receiving their] very meaning from that ensemble that it thus posits and presupposes rather than challenges" (Gasché, "Foreword" vii). This incompletion also underwrites Novalis' *Notes for a Romantic Encyclopedia* as a paradoxical project of a "book of books" meant to unite the irreducibly fragmented (in)completion of the sciences; Novalis writes that "One science can only truly be represented by another science" (*Notes* 6). Similarly his *Fichte Studies* (1795–1796), as Novalis' prolonged engagement with Fichte's *Wissenschaftslehre*, is structured as a system of fragments wherein "no individual pronouncement may be considered as conclusive [...] [C]ontradictions abound, self-corrective statements occur, [and] variations on the same themes are frequent" (von Molnár 27). This emphasis on atotality allows for the ambitious and audacious project of a total system of knowledge constituted by, and from within, its radical incompletion. And indeed, in a well-known *Athenaeum Fragment* Schlegel describes how "progressive universal poetry," as "a mirror of the whole circumambient world" unfolding a *poiesis* hovering between real and ideal, is the most potent philosophical concept for the purposive organisation of disparate and mutually (in)completing forces along a line of becoming without a teleological endpoint (*AF* #116). We will see that Schelling puts the opacity of this ungrounding atotality at the heart of his thought, and Jungian metapsychology also makes it crucial to the development of personality.

Closely connected to this emphasis on the productive nature of decentred knowledge is the reconception of language's proximity to thought in an epistemic shift away from what Foucault calls the "raw, primitive being" of Renaissance language on the one hand (that is, language which is interwoven with the natural world) and the taxonomical emphasis of the Classical episteme on the other. This shift pushes language toward its modern conception as a counter-science, an intransitive (un)working of other disciplines as it takes itself for its own object in a self-reflexive elusiveness. For Foucault, in what is almost a harkening back to the linguistic pantheism of the Renaissance, the "enigmatic density" (*The Order of Things* 298) of the modern episteme's language becomes an "enigmatic multiplicity," a "precarious being" which must be "mastered" through projects of "universal formalization of all discourse" (305), general theories of signs and other keys to the mystery of language. Hence the Romantic fascination with ur-languages and the search for language's ultimate origins, which to varying degrees also concerned Schelling and Jung, specifically in their formulation of mythology as primordial *poiesis* and their view of mythologies as its spontaneous manifestations. A.W. Schlegel conceives this *poiesis* as part of "a kind of original poetry of humanity, an original creativity of the human mind which underlies all specific, developed languages" (Behler 269). Yet unlike Foucault, whose ambivalent relationship to psychoanalysis leads him to disconnect this epistemic shift from the psyche, the Romantics often figured language protopsychologically as drive [*Trieb*] in a bid to reconcile the plenitude and density of Foucault's Renaissance language with the dilemmas of self-reflexivity posed by the modern episteme of the nineteenth century.

But Romanticism is, of course, far more than the quest for the "original power" of an ur-language. The freedom opened up by this "fall" from an original commensurability between word and world (and the desire to return to it) is crucial to a certain sort of existential play which reveals – indeed, at times dramatises the very impossibility of this return. Maurice Blanchot aligns Romanticism with this freedom in a "being of literature" that reads and writes not only the human sciences (for Foucault) but the ontological structures of reality itself:

> Romanticism, as the advent of poetic consciousness, is not simply a
> literary school, nor even an important moment in the history of art; it

opens an epoch; furthermore, it is the epoch in which all epochs are revealed, for, through it, the absolute subject of all revelation comes into play, the 'I' in its freedom, which adheres to no condition, recognizes itself in no particularity, and is only in its element–its ether–in the totality in which it is free. (168).

There is a grand synecdoche at work in Blanchot's prose. As the epoch of epochs, Romanticism's self-dramatisation is nothing less than the unfolding of the world in both its "pastness" and its future possibilities – the prophetic and prophesying nature of the "absolute subject of all revelation." The horizon of this unfolding futurity, the play of this Romantic "absolute subject" (Blanchot's glimpse of Romantic metasubjectivity) unbound by particularity, discourse, or paradigm, cannot be bound to metanarrative (Oedipal, infantile, or otherwise). Romantic thinking about language, on the one hand, is a complicated engagement with the Babelic multiplicity of discourse. On the other hand, it is a drive to regain an ur-language lost in the development of reason and self-consciousness – the pursuit of a lack which both unworks and constitutes the proliferation of discourses as alibis for a liminality between words and Being. But this "original language" must align with a psychic economy different from that of psychoanalysis.

As an implicit response to the critical psychodrama of a Romantic subject caught between a merely discursive self and the fantasy of a unified "I," Thomas Pfau's *Romantic Moods* (2005) turns from discursivity to "the (re-)construction of emotion as an aesthetic form, a 'voice,' [as] a more reliable mode of access to history than the garden-variety methods of associative and or contextual rumination" (24), thereby resisting the appropriation of affect as a screen for discursivity following what Andrea Henderson takes up as a "hermeneutics of suspicion" toward "the canonical Romantic model of 'deep' subjectivity" (3). Pfau does not abrogate personality or collapse the transcendent "back into a historical matrix against which [...] it had sought to establish itself" (24), but instead focuses on the traumatic historicity *underneath* history, so to speak – a general economy (following Bataille)[4] of productive forces from which the discipline and narratives of history emerge. In this sense, Romantic literature strives to connect with this historicity by orienting itself "toward an as yet unknown, perhaps unpresentable 'openness' " (25). But neither does Pfau return to the fantasy of a unified "I"; he describes the sublime experience,[5] for example, as "upheaval," an emotional "event" which "alerts the subject to its having been implicated all along in a seemingly uncontainable network of antagonistic historical forces" (31). If the sublime is apocalyptic revelation, it is the revelation of something closer to what Foucault calls the "historical *a priori*," a "condition of reality for [discursive] statements [which must] take account of statements in their dispersion, in all the flaws opened up by their non-coherence, in their overlapping and mutual replacement, in their simultaneity" (*Archaeology* 127). What Pfau describes without naming is a reframing of the sublime as an encounter with *historicity as such* – a traumatic historicity which describes, without circumscribing, a dangerous fluidity on which the flat surface of discourse composes and decomposes. This encounter is not with God or the moral law as transcendental signifiers, but with a "transcendent" historical empiricism from which the human psyche emerges. Pfau alludes to a non-psychoanalytic psyche which, moving through traditionally psychoanalytic economies of trauma and melancholy, approaches the psyche I explore here, one which emerges from such an "uncontainable network" of historical forces.

Joel Faflak writes that the psychoanalytic unconscious "marks the Romantic subject's alienation from himself" but also "a sublime imaginative *jouissance*" in which this subject "reimagines his psychic determinism within the interminable psychic process of finding his identity" (24). Similar to the Romantic subject traumatically (re)constituted through a metonymy of "pathological" substitute-formations (34), the Romantic metasubject exists under the burden of an impossible history, a genesis that can only be known through its traumatic effects – a genesis Schelling calls "unprethinkable" and which Jung narrates as emerging from the mists of human prehistory. Faflak points to a self-alienation that is not synonymous with Freud's answer to this metonymic trauma, which is to bind even *Nachträglichkeit*'s developmental impetus to a notion of primal phantasy which reinstates the past.[6] Romantic metasubjectivity theorises this pathology into a future to come for which psychoanalysis cannot fully account. This pathology is "perverse" and "monstrous" insofar as it is determined by the late eighteenth-century vitalist shift to epigenetic (self-generating) accounts of life in the Romantic sciences – a shift which unworks the hierarchical structures of preformation (the idea that all organisms had been predetermined by God) that had hitherto dominated the life sciences. As Richard Sha writes, in the Romantic period, epigenesis

> became widely accepted over preformation because it defined each new birth as a new formation, a theory that accounted for variability but implied the existence of an invisible vital force that could organise living matter into complex forms. [...] [N]ature was increasingly understood to be self-generating, [and] preformation had a hard time accounting for variation and monstrosity. [Epigenesis] gave the Romantics a way of thinking about the purposiveness of life without a predetermined form or purpose. In short, life itself was perverse. (19)

Put simply, then, Romantic metasubjectivity describes a purposive, *epigenetic* psyche in contrast to the teleology of a preformed goal inscribed in the organism.

The decentred nature of this epigenetic psyche also places Romantic metasubjectivity firmly in the dissociationist tradition of psychology, which holds that different clusters of images and affects in the psyche have their own autonomy and "personality." As I will discuss below, the dissociationist lineage can be traced back through Jung (as its most important twentieth-century thinker) to Schelling as one of its key philosophical precursors. Dissociationism provides the psychic territory upon which we may begin to map the "uncontainable network" of Pfau's Romantic historicity, and in the register of the psyche Romantic metasubjectivity asserts *materiality*, as a heterogeneous disturbance of all absolutes, against cultural *materialism* as "an absolutism of the empirical" (Rajan, "Introduction" 2). Pfau's conception of Romantic historicity reflects a concern beyond mere discursive play, and even the arch-associationist Hume admitted his inability to discern the laws governing the mind's organisation of external stimuli. And for Foucault, naming "the conditions of emergence of statements, the law of their coexistence with others, the specific form of their mode of being, the principles according to which they survive, become transformed, and disappear" does not bring him any closer to explaining these laws of discourse away from the "alien development" he wants to disavow (*The Archaeology of Knowledge* 127). Thus, Henderson's "hermeneutics of suspicion" toward notions of "depth" or the "deep subject" must *itself* be suspected. This suspicion *of* suspicion does not mean reinstating the canonical deep subject; it means rethinking its metaphors and operations in Romantic literature. This is not to say, however, that Romantic metasubjectivity points to a personified subject hiding in every Romantic work as a dramatic character (one could certainly not say this of, say, Wordsworth's Lucy poems). Rather, Romantic metasubject*ivity* gestures toward a wider Romantic universe whose impetus to self-organisation and purposiveness exists in both human and non-human forms, as Romantic scientists often observed; it marks a certain set of epistemological, psychological, and ontological perspectives within which the Romantic *metasubject* operates. Put briefly, and in terms I will articulate below: the Romantic metasubject is equivalent to what Novalis calls the "Self of one's self," what Jung calls the *Self*, and what Schelling calls the *absolute subject*.

Why Schelling? The absolute subject, or the logic of the third

Schelling's specifically Romantic intensity is reflected in a "darkening" shift in his thought, circa 1809, from an early idealist focus on the metaphysics of self-consciousness to a more Romantic concern with how we can gain knowledge of an unprethinkable Being and how the world of time and history comes to be. For Schelling, this shift is exemplified in Schelling's critique of Hegel's system of absolute knowledge. For Hegel, reflexive thought is ultimately capable of recognising and incorporating that which is other to it; the difference between thought and Being – in theory at least – is ultimately overcome in the revelation of absolute Spirit, and this Spirit is something which can be an object of knowledge. Being is always already determined by the dialectical movement of the Concept. This is the core of what Schelling calls Hegel's "negative philosophy" of abstraction, which "makes the truth of being a necessary consequence of thinking" (Bowie, *Schelling* 143). In contrast to this, Schelling's positive philosophy

> attempts to suggest a different path for philosophy, in the face of the impossibility of reason knowing what is absolutely other than it as ultimately itself. [...] [Its positivity] lies in the demand for an explanation [...] even in the case of geometry, or logic, of the fact that there can be self-contained *a priori* systems of necessity. *Such systems cannot, and this is the fundamental point, explain their own possibility:*

whilst geometry maps the structure of space, it cannot explain the existence of space. Schelling does not deny the internal necessity in geometry or logic, but demands to understand why it is necessary. The only possible answer to this is the fact that it is necessary, which does not allow of a further *logical* explanation. (Bowie, *Schelling* 142, 144; my first italics)

That is, for Schelling reflexive thought and knowledge rest on something irreducible to itself, a facticity, or plenitude of Being which recedes before attempts at knowledge just as it makes knowledge possible. As Bowie succinctly puts it, "the point is that the potential of thinking itself must first *be* in a way that it cannot itself explain" (166). We will see that as Schelling's oeuvre develops, he will turn to art as a means of accessing this plenitude.

This Romantic concern with the indeterminacy of Being is nascent in the natural philosophy [*Naturphilosophie*] of Schelling's 1799 *First Outline* and the transcendental philosophy of the 1800 *System*, but gains intensity with the *Philosophical Inquiries into the Nature of Human Freedom* (1809) and the third version of his *Ages of the World* (1815). Indeed, these texts foreground Schelling's unique conceptualisation of human freedom as the condition of possibility for all knowledge, unbinarised by oppositions between, for example, "fate" and "free will." That is, a consummately Romantic freedom does not vie for dominance against an opposed "fate" or "destiny" but rather becomes "a freedom without which neither determinism nor free will [nor ideology] could be supposed" (Ferris pars. 2, 3). But to simply label Schelling a "philosopher of freedom" is to miss the problematic yet constitutive tension between freedom and system present throughout his oeuvre. In the *Naturphilosophie*, infinite productivity is paradoxically circumscribed in a circle of possible forms; in the 1800 *System*, self-consciousness aims to contain the Nature in which it exists. The *Freedom* essay attempts to implicate an unruly freedom in an idealist narrative ending in love's ultimate resolution of all conflict, and the 1815 *Ages* develops a cosmological doctrine of potencies [*Potenzenlehre*] to explain the beginning of time and history while channelling this infinite productivity toward an ultimate unification of science and myth. In contrast to Hegel's insistence on dialectical Being and a terminus of absolute knowledge, Schelling turns to the *Potenzenlehre* to describe a non-logical being in non-logical terms, articulating the interaction of nonmolar forces oscillating in a rhythm that cannot be contained or understood in a reflective framework.[7] This interplay forms systems of knowledge, but we will see that they resist the transparency that Hegel attributes to them through dialectic's promise of completion (even if it is only a promise).

It was not without reason that Hegel dubbed Schelling the "Proteus of philosophy." The tension between an idealist drive toward systemic completion and a Romantic focus on what system cannot assimilate is perhaps most apparent in the *Naturphilosophie*, which Schelling develops from 1797 onwards and is crucial to understanding Schelling's thought as a whole. As we will see in Chapter 1, the productive yet problematic indeterminacy of Nature in Schelling's *First Outline* consists in Nature's ambivalence toward its own products – an ambivalence which both courts and resists the coalescence of this generative energy into a system. To this end, Grant argues that in response to a post-Kantian "antiphysics" which denudes Nature of its dynamism, Schelling's *Naturphilosophie* presents us with the groundwork of a *genetic* philosophy not of things but of *forces*, a project of *"unconditioning* the metaphysics of nature" (*Philosophies* 6). And as if anticipating the transferences between Schelling's *Naturphilosophie* and analytical psychology, Grant points out that *Naturphilosophie* puts metaphysics *itself* under analysis, confronting it with its molecular unconscious. That is, *Naturphilosophie*

> does not merely sit episodically amongst other systems and artifacts of the antiquarian intellect, but *challenges systems to reveal what they eliminate.* Insofar as philosophy still leaves nature to the sciences, it [fails this test] and becomes a conditioned, that is, a compromised antiphysics, an Idealism so 'powerful' [...] as to eliminate nature. (21)

For Schelling, it is precisely Nature's materiality that puts the Idealism of "antiphysics" under analysis, indeed opening up a space for an Idealism without absolutes as "a symbiosis between ideality and materiality" (Rajan, "Introduction" 1). This symbiosis, which makes Schelling so crucial for the concept of Romantic metasubjectivity, consists first and foremost in the idea of the *absolute subject* which is not only implicit in his work from the *First Outline* onwards but is also a trope for the individuative thrust of his oeuvre as a whole. Blanchot's "absolute subject of all revelation" is prefigured in Schelling's oeuvre, which can be read as a philosophical individuation, a circumambulatory approach to understanding the absolute subject both as it exists in, and recedes from, time and history. Where the "subject" is the human being interpellated by discourse, the absolute subject is Schelling's name for the organisational force that makes this subject possible. Because many of Schelling's important ideas constellate around the absolute subject, I will provide a brief shorthand of its presence in Schelling's work which will be amplified in the chapters that follow.

As Keith Peterson (xxviii) writes, the absolute subject is already implicit in the *Naturphilosophie* in Nature's desire for full self-realisation as what Schelling, in the 1799 *First Outline*, variously calls Nature's "absolute product" or "absolute organism" (*FO* 28). As the next chapter will demonstrate, this drive towards an absolute subject is far from a simple teleology, instead unfolding a rhythm[8] which becomes the fundamental basis for the purposive movement at the heart of Romantic metasubjectivity. While the absolute subject is also not named as such in the 1809 *Freedom* essay, it functions as a silent placeholder in the idea of copular logic with which the essay begins. According to copular logic, the statement "the ball is blue" is logically indefensible because a thing cannot be two things (a ball *and* blue) at the same time; *ball* cannot and does not own *blue* as part of its essence (or vice versa). Instead, there must be *something that is both a ball and blue*, but this "something" cannot be an object of knowledge because an object cannot be two things at once to consciousness. It is the *copula* (the *is*, or $=$ in "the ball *is* blue") which gestures toward this something as an unconditioned "object $=$ X" which cannot be defined by any of its predicates; this copula is "unprethinkable" because it is anterior to cognition, hence never fully available to it. But this unconditioned, absolute object $=$ X is also an absolute *subject* – that is, an unconditioned *subject* to which everything in Being is a *predicate*. Thus, the absolute subject is embedded in thought, so to speak, as the unspoken and unspeakable condition which makes it possible for us to think subject-predicate statements in the first place. Schelling's absolute subject is nearly synonymous with Romantic metasubjectivity's "Self of one's self," but as we will see, Romantic metasubjectivity evolves the un(der)developed psychology in Schelling's work and, through discerning its symmetries with analytical psychology, opens up the absolute subject's affinities with a more specifically Romantic dimension of thought.

In turning to this psychological tendency in Schelling's thought, we will see that this unknowable quantum of the absolute subject also becomes the essence of *personality* in the *Freedom* essay's discussion of the nature of evil. Here, personality is the link between man as selfish, particular being and man as spirit (33).[9] Put differently, in the *Freedom* essay's Romantic ontology, personality watermarks the unique dynamism between the individual and the *centrum*, or ground of Being as it exists in the person. This personality-dynamism through which human life unfolds recapitulates the creation of the world itself, which emerges through the dynamic between *ground* (or *Ungrund*, the ground-which-is-a-non-ground, Being before time and history) and *existence* (Being as the natural world of flux and process) in an unprethinkable moment which cannot be reduced to a logical concept or described by Hegelian dialectic. Indeed, this dynamic encrypts the answer to the question haunting Schelling's oeuvre: "Why is there something rather than nothing?"

Schelling's 1815 *Ages* also opens with Schelling's insistence that "the person is the world writ small, [thus] the events of human life, from the deepest to their highest consummation, must accord with the events of life in general" (3), implying a continuity between the absolute subject and the individual personality. In this spirit, a subject per se is absent yet liminally implied in the protopsychology invoked with magnetic sleep and Mesmerism. However, the absolute subject comes to the fore as reason confronts its Other in the form of God as freedom, which is "the negating force of the future," a future which can only be "intimated" (*Ages* xxxv). Here, the absolute subject is the Godhead as something beyond Being and non-Being. Put simply: for Schelling, the unapprehendable (non-)*ground* of existence [*Ungrund*] is *contractive*; it wants to shrink away from the tumult of Being into itself and refuse coming into being. This is the ground's death drive, so to speak – its "No" to existence. But this "No" is ineluctably entwined with the "Yes" of existence itself, the *expansive* principle, God's drive to enter Being and the play of natural products and forms which composes the world. Thus, this systolic-diastolic rhythm of Being unfolds Nature's antipathy and "unnaturalness" toward its own organic creations (*Naturphilosophie*), the tension between ego and *centrum* as the nonground of personality (the *Freedom* essay), and the potentiated, incomprehensible moment of creation, God's decision to enter Being (*Ages*). All of these iterations of Schelling's Romantic ontology orbit the Romantic metasubject's perennial suspension between the desire for system and the melancholic responsibility of freedom.

The *Freedom* essay and the 1815 *Ages* gesture to Schelling's later "On the Nature of Philosophy as Science" (1821) ["NPS"], which paves the way for Schelling's positive philosophy and Philosophy of Mythology. In "NPS," Schelling explicitly describes the absolute subject as that which engenders systems of knowledge while remaining irreducible to them – an organisational force *"proceeding through everything and not being anything"* (215). In the essay's philosophical psychology, the absolute subject moves within and through a fundamental disunity and "inner conflict" from which all systems of knowledge come, which Schelling calls a state of asystasy (210). Here Schelling offers a crucial experiential component of the absolute subject in the form of *ecstasy*, a dissociative experience where the ego is "placed outside itself" (228) closely resembling experiences of the Romantic sublime, but without the idealist optimism the Romantics often attached to the latter. This dissociative experience of the absolute subject, as the culmination of the nascent psychology in the *Freedom* essay and *Ages*, makes Schelling an important precursor to core concepts of analytical psychology.

Schelling's broader relevance to depth psychology has been explored in two recent studies of Romantic psychology which serve to build a critical history of Romantic metasubjectivity. Matt ffytche's *Foundation of the Unconscious* (2012) and Sean McGrath's *The Dark Ground of Spirit: Schelling and the Unconscious* (2012) can be counterposed, the former being a broadly constructivist approach, the latter being a more adventurous and philosophical exploration of Schelling's esoteric heritage. ffytche equates the unconscious with its dispersion across the disciplinary structures of the nineteenth century, which ultimately represses the conditions of its existence (12). McGrath, however, is more philosophically serious about the unconscious, arguing that while "clearly the unconscious is a constructed concept [...] we are not so sure that its constructed nature means that it does not in fact reference a real phenomenon" (*Dark Ground* 20). Thus, McGrath more directly engages with the ontological inscrutability of the unconscious which, for ffytche, is more illocutionary position than epistemological knot. Arguing that "Schelling is widely recognised for having been the first to posit a single ground of matter and mind, which cannot itself be conscious," McGrath places this "ground" (a notional term for the *Ungrund*) in a tradition extending through Jakob Böhme and Franz von Baader (74 n. 1, 44ff), two figures of whom Jung was certainly aware (see Dourley 124ff).[10] Reading the history of Schelling's oeuvre from within the cisionary grain of his own thought, McGrath sees a contrast between an early "Eckhartian reditus," "a return into the non-dual, unmediated point of origin of being," and a later "Boehmian exitus," "[a move] away from the non-dual toward differentiation, personalisation, history and mediation" (60). The concept of Romantic metasubjectivity is clearly more sympathetic to what McGrath calls a Schellingian "co-inherentism" between psyche and history, mind and nature (37). But where McGrath stops short of detailing its undiscovered theoretical country, Romantic metasubjectivity articulates the psyche which remains unspoken in both of these accounts.

Describing depth-psychology as "crypto-metaphysics," McGrath points to Schelling's anticipation of this tradition in psychology in his desire to conceive a medicine based not in clinical but *speculative* concepts such as his *Naturphilosophie*, so as to "fuse the *a priori* and the a posteriori element in psychology and *approach the empirical through the metaphysical*" (20). We must then consider the disciplinary transferences between psychology and philosophy as crucial to Romantic metasubjectivity. Freud's ambivalence toward philosophy and his construction of psychoanalysis as a surpassing of a "primitive" philosophy of nature is well known. While Jung often shares Freud's ambivalence toward metaphysics in insisting on his status as an empirical scientist, his thought is nevertheless multidisciplinary in ways Freud resisted. Indeed, the presence of the *religious* in Jung's middle and later writing, as well as his later research on alchemy, reflects an awareness of the interpenetration of religion, philosophy, and psychology. Despite this insistence on empirical science, in 1931 Jung writes that "philosophy and psychology are linked by indissoluble bonds which are kept in being by the interrelation of their subject-matters. [...] Neither discipline can do without the other, and the one invariably furnishes the unspoken – and generally unconscious – assumptions of the other" ("Basic Postulates" para. 659). In short, as a mirror image of Schelling's speculative thought, analytical psychology often approaches metaphysics from an empirical standpoint of clinical observation and interpretation and is crucial to thinking Romantic metasubjectivity's general psychic economy.

Why Jung? Anatomy of a difference

The cryptonomy of Schelling's oeuvre is a case study of depth psychology's self-analysis: in Schelling's work, there are aspects of both psychoanalysis and analytical psychology, and as such it sets in relief the theoretical break between Freud and Jung. In the history of depth-psychology, psychoanalysis emerges as a discipline plagued by the unsolvable problem of its own genesis. Confronted with the irresolvable problem of the unconscious and contracting, as it were, into an irretrievable (mythical) image of the past, its provisional solution to its constitutive problems is interminable analysis – a constant (re)finding of the primal scenes suggested by the complexes this analysis finds. Of course, analytical psychology (at least in its current form) would not exist had the momentous meeting between Freud and Jung in 1907 never taken place; indeed, Jung's *The Psychology of Dementia Praecox* (1907) opens with an indebtedness to "the brilliant discoveries of Freud" (3) which would later allow Jung to define analytical psychology as an independent science. But analytical psychology ultimately emerges from Jung's relationship with Freud and psychoanalysis as an *expansion* into a general economy of fluidity, in which this freedom can pursue its own line(s) of flight toward the plenitude of a potentiated unity which nevertheless remains unattainable, the receding terminus of a purposive unfolding. The complexes (re)found in psychoanalysis, which Freud at different times wants to bind to the *myth* of Oedipus or infantile trauma, are eclipsed by *mythology* as a decentred nexus of nonmolar forces, a view shared by both Schelling and Jung. Articulating Romantic metasubjectivity specifically against the backdrop of analytical psychology excavates Jung's crucial place in depth psychology's underexplored historical and theoretical continuities with Romanticism, which have often been overdetermined by psychoanalysis. Manfred Frank lays the foundations for individuality's resistance to mere (discursive) subjectivity on a normative level (see Appendix B), but we cannot conceive what this individuality *is*, and how it operates in more than its formal, socio-political sense, without the insights of analytical psychology.

Any discussion of Jung's relationship to contemporary thought must address a glaring question: given that Deleuze and other key contemporary thinkers (Bachelard, Simondon) clearly preferred Jung over Freud, why has Jung nevertheless been so consistently marginalised in contemporary theory? There are several possible answers – Jung's notoriously inexact and inconsistent language and the theoretical shallowness of much "Jungian" writing come to mind. But perhaps most importantly, the potency of Jung's thought for contemporary thought has been diluted significantly by a longstanding critical narrative which Sonu Shamdasani has aptly called the "Freudocentric legend." Perpetuated by many Freudians and Jungians for various reasons, in this narrative analytical psychology is a (typically inferior) derivative of psychoanalysis, and Jung is depicted as little more than Freud's errant Satan, a rebellious angel who left the psychoanalytic fold for a misguided career in starry-eyed "Romantic" mysticism (Shamdasani, *Jung Stripped Bare* 31).[11] In this psychoanalytic creation myth Jung is the ungrateful son in an uncanny Oedipal repetition of the primal scene, abjected from psychoanalysis to preserve its illusory purity; indeed, Jung was particularly singled out for scapegoating and retroactive "pathologisation" in efforts to discredit dissent (see Leitner 465, 481). And in this spirit, analytical psychology is marginalised by scholars who would never dream of reading Freud with the same critical inattention. Jacques Lacan, for example, describes the archetypal symbol as "the blossoming of the soul, and that is that" ("The Situation" 392). Slavoj Žižek similarly trivialises Jungian thought as a "New Age [...] resexualization of the universe ('men are from Mars, women are from Venus')" sanctioning "an underlying, deeply anchored sense of archetypal identity which provides a kind of safe haven in the flurry of contemporary confusion over roles and identities" (*The Ticklish Subject* 443–44). Elsewhere, Žižek incomprehensibly attempts to reabsorb Jungian thought into psychoanalysis with a purportedly "Jungian" reading of Wagner in terms of superego(!) symbolism, unabashedly superimposing psychoanalytic terminology over what he would have us believe is the Jungian paradigm ("Foreword" viii). And discussing the ways in which alchemical language and ideas have diffused into psychology, Christine Battersby paraphrases 12 years of Jung's research into alchemy as "a eulogy of the 'feminine' with a lethal bias against the merely female" (110), assuming that the masculine bias she perceives in the ancient alchemists was simply transferred to analytical psychology. Significantly, in none of these passages are Jung's works cited. You can lead scholars to Jung, but you can't make them think … sympathetically.

This said, some of the structuralist or essentialist allegations levelled at Jung are not entirely groundless. Jung's often religious or mythopoetic language at times suggests what I call, following Derrida, a *therapeutics of presence*[12] which casts analyst and analysand, and the archetypal forces investing their mutual encounter, as self-present forms in the interests of therapy and healing. In this sense, Jung writes that in dreams, literature, and mythology we encounter the Shadow (the Doppelgänger, or "dark side" of the conscious personality), the Anima or Animus (the figure of the woman in man or man in woman, respectively), the Wise Old Man/Woman (the figure of wisdom in the man or woman, respectively), and so forth. While useful in a therapeutic setting, this hypostasis often leads commentators to mistakenly cast Jung as primarily a thinker of "wholeness" or "the union of opposites" in a synecdochical reduction which reads Jung's idealism as the whole of his thought and elides the subversive valency of his metapsychology. But it is precisely this metapsychology which troubles this therapeutics of presence with a depth that psychologically (un)grounds Deleuze's notion of depth as multidimensional, "pure *implex* [...] the (ultimate and original) heterogeneous dimension [...] the matrix of all extensity [...] pure *spatium*" (*DR* 229–30). Irrespective of his occasional use of metaphors of depth and height to figure personality, Jung's metapsychology – that is, the plenitude of archetypal intensities Jung discovers but cannot contain – prefigures the differential depth Deleuze sees in the surface play of "length" and "breadth," where verticality is a mobile metaphor casting a small beam of light on a libidinal economy which exceeds the purview of any one metaphor. It is this "depth" which escapes and interrogates the understanding of "depth" informing the orthodox cultural materialist critique of the "deep subject."

For these reasons, if Foucault is correct that one day the twenty-first century will be known as "Deleuzian" ("Theatrum Philosophicum" 165), it is not implausible that, psychologically, it may be known as Jungian. Romantic metasubjectivity should be understood as a contribution to this reconsideration of Jungian thought: it is this "darker" Jung, whose metapsychology unworks the optimistic teleology of a therapeutics of presence, who is important to contemporary thought and whose ideas will be amplified in the following chapters. Jung is indispensable to the intellectual genealogy of Romantic metasubjectivity, and the Jungian lacuna in intellectual history necessitates a brief account of analytical psychology's key differences from psychoanalysis.

Freud's *Project for a Scientific Psychology* (1895) casts psychoanalysis as an empirical natural science which, through the discovery and (ideal) abolition of repression caused by primal scenes, would eventually isolate the "psychical processes" of the unconscious as "quantitatively determinate states of specifiable material particles" whose laws of interaction could be codified and ultimately made accessible to consciousness (295). In contradistinction to the "split subject" engendered by this perpetual agon between consciousness and the unconscious, Jung emphasises what ffytche calls the Schellingian "spirit of individuality" (276) which has been excised from psychoanalysis. That is, analytical psychology emphasises a compensatory relationship between consciousness and the unconscious that serves the individual human organism's current developmental needs: for example, a person wholly devoted to rational thinking in daily life is more likely to have an emotional, affect-driven unconscious that manifests itself in dreams and waking fantasies. Jung explains: "the role of the unconscious is to act compensatorily to the conscious contents of the moment. By this I do not mean that it sets up an opposition, for there are times when the tendency of the unconscious coincides with that of consciousness, namely, when the conscious attitude is approaching the optimum" ("The Role" para. 21). It follows from this that the unconscious need not smuggle dream contents past a censor into consciousness, as both consciousness and the unconscious are invested in the organism's well-being and preservation. Rather, the dream's symbolic language reflects its status as "a part of nature, which harbors no intention to deceive, but expresses something as best it can, just as a plant grows or an animal seeks its food as best it can" (*Memories* 161–62). Jung will elsewhere emphasise that "*the unconscious is nature, which never deceives*" (*Symbols* 62) – an alignment of the unconscious with Nature which pervades his oeuvre. Hence Jung's formulation of the *collective unconscious* as a stratum of the psyche common to all human beings and contiguous with Nature itself: "[t]he unconscious, as the totality of all archetypes, is the deposit of all human experience right back to its remotest beginnings. Not, indeed, a dead deposit, a sort of abandoned rubbish-heap, but a living system of reactions and aptitudes that determine the individual's life in invisible ways" ("The Structure" para. 339).

The mythopoeic register Jung so often uses to express the dynamism of this living system situates him in the literary-philosophical style Charles Schwab identifies with Manfred Frank's "antirationalist"/"neostructuralist" tradition inaugurated by Nietzsche. Neostructuralism underscores the ontologically productive nature of "metaphorically 'released'" language which "yields a thought all its own, or, more radically [...] only metaphorical procedures [that] are adequate to exhibit the dynamic, indeterminable, and multiple character of all semiosis or, if it is different, of reality at large" (Frank, *What is Neostructuralism?* xix). And we must not be snobbish about our metaphors: when Jung describes the unconscious as a "treasure-house [of] accumulated life-experiences" or as "[hiding] living water, spirit that has become nature" ("On the Nature of the Psyche" para. 352; "Archetypes of the Collective Unconscious" para. 50), when he describes regression as a dike damming up a mountain watercourse ("On Psychic Energy" para. 72), or when he warns those who would plunder "psychic riches" that "more than one sorcerer's apprentice has been drowned in the waters called up by himself" ("Archetypes of the Collective Unconscious" para. 31), he is not subscribing to nature-mysticism or diving headfirst into a metaphysics of presence. Rather, Jung's mythopoeic register establishes the profoundly *fabular* nature of these psychic dynamisms as anterior to logical thought. Jung writes: "The language I speak must be equivocal, that is *ambiguous*, to do justice to psychic nature with its double aspect. I strive consciously and deliberately for ambiguous expressions, because it is superior to unequivocalness and corresponds to the nature of being" (letter to Zwi Werblowsky, 17 June 1952, 70; trans. mod.). Schlegel writes that "one cannot really speak of poetry except in the language of poetry" (*Dialogue on Poetry* 54), and similarly Jung's ubiquitous references to fairy tales, myths, and literature to describe the phenomenology of the psyche reflect the quintessential Romantic emphasis on the aesthetic as the only authentic expression of absolute knowledge (we need only read the opening pages of Schelling's *Ages* to see his emphasis on the narrated nature of knowledge, which persists across all three revisions).

This compensatory dynamic between consciousness and the unconscious informs Jung's fundamental divergence from Freud concerning the nature of libido. Incest was the point of division: in 1912, Jung published *Wandlungen und Symbole der Libido* (*Transformations and Symbols of the Libido*; extensively revised as *Symbols of Transformation* [1952]), in which Jung argues that "[the incest taboo] has a much greater – and different – significance than the prevention of incest [...] [the taboo] is the symbol or vehicle of a far wider and special meaning which has as little to do with real incest as hysteria with the actual trauma, the animal cult with the bestial tendency and the temple with the stone" (letter to Freud, 17 May 1912, 506). Jung wrote *Wandlungen* knowing it would cost him his relationship with Freud (*Symbols* xxvi), who ultimately could not tolerate the dissent of the heir-apparent to psychoanalysis. Jung's *energic* conception of libido asserts its "generalised" quantitative aspect against Freudian libido, which is qualitatively defined by sexuality (Jung calls this the *mechanistic* approach). That is, Jungian libido is psychic energy in general, irreducible to any one instinct but measurable in principle through its *quantitative* potency and investment in objects or fantasies (which include, but are not limited to, the sexual):

[Libido] denotes a desire or impulse which is unchecked by any kind of authority, moral or otherwise. Libido is appetite in its natural state.

From the genetic point of view it is bodily needs like hunger, thirst, sleep, and sex, and emotional states or affects, which constitute the essence of libido. All these factors have their differentiations and subtle ramifications in the highly complicated human psyche. (*Symbols* 135–36)

The general economy of Jungian libido is conceptualised by the *archetype*, which is perhaps the best-known (and most misunderstood) concept of analytical psychology. Jung's anthropocentrism casts the archetype as a fundamental organisational force of human experience. Represented by images, objects, and affects while remaining unknowable in themselves, archetypes express the differentiations and varying intensities of libido performed in different forms at different times according to a culture's historical particularities. Archetypes can be dream figures or projections on to people in everyday life (mother, father, partner), or situations (birth, death, and other rites of passage). Jung's first reference to the archetype in 1919 is to "*a priori*, inborn forms of 'intuition'" in the collective unconscious, "the archetypes of perception and apprehension, which are the necessary *a priori* determinants of all psychic processes" ("Instinct" para. 270). As human beings, we exist in a rhythm of archetypal projection and recollection: we project archetypal patterns on to the objective world in order to organise and articulate our experience, but healthy adaptation also requires us to withdraw, or "recollect" archetypal material – to understand our own investment in projections and come to realise our psychic participation in what we see (Jung, "Psychological Aspects" para. 160). But while Jung's therapeutics of presence may present this rhythm as an unbroken harmony of interaction with symbols and natural phenomena on the way to "wholeness," Jung's darker metapsychology resists this teleological imposition. In Chapter 4 we will see, via Hölderlin, that this rhythm harbours a latent indeterminacy, a vulnerability to trauma which can bend and warp this line of flight into unpredictable or catastrophic directions.

Jung's early conflation of "archetype" [*Archetypus*] with vaguer terms such as "primordial image" [*Urbild*] ("Definitions" para. 747; see also Jung, "Instinct" para. 270 n. 7) has historically muddied the waters, as the German *Bild* is notoriously difficult to translate (it can mean "representation," "image," and "likeness," among other possibilities).[13] This, combined with Jung's at times rigid interpretations of myth and literature, has contributed to the understanding of the archetype as a fixed structural unit in a totalising literary-mythological encyclopedia of human experience. Moreover, Jung's early Kantian exposition of the archetypes distinguished between the *noumenal* "archetype in itself" and the archetype's *phenomenal* representation, which often presented the archetype as a static form strangely alienated from its manifestation. But the more indeterminate aspects of Jungian metapsychology radically unwork this orthodox conception: 1947 marks a turn in Jung's thinking on the archetype, a "further degree of differentiation" ("On the Nature of the Psyche" para. 419). Now, Jung conceives of the archetype as *psychoid* in nature, which is to say that its intensity ranges from the human psyche into the inscrutable materiality of biological processes. With the psychoid archetype, Jung's metapsychology moves decisively toward a general economy of dynamic creation which, as we will see, has compelling affinities with Schelling's *Naturphilosophie*. Indeed, straddling both mind and nature, ideal and real, the archetypes become unruly almost beyond definition: "you will never be able to disentangle an archetype. It is always interwoven in a carpet of related ideas, which lead ever further toward other archetypal formations, which constantly overlap and together knit the wondrous carpet of life" (*Dream Interpretation* 237). Thus, the Jungian archetype can best be defined as a centripetal force, attracting psychic and material contents (and perhaps other natural forces) to itself while remaining irreducible to any one of its representations. Always already implicated in a potentially infinite metonymy of representations, the archetype *happens* through unique constellations of ideas, images, and natural objects. Indeed, although Jung does not go this far, one can almost speak of the archetype as a constellation of *multiple energic centres*, much like the way Schelling describes comets as recapitulations of the "fiery electrical dissolution" of original matter, whose "individual center[s] of gravity [are] not reconciled with the universal center of gravity" and which embody the primordial systolic-diastolic rhythms of the cosmos without conforming to the set movement of "settled planets" (*Ages* 96–97). And following Jung's observation that archetypes are mutually entangled, it follows that archetypal *situations* constellate other archetypal symbols, affects, and forces as multiple energic centres. The question would then be: what makes this archetypal constellation "choose" particular manifestations in therapy and/or lived experience? This issue is broached in Chapter 4.

This centripetalism accounts for the Jungian archetype's *autonomous* nature. In dreams, altered states of consciousness and waking life archetypes can function as *dramatis personae*, individual personalities whose wishes do not always coincide with those of consciousness. Thus, where Freud's well-known second topography of the psyche features ego, id, and superego as *driven* yet impersonal constructs, the autonomy of the archetypes reflects Jung's indebtedness less to Freud and more to Pierre Janet[14] and the dissociationist tradition of depth psychology. As John Haule writes,

> Dissociationism accepted the notion that ideas and images tend to combine into complexes, but conceptualized the process very differently. Rejecting (forever) the concept of mental Newtonian forces, they held that every aggregation of ideas and images possessed, in some measure or other, its *own personality*. [Dissociationism] replaced the impersonal, atomic level mechanisms more appropriate to psychics and astrology with a kind of holistic personalism, which appears more adequate for understanding the experience and behavior of human individuals. [A] compelling adjunct to this was the fact that there exist lower life forms, well-known in biology, in which larger individuals are comprised of colonies of simpler individuals. (243–44, 245)[15]

We have seen how, in contrast to Freud, who "imposed a causal schema upon dissociationism's essentially teleological image of complex formation" (251),[16] Jung did not see libido as organised around a single instinct or primary cause. Nevertheless, for Jung individual development organises experience and knowledge according to an unfolding plan; the "voices" of the archetypes, if understood, suggest an epigenetic trajectory one's life should take (whether this *trajectory* is understood is another question). Jung's term for the process of discovering and attempting to follow this "plan" is *individuation*, which is the therapeutic goal of analytical psychology.

In simple terms (which we shall complicate in Chapter 4), Jungian individuation is the person's becoming who s/he is by negotiating both collective norms and particularities in a paradoxical "building up of the particular" which is "already ingrained in the psychic constitution" (Jung, "Definitions" para. 761). Individuation is the process of achieving the "optimum" compensatory relationship between consciousness and the unconscious. But as with the archetype, Jung's development of individuation as a concept emerges as a Deleuzian line of flight, cutting across traditions and disciplines while remaining unbound to any. Jung's earliest mention of the concept of individuation seems to have been in his *Septem Sermones ad Mortuos* ("Seven Sermons to the Dead"), published anonymously in 1916 and which is also a Gnostic fragment from *The Red Book*, Jung's self-authored and illustrated folio manuscript reflecting his imaginative engagement with his own unconscious following the traumatic break with Freud circa 1912. In this text, Jung refers to the "Principium Individuationis" (the principle of individuation) intrinsic to all creatures as a drive to resist the "primeval, perilous sameness" of the pleroma, Jung's Gnostic term for the "nothingness or fullness" from which "creatura" emerge (Jung, *Memories* 379–80).

But crucially, Jung elsewhere equates individuation with the *nonhuman*, which unworks any pretence to a teleological, linear understanding of individuation as proceeding tidily from one stage to another. Indeed, the following description illustrates the opposing tendencies of preformation and epigenesis which often inform Jung's articulation of individuation:

> [I]ndividuation is not an intensification of consciousness, it is very much more. For you must have the consciousness of something before it can be intensified, and that means experience, life lived. You can only be really conscious of things which you have experienced, so individuation must be understood as life. Only life integrates, only life and what we do in life makes the individual appear. [...] Individuation is the accomplishment through life. For instance, say a cell begins to divide itself and to differentiate and develop into a certain plant or a certain animal; that is the process of individuation. It is that one becomes what one is, that one accomplishes one's destiny, all the determinations that are given in the form of the germ; it is the unfolding of the germ and becoming the primitive pattern that one was born with. (*Visions* 2: 757–58)

On the one hand, individuation seems preformationist in nature (a matter of "accomplishing one's destiny" and the "determinations of the germ"). But on the other hand, it is precisely in the connection with "life" and the division of cells that individuation is opened up to the possibility of mutation, monstrosity, and deviation from categorical norms. Moreover,

Jung's further complication of individuation with the open economy of psychic "experience" moves individuation into more indeterminate territory – indeed, it is *psyche*, and its consanguinity with Nature, which ultimately undermines teleology in Jungian individuation: "The psyche is a phenomenon not subject to our will; *it is nature*, and [...] cannot be changed into something artificial without profound injury to our humanity" ("A Psychological View" para. 831; my italics). Jung will extend individuation even further into inorganic processes, with profound ramifications for the ethical possibilities of Romantic metasubjectivity we will explore in the Conclusion. But for now, let us observe that individuation's indeterminate, ateleological dimensions are also central to Schelling's thought beginning with the *First Outline*, which concerns itself with the question of how natural products individuate from within a primordial, undifferentiated fluidity. "The highest problem of the philosophy of nature," Schelling writes, is to explain how "Nature in general *evolves* with *finite velocity*, and so shows determinate products (of determinate synthesis) everywhere" (*FO* 77).

Analytical psychology's rhythms of progression and regression and archetypal projection and recollection, and its entanglement of psyche with Nature, allow us to conceive it as a supplement to psychoanalysis in the Derridean sense. Derrida takes up Kant's discussion of the *parergon* in the *Critique of Judgment* (1790), which is something that is both ornamental and augments a "complete object" (Kant's example is the relation between a picture frame and the "complete" painting which nevertheless needs the frame to complete it). For Kant, the *parergon* is always inessential to contemplating the complete work of art (*ergon*), but the "completion" of the object is called into question by its reliance on the *parergon*. In a word, the "complete" object relies on that which is outside it and which "incompletes" it. And just as the supplement "adds only to replace [...] intervenes or insinuates itself *in-the-place*-of" (Derrida, *Of Grammatology* 145) analytical psychology, emerging from psychoanalysis, "adds" a prospective, future-oriented element to depth-psychological theorising of the self and seeks to "replace" Freud's emphasis on the personalised subject by *also* reaching further back to the primordial origins of humanity, cast as the collective unconscious.[17] In this spirit, Todd Dufresne contextualises Jung's spectral presence in *Beyond the Pleasure Principle*: "Freud's attempt to ostracize Jung's generalized libido theory – to annul it in the eyes of psychoanalysis – with a 'generalized' death drive, only mirrored in reverse that very theory. As such, Jung's monistic vision of libido remains the *essential supplement*, the counterpart, to Freud's death drive and, consequently, the true structural partner to Freud's uneasy dualism of 1920" (*Tales* 23; my italics). More than this: by way of articulating Romantic metasubjectivity I will suggest in what follows that analytical psychology is, in fact, far more compatible with Derridean deconstruction than psychoanalysis and that the intellectual politics of Derrida's time inevitably point to a missed encounter between Jung and Derrida. But this missed encounter is also symptomatic of a broader resistance to theory which marks Jungian criticism. In the final section of this Introduction, I want to touch on some of the characteristically embattled Jungian sojourns into theory and philosophy as a means to suggest ways in which Romantic metasubjectivity opens a space for more productive engagements between Jungian thought and contemporary theory.

Jung and the resistance to theory

Begun in 1914 soon after the break with Freud and based in a series of traumatic (and arguably precognitive) fantasies preceding the First World War, *The Red Book* is a narrative of Jung's confrontation with the unconscious, written and illustrated in his own hand, depicting parables and dialogues with mythical figures after the style of Nietzsche's *Zarathustra* (*Red Book* 30, 88).[18] Its 2009 publication precipitated numerous discussions about its broader relevance to analytical psychology. Much of the *Red Book*'s reception reflects a pervasive Idealism in Jungian scholarship which often reduces the general economy of analytical metapsychology to an ontotheology of presence, which elides Jung's more radical thinking and closes down the possibilities of engagement with much contemporary theory. One such example deals with Schelling: Paul Bishop uses *The Red Book* to argue the quite valid point that "Schelling – and the intellectual debate of the period of German classicism and Romanticism [...] offers a framework within which we can better understand Jung's project in analytical psychology as a whole and in *The Red Book* in particular" ("Jung's *Red Book*" 337). But in designating *The Red Book* as Jung's "long-withheld masterpiece," Bishop repeats an auratic transference on to this "sacred text" symptomatic of a religious reading of Jung. Moreover, by categorising Schelling as idealist (337) Bishop obfuscates *Naturphilosophie*'s centrality to Schelling's thought by treating it as merely a preamble to the philosophy of art and the 1800 *System* which, following an orthodox and dated reading, he regards as Schelling's overarching system (347). In doing so, Bishop effectively closes analytical psychology off to the broader potential of a theoretical encounter with Schelling.

But the drive to idealise analytical psychology is particularly strong in the work of Wolfgang Giegerich, whose Hegelian reading of Jung empties analytical psychology of "irrational" factors such as the archetypes and the collective unconscious in favour of an alchemical-dialectical teleological movement of "Soul." For Giegerich, analytical psychology "is rooted in the Notion soul [...] explicitly set up [to give] (relatively) free play to the unfolding of the complexities of the Notion and harbors within itself, in implicit, germinal form [...] a *higher logical status of consciousness*, one that could be hoped to be able to match *the logical status our reality has long reached*" (*Soul's Logical Life* 53; my italics). Thus individuation, for Giegerich, is nothing more than a "Jungian power word," a subjective need eclipsing what he sees as the real (read: logical) substance of "the Jungian heritage" (85). For Giegerich, the labour of the Concept erases individuation as the core process of true psychology. Moreover, according to Giegerich Jung "hypostatized (substantiated) the unconscious" as a positive entity and "reified the archetypes" as "timeless factors" to the point where they are "positivized and logically removed from *within* the real psychic process and set up as external 'dominants' of this process" ("Love the Questions Themselves" 259). Jung's view of psychic illness as something potentially transformative is seen as a theoretical flaw. Indeed, assuming a Hegelian Archimedean point from which to survey history in its entirety, Giegerich negates the unconscious *itself* as something which "cannot be demonstrated and [...] could not possibly have been discovered," as only "an idea or construct in the minds of certain people. [...] Today, being able to see the crazes of the twentieth century from a historical distance, we no longer have to believe in the unconscious" (260).

Giegerich's dismissal of Jung's Romantic-dissociationist heritage centres on his notion of interiority – the idea that the soul's movement is absolutely "logical movement" with no Foucauldian thought of the outside. He writes: "There is nothing outside the psyche, no other, nothing new. The notion or logic of the soul precludes a beyond, an 'abroad.' [There is no] demarcation line separating what is inside the soul from what is out there. We are hopelessly stuck *in* the soul['s] absolute interiority" ("Is the Soul 'Deep'?" 136–37). The "conquest" of this absolute interiority's infinity consists in "the alchemical, logically negative process of an internal putrefaction, corruption, fermentation, sublimation of 'whatever is there' [in this infinity] deeper into itself" (139). History, which acquires for the Romantics a traumatic affinity with Being, is here merely the aftereffect of dialectic ("The Unassimilable Remnant" 445); all things "unconscious" are the misunderstandings of a "twentieth century craze," waste products of the soul's Hegelian teleological movement. Indeed, for Giegerich Schelling is an "ontotheological" thinker ("Jungian Psychology" 243) and, with excessive polemic, vehemently contests McGrath's view that Schellingian metaphysics is a "natural ally" for analytical psychology (McGrath, "The Question" 23). For Giegerich, "Schelling's project had always aimed, from beginning to end, for a grand system, an overall closed system" ("Jungian Psychology as Metaphysics?" 242). However, Giegerich's references to Schelling are overwhelmingly to the 1800 *System of Transcendental Idealism* and the 1801/1802 "Presentations" of Schelling's philosophy, none of which can be reasonably said to represent Schelling's oeuvre as a whole (indeed, Schelling himself not only consciously dropped transcendental Idealism after these brief forays but also returned to the *Naturphilosophie*). Giegerich dismisses a Schelling-Jung link altogether as an "emotional need" which leads people to establish links between *Naturphilosophie* and Jung, who for Giegerich can only be a thinker of alchemical teleology (244). As I will argue in Chapter 4, while there are teleological *moments* in Jung's alchemical studies and his desire to link stages of alchemy with stages of individuation, he ultimately unworks this teleology to make linear-alchemical progressions corpuscular, as part of a more fluid purposiveness.

As the following chapters will explore in more detail, Romantic metasubjectivity contests *tout court* such a Procrustean imposition of alchemical teleology on to Jungian thought and recovers the nonrational aspects of analytical psychology (the collective unconscious, the archetypes, the Self) which Giegerich abjects. Indeed, it involves reading Jung through the full compass of theoretical transferences informing his thought – away from the strictures of teleology and analytical psychology's therapeutics of presence and toward a specifically Romantic discipline of theory as "a field that lies midway between philosophy and criticism," between phenomenology (the study of the structures of consciousness and their expression in culture)[19] and deconstruction (as the interrogation of ontotheological "presence"), and thus partaking of both (Rajan, "Phenomenology" 158, 160). With this, let us turn to one recent theoretical relationship in Jung studies which has been subject to several problematic attempts at synthesis – the relationship between analytical psychology and Derridean deconstruction.

We have seen how theory can resist Jung; it remains an unfortunate fact that many Jungians also resist theory. Nevertheless, when Shamdasani refers to the collective unconscious as a Borgesian "library within" (*C.G. Jung* 49), he is touching on a fundamentally rhizomatic nexus within analytical psychology which situates it in close proximity to deconstruction. Deconstruction can be provisionally defined as the process of examining systems, methodologies, or other structures to reveal their constitutive incompletion, or the problems of their pretence to completion. Rajan defines deconstruction as "a transposition of phenomenological into linguistic models that retains the ontological concerns of the former" (*Deconstruction* 7) whose notion of writing (*écriture*) does not isolate the literary from the broader discourse of philosophical ideas. In other words, deconstruction calls for a sensitive reading (deconstruction) of structures and their less-than-stable relation to what lies outside their boundaries – attunement to the ways in which the "writing" of these structures, disciplines, and methodologies always already leaves them open to their unthought.

This theoretical sensitivity has often gone missing in Jungian criticism, which often prefers an interiority in which theory is (mis)translated into a Jungian rubric, resulting in the elision of analytical psychology's authentically deconstructive valency. For example, Polly Young-Eisendrath sees "little resonance" between Jung and deconstruction but adopts a somewhat dubious version of the latter as a "branch of postmodern theory" which "explicitly rejects a psychology of coherence, integration, or universal principles of development in favour of a psychology of discontinuity, lack of coherence, and local influences on development" (33). For her, deconstruction is "a political critique of human ideals and virtues [...] a skeptical philosophy of doubt and dismantling, based on a negative assumption that human lives are governed mostly by power arrangements" (79–80). Against this, she sees a "constructivist" Jung affirming *everything* as human interpretation. She denies the archetypes any part in this interpretive process because "even our very perceptions are interpretations, and so nothing is absolutely fixed and eternal in our phenomenal world." But in the next passage, she recapitulates a Kantian dichotomy between this phenomenal world and "universal aspects of our subjectivity" through which "we are all human beings who are universally constrained and endowed in certain predispositions to perceive ourselves and the world" (33). Susan Rowland makes some interesting observations regarding the tension in Jung between a logocentric, image-based Christian individuation process and an "Eros-based" narrative purportedly deconstructing a Logos-Eros inside/outside distinction. But she uses this to read Derrida – rather incomprehensibly – as "that other architect of mythical re-individuation" (106) who "emphasis[es] the goddess" (111), thus missing deconstruction's theoretical point and laying Derrida to rest on a Procrustean bed of mythical drama, constructing the very romance of unity which deconstruction fundamentally suspects. The mythical understanding of deconstruction here (as "son-lover" in the "Sky-Father/Earth-Mother" dyad) relapses into ontotheology at the expense of deconstruction's interrogation of presence. Indeed, just as prejudiced theorists often do not bother citing Jung, Rowland's substitution of other authors for Derrida's primary texts reflects this evasion of deconstruction's radical core instead of an earnest engagement with it.

Pellegrino D'Acierno and Karin Barnaby approach the issue more judiciously, rightly suggesting that Jung can "elucidate the psychological dynamics" suggested by "deconstructivist discoveries" (xxiii). Edward Casey takes up Jung's suspicion of the superstitious belief in "nebulous power-words" (Jung, *Alchemical Studies* 49) as a point of connection with Derrida's deconstruction of the language of metaphysics as part of a larger "recourse to the polyformity of phenomenology in flight from the monism of metaphysics" (Casey 320). And Ross Woodman's more sophisticated thematic alignment of Jung and Derrida regarding the significance of madness in symbolic orders preserves a phenomenological approach to Romanticism which, Rajan argues (*Deconstruction* xii–xiii), has been exorcised from American deconstruction: "Jung struggled less to imprison madness in an archetypal system than phenomenologically to transform it into an ever evolving consciousness evident in [Romantic] poetry" (Woodman 17). On the deconstruction side of the divide few seem to have specifically engaged with Jung, and he seems to have been predictably used as a term of derogation. In what could only have been an insult in the intellectual politics of the 1970s, Élisabeth Roudinesco compared Derrida's work with Jung's, which "flabbergasted" Derrida and led to a protracted falling-out between the two (Peeters 215, 365).[20]

It is important to do justice to the phenomenology of the psyche which Jung puts at the heart of analytical psychology (Jung, "Foreword to Jung" para. 742). But as "crypto-metaphysics," Jung's depth-psychological thought need not lead one to oversimplifying distinctions; contrary to Casey, "metaphysics" and "monistic" closure are not synonyms. Although both Jung and Schelling are in many ways "post-metaphysical" thinkers insofar as their oeuvres challenge the closure of system, their use of metaphysical concepts (often screened by psychology in Jung's case) points to the problem of demarcating metaphysics from its "post."[21] Romantic metasubjectivity's ontological terrain theorises what is missing in these more impressionistic accounts of Jung's affinity with deconstruction: a missed encounter between Jung and Derrida, a theoretical rapprochement heretofore elided by the *fort/da* with psychoanalysis which marked Derrida's intellectual milieu. This affinity articulates the subject Derrida might have found in this missed encounter, one which might have addressed his later dissatisfaction with psychoanalysis' own pleasure principles, the "large Freudian machines" which inhibit the productive psyche to the point of a closure he identifies with metaphysics. In the final year of his life, Derrida writes of psychoanalysis:

> the id, the ego, the superego, the ideal ego, the ego ideal, the secondary process and the primary process of repression, etc. – in a word, the large Freudian machines (including the concept and the word 'unconscious'!) – are [only provisional weapons] against a philosophy of consciousness, of transparent and fully responsible intentionality. I have little faith in their future. I do not think that a metapsychology can hold up for long under scrutiny [...] The grand entities (ego, id, superego, etc.), but also the grand conceptual 'oppositions' – which are too solid, and therefore very precarious – that followed those of Freud, such as the real, the imaginary, and the symbolic, etc. or 'introjection' and 'incorporation' – these seem to me to be carried away [...] by the ineluctable necessity of some 'difference' that erases or displaces their borders. [...] I am therefore never ready to follow Freud and his followers in the functioning of the grand theoretical machines, in their functionalisation. ("In Praise of Psychoanalysis" 172–74)

Jung's emphasis on the play of archetypal forces can be read as a general economy of symbolic writing – an ontological *écriture* which preserves the fundamental movements of Derridean *différance* which interrogate presence.[22] In other words, the grammatology of Being is synonymous with an *archetypal grammatology* which, unlike the psychoanalytic "machines," admits the play of *différance* among its constituent (archetypal) forces. It is this metapsychological convergence with deconstruction that allows for a more productive conception of the Jung-Derrida missed encounter. And indeed, Derrida was not concerned with eradicating the idea of the "subject" altogether; Manfred Frank suggests that even if subsequent Derrideans saw subjectivity as an epiphenomenon of *différance*, "Derrida does not repudiate the phenomenon of self-consciousness that is evident in itself; to do this would indeed mean falling into absurdity. What Derrida has in mind [is] a different, more illuminating explanation of that same phenomenon that is taken into consideration only within the framework of transcendental philosophy at the price of indissoluble aporias" (*What is Neostructuralism?* 257). The presence of the "self," as "proper word and unique name" (Derrida, "Différance" 160), is deferred – not deleted. Indeed, to see this nonknowledge (Bataille)[23] not for its own sake but as the conditions of possibility for knowledge itself against the closure of "organic totality," as Arkady Plotnitsky has compellingly argued ("Conclusion" 243, 248), is both quintessentially Romantic and a core tenet of analytical psychology. Archetypal grammatology articulates the absent subject of Derridean deconstruction because the Jungian Self is not hypostatised as a transcendental, self-present "I" but is rather a centripetal force of selfhood writing itself, as ontological *écriture*, through the symbolic unfolding of what Derrida calls *différance*. It is precisely these provisional constellations of knowledge from a nonmolar intensity which make *différance* possible. Thus, the Romantic metasubject is the "subject" Derrida, who remained stranded before the Law and doorkeeper of psychoanalysis, would perhaps have wished he had.

This book consciously proceeds via repetition with difference and a rhythm of regression-progression, harking back at times to the foundational work of earlier chapters and gesturing to the future of those concepts in what follows. The first chapter, "A First Outline of Romantic Metasubjectivity," reads the *Naturphilosophie* of Schelling's *First Outline of a System of the Philosophy of Nature* (1799) as a theoretical site of analytical psychology's distinction from psychoanalysis, indeed as a *Naturphilosophie après la lettre*. In this quasi-subjective space (one which lacks subjects but possesses a nascent absolute subject), the fundamental ambivalence of Schelling's Nature towards its products anticipates the dynamic of Jungian libido. This dynamic informs a Jungian (re)figuration of the death drive, what I call

Thanatopoiesis as, like Schelling's Nature, both a regression toward origins and a crucial drive *forward* which catalyses creativity and productivity in a futurity for which psychoanalysis cannot account. Chapter 2, "The Romantic Metasubjective Unconscious," tracks the theoretical transferences between *Naturphilosophie* and analytical psychology in more detail, articulating the Romantic metasubjective unconscious as coextensive with the specifically Romantic historicity which Pfau identifies at the cusp of modernity. To elucidate this unconscious, I turn to Schelling's exposition of the actant as non-molar (de)composing force in Schelling's *First Outline* to discern its remarkable isomorphism with the Jungian archetype. This isomorphism articulates Romantic metasubjectivity's radically historical psyche, a psyche underwritten by a rhizomatic unconscious which makes possible (without being reducible to) the materialist subject assumed by much Romantic criticism. And indeed, it is an under*writing* in the sense of a grammatology of Being, an open economy of signification and symbolisation constellated around the "Self of one's self" (Schelling's absolute subject, Jung's Self), which proceeds through this difference without simply *being* it.

Chapters 3 and 4 can be seen as complementary to each other. "Romantic Metasubjectivity: Experience," casts Schelling's "On the Nature of Philosophy as Science" (1821) as a philosophical psychology bound by the materiality of the *First Outline*'s Nature. It then traces the background of the phenomenological *experience* of Romantic metasubjectivity through Schelling's *System of Transcendental Idealism* (1800) as a text between Idealism and Romanticism which both courts and resists the *Naturphilosophie* of the *First Outline*. The *System* claims to have sublated *Naturphilosophie* in a transcendental system of self-consciousness akin to Fichte's subjectivism, but also remains eternally bound to Nature in a dynamic where two systems, to use a Jungian refrain to which I will return, "touch and do not touch" (Jung, "On the Nature of the Psyche" para. 418). From this anxiety of influence comes Schelling's formulation of *intellectual intuition* – the philosophical apprehension of the union of real and ideal (two decades later he will rethink this as *ecstasy*, which marks a more radical and traumatic encounter with the absolute subject which is not bound by the aesthetic). I also explore intellectual intuition's continuity with Jung's formulation of synchronicity, an acausal connecting principle which provides a therapeutical, developmental context for the experience of these energies – expressed by Schelling as the "ecstatic" contact with the absolute subject.

Chapter 4 turns to Schelling's *Philosophical Investigations Into the Essence of Human Freedom* (1809) and the 1815 *Ages of the World* to articulate individuation as the radically *a*teleological unfolding of personality which marks Romantic metasubjectivity. Paradoxically, it is precisely the traumatic experience of Romantic metasubjectivity that unworks any teleological possibility to individuation, even as this experience makes individuation possible in the first place. This experience is the confrontation between the person and the purposive force of self-organisation which constellates knowledge and experience. This chapter begins with the *Freedom* essay, which Schelling calls his theory of personality (*Freedom* 73) and which enacts *Thanatopoiesis'* regressive-progressive rhythm in a moral theatre. The *Freedom* essay explains the reality of evil as the energy of a rhythmic relation between the individual and the *centrum*, the (un)ground of all being as it exists in the individual. Cultivating this relationship is necessary for what Schelling calls "salvation," but evil consists in the individual breaking away from this relationship and being for-itself. This rhythmic attraction and repulsion is the index of personality and individuation. We then turn to Schelling's *Ages of the World* (1811–1815), whose textual history seems to reflect the darkening of his thought as the Idealism of the 1811 and 1813 versions mutates into something far more indeterminate by 1815, when psychoanalysis (in its broadest sense) emerges to traumatise teleology with the movement of the potencies [*Potenzenlehre*]. *Ages'* deployment of Mesmerism and magnetic sleep as dramatisations of the *Potenzenlehre* also uniquely position it as a proto-Jungian text, and so I turn to Jung to illustrate the remarkable degree to which these two texts of Schelling's prefigure individuation as well as the Jungian concepts of *inflation* (where the ego is taken over by archetypal energies) and the *transcendent function* (the creation of new knowledge in individuation). These Jungian concepts carry forward the undeveloped psychological tendencies of the *Freedom* essay and *Ages* to articulate a dissociative therapeutics based on a purposive, hence alinear model of individuation.

Chapter 5, as "applied Romantic metasubjectivity," focuses on mythology as the crucial expression of Romantic metasubjectivity's libidinal potentiation. Both Schelling and Jung think mythology not as stable pantheonic forms (Zeus, Christ, etc.), but rather as non-molar intensities, "theogonic processes" (in Schelling's Philosophy of Mythology) or Jung's archetypal mythologems. Schelling's Philosophy of Mythology was a crucial bridge to his later positive philosophy, "a historical philosophy that [...] integrates the orders of necessity that structure our existence" (Matthews, "Translator's Introduction" 30) against a Hegelian "negative philosophy" ultimately confined to conceptual thought.[24] Mythology assumes a similarly existential role in analytical psychology whose goal, stated simply, is to cultivate the individual's ability to "live their own myth" as the essence of individuation. With this in mind, this chapter reads William Wordsworth's *The Prelude* (1799–1850) and Percy Bysshe Shelley's *Prometheus Unbound* (1820) as two distinct yet related instances of what I call Romantic "Prometheanisms."

The Conclusion explores the contemporary ethical implications of this model of personhood, asking: can there be an ethics of Romantic metasubjectivity? I begin with Jung's late work *Answer to Job* (1952), which makes a case strikingly similar to Schelling's for evil's energic importance in the creation of the world. Indeed, Jung makes the crucial argument that even God must undergo Schelling's crisis of consciousness – even God must individuate. This non-human aspect of individuation aligns the human person with Nature in a way that makes a Romantic metasubjective *ethics* impossible. But this does not obviate the need for meaningful relation and obligation, a *morality* which resists the phantasy of overarching anthropocentric ethical paradigms in favour of the individual encounter. To this end I take up John Caputo's *Against Ethics* (1993), which offers a model of obligation and responsibility without recourse to ethical paradigms as a contemporary example of how Romantic metasubjectivity might operate in twenty-first-century culture. The non-human, hence non-ethical potency of individuation is a self-evident concern of the *Naturphilosophie*, taken up in both Schelling's engagement with nineteenth-century natural sciences and chemistry. But analytical psychology's radical non-humanism also leads Jung to Nature for examples of individuative self-organisation – particularly the crystal, which aligns Jung's thinking on individuation with Romantic crystallogeny as part of the nineteenth-century concern with self-formative forces in Nature. In turn, this individuative crystallogeny resonates profoundly with one of the twenty-first century's most infamous pop-cultural protagonists; thus, to crystallise this idea further I end with a brief analysis of Walter White, protagonist of the hit TV series *Breaking Bad* (2008–2013), who offers a particularly striking and timely representation of this non-human, non-ethical individuation. Walter White suggests a different, more contemporary Prometheanism than those of Wordsworth and Shelley, but one no less resonant with Romantic metasubjectivity, and with this brief, somewhat freehand analysis I hope to suggest ways in which Romantic metasubjectivity can contribute to contemporary cultural criticism.

A final word here on translating and citing Jung. Jung's *Collected Works* have arguably suffered more than other English translations from translator prejudices and errors: R.F.C. Hull, described by some as an "ardent rationalist," had difficulty understanding several of Jung's concepts and did not always follow Jung's directions, which led to a "silent correction" of Jung's texts without his consent which has had far-reaching consequences for the reception of some of his ideas. Moreover, the English *Collected Works* was released before the German and with material that was not added to the German edition (see Shamdasani, *Jung Stripped Bare* chap. 2). So while Hull has undoubtedly performed a great service in translating Jung for English audiences, like James Strachey's Freud translations the English texts must at times be read with healthy suspicion. For these reasons I have checked and, where necessary, modified each citation of Jung in this book; changes range from the cosmetic (relieving Jung of a certain nineteenth-century fustiness) to rectifying mistranslations which hinder the understanding of Jungian concepts. I gloss such changes where applicable and provide the original German for particularly significant terms (e.g. *Sinn* and the vexing problem of Jung's usage of *Psyche* and *Seele*). Significant issues in translation are glossed where appropriate. With the rare exception, I cite Jung's English *Collected Works* by paragraph number. Where indicated, I modify translations based on C.G. Jung's *Gesammelte Werke* (Patmos Verlag, 2011) and include all German sources in the References. Because paragraph numbers are not always interchangeable between the *Collected Works* and the *Gesammelte Werke*, I cite the German by volume and page number, for example, *GW* 4: 255. I am grateful to Jason Wirth for patiently fielding my many translation questions and his insights regarding particularly challenging concepts and passages; all shortcomings, of course, remain my own.

Notes

1. Jung first used the term "analytical psychology" in 1913 to differentiate his approach from Freudian psychoanalysis ("On the Doctrine" para. 1355 & n).

2. *Tel Quel* was a literary magazine begun in France in 1960, which published many seminal essays in deconstruction and post-structuralism (including contributions from Derrida, Blanchot, Foucault, and others).

3. For a particularly poignant example of how thinkers such as Élisabeth Roudinesco insisted on Nazifying Jung against facts proving otherwise (including Jung's WW2 enlistment as Agent 488 by the Office of Strategic Services [OSS; later the American CIA]), see Kirsch 152 and Bair 492–94.

4. Simply speaking, in *The Accursed Share* (1: 19ff), Georges Bataille defines a restricted economy as a relatively isolated system of operations where each agent has definable roles (e.g. changing a tire, ploughing a field), versus a general economy in which an excess of energy makes the boundaries of this system much more porous and indeterminate and demands the expenditure of this energy in irrational ways which may imperil the system (art and its potential to disrupt culture being one of Bataille's examples).

5. Generally speaking, the Romantic sublime is an overwhelming experience of powerful poetic rhetoric or of abject terror in the face of Nature's vastness (waterfalls, mountains, cliffs). Romantic-period thinkers overwhelmingly saw the sublime experience as culminating in the optimistic reassertion of the mind's power.

6. *Nachträglichkeit* is Freud's term for the analysand's revision of past events in the service of forward development. But in his analysis of the Wolf Man – ostensibly a response to Jung's critique of the primal scene as retroactively constructed – Freud binds *Nachträglichkeit* to the primal phantasy as the claim to origins, the demarcation of a single event which "dramatis[es] into the primal moment or original point of departure for a history. In the 'primal scene', it is the origin of the subject that is represented" (see Laplanche and Pontalis 113–14, 332).

7. See Beach 116ff. Indeed, from his earliest work Schelling is a thinker of potencies: magnetism, light, and electricity are conceived as potencies in the *First Outline* well before the *Potenzenlehre* of *Ages*.

8. While we typically understand rhythm as monotonous and regular, here it has a certain aleatorism which Hölderlin clarifies in his theory of rhythm and caesura (discussed in Chapter 4). In other words, rhythm here is *emergent* and not *immanent*.

9. Here and throughout I use "man" for the sake of expediency, as it was how both Schelling and Jung designated humanity in general. It should not be taken to exclude the non-masculine.

10. Robert Brown's *The Later Philosophy of Schelling: The Influence of Boehme on the Works of 1809–1815* (Cranbury, NJ: Associated UP, 1977) is a valuable study of Schelling's engagement with Böhme in the beginning phases of his positive philosophy.

11. Against this mythology, Dean Rapp (233) points out that British Edwardian intellectual circles overwhelmingly preferred Jungian thought to psychoanalysis.

12. For Derrida, Western philosophy is conditioned by a *metaphysics of presence*, which assumes that thought and language come from beings unproblematically and fully present to themselves, and that writing is secondary to speech, which retains the living "presence" of the speaking being. This metaphysics also conceives of Being *itself* in terms of this presence, making difference secondary or derivative, a "lack of presence," where Derrida sees it as constitutive *of* Being.

13. To make matters more confusing: in "Definitions," Jung's original German reads *das urtümliche Bild*. Hull translates this as "primordial image," but more accurately it means "natural" or "primeval" image, which does not have the same claim to absolute origins as "primordial." *Urtümlich* is closest to *ursprünglich* ("original"), and both carry the very specific sense of "from the beginning" or "from the origin." What makes it "natural" is that it remains true to its origin, as in a river whose course has not been artificially changed. It is thus "ancient" or "primordial," but in a strictly autochthonic sense. This does not make it static or unchanging: an *urtümlich* river continually flows, but it is ancient and originary, hence "natural" in this sense. For Schelling, *natura naturans* is *Urnatur* ("originary") and *urtümlich*, "natural."

14. Pierre Janet (1859–1947), founding figure in psychology whose work (particularly *Psychological Automatism* [1889]) helped develop the dissociationist approach to the psyche. See Ellenberger 358ff. and Shamdasani, *Jung and the Making* 122ff.

15. Despite dissociationism's chequered acceptance in the psychological community (Haule 245), Deleuzian-Guattarian schizoanalysis shares its fundamental understanding of the psyche. Schizoanalysis is the project of "tirelessly taking apart egos and their presuppositions" and "liberating the prepersonal singularities they enclose and repress" (*Anti-Oedipus* 362).

16. Although Jung's energic approach to libido is *not* teleological (e.g. there is no *telos* or final endpoint to its unfolding) but rather *purposive*, Haule clearly uses "teleological" in the latter sense here.

17. See Barentsen for a more detailed consideration of this supplementarity in Freud and Jung.

18. Put simply, *The Red Book* can be read as a poetic case study of Jungian individuation and specifically of active imagination, a concept we will explore in Chapter 4.

19. Apart from obvious exceptions, here and throughout I use "phenomenology" not as Hegel deploys it in service of teleology (a "phenomenology of spirit") but in its more unbound sense of potentiated (or libidinally charged) natural objects, which is also how Jung uses the term.

20. But Derrida's reading of Freud's agon with Jung in *The Post Card* (1980) perhaps signals a more leavened consideration of the latter. And by the time he writes "The Transcendental 'Stupidity'" (2007), Derrida has acknowledged Jung's significance via Deleuze: "Deleuze's absolute originality: in France, admiring Jung more than Freud" (37).

21. For a critique of the equation of metaphysics with "closure" see Bowie, *Schelling* 67ff.
22. *Différance* is Derrida's term for "the systematic play of differences, of the traces of differences, of the *spacing* by means of which elements are related to each other" (*Positions* 27).
23. Bataille sees "nonknowledge" as the anxiogenic non-ground of rational thought and knowledge from which emerge, according to inscrutable forces, organisations of knowledge and experience. I will say more about Bataille's nonknowledge in Chapter 3.
24. Edward Beach (107–8) offers a succinct discussion of negative and positive philosophies and their interrelation.

Chapter 1

A first outline of Romantic metasubjectivity

Contemporary scholarship (Grant, McGrath, ffytche) has recognised not only the multivalency of Schelling's oeuvre as a whole, but also the centrality of the *Naturphilosophie* he developed in the final years of the eighteenth century. Throughout his philosophical career Schelling returns to the *Naturphilosophie*'s core dynamics, remaining productively entangled in it to the extent that Iain Hamilton Grant writes: "Schellingianism *is* naturephilosophy throughout" (*Philosophies* 5). Ellenberger suggests that *Naturphilosophie* is an important basis for twentieth-century depth psychology: he writes that "there is hardly a single concept of Freud or Jung that had not been anticipated by the philosophy of nature" (205) but leaves this avenue unexplored. The "quasi-mythological nature" of metabiology in Freud's *Beyond the Pleasure Principle* (1920) leads Paul Ricoeur to argue for a defining relationship between Goethe's *Naturphilosophie* and Freud's libido theory as a whole (312f),[1] but this is where Freud's relationship to *Naturphilosophie* ends. For the nature of *Naturphilosophie* as a speculative physics positing fundamentally nonmolar, (de)composable forces behind the construction of matter itself is a concern far beyond Freud, who is at pains to distinguish his scientific project from the "mysticism" of nature philosophy ("Introductory Lectures" 20 & n. 1). In contrast to this, Romantic metasubjectivity marks affinities between *Naturphilosophie* and Jungian metapsychology which extend far beyond the personalist mechanisms of psychoanalysis. To elucidate this connection, this chapter frames the *Naturphilosophie* of Schelling's *First Outline* as a metaphysical site for the disciplinary *agon* between psychoanalysis and analytical psychology, reading Freud's *Project for a Scientific Psychology* (1895) and Jung's contemporaneous Zofingia lectures (1896–1899)[2] as engagements with the quasi-subjective space of Schelling's *Naturphilosophie*. These texts predate and prefigure the Freud-Jung schism, and in their wake I touch on other works as post-schismatic theoretical articulations. Freud's *A Phylogenetic Fantasy* (1915) is an early foray into the pre-human dimensions of libido which anticipates his extension of germ and cell theory into the speculative phylogenesis of *Beyond the Pleasure Principle* (1920), which I read in part as an engagement with the spectre of Jung.[3] Similarly, Jung's early critique of the hegemony of rational-empirical science prefigures his formulation of analytical psychology as he considers it in relation to the creation of world views [*Weltanschauungen*]. This formulation, which deconstructs other disciplines as a Foucauldian counter-science, culminates in *Symbols of Transformation* (1911–1912/1952) as the psychoanalytically heretical text which underwrites analytical psychology as a whole.[4]

Against this backdrop of *Naturphilosophie*, I also want to revisit the key issue in the Freud-Jung schism – the theory of libido – as the site of emergence for what I have described as *Thanatopoiesis*, the regressive-progressive, systolic-diastolic movement powering Romantic metasubjectivity. *Thanatopoiesis* reads Thanatos away from the yearning for inorganicity: libido is driven back to past experiences and the interiority of memory, but it is *also* impelled by present circumstances toward a horizon of self-development, a futurity that is always undecided and incomplete. In the words of Schelling's 1815 *Ages*, "all evolution presupposes involution" (83) – regression and progression entangled in a rhythm that can be intuited but which is never an object of knowledge. Indeed, the specifically Romantic quality of this bifurcated rhythm informs the ontopoetics of Schlegel's progressive universal poetry, which unfolds in precisely this manner as "capable of the highest and most variegated refinement, not only from within outwards, but also from without inwards" (*AF* #116). And the "progressive" nature of this universal poetry should be read not as a teleological progression but instead as a perpetual unfolding akin to Schelling's Nature; indeed, for Schlegel this poetry "should forever be becoming and never be perfected" (*AF* #116). The speculative physics of the 1799 *Naturphilosophie* thus allows one to trace the Romantic genealogy of *Thanatopoiesis* through Schlegel's progressive universal poetry to analytical psychology. Indeed, I will show that *Thanatopoiesis* establishes analytical psychology as a *Naturphilosophie après la lettre*, supplementing Freud's death instinct with a futurity marking the fundamental drive of Romantic metasubjectivity.

Schelling's *Naturphilosophie*: inhibition and "unnatural nature"

Tilottama Rajan judiciously reminds us that Schelling's *First Outline* "is not yet part of a history [and thus] brackets or re-idealises its more deconstructive insights" ("First Outline" 312). In a similar vein, Sean McGrath writes:

> The early Schellingian unconscious, developed in the nature-philosophy [...] is impersonal and immanent. It is not yet the dark side of God unveiled in the *Freedom* essay, not the underside of the personality of the *Stuttgart Seminars* [...] rather, it is the collective intelligence running through all of matter, and insofar as we too are material, running through us as well. [It is] the spirit of nature, nature spiritualized and given subjectivity, but of an impersonal quality. (*Dark Ground* 82)

This "collective intelligence" is, to use Lancelot Whyte's phrase, "potential mind" (116) not yet experientialised as psyche. It is *Naturphilosophie*'s version of the absolute subject (Peterson xxviii), and its dynamics are not yet part of the uniquely human history of suffering. It attempts to become object to itself as an abstract (if provisional) goal of Nature's infinite productivity. But although Schelling's unfolding "drama of a struggle *between form and the formless*" (*FO* 28) lacks *dramatis personae*, it is nevertheless linked to the forces of magnetism, gravity, and chemistry which occur in a temporal, historicised Being (albeit one bracketing time and space as markers of human history). Thus, *Naturphilosophie*'s dynamic unfolds not in a pre- or non-history but in a quasi-subjective space between world and psyche as it were, where the latter is *driven* to emerge as part of what David Krell calls Nature's tormented Idealism (*Contagion* 73ff). It is because of this emphasis on "thisness," the sheer facticity of Being and the attempt to think its emergence in *Naturphilosophie*, that neither Freud's personalist psyche nor his adherence to a Lamarckian inheritance of acquired characteristics can adequately articulate the *First Outline*'s protopsychology.[5]

In contrast to Freud's desire to conceive psychoanalysis as a natural science, Schelling's *Naturphilosophie*, as a dynamic "science of nature," is the foundation of a meta-physics – what he calls a "speculative" physics meant to discover the dynamic forces and drives behind Nature's infinite productivity. That is, *Naturphilosophie* "assumes that the sum of phenomena is not a mere world, but of necessity a Nature (that is, that this whole is not merely a product, but at the same time productive)" (*FO* 197). As such, *Naturphilosophie* unfolds in a register of process, drive, and compulsion: in the Introduction, Schelling writes that "Nature *can* produce nothing but what shows regularity and purpose, and Nature is *compelled* to produce it" (194). This Nature is one of "absolute activity," which is marked by "*the drive* [Trieb] *to an infinite development*" (18).[6] As necessity, Nature is also compelled, through this productive drive, to produce organic and inorganic natural products as part of a general economy of infinitely productive relations. And like Nature itself, the organism self-organises according to principles irreducible to a logical system, and the fact that each natural product performs within itself Nature's infinite productivity anticipates a mind-Nature parallelism with prototherapeutic properties which are taken up by Jung's model of the psyche. So even in the *Naturphilosophie*, this repetition of infinite production in the individual opens Nature to the bidirectionality of *Thanatopoiesis*. As Robert Richards writes, "[*Naturphilosophie*] suggested that nature might furnish a path back to the self [...] the exploration of nature might even be regarded as a necessary propaedeutic to the development of the self" (134). Nature is a Deleuzian fold, entangling interiority and exteriority: one finds oneself through Nature, but in going back "through" Nature one can move "forward" in self-development through Nature's "exploration."

Schelling's particular formulation of *Naturphilosophie* evolves from the broader field of German nature philosophy which encompasses Romantic biology and other disciplines. Writing that "all Romantic biologists were *Naturphilosophen*, but not all *Naturphilosophen* were Romantics," Richards argues that *Naturphilosophie* not only shifts away from eighteenth-century mechanist philosophy but also marks Schelling's move away from Kant within *Naturphilosophie* itself (8ff). The early *Naturphilosophen* included Kant, who conceived the archetypes of species as transcendental entities of an ideal reality. Schelling's *Naturphilosophie*, however, begins with natural (real) existence instead of (ideal) consciousness: "*the ideal must arise out of the real and admit of explanation from it*" (*FO* 194). Schelling moves against Kant's noumenal-phenomenal bifurcation of Being as well as Fichte's "absolute I," which makes nature an epiphenomenon of subjective consciousness. In the architectonic of Kant's *Critique of Pure*

Reason, the whole is subservient to the operations of its component parts; Kant's organicism is a regulative idea that denies Nature any genuinely aleatory force. In contrast, Schelling's *Naturphilosophie*, as "an *a priori* study of the 'Idea' of nature," holds that Nature "is not a mechanical system but a series of basic 'forces' or 'impulses' that mirror at the basic level the same kind of determinations that are operative in us at the level of freedom. [Thus *Naturphilosophie*] must construct an account of nature that is continuous with our freedom" (Pinkard 178, 181). And this continuity is also a repetition of the difference *between* Nature and human freedom, throwing open their contingent natures.

Richards writes, perhaps with some irony, that "the fundamental idea of Schelling's *Naturphilosophie* was simply that nature strove to achieve the absolute" (297) – hardly a simple idea, for although Schelling critiques Kantian formalism by conceiving nature as radical productivity, he does not jettison the *a priori*. Rather, anticipating Deleuze's conception of transcendental empiricism[7] and Jung's mature formulation of the archetype, Schelling relocates the *a priori* in experience. In the "Introduction to the Outline" he writes:

> *Not only do we know this or that through experience, but we originally know nothing at all except through experience, and by means of experience*, and in this sense the whole of our knowledge consists of the judgments of experience. These judgments become *a priori* principles when we become conscious of them as necessary, and thus every judgment, whatever its content may be, may be raised to that dignity, insofar as the distinction between *a priori* and *a posteriori* judgments is [...] a distinction made solely *with respect to our knowing* [...] every judgment which is merely historical for me—i.e., a judgment of experience—becomes, notwithstanding, an *a priori* principle as soon as I arrive, whether directly or indirectly, at insight into its internal necessity. [...] It *is not, therefore*, that WE KNOW *Nature* as *a priori*, but Nature IS *a priori*. (*FO* 198)

Written after the *First Outline*, and as an attempt to rein in Nature's infinite productivity by synchronising *Naturphilosophie* with transcendental Idealism's emphasis on the primacy of thought and self-consciousness (194), Schelling's Introduction wants to give Nature's productivity the sole task of "transporting" the real into the ideal world (193). But even here, in introducing psychology and appealing to *experience* as the criteria for *a priori* principles, Schelling does not rein in this indeterminacy so much as redouble it on the level of the psyche. And in stating that *"Nature* is *a priori,"* he folds the *a priori* back into contingency, which makes the *Naturphilosophie* forever resistant to encapsulation by self-consciousness.

So in the *Naturphilosophie*, the *a priori* is no longer separated from phenomena but is now imbricated with thought's (revisable) experience of natural objects as external stimuli. What Hegel will economise as dialectic becomes, with Schelling, dialects *of* dialectic as the absolute is now beholden to the intensity of interactions and events dictated by the individual's inscrutable grammatology of Being, written by "judgments of experience." These judgements are part of an anterior organisation, but this organisation is simultaneously, paradoxically constituted by its parts, in events where the individual realises a thought's "internal necessity." Indeed, this internal necessity offers a way through what would otherwise pose a logical problem for Schelling: how far one can move *from* the deductive principles of natural science *to* experiential Nature if "the ideal must arise out of the real and admit of explanation from it"? This movement is the sole means of discerning the *a priori* structures of Nature's infinite unfolding. Deleuze and Guattari describe this movement of concepts as syneidetic events, "fragmentary wholes" "jointed" together by "zones, thresholds or becomings" in relations of extensivity with other concepts: "every concept relates back to other concepts, not only in its history but in its becoming or its present connections. Every concept has components that may, in turn, be grasped as concepts" ("What is a Concept?" 16, 19, 20–21). Insofar as the *First Outline* speaks of an experiencing subject, Schelling anticipates this Deleuzian subject as a nodal point for these syneidetic events.

Schelling conceives the "regularity and purpose" of both Nature's productivity and thought's "internal necessity" (*FO* 194) in terms of a graduated scale of development [*Stufenfolge*]. The *Stufenfolge* is a development of increasing complexity in Nature's products, directed toward an *"absolute product"* that *"lives in all products, that always* becomes *and never* is, *and in which the absolute activity* [of Nature] *exhausts itself"* (16, 43n). This gradient is meant to culminate in man as its "greatest and most perfect form" (144), but the sexual generation of these beings both corroborates and troubles this *Stufenfolge*. Nature's crisis-autobiography (to use Abrams' term without its Hegelian tenor) emerges from within its own ontogenetic productivity – in essence, sexuality becomes a *pharmakon* to

Nature. Schelling writes of the separation of the sexes within the "infinite metamorphosis" of Nature that "each organism has a level of formation at which [this] separation is *necessary*. [But this] highest point of disturbed equilibrium is [also] the moment of the reestablishment of equilibrium" (36, 40–41). This describes the production of the genus against the individual in a systolic-diastolic movement of expansion and contraction foregrounded in Schelling's later work. But sexual separation does not fold the organism back into a teleological hierarchy of developmental stages. Instead, it opens the organism up to Nature's radical productivity: "from the moment of the diremption onward, the product no longer completely expresses the character of the stage of development at which it stood" (39). Schelling describes this as "derangement" [*Störungheit*], and this trope of illness marks the "most intense moment of natural activity" in the organism (39). Nature blossoms through "abortive" experiments on itself, seizing on its own aberrations, "pursuing" its individuative derangement as far as possible in a given manifestation (41n). Precisely this derangement, this illness, drives one toward absolute knowledge as "a following of the particular wherever it might lead, regardless of its consistency with a larger whole" (Rajan, "First Outline" 315). Each organism is a tumescence, a derangement of the *Stufenfolge*, a symptom of radical auto-alterity in Nature which resists Schelling's attempt, in the later Introduction to the *First Outline*, to contain it as an anterior organisation which "must have existed as a whole previous to its parts" (*FO* 198). We will see that Jung later conceives the collective unconscious along precisely these lines: as a universal stratum of the psyche, "transcendental" in that it cannot become an object of knowledge but nevertheless constituted by the historicity of its evolving archetypal matrix. But just as Jung will face the question of how consciousness emerges from the depths of the unconscious, Schelling faces an analogous problem: how does Nature come to *be* from this fluidity, "the *most primal fluid*—the absolute noncomposite, and for that reason the absolute decomposite" (6)?

For the Nature of Schelling's *First Outline* it is *inhibition* – a primordial self-limiting force intrinsic to Nature – which brings about the phenomena of the natural world. As a homogeneous "universal organism" (*FO* 6) Nature, as "absolute activity" (16), is "inhibited at sundry stages" (6) which produce natural objects. Inhibition is at the root of all conflict and difference as "an *original diremption* in Nature itself [...] that original antithesis in the heart of Nature, *which does not* [...] *itself appear*" but nevertheless constitutes

Nature as object to itself (205; my first italics). As the force of Nature's auto-alterity and the paradoxical differential movement within an always already universal organism, inhibition infinitely counterbalances Nature's infinite productivity: "*If nature is absolute activity, then this activity must appear as inhibited ad infinitum. (The original cause of this inhibition must only be sought in [Nature] itself, since Nature is* ABSOLUTELY *active)*" (16).[8] Schelling is well aware of the "irresolvable difficulty" of this infinite deadlock between activity and inhibition (17), and Krell sums up the problem in terms of Freudian Eros and Thanatos:

> Schelling [must] conceive of an original duplicity, a *dyas*, in which infinite activity and infinite inhibition work together to produce the natural world. [But sexuality and its relation to illness disturb this balance. Both] alike tend toward the universal and the infinite. It is as though infinite activity itself, the absolute as such, were both sexually active and subject to ultimate passivity and even an inevitable infection or malignancy. *It becomes difficult, if not impossible, for Schelling to locate the duplicitous source of life without colliding against the ultimate source of illness and demise.* ("Three Ends" 65; my italics)

Here Krell emphasises sexuality and illness as markers of the organism's highly ambivalent, indeed "unnatural" relationship with Nature. With sex, both the Erotic drive toward the absolute product and the Thanatotic drive back to universal indifference explode on to this primal site. Nature longs for its original state of indifference, a zero-point which can only be hypothesised behind the always already extant original diremption. In this quasi-subjective death drive, "Nature contests the Individual; it longs for the Absolute and continually endeavors to represent it. [...] Individual products, therefore, in which Nature's activity is at a standstill, can only be seen as *misbegotten attempts* to achieve such a proportion" (*FO* 35). But just as the *Stufenfolge* is disrupted by the sexual proliferation of beings, each "misbegotten attempt" also recapitulates Nature's intrinsic dynamism (25). As a result, sexuality's propensity to reproduce such misbegotten attempts (and consequently Nature's inhibition) makes it a hostile, pestilent force to a Nature yearning for primordial, absolute indifference.

This originary "not-Nature" within Nature is transferred to the dynamic interplay of forces in the production of natural phenomena. Schelling describes the activity of life (as the effect of inhibition) in terms of *actants* [*Aktionen*], combinatory forces in the natural world. Themselves irrepresentable, actants collectively constitute an "infinite homogeneity" which combine in various relations and ratios to form different natural products:

> [Actants are] the most originary points of inhibition of Nature's activity. [As] the most originary negative presentations of the unconditioned in Nature [they] are not themselves *in space*; they cannot be viewed as *parts* of matter. [They are, rather,] *action* in general. (*FO* 19–21)

We will see in the next chapter that, more than Kant's thing-in-itself, Schelling's actant is a crucial metaphysical analogue to the Jungian archetype, which performs Schelling's "drama of a struggle *between form and the formless*" (28) in the register of the Romantic metasubjective psyche. What is significant for us here is that "these [combinatory] actions, presented collectively, *strive toward one and the same product*; for all natural activity aims *toward an absolute product*" (24; my last italics). There is a compulsion in Nature which is recapitulated in Nature's persistent strife with its "misbegotten attempts," and perhaps nowhere is this made clearer in the *First Outline* than in Schelling's admission, repressed into the margins of the "Introduction to the Outline" in a lengthy footnote, that

> Nature hates sex, and where it does arise, it arises against the will of Nature. The separation into sexes is an inevitable fate, with which, after Nature is once organic [...] it can never overcome.—By this very hatred of separation it finds itself involved in a contradiction, inasmuch as what is odious to Nature it is compelled to develop in the most careful manner, and to lead to the summit of existence, as if it did so on purpose; whereas it is always striving only for a return into the identity of the genus, which, however, is enchained to the (never to be canceled) duplicity of the sexes, as to an inevitable condition. [...] Nature develops the individual only from compulsion. (231n)

Thinking Nature's compulsive auto-alterity and productive self-division on the level of psyche, Jung writes that "together with 'life' itself, [the soul is] the only natural factor which can transform natural laws, that is, statistical organizations, into 'higher' or rather 'unnatural' states, in contrast to the law of entropy which governs inorganic nature" ("On the Nature of the Psyche" para. 375; trans. mod).[9] The Jungian psyche is a generative "natural factor" which Nature's auto-alterity both courts and resists.

Thus, Nature is hostile to the organism because it is an obstacle to its regressive yearning for original indifference. But the organism is also *necessary* for the progressive unfolding of an absolute product which already exists as potential in Nature but is nevertheless paradoxically open to the mutations and transformations of its parts. Indeed, faced with this *pharmakon* which cannot be limited to a Thanatotic drive for a *previous* state of indifference, Schelling's task is now to "*find the point in which this infinite multiplicity of diverse actants can be unified in Nature*" (*FO* 24). But with Schelling's desire to find this zero-point of unity we return to the idea of the absolute subject as Schelling's gesture, within the *First Outline*'s quasi-subjective space, toward the seeming paradox of the absolute organism as perfected nature *within* Nature (*FO* 28). This search for Nature's zero-point of indifference is where we locate Schelling's relevance for depth psychology. In different ways, Freud and Jung attempt to theorise this subject's unfolding; in different ways, they attempt to write the drama between form and formless. For Freud, *Beyond the Pleasure Principle*'s drama of the germ-plasm moves boldly past the earlier *Project* and into the speculative; it ultimately pits Eros against the death instinct's nostalgic drive for inorganicity, a drive reminiscent of Schelling's sex-hating Nature. In contrast, Jung's *Symbols of Transformation*, and the energic model of libido it proposes, supplements this drive with a bidirectionality that recapitulates the productive ambivalence of Schelling's Nature in ways that surpass the bio-nostalgia and personalism which mark psychoanalysis. Absolute knowledge remains on a promissory horizon, but this Romantic metasubjective psyche can think this horizon in ways the psychoanalytic subject cannot. With this, let us turn to Freud's early theoretical narrative.

Freud and Jung: borders and border zones

Freud's *Project for a Scientific Psychology* (1895) can be called a first outline of psychoanalysis, auguring in microcosm its history and dynamic. Posthumously published, the spirit of its letters haunts Freud's writing on psychoanalysis until his death[10] and informs the subsequent unfolding of Freud's theories through their own interminable self-analysis. The *Project* opens with Freud's casting of psychoanalysis as a "natural science" which will "represent psychical processes as quantitatively determinate states of specifiable material particles, thus making those processes perspicuous and free from contradiction" (295). This natural-scientific project becomes one of the more salient points of difference between Freudian and Jungian metapsychologies, a difference prefigured by Schelling's critique in the *Naturphilosophie* of the "mere world" of mechanism as a quantitative aggregate of products (*FO* 202). Freud's drive toward a *natural science* (an atomist science of "material particles") is thus contrary to Schelling's conception of *Naturphilosophie* as a *science of nature* which explores the play of forces which generates Nature's products.[11] Schelling begins the Outline to the *First Outline* by writing that "to philosophize about nature means as much as to create it" (*FO* 5), a resounding statement which ontologises thought to foreground the uncanny affinity between mind and Nature. Moreover, we have seen that *Naturphilosophie*'s emphasis on Nature's dynamic processes recapitulates this dynamism on the level of the individual object, which is subject to the same drive to infinite development as the Nature engendering it: "even if [infinite productivity] should result in finite products, these can only be apparent products; i.e., *the tendency to infinite development must lie once again in every individual*; every product must be capable of being articulated into products" (5; my italics).

Of course, Freud does not remain strictly biological in his approach: the natural-scientific principles of the *Project* are dispersed and transformed across the history of psychoanalysis, a history which includes his "second topography" of ego/id/superego as well as *Beyond the Pleasure Principle*. More specifically, *Beyond* attempts to map its more speculative terrain with Victorian biologism in the form of the biodrama of the germ plasm; indeed, this biodrama is *Beyond*'s textual centripetal force, pressing other narratives (little Ernst's *fort/da* game, the sexual theogony of Plato's *Symposium*) into its service. Biology reins in the plasticity of psychoanalytic discourse. This difference between a natural science aiming toward a closed, measurable system of natural "particles" and *Naturphilosophie*'s speculative physics is the first point of divergence between Freudian and Jungian metapsychology. Indeed, the spectre of Jung in *Beyond* manifests as Eros, the mythological unifying principle which imperils Freud's system with a speculative futurity it cannot digest. Jung's earliest metapsychological text, "On Psychic Energy" (1928), contrasts the "purely causal" mechanistic view with an "energic point of view [...] which understands the event as following from an energy which underlies the changes in phenomena [and which is] founded not on the substances themselves but on their relations" (para. 3; trans mod). And as I will discuss later, Jung's earliest conception of the archetype as a "complex," and its evolution into a transcendental-empiricist component of human knowledge, comes to emphasise the infinite productivity of psychological processes in ways resisted by psychoanalysis.

As the soil from which analytical psychology would germinate, "The Border Zones of Exact Science" (1896) is roughly contemporaneous with the *Project*. As a critique of scientific rationalism, this early essay is theoretically counterpositioned to Freud's biologism and sets the stage for Jung's later development of analytical psychology as the border zone in which psyche and Nature "touch and do not touch." Full of youthful arrogance and confidence, roughly half the essay attacks materialists, "Mammonists," and careerists as agents of "stupidity," cultural manifestations of the "principle of inertia" (para. 13). And perhaps this is what leads Jung to discuss not borders per se, but border *zones* as permeable boundaries that resist intellectual inertia. Important for Jung's later metapsychology, however, is his emphasis contra mechanism on a "preexistent vital principle" necessary "to explain the world of organic phenomena" (para. 63). Here, Jung argues that rationalism's attempt to trace the origins of organic life exhausts itself in an infinite regress to end in the paradoxical observation that "the creation of the first cell must have come about through contact with preexistent life" (para. 57). This regress unworks the claims of causal logic to explain the organic, leading "the critical examination of rational scientific claims" into "an immaterial or metaphysical realm" (para. 57). Indeed, in "Thoughts on the Nature and Value of Speculative Inquiry" (1898) Jung writes, with words reminiscent of Schelling's emphasis on the *a priori* nature of experience in the *First Outline*, that "every *a priori* structure *which abstracts from all experience* can only lead to error" (para. 175; my trans. and italics).

Freud's *Project* inaugurates the particular materialism that persists throughout psychoanalysis, but Jung's dual polemic against philosophical abstraction and stark materialism anticipates his later development of synchronicity, Jung's concept for the experience of the archetypal as real-ideal, a rupture in the boundary between Nature and mind (which he recasts as "physical" and "spiritual"). One key milestone in this development is Jung's idea of "psychic reality" in "Basic Postulates of Analytical Psychology" (1931),[12] which does not resolve but rather expands Schelling's question of why there is something and not nothing into the domain of a psyche which cannot escape entanglement with Nature. In other words, Jung's attempt to develop psychic reality as a domain of mental "psychic images" brings him up against the conundrum of sheer facticity that underwrites Schelling's guiding question. Recognising "the paradox of psychic life," Jung's essay tries to negotiate a path between the Scylla of spiritual monism and the Charybdis of a "*modern* [empirical, objective] brand of nature philosophy" that explains existence in purely physical terms. Jung begins with the assertion that we are "so wrapped about by psychic images that we cannot penetrate at all to the essence of things external to ourselves," and that the indeterminate something $= X$ of the psyche, "because it alone is immediate, is superlatively real" (para. 680). Yet he contradicts himself by attempting to dissect psychic reality into content "derived from a 'material' environment to which our bodies belong" and those "in no way less real, [which] seem to come from a 'spiritual' source which appears to be very different from the physical environment" (para. 681). Jung finds himself caught in the conundrum of speaking about a psyche which, in the end, is an "incomprehensible 'something'," and to make any statements about it at all we must "be willing to contradict ourselves" (as he does!) to do justice to something to which Jung gives the proper name "psyche" but whose excess suspends his efforts to *psychologise* this psyche (para. 680).

While Jung invokes the sole validity of the psyche – still an indeterminate "something" – to end "the conflict between mind and matter, spirit and nature, as *contradictory* explanatory principles" (para. 681), he nevertheless removes his qualifying quotes from the "'material' environment" when he admits that beyond the domain of psychic images there are "*physical process[es] whose nature[s] [are] ultimately unknown*" (para. 681; my italics). Jung wants to distinguish between psyche and matter, to resolve all experience into an unknowable psychic reality which nevertheless inexplicably "still exists in its original oneness, and awaits man's advance to a level of consciousness where he [...] recognizes both as constituent elements of one psyche" ("Basic Postulates" para. 682). But "psyche," as something that resists all of Jung's predications and boundaries, collapses into the plethora of its own facticity, its own being, even as it encompasses all human experience ("All that I experience is psychic" [para. 680]). In this ontoaesthetics[13] of intensity where psychic reality unfolds in Being as unique symbolic forms and metaphors, art is not only the organ of philosophy but the primary organ for the individuation of the *organism*.

Indeed, Schelling's overarching task in the 1815 *Ages of the World* will be to potentiate and dramatise this individuation cosmogonically.

But what does it mean to read the *First Outline* "aesthetically"? To "narrate" Nature in Schelling's speculative physics is to make aesthetics a tacit ontoaesthetics in an "outline" meant for the organic form of the lecture (as rhizomatic genre of the line of flight – the pursuit of knowledge along any number of abstract paths) instead of an analytic treatise (*FO* 3). Indeed, as a series of lecture notes, the text of the *First Outline* has a plasticity which causes it to derange itself into productive paths of copious footnotes and digressions. Nature's hatred of Eros (as sex) and corresponding ambivalence toward its products establish one thread in *The First Outline* in part as an ur-text of what Peter Brooks calls "Freud's Masterplot" (285). This narrative seeks to avoid deranging "short-circuits" in the service of, in Freud's words, "restoration of an earlier state" (*Beyond* 76), and in this sense the *First Outline*'s "ending" truly is the beginning in the form of the Introduction. Indeed, in Brooks' sense that beginnings presuppose endings (283) the ending is *before* the beginning: the *First Outline* begins with an "Outline of the Whole" and ends not with an Introduction, but an "Introduction to the *Outline* of a System of the Philosophy of Nature," a "beginning-again" that tries to contain the deranging short-circuits of Schelling's Nature by tethering it to transcendental Idealism (*FO* 193).

But Nature exists here as an unruly organ, an appendix whose ontoaesthetics unwork the body of this Freudian masterplot, and so as an heuristic narrative of Romantic metasubjectivity the *First Outline* must be read against this teleological grain, as a site of ateleological displacement. In this light, Schelling's graduated stages do not simply narrate the desire for an earlier, inorganic state but rather follow a progressive "stream of consciousness" unique to the organism – a line of development discernible only in its unfolding between the poles of regression and progression, recollection and repetition. Brooks gestures toward this possibility, if only through the lens of a bleak Freudianism: "It may finally be [...] that repetition speaks in the text of a return which ultimately subverts the very notion of beginning or end [...] that the interminable never can be finally bound in a plot. [...] Narrative, that is, wants at its end *to refer us back to its middle, to the web of the text*: to recapture it in its doomed energies" (297; my italics). Put differently, Romantic metasubjectivity is the articulation of an organic "plot" through its own excess, a surplus of *Trieb* whose general economy unfolds the organism by means of a narrative readable only in its wake; its purposiveness breaks through narrative teleology. If this is "doomed" energy, as Brooks argues, then it is doom as "fate," as a distinctly Nietzschean tragedy in terms of

> [t]he metaphysical solace [...] we derive from every true tragedy, the solace that in the ground of things, and despite all changing appearances, life is indestructibly mighty [as] that core of being [which exists] despite the constant destruction of the phenomenal world. (Nietzsche, *The Birth of Tragedy* 39, 41)

For psychoanalysis, then, ontology becomes aetiology – a Being which is a sickness unto death striving toward a primordial inorganicity which has been and *must be again* as a return of the Same. This return transpires in what Deleuze calls the theatre of representation, where repetition is explained by (and contained in) an overarching external concept (the past, Oedipus). Deleuze describes the differences between a repetition of the Same and a repetition serving the auto-alterity of the Idea itself, or what he provocatively calls "the Self of repetition":

> [W]e must distinguish two forms of repetition. [...] in one case, the difference is taken to be only external to the concept; it is a difference between objects represented by the same concept, falling into the indifference of space and time. In the other case, the difference is internal to the Idea; it unfolds as pure movement, creative of a dynamic space and time which correspond to the Idea. The first repetition is repetition of the Same, explained by the identity of the concept or representation; the second includes difference, and includes itself in the alterity of the Idea, in the heterogeneity of an "a-presentation". One is negative, occurring by default in the concept; the other affirmative, occurring by excess in the Idea. [...] One is material, the other spiritual, even in nature and in the earth. One is inanimate, the other carries the secret of our deaths and our lives, of our enchantments and our liberations, the demonic and the divine. [...] One concerns accuracy, the other has authenticity as its criterion. (*DR* 23–24)

For Deleuze, Nietzsche's "indestructibly mighty core of being," whose productivity cannot be reined in by a nostalgia for origins, is figured as the excess of "a-presentation" intrinsic to an unfolding Idea unconfinable to an atomistic "materialism" but readable only through a "spiritualism" encompassing the earth as a secret pulsation of dynamic polarities (death/life, enchainment/liberation, demonic/divine). Put differently, where the first repetition is really only the (Hegelian) play of the Concept with itself in which it always returns to itself through its own differences, the second repeats the difference of the (Deleuzian) Idea's auto-alterity; it reflects the Idea's indwelling desire to know itself, but this desire unfolds through fluctuations between polarities to generate knowledge that never fully returns to itself.

We can align Deleuze's two fundamental movements of repetition with two fundamental ways to read the seething ontoaesthetic "narrative" of the *First Outline* and, *mutatis mutandis*, the movements of libido distinguishing psychoanalysis from analytical psychology. What for psychoanalysis is the mere aetiology of representation and the Same – the Thanatotic drive toward an impossible object – is, seen through the Thanatopoietic lens of Romantic metasubjectivity, always already supplemented by the difference within repetition's emergence. "Spiritual" repetition can never reach the Same. Romantic metasubjectivity figures Brooks' narrative return as an eternal return which "ultimately subverts the very notion of beginning or end"; the "web of the text" at every purported end is a return to the indestructibility of narrative *itself* (Brooks 297). Against the Hegelian theatre of representation, in the (Kierkegaardian/Nietzschean) theatre of repetition

> we experience pure forces, dynamic lines in space which act without intermediary upon the spirit, and link it directly with nature and history, with a language which speaks before words, with gestures which develop before organised bodies, with masks before faces, with spectres and phantoms before characters – the whole apparatus of repetition as "terrible power." (*DR* 10)

The tension between these two readings offers us a history of Romantic metasubjectivity's genesis from the dynamic between Freud and Jung, and Jung's emergence from within the fluid early days of depth psychology. Thus, to amplify and detail the issues at stake here, we turn to *Beyond* and *Symbols* as key statements of Freudian and Jungian metapsychology to articulate this emergence against the backdrop of Schelling's *Naturphilosophie*. These two texts are antipodal attempts to think the psyche toward the pre-subjective origins of Schelling's *First Outline,* framed through the questions of the nature of libido and drive which preoccupy both texts. Like psychoanalysis, analytical psychology constitutes a "poetics of the baneful" (Krell, *Contagion* 53) in its pathological relationship to knowledge; in turning to Jung to articulate Romantic metasubjectivity, however, it becomes apparent that this pathology is deployed in a different economy and to a different end.

Freud: the pleasure principle…and beyond

In 1962, Lancelot Whyte was perhaps the first to discern in Schelling's thought a "single unconscious formative energy" organising both mind and nature while remaining irreducible to either (116–17). With this monistic principle, Schelling prefigures what Freud and Jung both develop in different directions as libido. However, only with *Beyond*'s phylogenetic speculations does Freud's speculation about the origins of life approach the *Naturphilosophie* he previously disavows to make *Beyond* a nerve cluster in the body of Freud's writing, a curious text which tacitly extends the biologism of germ and cell theory to the speculative terrain of Schelling's *Naturphilosophie*. It retraces its steps, even as its depersonalisation of sexual libido as Eros moves resistantly toward some of the Jungian ideas Freud disavows, thus performing the very detours and short-circuits it theorises in a bid to master its own drive. A text about the death instinct as the culmination of Freud's final metapsychology, *Beyond* wants nothing more than to (impossibly) fulfil its own pleasure principle as a culmination and completion of psychoanalytic metapsychology which bridges Freud's early biologism and his later psychology. Todd Dufresne suggests as much when he describes *Beyond* as "the Rosetta Stone of Freudian theory—the key that unlocks the psychological theories of the late works precisely because it provides a translation of the biological theories of the earliest" ("Introduction" 26). And even where Ellenberger, for example, reads Freud's nod to Fechner[14] as a decisive influence (512ff), perhaps nowhere else in his writings is Freud struggling more with Jung. And Dufresne's suggestion that *Beyond* is an attempt to "exorcise" Jung (*Tales* 22) is more exact than one may think if one also takes into account the suitably archaic definition of exorcism as "the action of *calling up* spirits" (*OED* 1b; my italics); the word's uncanny bivalency as something that expels, but with a residual threat of "contamination" (the way out is the way in, so to speak), aptly describes the dynamic of *Beyond*'s Jungian agon. As "a traumatic rupture point in the history of psychoanalysis" (Dufresne, *Tales* 26), *Beyond* does not quite scuttle the good ship Psychoanalysis (even if it does make the crew wonder where magnetic North is). But as the site where "metapsychology subverts psychoanalysis," Dufresne writes that *Beyond* is "the name of the trauma Freud inflicted on psychoanalysis, playfully or otherwise, from a position within psychoanalysis" ("Introduction" 28). As such, it brings Freud dangerously close to the "black tide of mud of occultism" against which he enlisted Jung's aid in the halcyon days of their collaboration (*Memories* 150) and which Freud would hang around Jung's neck after their break.

It is 1911, and the Freud-Jung partnership is in its terminal phase. Freud writes Jung a characteristically ambivalent letter – a précis, to be sure, of their professional break, but also of the *fort/da* game Freud would play with the figure of Jung, carried through the metapsychological papers of 1914–1915 and culminating, perhaps, in *Beyond*. In this letter, Freud writes to Jung referring to him in the third person:

> One of the nicest works I have read (again), is that of a well-known author on the "Transformations and Symbols of the Libido." […] it is the best thing this promising author has written, up to now, though he will do still better. […] Not least, I am delighted by the many points of agreement with things I have already said or would *like* to say. […] it is a torment to me to think, when I conceive an idea now and then, that I may be taking something away from you or appropriating something that might just as well have been acquired by you. When this happens, I feel at a loss. (letter to C.G. Jung, 12 Nov. 1911, 459)

In this magnificently understated and overlooked passage Freud admits that Jung says what he *would like to say* – but cannot. What exactly *is* it Freud would *like* to say? What makes him incapable of saying it? The answer to these questions is, of course, a sphinx-like silence. Jung's response is equally prescient: "You are a dangerous rival—if one has to speak of rivalry. Yet I think it has to be this way, for *one cannot stop something which is natural, nor should one try to change it.* […] Because of the difference in our working methods we shall undoubtedly meet from time to time in unexpected places" (letter to Freud, 14 Nov. 1911, 460; trans. mod.; my italics). The degree to which Freud was – susceptible to? tolerant of? struggling against? – Jung's ideas will remain a matter of speculation and debate. But Jung's insistence on the irrevocable unfolding of a *natural* development foreshadows his later theoretical emphasis on prospective, forward movement. And this prospective *Trieb* would encounter the final phase of Freudian metapsychology against the metaphysical backdrop of Schelling's *Naturphilosophie* – a theoretical meeting place neither Freud nor Jung would have expected.

A few years after the fateful break, Freud's strange bids on the phylogenetic and pre-subjective begin with *A Phylogenetic Fantasy* (1915) – a metapsychological metanarrative contiguous with the work begun in *Totem and Taboo* (1913) on the primordial origins of the human race. *A Phylogenetic Fantasy* can be read as a response to Jung's *Symbols*, and the Thanatotic quality of its textual drive makes it a stepping stone to Freud's later flirtations with phylogeny in *Beyond*. *A Phylogenetic Fantasy* is Freud's project of "[representing] forcefully the interests of early infantile acquisitions" while constituting a "phylogenetic series" "which relates the development of each illness [dementia praecox, paranoia, melancholia-mania] in the individual (ontogeny) to specific events in the prehistory of mankind (phylogeny)" (Hoffer 518). And here Freud comes closest to extending this narrative beyond phylogenetic history toward something like the quasi-subjectivity of Schelling's Nature: "The developmental history of the libido recapitulates a much older piece of the [phylogenetic] development than that of the ego; the former perhaps recapitulates conditions of the phylum of vertebrates, whereas the latter is dependent on the history of the human race" (*Phylogenetic Fantasy* 11–12). If Schelling's three versions of *Ages of the World* never quite get beyond the past, and if this past's ineluctable nature is part of *Ages'* "invention" of psychoanalysis in its broadest sense (Rajan, "First Outline" 312), one can see an analogous quandary in Freud's phylogenetic fantasy. Here, Freud's ages of the libidinal world remain tied to the "anxiousness of the beginning of the Ice Age" (*Phylogenetic Fantasy* 14), even as successive epochs of human development provide the psychic foundation for modern neuroses and psychoses. The text ends with a similar recapitulation, summarising the phylogenetic narrative as something that "may be no more than a playful comparison" but whose promise, in an apt moment of deferred action, "should properly be left to further investigation, and illumination through new experiences" (19). Thus the *Fantasy*'s *Nachträglich* coda, with the phylogenetic narrative as binding primal phantasy.

This phylogenetic fantasy frames Freud's later theorising of both origins and the return *to* those origins in *Beyond*'s metapsychology. Yet *Beyond* reaches back beyond the phylogenetic fantasy to a space where there is no thinking subject or racial history but instead the genetic drama of the germ-cells, the very beginnings of life and markers of potential immortality which Freud invokes in a way that both corroborates and troubles *Beyond*'s metanarrative. As the urge to restore inertia, the death instinct is "the expression of the *conservative* nature of living matter" contrary to "factor[s] pressing toward change and development" (*Beyond* 75–76). Freud's disavowal of *prospective* movement aligns with both the dying organism's "greater and greater deviations from its original path of life and toward more and more complex detours" and his formulation of deferred action [*Nachträglichkeit*] in service to primal phantasy.[15] The subject is constituted as Nature's primary "misbegotten attempt," driven backward to annihilation and primordial inorganicity. Indeed, as formulated by Freud, the death instinct ultimately suggests a melancholic drive within Nature *toward* Nature as inorganicity not unlike what Geoffrey Hartman sees as the *pharmakon* element in Romantic self-consciousness, where this "death-in-life" is its own antidote as a "middle-term, the strait through which everything must pass" in the circuitous journey of the detour (Hartman, "Romanticism" 50–51). Freud's Thanatotic bionarrative begins in a similar vein:

> At some time, and through the influence of a completely inconceivable force, the characteristics of life were awakened in nonliving matter. Perhaps this was a process similar in type to that other process which later brought about the emergence of consciousness in a particular layer of the living matter. The tension then arising in the previously inanimate substance strove toward equilibrium. Thus arose the first drive: the drive to return to the nonliving. (*Beyond* 77)

Here Freud narrates the Romantic impetus toward "anti-self-consciousness," but it is *Beyond*'s drama of the germ-cells which both corroborates and troubles this narrative of inorganicity, recapitulating the "wavering rhythms" of the organism it describes (79). This drama also performs Freud's Jungian agon, a *fort/da* moving him both toward and away from Jung as Freud is driven to reduce Jung's "libidinal" presence (the presence of Jung's rhythmic libido) in this metapsychology to a zero-point of influence.

Freud's discussion of the germ-cells begins with a telling *peripeteia* – "this cannot be so" (78) – which is indeed a *turn*; not a turning-away from, but perhaps a looking-askance at the conservative formulation of the death instinct. It is also the point of departure for the germ-cells' dramatisation of what for Schelling's speculative physics is the ambivalent bidirectionality, the lifedeath of Nature. Yet in precisely this ambivalence we can read what Freud would like to say, but ultimately cannot. As Freud's markers for the "potential immortality" (79) of organic matter apart from "the developmental path all the way to natural death" (78), the germ-cells participate in both a "fall[ing] back on the beginning of development" and a "development to the end" (79). As the "wavering rhythm" (79) of the organism, *Beyond* deploys the trope of the uncanny to articulate both the germ-cell's fundamental division against itself *and* its drive to "[merge] with another [cell] similar yet different from it" (79). In this rhythm, "one group of drives storms forward to reach the final goal of life as soon as possible, but the other group shoots back to a certain location on the path to retrace it from a given point, thus prolonging the journey" (79). This *heimlich-unheimlich* nature of the germ-cell – its desire for something simultaneously identical with and foreign to itself – constitutes an uncanny remainder which troubles Freud's narrative. The labyrinthine paths of his metapsychology here lead Freud to remark that the sexual drive "came into operation at the very start," which brings him very close to the Jungian monism he later derides, irrespective of the distinction between sexual and ego-instincts that is unworked later in *The Ego and The Id* (1923) (*Beyond* 79, 89). Thus, while the death instinct and its phylogenetic narrative constitute the Romantic subject of diseased self-consciousness which "seeks to draw the antidote to consciousness from consciousness itself" (Hartman, "Romanticism" 48), in detouring back to inorganicity it never reaches its origin. But even though the death instinct is forever frustrated by its uncanny remainders, it does not serve the "vital, dialectical movement of 'soul-making'," the infinite productivity Hartman sees as central to the Romantic project (49). What Freud *would like to say, but cannot* resides in the uncanny remainder unsettling the death drive.

This remainder is *Eros*, the drive "to combine the organic into larger and larger unities" (*Beyond* 81). At one point Freud seems to construct Eros as a *Stufenfolge*, only to dismiss it as impossible, seeing it as a substitute for a human "drive toward perfection" which cannot be realised (80). But in a lengthy footnote at the end of *Beyond*, Freud notes that the "findings of psychoanalysis" lead him to decouple sex drives from reproduction, indeed to see the sex drive as "Eros, which seeks to push together and hold together the parts of living substance" (97 n. 1). And in admitting that death drives are always already entangled with life drives (93), Freud closes down his scientific investigation as "a darkness into which not one ray of hypothesis has penetrated," turning to Plato's *Symposium* and the *Upanishads* to corroborate his original hypothesis (93, 94 n. 2). This transition from Victorian biologism to "the Eros of the poets and philosophers" (87) is watermarked by Jung's presence, specifically in Freud's reference to "critical and far-seeing minds" which "had long ago objected to restricting the concept of libido to the energy of the sex drives directed toward an object" (88). But just as quickly as this speculative expansion of psychoanalysis appears it is closed down, as such minds have nothing to provide orthodox psychoanalysis (88). Now, as the promulgator of "monistic libido" (89) Jung is sidelined, along with the futurity of Eros as combinatory force. *Beyond* can only access this speculative potency through forays into mythology, religion, and philosophy, which are ultimately repressed in Freud's scientific economy.

Inter-section: Deleuze's perversion of libido

Deleuze offers a useful framework through which to approach Jung's energic reconception of libido and implicit reformulation of the death drive. In *Coldness and Cruelty* (1967), Deleuze attempts to get at what is "really" beyond the pleasure principle – the "second-order [transcendental] principle,"[16] "the highest authority which subjects our psychic life to the dominance of this principle," "the absolutely unconditioned, the 'ground-less' from which the ground itself emerged" (112, 114). For Deleuze, this (un) grounding principle is *perversion*, the "structural split" in "the functional interdependence of the ego and superego" (116f) marking *desexualised* libido (freely mobile energy) according to Freud's own observations on libido's desexualisation in the narcissistic ego (idealisation) or the superego (identification). That is, desexualised libido is an indifferent energy that can be either Eros or Thanatos and which enables love to become hate and vice versa – Freudian libido's repressed third term, as it were. In perversions such as sadism and masochism, the desexualisation of idealisation/ identification is resexualised "in coldness" – in other words, the original desexualisation "has become in itself the object of sexualization" in a way that does *not* sublate the original desexualisation, which persists as an unassimilable remainder (117).

Contrary to Freud's assertion that this desexualised libido serves the pleasure principle (*The Ego and the Id* 135), the repetition "beyond the pleasure principle" becomes unbound. In perversion,

> repetition runs wild and becomes independent of all previous pleasure. It has itself become an idea or ideal. Pleasure is now a form of behavior related to repetition, accompanying and following repetition, which has itself become an awesome, independent force. Pleasure and repetition have thus exchanged roles, as a consequence of the instantaneous leap, that is to say the twofold process of desexualization and resexualization. (*Coldness* 120)

The pain in sadism and masochism now "represents a desexualization which makes repetition autonomous" in a way which does not annul the pleasure principle, but rather releases repetition into a wider economy in accordance with the "perverse" second-order principle governing the field of the pleasure principle (120). We can read this dynamic away from its personalised Sadean register: in appealing to perversion as the (un)ground of this wider economy of repetition, Deleuze reads in Freud a polymorphous perversity leading *away* from the sovereignty of past pleasures and toward autonomous repetition. And although Jung criticises Freud's formulation of "polymorphous perversity" in children in its literal, sexual sense ("Psychic Conflicts in a Child" 5), the kernel of desexualisation Deleuze sees in Freud leads toward Jung's definition of the archetype as a centripetal force of *repetition*, "impressions of ever-repeated typical experiences [which simultaneously] behave empirically like agents that tend towards the repetition of these same experiences" (*On the Psychology* para. 109). The following chapter will show that what Jung *therapeutically* criticises in Freud recrudesces as the impersonal and cosmic polymorphous perversity of the archetypes in Jung's metapsychology.

In *Difference and Repetition*, Deleuze thinks Thanatos beyond the phylogenetic return to a previous state and toward death as an "empty form of time" separate from negation, uniting past, present, and future in a sort of "death" drawing the ego narcissistically into itself through "the essentially lost character of virtual objects and the essentially disguised character of real objects" (110). This ego re-emerges as Deleuze's larval subject, a narcissistic ego "related to the form of an I which operates upon it as an 'Other'" constituted by displacements forming a house of mirrors through which the larval subject is constituted (110). As Constantin Boundas puts it, here "the subject is the tensive arrangement of many larval subjects. A self exists as long as a contracting machine, capable of drawing a difference from repetition, functions somewhere" (274). That is, Deleuze's notion of "transcendental synthesis" releases Thanatos from nostalgia into a futurity that Freud represses:

> From a transcendental viewpoint, past, present and future are constituted in time *simultaneously*, even though, from the natural standpoint, there is between them a qualitative difference, the past following upon the present and the present upon the future. [...] These two correlative structures [of past and present] cannot constitute the synthesis of time without immediately opening up to and making for the possibility of a future in time [...] that saves or fails to save, depending on the modes of combination of the other two. (*Coldness* 115)

Deleuze's indication of "a monism, a qualitative dualism and a difference in rhythm" in Freud's work on the death instinct gestures toward a futurity which reads Thanatos not only toward the spectre of Jung in Freud's thought as Eros, but also toward that aspect of *Trieb* in Schelling's Nature which does not hark back toward sex-hating indifference. Thus, Deleuze offers a way of mapping the temporal topography of *Thanatopoiesis* and Romantic metasubjectivity; his exposition on death in *Difference and Repetition* leads it away from a binary opposition with Eros and toward the "neutral, displaceable energy" that Freud repudiates in Jung. Invoking the dissociationist psyche (whose topography I will trace in the following chapter), Deleuze puts the subject under erasure as an amalgam of larval subjects in order to think the death drive, as desexualised, neutral libido unbound by the erotism of the pleasure principle, towards Schelling's *Naturphilosophie* and Jung's collective unconscious.

The "natural development" which signals Jung's break with Freud also augurs the movement of supplementarity by which Jungian metapsychology releases the Thanatotic drive of the pleasure principle into a broader dynamic field. Schelling's *Naturphilosophie* conceptualises this agon, but Romantic metasubjectivity marks Jung's close relationship to the bidirectionality of Schelling's Nature. Where *Beyond* sublates the Romantic subject into the "urge inherent in living organic matter for the restoration of an earlier state [as] the expression of inertia […] to reach an old goal by ways old and new" (75–77), Romantic metasubjectivity emerges as an anamnesis of *Naturphilosophie*'s rich ambiguity through its Jungian analysis. We have seen how in Schelling's *Naturphilosophie*, Nature's developmental drive toward the absolute product stalemates Nature's backward movement with a promissory horizon of unity, paradoxically substantiated by the same organic life which unworks it. This bidirectionality underwrites the *Thanatopoiesis* of Romantic metasubjectivity, which names the ontoaesthetic "ambitendency" of Jungian libido (*Symbols* 173).[17] *Thanatopoiesis* articulates the Romantic metasubjective psyche's ontoaesthetic rhythms of projection and recollection, progression and regression as it recapitulates, stepwise through time, its uncanny affinity with a Nature ambivalent toward its products. With this, we turn to Jung in order to examine how analytical psychology emerges as a very different kind of science and opens itself to the speculative terrain unavailable to psychoanalysis.

Jung: analytical psychology, *Weltanschauung*, and the fluidity of Being

The project of Schelling's *First Outline* begins, in essence, from the standpoint of a philosophical unconscious figured as Nature's preindividual fluidity. Within this *"most primal fluid*—the absolute noncomposite [and] absolute decomposite […] receptive to every form […] a mass wherein no part is distinguished from the other by figure"* (*FO* 6), the actants, as combinatory forces, both coalesce and resist each other. This "drama of a struggle *between form and the formless"* (27–28), between individual force and "the chora, the (un)ground of new formations" (Rajan, "First Outline" 314), is doubled on the level of psyche as the "original, undifferentiated polyvalency" of regressed libido in Jung's collective unconscious (*Symbols* 159). Analytical psychology's constitutive fluidity and its reconception of the death instinct as *Thanatopoiesis* align it with what Foucault calls a counter-science – a science which directs positivist sciences "back to their epistemological basis" to "unmake" that positivity (*The Order of Things* 379). That is, a counter-science

> traverse[s], animate[s], and disturb[s] the whole constituted field of the human sciences [by] overflowing it both on the side of positivities and on that of finitude [to] form the most general contestation of that field.

[It] make[s] visible, in a discursive mode, the frontier-forms of the human sciences[, situating] its experience in those enlightened and dangerous regions where the knowledge of man acts out, in the form of the unconscious and of historicity, its relation with what renders them possible. (381)

This fluidity also constitutes analytical psychology as a psychic afterlife of the Romantic *Trieb* toward unconditional knowledge represented in the *First Outline*, in which Nature is *itself* a force which unworks the positivity of the positive sciences. Indeed, this distinction informs Jung's essentially Romantic conception of science against Freud's fundamentally Victorian-scientific understanding. *Beyond* folds even the "potential immortality" of the germ-cells into the primal phantasy of inorganicity as "only a lengthening of the path toward death" (79), but analytical psychology seeks the very fluidity of a science "receptive to every form" insofar as it lacks an Archimedean point of reference in recapitulation of Schelling's "'absolute activity' of Nature as the 'unconditioned'" (Rajan, "First Outline" 313–14). Analytical psychology sounds the full depth of Nature's lifedeath by measuring the fluidity of Schelling's Nature through the regressive-progressive rhythm of libido.

We can begin to probe analytical psychology's fluidity with Jung's essay "Analytical Psychology and 'Weltanschauung'" (1931), in which Jung articulates analytical psychology as a "science," which is different from both psychoanalysis as "natural science" and a *Weltanschauung* (a philosophy of life or, as Jung defines it, "a conceptually formulated attitude" [para. 689; my trans]). But while Jung attempts to distinguish between such terms as "*Weltanschauung*," "science," and "picture of the world" (para. 698), all of these terms are drawn together in a fluidity from which analytical psychology ultimately emerges as a science of life, a psychology of experience which prioritises what Schelling has called the *a priori* "internal necessity" of one's judgments in Nature (*FO* 198). Thus, in separating analytical psychology from *Weltanschauung* Jung ends up equating them as the force of difference between systems which *creates* systems; indeed, this counter-scientific fluidity constitutes the "Weltanschauung" essay in many ways as Jung's own "First System Programme."[18]

The "Weltanschauung" essay is bookended with discussions of the relationship between analytical psychology and *Weltanschauung*, but the middle is weighted with an exposition of analytical psychology contra psychoanalysis. Here, Jung aligns the inherited nature of archetypes with the collective unconscious as "an inherited system identical with the ancestral constitution, which will unfailingly function in the same way as before. Consequently, the possibility that anything new and essentially different will be produced becomes increasingly small" (para. 717). Left here, the Jungian psyche reads like a restricted economy of "inherited possibilities," a structuralist pantheon of archetypes whose limits are always already delineated. But Jung continues, describing the collective unconscious as

> the all-dominant deposit [*der alles beherrschende Niederschlag*] of ancestral experience accumulated over countless millions of years, the echo of prehistoric world events to which every century adds *an immeasurably small amount of variation and differentiation.* [It is ultimately] a deposit of world events expressed in the structure of the brain and the sympathetic nervous system, [constituting] in its totality a type of timeless and eternal world-image. (para. 729; trans. mod.; my italics)

This is to say that the "inherited system" recapitulates, but encrypted within this "sameness" is a kernel of difference, a quantum of variation which makes the "mighty deposit of ancestral experience" an evolutionary remainder in the economy of the psyche. This kernel of difference is carried over into the "Weltanschauung" essay's attempt to articulate the relationship between analytical psychology and *Weltanschauung*. As a worldview or philosophy of life, Jung defines a *Weltanschauung* as

> something which embraces all sorts of attitudes to the world, including the philosophical. [...] [It is a person's] serious attempt to formulate his attitude in conceptual or concrete form [...] a widened or deepened consciousness [...] To have a *Weltanschauung* means to create a picture of the world and of oneself [with] the best possible knowledge—a knowledge that esteems wisdom and abhors unfounded assumptions, arbitrary assertions, and didactic opinions. Such knowledge seeks the well-founded hypothesis, without forgetting that all knowledge is limited and subject to error. (pars. 689, 694–96, 698)

But while a *Weltanschauung* is based in a conscious creation of one's "picture of the world," this picture is nevertheless predicated on one's "unconscious attitude" (para. 697). That is, as the conscious articulation and cultivation of one's attitude, a *Weltanschauung* is nevertheless always already rooted in the unconscious, purposive aspects of personality – one's attitude as the "particular arrangement of psychic contents *oriented towards a goal or directed by some kind of ruling principle*" (para. 690; my italics).

Jung sees psychoanalysis as a *Weltanschauung* of "rationalistic materialism [...] a fundamentally practical natural science" (para. 707; trans. mod).[19] In contrast, analytical psychology is "*not a Weltanschauung but a science* [...] an experiment in *Weltanschauung*" which provides tools to construct *Weltanschauungen* (pars. 730–31; trans. mod), but as much as Jung wants to cast analytical psychology as a science separate from *Weltanschauung* (making the former irreducible to the latter as "experiments" in it), it is precisely the *experiment* which fuses them together. For Jung's exposition of analytical psychology's *concepts* and *hypotheses* of the autonomous complex and the collective unconscious in the middle of the essay are fundamentally a case study of the formation of the "well-founded hypothesis" both analytical psychology and *Weltanschauungen* depend on. This said, there is nevertheless a desire in Jung's essay to release analytical psychology from the conceptual economy it shares with *Weltanschauungen*: in the end, the generation of a *Weltanschauung* (which is necessary for life) requires that one "leave behind science," because "now we need the creative resolve to entrust our life to this or that hypothesis" (para. 740). This creative resolve casts analytical psychology as a psychology of experience – as what we might call an *Urweltanschauung*, a set of crafted hypotheses which folds back into Being as something resistant to reifying concepts.

Roughly 15 years later, Jung thinks analytical psychology closer to a counter-science of the unconditioned in "On the Nature of the Psyche" (1947).[20] Here, Jung frames analytical psychology as nothing less than a disciplinary individuation process which recapitulates the dissociative potentiation of individual development. Just as the individual's goal is the depotentiation of the ego in service to integrating "objective," autonomous archetypal content, analytical psychology's goal is ultimately to, in a word, dissociate – *to become its own subject through becoming the very object of its knowledge*:

> [Analytical psychology] is in a difficult situation compared with the other natural sciences because it lacks a base outside its object. It

can only translate itself back into its own language, or fashion itself in its own image. The more it extends its field of research and the more complicated its objects become, the more it feels the lack of a standpoint distinct from those objects. And once the complexity has reached that of the empirical man, his psychology inevitably merges with the psychic process itself. It can no longer be distinguished from the latter, and so turns into it. But the effect of this is that the process attains to consciousness. In this way, psychology actualizes the unconscious urge to consciousness. [Analytical psychology] is the coming to consciousness of the psychic process but not an explanation of this process in a deeper sense, for *no explanation of the psychic can be anything other than the living process of the psyche itself. Psychology is doomed to cancel itself out as a science and therein precisely it reaches its scientific goal.* ("On the Nature of the Psyche" para. 429; trans. mod.; my italics)

Schelling's World-Soul unfolds in "the tension of infinite individuation of matter and the un-conditioning of experience as it moves from recording to producing further individuation" in an infinite "feed[ing] back on itself" (Grant, "Philosophy Become Genetic" 133). Similarly, analytical psychology's speculative archetypal physics is a self-unfolding indistinguishable from its objectification in Nature, a "progressive universal poetry" which writes itself mythopoeically and phenomenologically in the world – Jung's version of Schelling's *a priori* Nature. Novalis makes similar claims for philosophy: "We cannot measure the content of reason by its form, or its form by its content – both are unending – and philosophy can never be *primal history*, but rather must be, and remain, the law of unmediated existence. […] It may not pursue its ideas, but only represent them" (*Fichte Studies* #472).

This bold mission statement declares nothing less than analytical psychology's counter-scientific desire not simply to be one *Weltanschauung* contending among others but the fluid economy from which *Weltanschauungen* come – which, ironically, unites the projects of analytical psychology and *Weltanschauungen*. Jung's vision of psychology as "the discipline to unite the circle of the sciences" (Shamdasani, *Jung and the Making* 18) mutates into a psychic analogue of the Romantic encyclopaedia as analytical psychology's intrinsic resistance to form both underwrites and dissolves this circle of knowledge. Schelling puts in relief the possibility of this system as the opening of an intellectual infinity imbued with the forces and processes of the natural world. That is, the possibility of this unifying science is encrypted into its very unworking in a text as dynamic as the Nature it tries to explain:

> The *empirically infinite* [of Nature] is only the external intuition of an *absolute* (*intellectual*) *infinity* whose intuition is originally in us, but which could never come to consciousness without external, empirical exhibition [...] through a *finitude* which is never complete, i.e., which is *itself infinite*. In other words, it can only be presented by *infinite becoming*, where the intuition of the infinite lies in no individual moment, but is only *to be produced* in an endless progression. (*FO* 15)

This idea of subject-object/mind-nature consubstantiality informs the idea of the *unconscious* as the crucial point of convergence for Schelling, Jung, and Deleuze and Guattari; we will later see that its specifically human materiality emerges in Schelling's 1800 *System*. Jung's scepticism about unifying the circle of the sciences is encrypted in his reminder that "there is no conscious content which can with absolute certainty be said to be totally conscious, for that would necessitate an unimaginable totality of consciousness. [Thus] the paradoxical conclusion that there is *no conscious content which is not in some other respect unconscious*" ("On the Nature of the Psyche" para. 385).[21] Writing at the point of his crucial turn in thinking on the archetypes (which I discuss in the following chapter), this fluidity moves Jung decisively away from Kant and Hegel and aligns the *a*teleological project of analytical psychology closely with Schelling's thought. Let us turn, now, to Jung's specific formulation of libido which caused the break with Freud and which powers the dynamics of Romantic metasubjectivity.

"Sexuality is not mere instinctuality; it is an indisputably creative power [...] sexuality seems to us the strongest and most immediate instinct, standing out as *the* instinct above all others" (Jung, "On Psychic Energy" pars. 107–8). This may sound quasi-Freudian, but here Jung is already thinking sexuality away from Freudian biologism; sexuality is in dialogue with spirit, both of them as what Schelling called, in his earlier *Ages*, questioning and answering beings. Thus Jung writes:

> the spirit senses [*wittert*] in sexuality an equal, indeed a related counterpart to itself. For just as spirit would like to subordinate

sexuality to itself like all other instincts, so sexuality has an ancient claim upon spirit, which it once—in procreation, pregnancy, birth, and childhood—contained within itself, and whose passion the spirit can never dispense with in its creations. (para. 107; trans. mod)

this is not, of course, the sublation of sexuality into spirit. Rather, sexuality becomes a catachresis for desire in general, but as a speculative Eros in a dialogue with spirit which psychoanalysis cannot decrypt. Sexuality becomes susceptible to blockage, the involution which precedes evolution:

> If an instinct is checked or inhibited, it gets blocked and regresses. Or to be more precise: if there is an inhibition of sexuality, a regression will eventually occur in which sexual energy abandons the current area of application and activates, or communicates with, a function in some other area. In this way the energy changes its form. [...] The presexual, early infantile stage to which the libido reverts is characterized by numerous possible applications, because there libido regains its original undifferentiated polyvalency. (*Symbols* 158–59; trans. mod.)

This "original undifferentiated polyvalency," as a fluid reservoir of intensity, allows Jung to depotentiate the specifically biological aspect of incest, the issue which so vexed the Freud-Jung relationship. Thus, incest has a metaphoricity which makes it less about sexual taboo and more about transformation: "The effect of the incest-taboo and of the attempts at canalization is the essence of imagination which, in creating possibilities, gradually produces possible avenues for the self-realisation of libido. In this way the libido becomes imperceptibly spiritualized" (224; trans. mod).[22] Jung releases libido from the work of nostalgia into a wider energic economy, articulated by the Thanatopoietic movement of regression (to the mother, symbolic or otherwise) and progressive (purposive) creation of new libidinal avenues unconstrained by metanarrative or teleology.

This Thanatopoietic dynamic unfolds quantitatively, in relations of intensity which Jung consciously develops as a ruling concept in analytical psychology:

> Experience shows that instinctual processes of any kind are often intensified to an extraordinary degree by an afflux of energy which can come from anywhere. [...] One instinct can be temporarily depotentiated in favour of another, and this is true of psychic activity

in general. [Thus] it is not the sexual instinct but a fundamentally indifferent energy which gives rise to symbols such as light, fire, sun et cetera. (*Symbols* 138–39; my trans.)

Indeed, where Schelling writes in the *Naturphilosophie* that "beyond matter is pure intensity" (*FO* 21n), Jungian libido is nothing less than "*subjectively perceived intensity* [*die subjektiv wahrgenommene Intensität*]" (*Symbols* 165; my trans). And in a strongly proto-Deleuzian passage, Jung writes that libido only manifests

in the form of a "force," that is, as a particular energetic charge of "something," for example a moving body, chemical or electrical tension, etc. Libido is therefore tied to definite forms or states. It appears as the *intensity* of impulses, affects, actions, and so on. In this respect these phenomena are never impersonal; they manifest themselves as parts of the personality. (328; my trans.)

Jung sometimes lapses into a psychological Kantianism in attempting to distinguish between a noumenal archetype-in-itself and its phenomenal manifestation. But Deleuze takes up Jungian libido in its intensive dimension, as transcendental empiricism, in a move *against* the Kantian subject as a locus of quantity, quality, relation, and modality as the categories of pure reason defining all possible experience. Indeed, given that at least some of *Difference and Repetition*'s key concepts are "explicitly indebted to Jung" (Kerslake, "Desire" 78), it is plausible that Deleuze's notion of intensity is derived directly from Jung's formulation of libido (see Kerslake, "Rebirth Through Incest" 142). Deleuze takes up the Jung who is concerned not with the qualities of *possible* experience (the Jung that would stop at a "closed system of inherited possibilities") but instead with articulating *actual* experience in a phenomenological economy. Indeed, Jung does not limit libido to progressive-regressive bidirectionality but superadds the tension between introverted and extraverted experiences: Jungian libido thus "moves not only forwards and backwards, but also outwards and inwards" ("On Psychic Energy" para. 78).

Jung thus gives libido a multidimensionality Deleuze later takes up as the "pure *implex*" of depth resisting metaphors of verticality. And it is perhaps not surprising that Deleuze specifically invokes Schelling with regard to this depth: "[Schelling] said that depth is not added from without to length and breadth, but remains buried, like the sublime principle of the *differend* which creates them. [...] Depth and intensity are the same at the level of being, but the same in so far as this is said of difference" (*DR* 230–31). The indifferent energy of Jungian libido is aligned with Deleuzian intensity as the precursor of empiricism itself. Deleuze writes:

> [As opposed to an empirical energy,] energy in general or intensive quantity is the *spatium*, the theatre of all metamorphosis or difference in itself which envelops all its degrees in the production of each. In this sense, energy or intensive quantity is a transcendental principle, not a scientific concept. [...] An empirical principle is the instance which governs a particular domain [as] a qualified and extended partial system, governed in such a manner that the difference of intensity which creates it tends to be cancelled within it (law of nature). [...] On the other hand, there is an intensive space with no other qualification, and within this space a pure energy. The transcendental principle does not govern any domain but *gives the domain to be governed to a given empirical principle.* [Thus] [t]he domain is created by difference of intensity, and given by this difference to an empirical principle according to which and in which the difference itself is cancelled. It is the transcendental principle which maintains itself in itself, beyond the reach of the empirical principle. (*DR* 240–41)

In Jungian terms, libido is the intensive field through which empirical concepts arrange and govern knowledge. And in the absence of these specifically human domains, intensity is the *First Outline*'s fluidity; it is "pure energy," what Schelling will later call the differential *asystasy* which recedes with the creation of systems of knowledge. "Domains" emerge to occlude their intensive (un)grounding just as *Weltanschauungen* are constructed from within the matrix of analytical psychology as their "transcendental principle" and, for Foucault, positive sciences emerge from the epistemological bases they repress. This differential principle is the counter-scientific concept which analytical psychology both strives towards and relentlessly deconstructs through its matrix of archetypal forces.

In the final pages of *The Order of Things*, Foucault speculates about the potential of a "third counter-science" between psychoanalysis and ethnology, lauding the possibilities of an ethnology whose object of inquiry was not "societies without history" but "the area of the unconscious processes that characterize the system of a given culture [so as to] bring the relation of historicity, which is constitutive of all ethnology in general, into play within the dimension in which psychoanalysis has always been deployed" (379–80). In other words, Foucault wonders about a psychoanalysis "with the dimension of an ethnology" guided by "the discovery that the unconscious also possesses, or rather that it *is* in itself, a certain formal structure" (380). The forms of "the unconscious and of historicity" (381) Foucault attributes to such a counter-science are uncannily prescient of analytical psychology which, more than psychoanalysis, sought to "rework psychology radically on the basis of ethnopsychology" (Shamdasani, *Jung and the Making* 297) and primarily through the very phenomenon of mythology which Foucault saw reflecting the "formal transformations" of this (to Foucault) hypothetical structure (*The Order of Things* 380). We may lament yet another missed encounter between Jung and twentieth-century theory, but Romantic metasubjectivity opens up a space for us to consider how analytical psychology specifically names this counter-scientific historicity. Moreover, while Foucault remained largely entrenched in discourse and linguistics, Romantic metasubjectivity also allows us to conceive the *psyche* to which Foucault's historicity gestures. The articulation of this psyche is the subject of the following chapter, which returns to the *First Outline* and the Jungian archetype in order to explore their continuity in more detail and articulate the dissociative matrix from which Romantic metasubjectivity emerges.

Notes

1. Ricoeur is talking specifically about Goethe's *Naturphilosophie* which, Robert Richards argues, emerges at least in part from a reciprocal influence between Goethe and Schelling (464f).
2. The Zofingia Lectures were a series of talks given by Jung at the weekly club meetings of the *Zofingiaverein*, a Swiss student fraternity to which Jung belonged during his medical studies at Basel University.
3. This largely unexplored domain of Freudian scholarship is developed further by Dufresne (*The Late Sigmund Freud* 229ff).
4. Although the original *Wandlungen und Symbole der Libido* was published in 1912 before the other theoretical works I take up here, its substantial revision in 1952 also makes it a later Jungian text, a theoretical substructure of Jung's oeuvre as a whole. The first English translation (*Psychology of the Unconscious* [1912], trans. Hinkle) is generally considered unreliable.

5. George Hogenson argues compellingly that not only did Jung not endorse Lamarckism but was more closely aligned with the contrasting thought of Conway Lloyd Morgan and James Mark Baldwin, whose "Baldwin effect" argues, contrary to Lamarck, that "one result of evolution is the organism's ability to alter the environment and thereby shape the circumstances of evolution by natural selection" (596). This crucial idea of "behavioural plasticity" (596) actuates, in the domain of evolutionary science, what Foucault sees as the elusive "historical a priori" laws governing the heterogeneity of social discourse; we will see that it is also essential to understanding the genesis and development of the Jungian archetype.

6. Schelling often uses *Bildungstrieb* ("formative drive") instead of *Trieb* to describe Nature's production in the *First Outline*. However, Frederick Beiser perceptively points out two somewhat contradictory meanings of *Bildung* ("building," "forming," "culturing," "education") in early German Romanticism. On the one hand, *Bildung* "must arise from the free choice of the individual [and] reflect his own decisions. The self realises itself only through specific decisions and choices, and not by complying with general cultural norms and tradition. *Bildung* cannot be the result, therefore, of some process of education or conditioning imposed by a culture or state" (*The Romantic Imperative* 29). On the other hand, "the importance, and indeed urgency, of *Bildung* in the early Romantic agenda is comprehensible only in its social and political context" and that (contrary to the outcome of the French Revolution) *Bildung*'s apogee lies in a republic of "responsible, enlightened, and virtuous citizens" (88–89). Ultimately neither teleological nor sociopolitically subject-ed, *Bildung*'s individual and collective aspects are left unresolved, as they must be to reflect the specifically Romantic problem of freedom. For this reason, I use *Trieb* throughout as the radicalised force which emerges from this tension.

7. For Deleuze, transcendental empiricism is tied to "the very being of the sensible": "Empiricism is by no means a reaction against concepts, nor a simple appeal to lived experience. On the contrary, it undertakes the most insane creation of concepts ever seen or heard" (*DR* xx, 57). In a similar vein, Schelling writes of *Naturphilosophie* that it is "empiricism extended to include unconditionedness" (*FO* 22).

8. Krell's translation of this passage ("Three Ends" 63) is clearer about the source of inhibition being in Nature itself.

9. The German *Seele* is difficult to translate: in the past it was rendered as both "mind" and "soul" in English, but its meaning is now generally confined to "soul." In the quoted passage, Hull erroneously synonymises *Seele* with *Psyche* when Jung clearly distinguishes between them. In the original German (*GW* 8: 207) Jung begins the paragraph referring to *Psyche*, stating that "all psychic processes [*psychischen Vorgänge*] available to observation and experience are somehow bound to an organic substrate. [. . .] This in no way means that the psyche [*die Psyche*] should be exclusively derived from the domain of

the drives and thus from its organic substrate" (my trans). Jung then shifts to what is conspicuously the only reference to *Seele* in this paragraph (the quote provided with this note): "For this very reason the soul as such [*die Seele als solche*] cannot be explained by physiological chemistry, because if anything it [*sie*, referring to *Seele*], with 'life,' is the only natural factor..." The rest of the paragraph refers to *Psyche*. Moreover, in his earlier *Psychological Types* (1921) Jung distinguishes between psyche ("the totality of all psychic processes, conscious as well as unconscious") and soul ("a clearly demarcated complex of functions that can be best described as a 'personality'") ("Definitions" para. 797; last trans. mod). Thus *Seele*, as "personality," means something *other* than "mind" or strictly psychic processes, and personality's ability here to create "unnatural" states from *within* Nature makes Jung's understanding of personality key to understanding the psychic aspects of the auto-alterity of Schelling's Nature, which will be taken up in Chapter 4.

10. The *Project*'s textual history shows Freud's ambivalence toward it during its composition. At one point, Freud writes to Wilhelm Fliess that while composition promised success, "nothing certain can be said as yet. To make an announcement on this now would be like sending the six-months' foetus of a girl to a ball" (284). However, Freud would later reformulate the *Project*'s ideas into the core precepts of psychoanalysis.

11. *In the Psychopathology of Everyday Life* (1901) Freud describes psychoanalysis as the project of "transforming metaphysics into metapsychology," but the original German ("*die Metaphysik in Metapsychologie umzusetzen*" [*GW* 4: 288]) points to an interpretive knot. *Umzusetzen* (or *umsetzen*) can mean "transform," "turn into," "transpose," or "implement," but it can also mean "translate." While "transforming" metaphysics into metapsychology implies a change in nature without remainder, "translating" metaphysics into metapsychology suggests *deriving* metapsychology from a metaphysics which retains some foundational authority. Like Strachey, Anthea Bell translates this passage as "turning *metaphysics* into *metapsychology*" (245).

12. The English title of Jung's essay is misleading. The original German title, *Das Grundproblem der gegenwärtigen Psychologie*, is properly translated as "The Fundamental Problem of Modern Psychology" – in other words, the problem of psychic reality which is the focus of the essay and not a survey of "basic postulates." I refer to Hull's translated title for the sake of convenience and clarity.

13. "Ontoaesthetics" merges ontology and aesthetics to express the importance of metaphoricity not only for literary poetry and art but also for articulating Being.

14. Gustav Theodor Fechner (1801–1887) developed the theory of psychophysical parallelism (which established a causal link between physical stimuli and psychological reactions, e.g., sensations) and the theory of the "tendency to stability" by which psychic energy always seeks the lowest and most stable form or state. See Ellenberger 218.

15. Although Laplanche and Pontalis (122) defend *Nachträglichkeit* against criticisms that psychoanalysis reduces all human actions and desires to the infantile past, they do not differentiate *Nachträglichkeit* from the regressive movement of the death instinct. As a result, the "pathogenic force" with which the neurotic subject revises past events is not the same as Jung's prospective hermeneutic.

16. "Transcendent in no way means that the faculty addresses itself to objects outside the world but, on the contrary, that it grasps that in the world which concerns it exclusively and brings it into the world" (Deleuze, *DR* 143).

17. Jung coins "ambitendency" from Bleuler, who introduces the term in a 1911 paper "*Zur Theorie des schizophrenen Negativismus*" ("On the Theory of Schizophrenic Negativity") to describe the psychological counterbalancing of a tendency by its opposite. For more on "ambitendency" see Jung, *Introduction to Jungian Psychology* 92–93.

18. The "Oldest System Programme of German Idealism" (1796), attributed to several authors (including Schelling), was a reaction to the restrictions on human knowledge set by Kant's *Critique of Pure Reason*. Its heavy emphasis on organicism contra mechanism and its call for philosophy's "sensualisation" for a future "mythology of reason" are crucial to Romanticism's development out of German Idealism.

19. Jung's original German (*GW* 8: 403, 413) defines psychoanalysis as *Naturwissenschaft* and analytical psychology as *Wissenschaft*. Presumably Jung wants to separate analytical psychology from the materialist dimensions of Freud's "natural science."

20. The original German title of this essay is *theoretische Überlegungen zum Wesen des Psychischen* ("Theoretical Reflections on the Nature of the Psychic"), which retains the bold speculative nature of Jung's project lost in Hull's English translation. Again, I use the original title for consistency.

21. Jung emphasises this statement in the original German. Hull often omits these emphases in the *Collected Works*.

22. "Canalization" is Hull's translation of *die Überleitungsversuche*, which can be rendered more literally as "attempt at transition," or the compensatory act of creating new and more productive avenues ("canals") of libidinal flow ("transit").

Chapter 2

The Romantic metasubjective unconscious

Dissociation, historicity, trauma

"The psyche, like the body," writes Jung with emphasis, *"is an extremely historical organism"* ("Foreword to Perry" para. 837; trans. mod.).[1] Jung goes further to suggest a synthesis of individual contingency and the purposiveness of Being when he writes that "history is *prepared* in the collective unconscious of the individual" (*Tavistock* para. 371; trans. mod.; my italics). It is now commonplace to conjugate Romanticism with the so-called "rise of history," but narratives of a "Romantic" Jung do not take this into account. Jung's extended analysis of Hölderlin's poetry as a literary case study of energic libido in *Symbols* (398ff), and his focus on Schiller and Goethe in his theory of psychological types, are enough to make us suspect his disavowal of Romanticism.[2] Moreover, in 1918 Jung insists that the productive-dissociative unconscious, which "[holds] that every aggregation of ideas and images possesse[s], in some measure or other, its *own personality*" (Haule 243–44), "can be traced back to the time of the French Revolution, [with] the first signs of it [to be found in] Mesmer" ("The Role" para. 21). Like the Romantics, Jung saw the French Revolution as more than merely a major socio-political event: it was an irruption of the "unconscious destructive forces of the collective psyche" which deposed Christianity to make "a tremendous impression on the unconscious pagan in us" (para. 22). With his characteristically mythopoeic expressiveness, Jung offers us a psychological analogue of the Deleuzian event. For Deleuze, an event is the unique expression of a nexus of "prehensions," his term for constellations of objects and perceptions (e.g. the event of the living organism "prehends water, soil, carbon, and salts") (*The Fold* 88). Furthermore, "the event is inseparably the objectification of one prehension and the subjectification of another; it is at once public and private, potential and real, participating in the becoming of another

event and the subject of its own becoming" (88). The Jungian analogue to this is the unique emergence of archetypal forces from the collective unconscious into human history, which subtends individual and group "prehensions" and the variations in intensity that express themselves as the objectification or subjectification of these forces. These prehensions are part of an event's becoming, but cannot conclusively determine the law or laws of its emergence.

More than this, however, this irruption catalysed the rise of empiricism's concern with materiality *itself.* Leaving to one side Jung's highly impressionist rendering of this history, its trajectory leads humanity's inquiry into "the roots of life itself" from alchemy to scientific materialism, social realism, and finally to contemporary inquiries into "the 'dark' side of matter itself" (232). The importance of this trajectory should not be understated, for it also maps the profound shift in intensity within Jung's own thinking, particularly with respect to the archetypes. Where Jung's early thought inhibits the archetype in a Kantian noumenal-phenomenal architectonic, his later formulation effectively unworks this boundary to entangle the archetype in both psyche and Nature as a point of intensity in a dissociative matrix synonymous with the psyche's nature as an "extremely historical organism." This organism, then, is grounded in the "dark side of matter," the materiality and historicity from which the discipline of history emerges.

This shift in Jung's thought is ironically prefigured in expositions of Hegel and Schelling in one of depth psychology's key historical texts – Eduard von Hartmann's *The Philosophy of the Unconscious* (1869), which exerted a profound influence on European culture at the end of the nineteenth century and which both Freud and Jung knew well. Steeped as it was in the German Idealism of the time, and as much as it may ultimately have corroborated the philosophical narrative which put Schelling under Hegel's shadow, von Hartmann's text privileges both Hegel *and* Schelling as forerunners of the unconscious; in so doing it embeds, in the history of the unconscious, a voice for the Romanticism emerging from Idealism. Von Hartmann's Idealism emerges most clearly in his goal of "[elevating] Hegel's unconscious Philosophy of the Unconscious into a conscious one" (1: 28). And von Hartmann's Hegelian analytic of the unconscious is inscribed in a strikingly proto-Freudian framework: his metaphysical unconscious is demonic and indeterminate but ultimately beholden to consciousness, offering up its first fruits of "feeling for the beautiful and artistic production" to specifically further the "conscious process of thought" and to "preserve" and "guide" the organism (2: 39). To this end von Hartmann writes: "wherever consciousness is able to replace the Unconscious, it *ought* to replace it, just because it is to the individual the higher" (2: 41). Strange, then, that von Hartmann, whose work watermarks Jung's early Zofingia Lectures, writes in almost the same breath that only with Schelling does one find "the Unconscious in its full purity, clearness and depth" (1: 24). Stranger still that Jung should miss this aspect of von Hartmann's thesis, reducing Schelling to a minor waypoint en route to Carus, Schopenhauer, and von Hartmann himself (*Transformation Symbolism* para. 375). Indeed, significant lacunae in Jung's account are von Hartmann's focus on Schelling's important critique of Fichtean subjectivism (1: 24; trans. in Schelling, *On the History* 108ff.) and von Hartmann's identification of Schelling as the first to explore the question of "[w]hether, and how far, the obscure ideas without any consciousness are to be explained by the penetration of the original intellectual intuition of the primordial Being into the derived human understanding" (1: 23). This latter point crucially anticipates Jung's later thinking on the archetypes and the collective unconscious, particularly as it feeds his development of synchronicity as a core concept of analytical psychology.

Von Hartmann's identification of Schelling as the explorer of an original "intellectual intuition of the primordial Being" is an early hint of his importance to the development of the dissociationist model to the mind, a line of thinking which extends from Schelling through Reil,[3] Bergson, Janet,[4] and Jung, to Deleuze and Guattari (who were closely aligned with the anti-psychiatry movement of the 1960s, which included R.D. Laing and Foucault). Indeed, McGrath views Schelling as an important metaphysical precursor to dissociationism's view of the person as *"constitutively plural"* ("Schelling and the History" 53 n. 2).[5] And Christian Kerslake sees dissociationism as a crucial point of difference between Jung and Freud: against Jung's metapsychology of intensive variation, he writes that Freud's "discovery" of the unconscious consists in his being the first "to create a strictly 'molar' opposition between consciousness and the unconscious" which led to "the loss of demarcations between different kinds of *states of consciousness*" (*Deleuze* 58–59). Dissociationism's constitutive plurality and its amenability to the nexus of prehensions which define authentic events – the voices it gives to the "dark matter" and pure depth of the unconscious – make it the essential terrain on which the historicity of the Romantic metasubjective unconscious unfolds.

Jung was no historian; one quickly sees that his sense of history is overdetermined by his theory of the archetypes, and as a result historical events are often read as tangential points in the unfolding of the collective substratum of the human psyche. Indeed, Jung casts this history mythopoeically as the transition from Gnosticism to alchemy, a repetition of the Gnostic Nous "who, beholding his reflection in the depths below, plunged down and was swallowed in the embrace of Physis" (*Aion* 232–33). Nevertheless, Jung's concern with the "dark side" of matter alludes to what Pfau calls the transferential "affinities" on which contemporary Romantic scholarship predicates the rise of history:

> Moments of rhetorical instability [in Romantic texts] ought to be grasped [...] as symptomatic condensations of a larger historical dilemma. Indeed, it is only on the basis of a deeper affinity between formal-aesthetic and historical processes that we can begin to grasp romanticism as a specific phase in the evolution of modernity. Above all, we find the period conceding interiority to its post-Enlightenment subjects only in supplemental form. Rather than collapsing inwardness into a purely imaginary order–a quasi-maternal and allegedly unimpeachable, affective origin–romanticism during the Napoleonic era and beyond stages the inwardness of its subjects as *a progressive awakening to their traumatic history*. (242; my italics)

What Pfau describes in a less explicitly psychological framework than Jung is Romanticism's ever-shifting tectonics of language and history, whose "affinities" nevertheless serve to recapitulate their difference in a dynamic encrypting, "staging" the interiority of the subject (Pfau's dramatic language here is surely not accidental). In other words, what Pfau calls traumatic *history* is history's subjection to the indeterminacy of *historicity* – what Schelling would call history's derangement. And while critical history still too often associates Jung with this "purely imaginary order," we have seen that the Jungian collective unconscious is *historicity itself*, the recapitulation of an infinitesimal kernel of difference and variation in its "deposit of world-processes" resulting in a "type of timeless, to some extent eternal world-image which counterbalances our conscious, momentary picture of the world" ("Analytical Psychology" para. 729; trans. mod).

But what is a "type of timeless or eternal world-image"? How, or perhaps *why* does timelessness resolve itself into a "type"? Jung's imprecise language suggests a timelessness which is nevertheless in and of the world, an equivocal eternity which has always already fragmented into what consciousness can only fumble with using concepts.[6] In this sense, Jung offers a colloquialism for the difference within repetition that here marks the unconscious, a repetition that "appears as difference without a concept, repetition which escapes indefinitely continued conceptual difference. It expresses [...] *a stubbornness of the existent in intuition, which resists every specification by concepts*" (*DR* 13–14; my italics). Put differently, this timelessness marks the imbrication of ideal and real, the repetition of what does not rest entirely in concepts of either singularity or difference – the paradoxically productive lack underwriting the enantiodromia[7] between them in a "moment" which is always happening. Jung's collective unconscious is the paradox of "sheer objectivity" which takes the subject out of itself to make it the "object of every subject, in complete reversal of [...] ordinary consciousness, where [...] the subject [always] has an object" ("Archetypes" para. 46). But it also makes the self part of the *world* in a continuum which consciousness cannot perceive. In other words, as Jung's version of Schelling's *a priori* Nature, the collective unconscious names the nonmolar matrix of historicity from which history unfolds. It is that "in" the person as ego (figuratively speaking) which connects them with the intensities of the archetypes, which the concept "collective unconscious," like Schelling's "universal hierarchy" (*FO* 34), attempts to circumscribe only to find its boundaries infinitely porous, defined by the very excess it tries to contain.

Within this dissociative seethe, the "coming to presence" of every organism shares what Wirth calls a terrible solitude at the heart of its coming into existence, its own "awful secret of the absolute as *natura naturans*" (*Schelling's Practice* 4), its singular burden of Nature's infinite productivity which is nevertheless paradoxically shared by all organisms. Indeed, Wirth's observation that "the community that is [Schelling's] nature, a terrible belonging together, is the strange *one* – in no way to be construed as one thing or being – expressing itself as the irreducibly singular proliferation of the *many*" (5) resonates uncannily with Jung, who suggests that if "the unconscious can contain everything that is known to be a function of consciousness, then we are faced with the possibility that it too, like consciousness, *possesses a subject, a sort of ego*" ("On the Nature of the Psyche" para. 369; my italics). For Jung archetypes, and individuals as amalgamations of archetypal intensities, all manifest as singular proliferations of an unprethinkable materiality. The dissociative matrix of Nature and historicity is what engenders the trauma of becoming for each of Nature's organisms; left to individuate in and through time and history, and powered by forces which recede before the purview of consciousness (or which dwell and circulate through the non-human animals consciousness encounters), each organism lives, consciously or not, this secret of the Absolute. And for our species, to experience this awe and terror is to experience that which cannot be *named* as such.

As the dissociative framework of the Romantic metasubjective unconscious, the isomorphism between Schelling's Nature and Jung's collective unconscious offers a way through Jung's early embattled attempts to articulate "psychic reality" which, as we saw in the last chapter, come up against the psyche's unassimilable fluidity and resistance to a psyche-Nature binarism. Schelling's actant is a hypothesis, a heuristic unit which does not "exist" but which must be postulated in order to think Nature. And Schelling's only way to think the actant's dynamism is in the protopsychological rubric of *Trieb* which, even in this prehuman space, invites an analogy with the collective unconscious. Archetypes, on the other hand, *are* figured within an ontoaesthetic space as images, affects, situations, and experiences, even if their symbolic economies can only gesture toward the archetype's unknowable core. Thus, Jung's archetype in effect translates[8] the dynamism of Schelling's actant into the economy of the dissociationist psyche, but this should not be understood as a relapse into a Cartesian distinction between (Schellingian) Nature and (Jungian) psyche given Jung's mature formulation of the archetype in line with Jung's conception of analytical psychology as a (counter-scientific) science of historicity. The actant articulates the coalescence of Nature's infinite productivity into dynamic products; the archetype articulates knowledge and experience *of* this emergence as images, affects, experiences, and situations which variously, infinitely recapitulate this emergence and its "terrible belonging together" in solitude.[9] Jung ultimately grounds the archetype in a notion of *language* approaching the "enigmatic density" Foucault attributes to modern language in *The Order of Things*. Unlike the density given to language in the Renaissance, with modern language "now it is not a matter of rediscovering some primary word that has been buried in it, but of disturbing the words we speak, of denouncing the grammatical habits of our thinking, of dissipating the myths that animate our words, of rendering once more noisy and audible the element of silence that all discourse carries with it as it is spoken" (298). This silent derangement allows us to conceptualise the grammatology of Being, the symbolic *écriture* through which Romantic metasubjectivity's "Self of one's self" unfolds. We begin, then, with Schelling's notion of the actant, which must be seen in terms of the interlocked concepts of derangement, drive, and disease which inform Schelling's Nature.

Schelling's actant: derangement, drive, disease

The *First Outline*'s structure is rhizomatic, a body without organs consisting of intersecting and mutually determining systems and disciplines which are constellated in a text with "undeveloped tendencies" (Rajan, "First Outline" 329–30). Indeed, the "rhetorical instability" Pfau diagnoses in Romantic texts is reflected in the *First Outline*'s performativity, which (un) grounds Schelling's oeuvre as its metaphysical unconscious, the "fluidity" (*FO* 29) from which the other strands of his philosophy emerge and in which they are entangled. Schelling never fully plumbs the depths of his Nature, but in opposition to Hegel's philosophy of nature, which is "structured by an anthropomorphism that reads nature as pathologized spirit" (Rajan, "Philosophy as Encyclopedia" 9), Schelling will privilege Nature's productive aporias in subsequent works and phases of his thought. Indeed, Wirth offers a compelling case for considering the *Naturphilosophie*, if not *as* psychology, nonetheless *psychologically*; bridging the gap between the *Naturphilosophie* and Schelling's later protopsychological works, he writes that "doing *Naturphilosophie*" is not "doing a science," but rather "doing philosophy in accordance with nature," as "a gateway into the originating experience of philosophizing" itself (*Schelling's Practice* 17). To plumb the depths of Nature is to sound the depths of one's *own* nature. And while Schelling does not use the term "absolute subject" in the *First Outline*,[10] it is nevertheless nascent as the "Proteus" of a philosophical creation myth drawing all possible forms into a circle "determined for it in advance" (*FO* 28). This gathering requires "infinitely many attempts" (28), making the circle both determinate and immanent. This Protean appearance in the *First Outline*'s speculative physics is, in fact, a precursor of the constellating force of the Self which Jung will articulate much later. But to articulate the dynamic of how this "gathering" comes about, we must examine in more detail the actant as the constituent part of this dynamic productivity.

In the first of the *First Outline*'s three Divisions, Schelling develops the actant [*Aktion*] as the nonmolar, monadic force articulating Nature's absolute productivity, which is the first principle of the *Naturphilosophie*'s "dynamic atomism" (*FO* 5). Although the actant briefly reappears in his retrospective Introduction to the *First Outline* and the second Division, Schelling does not revisit the concept elsewhere in his oeuvre. Nevertheless, the actant occupies an important role in the *First Outline* as the fundamental component of "the original multiplicity of individual principles in Nature [...] Each [actant] in Nature is a fixed point for it, a seed around which Nature can begin to form itself" (*FO* 21 n. 1). And just as Nature "forms itself" around the actant in the phenomenal world, so Schelling surrounds the actant with a proliferation of textual predicates in an attempt to define it: actants are "dynamic atoms," "*pure intensity*," "originary qualities," "simple productivities" of Nature – and yet their "simple" nature proves unruly as their *Trieb* drives them from text into subtext and back again in the form of lengthy footnotes complicating this "simplicity" (*FO* 21 n., 208). Indeed, as if embedding the actants' dynamism in the texture of language, Schelling's text itself recapitulates the "infinite multiplicity of original actants" (28).

Taking up atomism to define the actant as a factor of Nature's dynamic productivity, Schelling concedes that the intangibility of the actants is precisely what makes them necessary:

> Our opinion is [...] not that *there are* such simple actants in Nature, but only that they are the ideal grounds of the explanation of quality. These simple actants do not really allow of demonstration–they do not *exist*; they are what one must posit in Nature, what one must think in Nature, in order to explain the originary qualities. [...] [S]uch simple actions must be *thought* as ideal grounds of explanation of all quality. (*FO* 21 n.)

Not existing in space or as matter (but nevertheless "constituent factors of matter"), and "truly singular" like Leibnizian monads yet decomposable to an indeterminate degree (*FO* 21 & n.), the actant occupies a liminal space between the ideality of the unconditioned and the materiality of space. To complicate matters further, after defining the actant as "action in general"

Schelling goes on to define matter *itself* – in the footnoted margins to his own philosophy – in terms of "repulsive and attractive forces" (*FO* 21, 22–23 n). Schelling's aporia here is the undecidable relationship between actant and matter, analogous to Jung's realisation that "the nonpsychic can behave like the psyche, and vice versa, without there being any causal connection between them. Our present knowledge does not allow us to do much more than compare the relation of the psychic to the material word with two cones, whose apices, meeting in a point without extension – a real zero-point – touch and do not touch" ("On the Nature of the Psyche" para. 418).

Yet the First Division of the *First Outline* attempts to work through the trauma of its textual excess by turning from the metaphysical overgrowth of the first section on the actants ("The Original Qualities and Actants in Nature") to something closer to dramatic narrative in the following section ("Actants and Their Combinations"). Here, Schelling describes the creation of matter as "the drama [*Schauspiel*] of a struggle between *form and the formless*" (*FO* 28). For Schelling, Nature's universal fluidity is always already inexplicably "solidified" by the actants in this drama without beginning, which transpires in "infinite multiplicity" between fluid and solid. The actants, in their creation of natural products, are always already subject to a drama of (de)combination in their infinite multiplicity:

> While the actants are *decombined*, left to itself each one will produce what it must produce according to its nature. To that extent, in every product there will be a constant drive toward free transformation. While the actants are continually *combined* anew, none of them will remain free with respect to its production. Thus, there will be compulsion and freedom in the product at once. Since actants are constantly set free and recaptured, and since infinitely various combinations of them are possible (and in every combination a slew of various proportions are possible), then continually *new* and *singular* materials will be *originally* produced in this product. (*FO* 33)

This dynamic of (de)combination, coalescence, and dissolution is ultimately pathologised by Schelling as the actants' "mutual derangement" [*sich stören*] of each other into universal fluidity, which is in turn resisted by the actant's individuality (*FO* 26). This derangement describes what we saw in Chapter 1 as Nature's auto-alterity, the ambivalence of a Nature divided against itself yet compelled to form products in a tension which creates generative fibrillations in Nature. The psychological language Schelling uses to describe this deranging moment is significant: the actant's "constant drive [*Trieb*] toward free transformation" is inhibited by the "compulsion" [*Zwang*] of its combination with other actants (33). In Jungian parlance, free drive enantiodromally turns into the compulsion to bind to other actants in two "moments" imperative to Nature's dynamism.

Jung, too, recapitulates this derangement's productivity as the dissociationist psyche and its bustling *dramatis personae* of personification, sense, and image. Indeed, in a psychic economy where archetypes cannot be disentangled,

> the unconscious depicts an extremely fluid state of affairs: everything of which I know, but of which I am not at the moment thinking; everything of which I was once conscious but have now forgotten; everything perceived by my senses, but not noted by my conscious mind; everything which, involuntarily and without paying attention to it, I feel, think, remember, want, and do; all the future things that are prepared in me and will later come to consciousness. ("On the Nature of the Psyche" para. 382; trans. mod.)

Indeed, the fluid derangement of Schelling's actants provides Jung with an "answer" to the "question" of Nature; it gives analytical psychology the metaphysical foundation Jung thinks it lacks, while preserving the power of this "questioning" Nature as a force analogous to Jung's idea of the unconscious.[11] Indeed, just as the question of Nature dogs Schelling's metaphysics, its infinitely productive question is recapitulated in Jung's collective unconscious as an uncanny mirroring of Schelling's Nature:

> [In medical psychology] the object puts the question and not the experimenter. The experimenter, the doctor is confronted with facts which he has not chosen and which he probably never *would* choose had he the freedom to do so. The sickness or the patient himself asks the decisive questions, which is to say that Nature experiments with the doctor and, in so doing, expects an answer from him. (*The Undiscovered Self* para. 532; trans. mod.)

Here Jung is getting at the transferential nature of the medical-psychological experiment (in the form of the object as "questioning analysand"), which requires relinquishing the *a priori* assumptions of science as much as possible to approach the unconditioned "derangement" of the forces behind the "crucial questions" of the analytic encounter. But what kind of questions does a deranged Nature ask? What does its facticity present to us? The natural products we see in the world are, after all, "nothing other than productive Nature itself determined in a certain way" (*FO* 34), inhibited by inscrutable laws into the unique, terrible, and solitary forms which surround us. Each one of them is part of Schelling's *Stufenfolge*, the graduated series of stages through which Nature craves the "Absolute," "the most universal proportion in which all actants, without prejudice to their individuality, can be unified" (*FO* 35). Yet each one of them is also a *"misbegotten attempt"* at this proportion (35): as we saw in Chapter 1, each product is a wayward line of flight away from the absolute ideal for which Nature strives but can never achieve, caught in an "infinite process of *formation*" (35). Nature is caught within the dynamics of its actants – caught in the derangement of a free drive to create infinite products and the compulsion to combine them into a "universal proportion," and it is from this derangement that the materiality and historicity of Being emerge. It is to this historicity that Jung replies when he writes that, ultimately, Nature experiments with the doctor: "When all is said and done, our own existence is an experiment of nature, an attempt at a new combination" ("Analytical Psychology" para. 730; trans, mod).

And for Jung, the products of this derangement coalesce around the individuation process. To be sure, Jung describes individuation in part as one's "becom[ing] what one is [...] one['s] accomplish[ment of] one's destiny, all the determinations that are given in the form of the germ" (*Visions* 2: 758) in what reads like a preformationist understanding. But in the same breath Jung also states that individuation is when "a cell begins to divide itself and to differentiate and develop into a certain plant or a certain animal" (*Visions* 2: 758), which opens the organism to mutation and indeterminacy. Indeed, to this end Jung likens the processes of the unconscious to *teratomata* (*Introduction* 39) – rogue growths in the body caused by independent germ cells being for-themselves, cells embarking on their own lines of flight away from the organism's "proportion." Similarly, in the experience of *Naturphilosophie* as "doing philosophy according to nature," the philosopher experiments on Nature, but paradoxically as one of Nature's own "abortive experiments" (*FO* 41 n.) confronting Nature's derangement. These two views mirror each other in what both Schelling and Jung would aver is the "infinite task" of discovering the "intermediate links in the chain of Nature" or the psyche (*FO* 199).

This infinitely productive derangement of the actants is the basis of the *aetiology* of the ontoaesthetic, which Schelling locates in disease. Disease, for Schelling, is coterminous with life itself: because disease "is produced by the same causes through which the phenomenon of life is produced[, it] must have the same factors as life" (*FO* 160). Thus, although in the *First Outline*'s Appendix on disease (*FO* 158ff) the term *Aktion* is not used, Schelling in effect transposes the actants' deranging dynamism of activity and receptivity on to physiology: here, the organism exists not as a static "being" but as "a perpetual *being-produced*," an "activity mediated by receptivity" (*FO* 160) against a series of external stimuli which prevent the organism from "exhausting" its activity in a final (dead, inorganic) object.[12] In this "being-produced," the organism reproduces an "original duplicity" whereby it generates itself "objectively" in response to external conditions (its receptivity to the world) as well as "subjectively" as an object *to itself* (its activity). This is what Schelling calls the organism's "excitability," its capacity to define itself *against* Nature but also *for itself* with a self-organisational interiority that cannot be directly influenced by external factors (*FO* 106 & ff). Indeed, for Schelling excitability is the source of both life and disease (161). Disease is precisely the "othering" of the organism's presence to itself as object, a "disproportion" within the economy of excitability (169). And this force of disease is ultimately predicated on a "uniformly acting external force" which acts on the organism while at the same time it "seems to sustain the life of universal Nature just as much as it sustains the individual life of every organic being (as the life of Nature is exhibited in universal alterations)" (171).

Both life and disease, then, emerge from a constitutive tension between the world of external forces and a higher-order dynamical force which sustains the organism against the barrage of stimuli from without (*FO* 161). Schelling will later cast this tension psycho-theologically in the *Freedom* essay as the relationship between self (the individual in time and history) and *centrum* (the individual's unique relationship with the Absolute, marked by personality). And as a *Naturphilosophie après la lettre*, analytical psychology takes up actantial dynamism as the libidinal economy of the archetypes to furnish Schelling's project with the (meta)subject upon which its predicates must ultimately hang. Where Schelling's *Naturphilosophie* deals with Nature's primordial derangement and its manifestation in the organism's economy of excitability, analytical psychology conceives this derangement on the level of the psyche, giving it a materiality which brings it into the domain of Nature as an "extremely historical organism." With this, we turn to Jung's formulation of the archetype as the formative force behind analytical psychology's symbolic economy of psychic production.

Jung's archetype: dissociation

Jung's thinking on the archetype evolves from its origins in language via his early word-association experiments and their demarcation of dissociative complexes, through problematic attempts to delineate noumenal and phenomenal dimensions of the archetype, and finally to Jung's mature formulation of the psychoid archetype as a force which is both psychic and material, ideal and real. This mature formulation opens up the psyche encrypted in the dynamics of the *First Outline*'s Nature. In this spirit, McGrath's description of Schelling's move away from Fichte and Hegel prefigures Jung's shift away from Kant toward the fundamentally non-rational basis of his metapsychology, which finds expression in the archetypes and the collective unconscious:

> Fichte had shown that if one takes away the ghost of a thing-in-itself which forever relativizes a priori judgements, the categories of reason become categories of being. [...] Schelling sees in [this] the undermining of every rationalism: no longer a secure possession of the self-reflecting subject, the a priori is the ground that always recedes from the reflective gaze; instead of serving as the transparent logical pre-structure of the Cartesian "I think," the a priori coincides with the unconscious, or at least that part of it that can be indirectly deduced. *Material nature now tells us as much about the structure of the subject as the structure of the subject tells us about nature.* [Schelling's method] *underscores the role of psychological introspection in Schelling's nature-philosophy, indeed the origin of the latter in the former.* ("Is Schelling's" 11–12; my italics)

Working through the history of Jung's thinking about the archetype reveals both his precarious allegiance to Kant's noumenal-phenomenal distinction and his turn to a more Schellingian account of production.[13] And although Jung at times represses this materiality by attempting to rein it in under a Cartesian mind-Nature distinction, this materiality provides the psychic bedrock, the symbolic grammatology with which the Romantic metasubject Thanatopoietically converses with the "unconscious productivity [...] whose mere reflection we see in Nature" (*FO* 194).

Jung's theory of the archetypes emerges from his earlier theory of complexes which, as we have seen, is firmly rooted in the dissociative tradition in psychology. Dissociationism's specifically Romantic lineage can be traced to nineteenth-century Romantic scientists including Schelling but also Reil, whose *Rhapsodien* (1803) advanced a theory of insanity as self-fragmentation which was foundational to Romantic psychiatry. We have seen how dissociationism sees the psyche as decentred, composed of various autonomous forces with "egos" or "personalities" of their own. These "sub-egos" are somehow constellated into a coherent order (personality), but because we are not entirely conscious beings this organisation cannot be made fully transparent to the ego. Put differently, this "multëity in unity" (to borrow a term from Coleridge ["Essays" 372]) is organised through an inscrutable dialectic of conscious and unconscious aspects of the psyche. And akin to what Novalis saw so clearly in disease, this dialectic is one of contagion, the interaction of things which "touch and do not touch." Jung's full description of the complex, worth quoting at length, is a contemporisation of Romantic polypsychism[14] which informs his theory of the archetypes and the collective unconscious:

A complex is an agglomeration of associations—a sort of picture of a more or less complicated psychological nature—sometimes of traumatic character, sometimes simply of a painful and highly toned character. [...] *A complex with its given tension or energy has the tendency to form a little personality of itself* [with a localized] body, a certain amount of its own physiology. [...] Because complexes have a certain will-power, a sort of ego [...] [t]hey appear as visions, they speak in voices which are like the voices of definite people. This personification of complexes is not in itself necessarily a pathological condition. In dreams, for instance, our complexes often appear in a personified form. [...] All this is explained by the fact that the so-called unity of consciousness is an illusion. [...] We like to think that we are one; but we are not, most decidedly not. [...] [The collective unconscious] consists of *an indefinite, because unknown, number of complexes or fragmentary personalities.* This idea explains [the poet's] capacity to dramatize and personify his mental contents. When he creates a character on the stage, or in his poem or drama or novel [...] that character in a certain secret way has made itself. (*Tavistock* pars. 148–52; my italics)

"Feeling-toned complexes," Jung writes, are part of what he calls the personal unconscious – that stratum of the unconscious reflecting the individual's unique psychic life ("Archetypes" para. 4). As such, they constellate archetypal material: a father-complex can constellate the archetypal image of the father (as tyrant, saviour, etc.) but also an innumerable amount of archetypal father-situations (including, but not limited to, literal or symbolic incest). Moreover, the detour into art with characters that autonomously "make themselves" establishes Jung's complex theory as not only a therapeutic organisation of dissociative material but also a post-Romantic aesthetics ventriloquising the productive-dissociative unconscious through art.[15]

Jung's complex theory evolved from his word-association experiments of 1900–1905, in which patients had to respond to single (hence ambiguous) words with another word. Longer reaction time indicated that the test words were connected to a complex, and using this method a list of associations could theoretically isolate it. We shall have cause to return to this importance of *language* as an (un)ground for both the complex and the archetype; for now, let us note that this was the intellectual-historical backdrop against which, as early as 1907, Jung was reading Freud through a Janetian-dissociative lens (Haule 255). Haule writes that Jung formulated the archetype as "the completion of the complex theory" (256), but Jung's theory of archetypes ends up deconstructing, and not completing, his metapsychology. Jung eventually conceives the archetype as inextricably entangled with psyche and material Nature, but it is also entangled within its own intellectual history; Haule discerns no fewer than six "partly complementary, partly contradictory" meanings of the archetype (256f), and in these examples terminology proliferates in a manner harking back to Schelling's effusive attempts to define the actant. Like Wordsworth's "hiding-places of Man's power" which close whenever the Poet tries to approach (*1850 Prelude* 12.279), the archetype recedes as Jung attempts to approach and define it in an interminable ventriloquism.

Jung's 1919 reference to the archetype as an "*a priori*, inborn [form] of 'intuition'" embeds it in the dissociative tradition. As the force which "[channels] perception and apprehension into specifically human patterns," the archetype is

> the *instinct's perception* [*Anschauung*] *of itself*, or [...] the self-portrait of the instinct, in exactly the same way as consciousness is an inward perception of the objective life-process. Just as conscious apprehension gives our actions form and direction, so through the archetype the unconscious determines the form and determination of instinct. ("Instinct" pars. 277; trans. mod.)

This passage inaugurates some of the central tensions in Jungian metapsychology: instinct is given self-awareness as consciousness is made into an epiphenomenon of Nature, even as Jung attempts to salvage a certain freedom of "conscious apprehension" alongside instinct's own strange "consciousness." We are misbegotten attempts of Schelling's Nature and attempts at a new synthesis in the experiments of Jung's Nature. Already we see the profound liminality between Nature's "objective life-processes" and "inward perception" which unworks Jung's attempts elsewhere to resolve the psyche into a Cartesian inside/outside polarity, for example when he writes that "it is the function of consciousness not only to recognize and assimilate the external world through the gateway of the senses, but to creatively translate the inner world into visible reality" ("The Structure of the Psyche" para. 342; trans. mod). Yet how does consciousness, as "perception," a passive aftereffect of natural processes, assimilate and "translate" into/for Nature (especially given the conundrums of translation we have pointed out)? Consciousness clearly estranges the psyche from natural processes enough to allow a certain reflexive assertion of (in Lacan's terms) the Symbolic over the Real; enough to create "'higher' or 'unnatural' states" in opposition to inorganic entropy ("On the Nature of the Psyche" para. 375). But this boundary is troubled by a fluidity which depotentiates the ego to make consciousness a marker of Nature's autoerotism, an "aftereffect" necessary for Nature's self-differentiation. Just as Schelling sees reason as the epiphenomenon of natural processes (*FO* 195), Jung's consciousness translates Nature back *to* itself but also keeps a portion of this Nature *for* itself in contagious exchange, assimilated and transformed into Nature's uncanny self-perception, a mirror-state where consciousness mirrors Nature to itself in an image both identical and transposed. This contagion persists throughout Jung's attempts to define the archetype, and perhaps this is where Schelling's isomorphic account of the actant productively supplements Jung's embattled psyche-Nature connection. Where Jung talks of psyche and archetype, the actant steps in to remind us that Nature, too, emerges from a dissociative matrix – something Jung will acknowledge in his mature formulation of the archetype, but also in his later (1958) statement that psyche *is* Nature ("A Psychological View" para. 831).

Consciously appropriating Kant, Jung defines the archetype in 1921 as "the noumenon of the image which intuition perceives and, in perceiving, creates" (*Psychological Types* 401). Anthony Stevens suggests that this Kantianism perseveres until 1947, when Jung resolves the archetype into "a clear distinction between the deeply unconscious and therefore unknowable and irrepresentable *archetype-as-such* (similar to Kant's *Ding-an-sich*) and the archetypal images, ideas and behaviours that the archetype-as-such gives rise to" ("The Archetypes" 77). But in fact, Stevens' account recapitulates a Kantian binarism that is not borne out by Jung's post-1940 thinking. Indeed, Jung's fraught engagement with Kant ends up taking him "not only back to pre-Kantian thought but also beyond the critical philosophy into the post-Kantian realms of late German Idealism and Romantic philosophy" (Bishop, "The Use of Kant" 137).

Jung's turn in thinking on the archetype begins with *On the Psychology of the Unconscious* (1943) and culminates in his 1947 supplementation of the archetype's "merely psychic" operations with "a further differentiation of the concept" ("On the Nature of the Psyche" para. 419; trans. mod.) – the archetype's *psychoid* nature which, he emphatically writes, has "a nature which *cannot with certainty be designated as psychic*" (para. 439). This shift in thinking releases analytical psychology from a Kantian architectonic and moves it closer to the quasi-subjective space of Schelling's *Naturphilosophie*. Jung uses a natural-scientific analogy of light to describe the archetype's relation to instinct:

> Just as the "psychic infra-red," that is, the biological life instinct, gradually passes over into the physiology of the organism and thus into its chemical and physical conditions, so the "psychic ultra-violet," the archetype, describes a field which on the one hand exhibits none of the peculiarities of the physiological and on the other hand can no

longer be regarded as psychic, although it manifests itself psychically. But physiological processes behave in the same way, without on that account being declared psychic. Although there is no form of existence that is not mediated to us psychically and only psychically, nevertheless one cannot explain everything as merely psychic. (para. 420; trans. mod.)

This passage reflects Jung's difficulty in keeping the archetype within a "psychic light spectrum" as it slips into Nature, dragging psyche with it. Our experience comes to us only through the psyche, Jung writes, but what this psyche *is* has now radically altered, a difficulty compounded by the connection the archetype now has with "the organic-material substrate" (para. 380). Jung explains this radical materiality "by assuming [archetypes] to be *deposits of the continuously repeated experiences of humanity* [...] subjective fantasy-ideas *aroused by the physical process*" (*On the Psychology* para. 109; trans, mod.; my italics).[16] Archetypes are embedded in materiality; in Schelling's words, Nature is *a priori*. And the metaphysics often consigned to the margins of analytical psychology come to the fore in a crucial footnote: "[The archetypes are] the effect and deposit of experiences that have already taken place, *but equally they appear as the factors which cause such experiences*" (para. 151 n. 3; my italics). With this paradox, the archetypes and the collective unconscious open into an uncontainable fluidity which articulates the materiality of Being. Indeed, two years before his death in 1961 Jung writes, somewhat convolutedly, that the archetype is "an image of a probable sequence of events, *an habitual current of psychic energy* [*Strömungs-System*], so to speak" (letter to Herr N., 9 May 1959, 505; my italics); the mind's eye is led from "image" to "probable sequence" to intangible "current" as the archetype recedes from cognitive view, elusive like Schelling's actant.

Jung figures this unconscious in strikingly Schellingian terms. The stratum of drives, much like the primordial fluidity of Schelling's Nature and its seethe of actants, is an unmanageable chaos in itself. Where Schelling sees the inscrutable agency of inhibition at the point of Nature's genesis, for Jung it is consciousness, which emerges inexplicably from the dark mists of the unconscious (but is nevertheless connected to it):

The system of drives is not a harmonious composition, but is exposed to numerous internal collisions. One drive deranges and represses [*stört und verdrängt*] the others, and although the drives as a whole make individual life possible, their blind compulsive character [*blinder Zwangscharakter*] frequently causes mutual disturbances. The differentiation of function from the inevitable compulsion of the drives [*der zwangsläufigen Triebhaftigkeit*], and its voluntary application, is vitally important with regard to the maintenance of life. But this differentiation increases the possibility of collision and creates disruptions – precisely those dissociations which time and again put into question the unity of consciousness. ("On the Nature of the Psyche" para. 378; trans. mod.)[17]

Here Jung takes up, on the level of psyche, Schelling's demand in the *First Outline* that *Naturphilosophie* "accompany its *a priori* constructions with corresponding external intuitions" (*FO* 19); indeed, the Jungian system of drives is the mirror-image of Schelling's fluidity, its dark aspect. Schelling can only describe the actants' impetus to free transformation as *Trieb* (*FO* 34), which already gives Nature's bidirectional ambivalence a taint of temporality and purposiveness. And in the *First Outline* the actant's *Trieb* is bound by compulsion [*Zwang*], making it receptive, bound to other actants according to a "universal hierarchy." But in Jung's version of this economy, the drive's binding *Zwang* is one of discord and disruption; psychological functions must separate from this compulsive derangement in the service of consciousness and life. Thus, Jung and Schelling describe two complementary aspects of Nature's motile moment. These mirror-images – Schelling's "universal hierarchy" and Jung's disturbed, repressed, and disruptive "system of drives" – punctuate the melancholic incommensurability between mind and Nature. Indeed, this psyche puts into relief the fundamental problems with this correspondence: actantial drive perpetuates the unifying "prehension" binding them, and conversely Jung's unifying "differentiated functions" of consciousness perpetuate the deranging "dissociations" they are meant to order and contain. As a result, both *a priori* constructions and external intuitions (Jung's drives and functions) become barely distinguishable from each other in the transcendental empiricism (empiricism "extended to the unconditioned" [*FO* 22; my trans.]) which frames Nature and psyche in a relationship of repetition and difference. Consciousness may be able to defy natural law and entropy to some degree, but it is never completely free from the possibilities of disease intrinsic to the derangement of (actantial, archetypal) forces (un) grounding the psyche.

As a "condensation [*zusammenfassender Ausdruck*] of the living process" ("Definitions" para. 749) the archetype is a centripetal force, gathering and combining specific materialities, "natural products" to itself while remaining irreducible to the metonymy of their possible representations. And we must emphasise the plural, for Jung also writes that the archetype is not merely one energic centre, but "bipolar" (*Psychology and Alchemy* 471) like the ambitendent nature of psychic energy itself and the actants' dual tendencies of autonomy and receptivity. Because of this, Jungian taxonomy strains under the excess of "an indefinite number of archetypes representing situations" (*On the Psychology* para. 185; trans. mod.). Indeed, similar to Schelling's problem of finding the laws whereby actants coalesce into their own lines of "free transformation" (*FO* 33), Jung's problem is that of type *itself* – of *how* Being coalesces into the archetypes, or how to conceive an archetypal taxonomy at all. We have seen how Schelling sees the actants as necessary constructs in order to think Nature; he also knows he cannot ultimately explain how actants, as "pure intensities" (*FO* 208), coalesce into "simple qualities," or the law(s) by which they are "completely dissolved" (31). Jung clearly faces a similar dilemma:

> An archetype, in its quiescent, unprojected state, has no exactly determinable form but is itself an indefinite shape which can assume definite forms only in projection. This seems to contradict the concept of a "type." [...] As soon as one divests these types of their casuistic phenomenology and [tries] to examine them in relation to other archetypal forms, they expand into symbolic contexts so extensive that one comes to the conclusion that *the basic psychic elements are indeterminate and enigmatic in ways which exceed the human imagination.* Empiricism must therefore content itself with a theoretical "as if." ("Concerning the Archetypes" pars. 142–43; trans. mod.; my italics)

Thus, both Schelling's actant and Jung's archetype are constituted by a rhizomatic indeterminacy, where specific forms become visible as fluctuations in relationality and intensity between an infinite proliferation of nodal points. Schelling's "universal hierarchy" and Jung's collective unconscious are always already provisional circumscriptions of the primordial fluidity of Being.

This fabric of indeterminacy is the canvas of Romantic *poiesis*. For in Romanticism "language and poetry [are] the *material* that Idealism can never fully assimilate or marginalize in its formation of an absolute" (Plug 17), and this materiality underwrites what David Clark gracefully calls, with Derridean (and Jungian) flavour, Romanticism's paleonymic nature – "at once haunted by sedimented histories and beckoning towards undetermined futures" (166). Indeed, the nonmolarity which the archetype shares with the actant is poeticised in Novalis' unfinished *Novices of Sais* (1798), which can be read as a condensation of analytical psychology. Its second division, "Nature," narrates the emergence of consciousness and an Idealist impetus to unite man and Nature, but against the backdrop of Nature's "infinite divisions" which poeticise the drama of the actants in Schelling's *First Outline*:

> Never can we find the smallest grain or the simplest fiber of a solid body, since all magnitude loses itself forwards and backwards in infinity, and the same applies to the varieties of bodies and forces; we encounter forever new species, new combinations, new phenomena, and so on to infinity. (39)

The rhizomatic yearning Novalis describes here – the "mysterious force" in us "that tends in all directions, spreading from a center hidden in infinite depths" (29) – marks Romantic metasubjectivity's cryptic exotropism. This differential articulation is open to any direction pointed out by its own unfolding, but emanates from a nucleus which persists only under the erasure of its own becoming. This unfolding can only proceed in a psyche deeply implicated in the work of futurity, of *Thanatopoiesis* – a psyche which is

> [a] living phenomenon [...] always indissolubly bound up with the continuity of the vital process [...] so that although on the one hand it is always something which has become, on the other hand it is always something which is creatively becoming. The psychological moment has a Janus-face which looks backwards and forwards. As it becomes, it also prepares the future. (Jung, "Definitions" pars. 717–18; trans. mod.)

The systole-diastole of Jung's "Janus-faced" psyche, its Thanatopoietic enantiodromia between past and future, is emphasised by the psyche's archetypal grammatology which, like Schelling's chemical elements (*FO* 33), figures the inscrutable combinations of natural materials and forces which unfold Being. We can now examine how this grammatology is articulated in a psyche that is structured like a language, but whose dissociationist matrix resists structuralist impositions.

The grammatology of Being

In *Of Grammatology* (1967), Derrida conceives grammatology as a "science of writing" which interrogates the privileging of speech over writing (the "absolute privileging of voice and being, of voice and the meaning of being" [12]) named as logocentrism but also more generally the idea of Being as presence, as onto-theological truth present to itself before all writing and signification (14). Arguing against the idea of a transcendental signified that separates signifier and signified, grammatology makes a case for the motility of signification itself. In other words, grammatology's essence is an "arche-writing," a "movement of differance," of traces[18] which "cannot, as the condition of all linguistic systems, form a part of the linguistic system itself and be situated as an object in its field" (60), and this differential movement prevents elements in a linguistic system from congealing into Being as presence. A year earlier, in "Freud and the Scene of Writing" (1966), Derrida radicalises the idea of the (Freudian) trace outside of its logocentric articulation in institutionalised psychoanalysis. Anticipating grammatology, he calls for a "psychoanalytic graphology," "a psychoanalysis of literature respectful of *the originality of the literary signifier*" versus the "analysis of literary *signifieds*" or "*nonliterary*" signified meanings," self-present meanings which purport to transcend the differential matrix of signification (230). Thus, grammatology is the science of *écriture*, of a writing which makes historicity possible before "being the object of a history [or] of an historical science" (*Of Grammatology* 27). In short, grammatology raises the question of a science's genesis in writing, which is repressed by sciences in their formation (28).

However, in privileging psychoanalysis as a discipline of the future which interrogates "being in its privilege" (21), Derrida grafts grammatology on to a positive science which ultimately resists the undecidability on which the general economy of the trace is predicated. That is, a science which "runs the risk of [...] never being able to define the unity of its project or its object [or] describe the limits of its field" (4), as well as the "danger" of its undecidable future (5), is paired with a psychoanalysis whose radical traces bear the burden of a nostalgia which watermarks even its most *nachträglich* moments and movements. Perhaps this is why Derrida takes care not to simply equate the two, cautioning that "Despite appearances, the deconstruction of logocentrism is not a psychoanalysis of philosophy" ("Freud and the Scene of Writing" 196). In contrast, the grammatology of Being which underwrites Romantic metasubjectivity reflects Derrida's missed encounter with analytical psychology, which is precisely a science that can describe neither the limits of its field nor that of its object but which is, as we have seen, driven to *become* that object. The grammatology of Being gives Derrida's formulation a materiality more commensurate with his interrogation of the signifier/signified binarism as part of "the play of signifying references that constitute language" (7), but also with his extending this question to the repressed "ontophenomenological question of essence" (28) within organisations of knowledge. This encounter is formulated in Romantic metasubjectivity, which articulates the subject that goes missing in Derrida's account of *différance*. And this subject emerges from precisely the isomorphism between Schelling's actant and the Jungian archetype, which put the ideas of play and trace into a general economy more amenable to the futurity which marks both Derrida's grammatology and Romanticism's paleonymic nature. In this, analytical psychology offers a model of the psyche which provocatively resonates in contemporary theory.

To use a phrase Krell invokes so lucidly with reference to Novalis: in the Romantic view there is, between language and Being, a "touching at a distance" which defines the very desire for the object within language (*Contagion* 59). Language is infected with Being. In a more Jungian sense, this contagion is precisely divine hypochondria, a symptom of the convergence of conscious and unconscious, of egoic existence and archetypal experience which "touch and do not touch" in the form of the symbolic, which gives all language a numinous texture. In language, this derangement means that any signifier can become a signified, a symbol infused with libidinal intensity – indeed, it all but nullifies the signifier-signified distinction altogether. The "illness" here is the ineradicable proximity of life and death, language and Being – which yields spiritual knowledge (for better or worse) if we learn to see it as such, and of which individual illness (as melancholy) is the representative. We will see in the following chapter that this experience is a limit-encounter of reason, a trauma which Pfau places at the core of Romantic historicity.

Thus the Romantic metasubjective unconscious is, to borrow Lacan's famous phrase, "structured like a language," but the *historicity* of the Romantic metasubjective psyche demands that we depotentiate the idea of "structure" in favour of "language." Indeed, Jung does more than simply mark the phylogenesis of the psyche through physiology. Appealing to the experience of meaning, Jung progresses through, only to deconstruct, the stages of the therapeutics of presence[19] that elsewhere characterises the analytical process:

> The anima and life itself are meaningless in so far as they offer no interpretation. Yet they have a nature that can be interpreted, for in all chaos there is a cosmos, in all disorder a secret order, in all caprice a fixed law, for all action is based on opposition. [...] Only when all props and crutches are broken, and no cover from the rear offers even the slightest hope of security, does it become possible for us to experience an archetype that had hitherto lain hidden behind the meaningful absurdity [*bedeutungsschweren Sinnlosigkeit*] of the anima. This is the *archetype of meaning* [*der Archetypus des Sinnes*]. ("Archetypes" para. 66; trans. mod.)

But what does this meaning *mean*? Jung's answer in the following paragraph breaks with the linearity of this therapeutics:

> From what source, in the last analysis, do we derive meaning? The forms we use for assigning meaning are *historical categories* that reach back into the mists of time—a fact we do not take sufficiently into account. Interpretations make use of certain *linguistic matrices that are themselves derived from primordial* [urtümlichen] *images. From whatever side we approach this question, everywhere we find ourselves in the history of language and motifs, which always leads back straight away into the primitive wonder-world.* ("Archetypes" para. 67, trans. mod.; my italics)

In one fell swoop therapy's teleology opens out on to radical *atelos*. Analytical psychology becomes an *archetypal grammatology*, and this grammatology marks Jung's a prioritisation of historicity itself through the isomorphism between language and the archetypes: both are imbued with a materiality which marks the operations of the collective unconscious beneath discourse, as it were.

This unconscious operates with a motility akin to the enigmatic density of modern language in *The Order of Things*; however, aligned with Schelling's actants as the forces of a bidirectional Nature, the corresponding ambitendency of the archetypes unfolds with a purposive self-organisation which supplements Foucault's discursive narrative. Indeed, with Novalis, one might say that the transcendental empiricism of the archetypes and the collective unconscious approaches the "*sympathy* of the *sign* with the signified" (*Notes* 23). Novalis also puts this empiricism at the core of the "grammatical mysticism" which underlies Being: "Everywhere there is a grammatical mysticism [...] It is not only the human being that speaks— the universe also speaks—everything speaks—unending languages" (qtd. in Weeks 223).[20] This speaking in tongues constitutes the "sick" narrative of Novalis' magical Idealism as a "poetics of the baneful," infused with the melancholic illness of nature and history (Krell, *Contagion* 53). But nevertheless, *something speaks* – the motile force behind the intensive unfolding of these archetypal-grammatological forces. With the grammatology of Being, Romantic metasubjectivity gives an experiencing psyche to what Foucault sees as the "enigmatic and precarious being" of language itself (*The Order of Things* 305). It symbolises the plenitude of a general economy which "[denounces] the grammatical habits of our thinking, [dissipates] the myths that animate our words, [renders] once more noisy and audible the element of silence that all discourse carries with it as it is spoken" (298). But these myths are not dissipated *into* words; the symbolic, no longer bound to the Providence of a divine Word, instead speaks a derangement of myths, motifs, and words. The myths, the gods are not dead; they are just implicated in the textures of sense and the event which constellate language and Being.

The *Thanatopoiesis* of Romantic metasubjectivity puts under analysis the liminality between Being and language to make its historicity *felt*, as *affective* contagion, through the performativity of the poem as event. Indeed, for Novalis language is caught up in the Romantic potentiation of the world, and Schelling will devote *Ages* to, among other things, a cosmological dramatisation of potencies in the creation and *narration* of knowledge. In a well-known passage Novalis writes:

> The world must be made Romantic. [...] To make Romantic is nothing but a qualitative raising to a higher power [potentization]. In this operation the lower self will become one with a better self. Just as we

ourselves are such a qualitative exponential series. This operation is as yet entirely unknown. By endowing the commonplace with a higher meaning, the ordinary with mysterious respect, the known with the dignity of the unknown, the finite with the appearance of the infinite, I am making it Romantic [...] Romantic philosophy. *Lingua romana.* Raising and lowering by turns. (*Logological Fragments* 1, #66)

Chapter 4 will investigate how this poetics of potentiation anticipates the movement of the potencies in Schelling's *Ages* and Jung's articulation of the individuation process. But germane for us here is how Novalis figures this "potentization" in the specifically *linguistic* terms of his "grammatical mysticism [which] lies at the basis of everything," and it is precisely the mysterious which "incit[es] potencies" (*Notes* 23). This grammatical mysticism underlies the Romantic presumption that poetry is the supreme art among arts. But Novalis' consideration, like Schelling's, of his own idealist "Golden Age" reads language away from poetry and into the fabric of Being itself – "a Golden Age, when all words become— *figurative words*—myths—And all figures become—linguistic figures— hieroglyphs—When we learn to speak and write figures—and learn to perfectly sculpt and make music with words" (*Notes* 206).

What Novalis sees as the Romantic potentiation and figuration of words which imbricate them with Being, Deleuze conceives as the "linguistic precursor," his understanding of the psyche's isomorphism with language (*DR* 122). The linguistic precursor is an "event" analogous to the centripetal force of what Deleuze elsewhere calls the dark precursor as the "in-itself of difference," an enigmatic force impelling the differential communication between disparate series which makes all difference possible (we will take up the dark precursor in Chapter 3) (117). That is, the linguistic precursor is an "esoteric word" that marks the *sense* of language – the irruption of an affective texture in the word which troubles its place in its chain of signification. Deleuze cites the (Joycean) portmanteau word[21] as a contemporary example of such a word which expresses "both itself and its sense" (155). Thus, the linguistic precursor marks this limit-experience of sensibility before the being *of* the sensible:

the linguistic precursor belongs to a kind of metalanguage and can be incarnated only within a word devoid of sense from the point of view of the series of first-degree verbal representations. [...] This double status of esoteric words, which state their own sense but do so only by representing it and themselves as nonsense, clearly expresses the perpetual displacement of sense and its disguise among the series. In consequence, esoteric words are properly linguistic cases of the object $= x,$ while the object $= x$ structures psychic experience like a language *on condition that the perpetual, invisible and silent displacement of linguistic sense is taken into account.* In a sense, everything speaks and has sense, on condition that speech is also that which does not speak – or rather, speech is the sense which does not speak in speech. (*DR* 123; my italics)

The linguistic precursor's "metalanguage" is that which suspends "first-degree" conceptual representation. "Esoteric words" mark the irruption, in language, of the object $= x$ which unites the word's morphemes in non-sense and, as with the confrontation with an archetypal intensity, one must encounter and decipher this experience for oneself in the raw data of sense.

Deleuze's understanding of sense through the linguistic precursor, as fundamental unity of difference within the series-unity of discourse, thus harks back to the non-ground of sense and Being from which all discourses coalesce. The Yes and No of Schelling's expanding and contractive forces are perhaps the first, best portmanteau words; they are "shifters," or "indexicals," which "[draw their] entire energy from [their] site[s] of enunciation" (Comay 250). Language at its most authentic is schizophrenic, open to and entwined with the potentiation of Being. Indeed Romantic poetry, which understood literature as a fundamentally *embodied* vocation, sought to engage with *and experience* this kind of Deleuzian sense – whether it is both courted and resisted (Coleridge) or more enthusiastically explored by the so-called "Younger Romantics" such as Keats and Shelley (Mitchell 44–45). Chapter 5 will examine Shelley's *Prometheus Unbound* as a poetic metapsychology of Romantic metasubjectivity demonstrating this sense-power of language not only as it invokes the power of political discourse, but also as it more fundamentally represents actantial-archetypal dynamics in the emergence of the dissociative psyche. But we must first explore this "sense-power" as it is articulated by Schelling and Jung, and this leads us to the question of *experience* as a crucial index of Schelling's difference from Hegel but also the central concern of analytical psychology. What is the experience of this grammatological entanglement? What is the experience of Romantic metasubjectivity?

Notes

1. Jung appears to have written this Foreword in English, and the *Collected Works* read "extremely historical structure." The German edition reads: *"ein äußerst historischer Organismus" (GW* 18.1: 384). I retain *Organismus* ("organism") throughout, as "structure" does not do justice to Jung's thinking about the fluidity of psychic evolution.
2. For more on Jung's ambivalence toward his "Romanticism," see "Foreword to Mehlich" pars. 1732ff. and "Foreword to von Koenig-Fachsenfeld" pars. 1739–40.
3. Johann Christian Reil (1759–1813) actively took up Schelling's thinking to develop a theory of insanity as self-fragmentation closely aligned with the "polypsychism" of nineteenth-century magnetists (Ellenberger 146ff; Roberts 263). Generally, polypsychism conceived the individual as composed of a multitude of different entities ("souls," psychological forces, etc.) and is a direct ancestor of dissociationism.
4. Jung attended Janet's lectures in Paris in 1902 – five years before he met Freud – and counts Janet as one of his most important teachers along with Bleuler and Flournoy (Shamdasani, *Jung and the Making* 47, 93). For a more detailed study of Janet's presence in Jung see Monahan 40ff.
5. McGrath elsewhere makes the important point that Schelling's copular logic is by definition dissociative, something "which conjoins but also disjoins." When one says "A *is* B" (or "the ball *is* blue"), one always points to the unnameable copula. In other words, "in all acts of self-consciousness or self-identification, some aspect of the self goes unnamed, an anonymous indifferent ground withdraws from the identification and is never denominated by either the subject (the I) or the predicate (whatever the I happens to identify itself with)" (*Dark Ground* 121). Schelling also notably called the concept of freedom in the *Freedom* essay only one of his system's "ruling centrepoints" (*Freedom* 9), which anticipates "NPS'"s later ungrounding of knowledge in what can be called Schelling's systemic dissociationism.
6. For this reason I do not subscribe to the view, held by some Jungians, that Jung sees the collective unconscious as ultimately "timeless" in a transcendental sense. While Jung sometimes intimates as much, Jung does not ultimately hypostatise either the collective unconscious or the archetypes. Jung's mature view is that they are "timeless" in precisely the sense of Schelling's "empirically infinite" Nature whose "infinite becoming" reflects an "absolute (intellectual) infinity" originating in the mind (*FO* 15). Put differently, the collective unconscious is timeless in a transcendental-empirical sense.
7. Jung takes up enantiodromia from Heraclitus, as a principle whereby a thing (or position or outlook), taken to its extreme, transforms into its opposite. Psychologically, Jung defines it as "the emergence of the unconscious opposite in the course of time [which] always occurs when an extreme, onesided tendency dominates conscious life; in time an equally powerful counterposition is built up" ("Definitions" para. 709).

8. Indeed, the conundrum over "translation" – does one *translate from* an original, or *transform* the original *into* something different? – is no less present here than with Freud (see Chap. 1, note 11, above). However, the point here is that the chiastic theoretical dialogue between Schelling's actant and the Jungian archetype reveals the former's psychological potency and the latter's material potency beyond Jung's sporadic attempts to make Cartesian distinctions between psyche and Nature.

9. Jung's mature formulation of the archetype *does* have a distinctly material aspect which we will explore later in the form of the crystal analogy. But Schelling's *Naturphilosophie* clearly goes further than Jung in thinking the self-organisation of Nature in relation to forces such as gravity and electricity.

10. However, Schelling *does* explicitly equate *Naturphilosophie* with the absolute subject in his later lectures on the history of modern philosophy. Here he explains that *Naturphilosophie* moved away from Fichte in beginning not with the human "I," but "the infinite subject [. . .] the absolute *subject, because* it alone is *immediately* certain [and] the subject which can *never* stop being subject, can never be lost in the object, become mere object" (*On the History* 114).

11. Deleuze relies heavily on Jung's formulation of the unconscious to argue that "Problems and questions [. . .] belong to the unconscious, but as a result the unconscious is differential and iterative by nature; it is serial, problematic and questioning" (*DR* 108).

12. See also *FO* 56f., where Schelling more specifically deduces the dynamism of activity and receptivity.

13. For an early critique of Jung's relationship to Kant, see de Voogd. Following this critical tradition, Paul Bishop concludes that "whilst claiming to remain within Kantian boundaries, Jung shows his true Romanticism in constantly yearning to go beyond them" (*Synchronicity* 162ff, 185).

14. For polypsychism, see note 3, above. Significantly, polypsychism (and by association, dissociationism – pardon the pun) figures in Graham Harman's object-oriented ontology (OOO), which is an important contribution to the contemporary philosophical perspective known as Speculative Realism. I shall risk gross oversimplification to define OOO as a view that everything is an "object," objects being entities that cannot be reduced to either manifestations of a universal vitalist essence or substrate or to their perception by the human mind. There are many different thinkers with divergent views in Speculative Realism (of which OOO is one, Iain Hamilton Grant's work on Schelling another), but they all share a pointed criticism of the correlation between thought and Being, which they see as having conditioned the vast majority of Western thought. To this end, Harman endorses a polypsychism "which must balloon beyond all previous [psychological] limits, but without quite extending to all entities" in service to a "speculative [Schelling might say "cosmic"] psychology, [which may one day lead] philosophy to the tectonic plates that separate atoms from gold, moss, mosquitoes, Neanderthals, and

bears" (122). Exploring what Jung, or indeed Romantic metasubjectivity, has to offer Speculative Realism is a fertile ground for future study.

15. Jung's mythopoetic register is predicated on the generic shift from scientific treatise to literary art in Reil's *Rhapsodien* (1803), "perhaps the most influential work in [the] shaping of German psychiatry before Freud" (Richards 263–64).

16. This idea had, in fact, been present in Jung's thinking as far back as 1928 in "The Unconscious in the Normal and Pathological Mind," the first essay in the Baynes translation of *Two Essays on Analytical Psychology*. At that time it was relegated to a footnote (71–72), where at this stage in Jung's thinking it is brought to the fore.

17. Hull is by no means consistent in his translation of *verdrängen* in the *Collected Works*; here he translates it as "displace," but "repression" retains the dynamism between drives which Schelling reads into the actants. Like Strachey's translation of Freud's *Standard Edition*, Hull also seems to equate "instinct" with "drive," where Jung tends to distinguish the two.

18. For Derrida, the "originary trace or arche-trace" (*Of Grammatology* 61) is the primordial difference that marks the constitution of objects. Because entities can be conceived only relative to what they are not, e.g., to other entities, any entity must retain a trace of its "others." This originary trace is synonymous with *différance* (62).

19. This tension between therapeutics and metapsychology can be represented in Jean-François Lyotard's figural terms as a tension between the *figure-image* as "that which I see in the hallucination or the dream [. . .] an object placed at a distance, a theme [belonging] to the order of the visible," and the *figure-matrix*, which is an "object of originary repression," an astructural "violation of the discursive order" whose unconscious origins instantly recede before the "schema of intelligibility" imposed on it from without (268). Although Lyotard deploys these figures in a Freudian framework, they nevertheless map the tension between a therapeutics of presence which works within an economy of figure-images that inhibit difference into "quasi-oneiric" (268) outlines of personal narrative in the therapeutic setting, and the figure-matrix as the differential general economy of the collective unconscious, the mutual imbrication of archetypal forces that resists the "scheme of intelligibility" which reifies them into figure-images.

20. For Novalis, "mysticism" is neither *Schwärmerei* (starry-eyed religious enthusiasm) nor the religious desire to transcend the material world. Rather, by mysticism he means the outcome of a "syncriticism" which unites the real and the ideal (*Notes* 75). To this end, he dismisses "the faith in fathoming the thing-in-itself" as "false mysticism," the misled belief in spiritual knowledge which annuls Nature (*Notes* 161).

21. Portmanteau words are combinations of two or more other words but with a meaning and sense of their own. For example, in *Finnegans Wake* Joyce uses *fadograph*, which combines "faded" and "photograph" without being synonymous with either.

Chapter 3

Romantic metasubjectivity: experience

"Everything about [analytical psychology] is essentially experience; the theory itself – even at its most abstract – *comes directly from experience*" (Jung, *On the Psychology* para. 199; trans. mod.; my italics). Jung's words recall a similar statement of Schelling's in the *First Outline*: "*Not only do we know this or that through experience, but we originally know nothing at all except through experience, and by means of experience*" (198). We have seen how, for Schelling, the intensity of experience becomes the royal road of insight into Nature's *a priori* existence in the *Naturphilosophie*; indeed, reason itself is seen as a product of natural processes. The previous chapter read this emphasis on experience forward to Jung, whose conception of the archetype developed out of the theory of complexes and word-association experiments – the *affective* experience of language that ultimately constitutes an archetypal grammatology of Being which unfolds through the experience of symbols and objects. This turn in Jung's thought is inevitable in analytical psychology, whose object of knowledge is "pure experience" ("Foreword to von Koenig-Fachsenfeld" para. 1738; trans. mod.) and whose goal is to "release an experience that grips us or falls upon us as from above" (*Introduction* 87). And Jung's emphasis on the phenomenology of the psyche brings this grammatology that much closer to Schelling's concern with the general economy of nonmolar forces from which natural products emerge.

This chapter focuses on the *experience* of Romantic metasubjectivity, which bears an intimate and complex relation to the purposive *individuation* process articulated in the following chapter. The understanding of experience which I will discuss, which is crystallised in "On the Nature of Philosophy as Science" (1821) ["NPS"], underscores an aleatorism which troubles individuation's teleological drive to organise experience according to the *Stufenfolge*. In this limit-experience of reason, the reflexive epistemology of consciousness encounters its own materiality as that which it cannot assimilate or contain in reflection. Reason encounters its genesis in Nature (for Schelling, the ideal's "arising from the real" [*FO* 194]); knowledge is confronted with its genesis in archetypal formations which are paradoxically both producers and products of the human organism's experience of material nature – archetypes of "perception and apprehension" [*Wahrnehmung und Erfassung*] rooted in *sense* (Jung, "Instinct" para. 270). The experience of Romantic metasubjectivity, as the self's encounter with the "Self," is thus the ineffable point where ideal and real, mind and Nature, touch and do not touch, the encounter with the "third" of Schelling's copular logic which grounds all subject-predicate and subject-object relationships. And anticipating the concept of individuation discussed in the following chapter, it is an intuition, an awareness that one is "on the right path" *while never allowing knowledge that one is on the right path*. This is precisely the condition of Romantic metasubjectivity: what one *knows* about one's path is always left behind the minute one *walks*, experiences, *feels* the path one is on after its happening. But this happening always leaves clues to lead knowledge forward and backward, beyond itself, *beside* itself.

In what follows, I track the development of this limit-experience through Schelling and Jung. Schelling's thinking of this limit-experience centres around intuition – specifically, the fundamental (and fundamentally problematic) idea of *intellectual intuition* [*intellektuelle Anschauung*][1] as developed in the 1800 *System of Transcendental Idealism*. There, intellectual intuition is the experience of contact between real and ideal which grounds the *System*'s idea of self, and this experience undergoes a crucial transformation in Schelling's later thinking. It is a free act of intuition (i.e. one that does not require proofs) in which the self recognises itself as it constructs itself as object. But because consciousness cannot be completely responsible for self-construction, a catalyst, an "alien" presence, reveals itself in relation to consciousness. As such, this intuition is an *unconscious* quantum which both constitutes and unworks the profound emphasis on consciousness and thought in the *System*'s transcendental philosophy. In the later "NPS" intellectual intuition becomes *ecstasy*, as the experience of the absolute subject moving through knowledge to organise it without being concretised in it; thus, intellectual intuition's "intellectuality" is deconstructed, returned to its basis in embodied nature – returned, in effect, to its status as the *organ* of transcendental philosophy (*STI* 27) but with an unruliness previously repressed by the *System*'s Idealism.

In the closing pages of the *System* Schelling attempts to harmonise the disruptive potential of intellectual intuition, and the productive unconscious it marks, by sublating its unruly energies into *aesthetic* intuition as the objectification of these energies in the work of art. This aesthetic Idealism leads to a missed encounter with the productive force of intellectual intuition – a force whose potential is lost until its recovery in the cosmological imagination of the 1815 *Ages*. This drive to repress intellectual intuition's aleatory materiality is the locus of the *System*'s textual neurosis, a neurosis which speaks to Schelling's ambivalent (and quite possibly ironic) desire to close the circle of the *System*'s knowledge at all costs, and ostensibly against his earlier resistances to the idea of a system. Contrary to dated views of Schelling as a thinker of the "overall closed system" (Giegerich, "Jungian Psychology as Metaphysics?" 242), as early as 1795 Schelling insists that authentic philosophy does not and cannot result in an overarching system:

> Nothing can rouse the indignation of the philosophical mind more than the declaration that henceforth all philosophy shall be detained in the fetters of a single system. The genuine philosopher has never felt himself to be greater than when he has beheld an infinity of knowledge. The whole sublimity of his science has consisted in just this, that it would never be complete. He would become unbearable to himself the moment he came to believe that he had completed his system. That very moment he would cease to be *creator* and would be degraded to an instrument of his own creature. (*Philosophical Letters* 172)

In this spirit, the *System*'s ironic drive toward a complete system should be read against Schelling's oeuvre as a whole: certainly by 1809 he is unconcerned with creating anything remotely resembling an "overall closed system," and this "darkening" focus on the indeterminate has its roots in the quasi-subjective space of the *Naturphilosophie* but also the *System* as a narrative of "epochs of consciousness" watermarked by what consciousness cannot assimilate.

Jung's early thinking about intuition as unconscious perception, "the unconscious, purposive apprehension of an often highly complicated situation" ("Instinct" para. 269; trans. mod.), is drawn from the same nonrational basis as intellectual intuition. He will later articulate this experience as synchronicity, an "acausal connecting principle" where circumstances in the external world and archetypal constellations in the psyche converge in an event wherein cause and effect are suspended – an event which reveals that psyche *is* Nature. But this encounter with infinite dynamism and productivity is also a site of strange chiasmus in Schelling and Jung's silent partnership. Schelling's turn to the ecstatic admits a quasi-mystical element into his thinking as part of what would become his positive philosophy of existence;[2] in contrast, Jung's discussion of synchronicity is embedded in the genre of the twentieth-century scientific experiment. That is, where Schelling positively affirms ecstasy as a nonrational basis for systems of knowledge, Jung expresses this nonrationality negatively, as an experiment which ultimately shows the limits of the statistical method in explaining "*immediate creation [unmittelbaren Schöpfungsakt]* which manifests itself within a certain latitude of chance" (letter to Markus Fierz, 2 March 1950, para. 1198; trans. mod). Just as the *System* attempts to rein in the limit-experience of intellectual intuition through an aesthetic Idealism, Jung attempts to contain synchronicity's aleatorism in an experiment, watermarked by Cartesianism, which interrogates Nature. Yet this does not diminish synchronicity's potency, which recrudesces in Jung's ideas of the transcendent function and active imagination as core ideas of individuation (which I discuss in the next chapter). Indeed, in spite of Jung's imposing questions on Nature one wonders if, leading him into a labyrinth of statistics and numbers, Nature once more experiments with Jung in expecting an impossible answer. Let us begin with "NPS," which offers up a philosophical psychology that both harks back to the past of the *System* and gestures to the future of the positive philosophy.

On the "nature" of "philosophy" as "science"

Schelling's "On the Nature of Philosophy as Science" is a lecture given in 1821 at Erlangen which takes up the question of philosophy's status as a unified system of knowledge. As such, "NPS" is an implicit response to Hegel's construction of philosophical knowledge as a unity composed of its different historical manifestations. In response to Hegel's demand for systemic unity, Schelling develops the idea of freedom first articulated in the 1809 *Freedom* essay (contemporaneous with Hegel's *Phenomenology of Spirit* [1807]): freedom is neither absolute indeterminacy nor the teleological determination of absolute spirit but rather the freedom to *be determined* in a unique unfolding which cannot be articulated by teleology, an unruliness behind and beneath systemic unity. Schelling's lecture focuses on this freedom and its experience. Seen in this light, "NPS" is an afterword to the "system" Schelling envisioned, tantamount to the "growth of a philosopher's mind" unbound by Hegelian teleology or the rhetoric of self-making that marks Wordsworth's "egotistical sublime."[3] Indeed, looking back in Schelling's oeuvre while looking forward to the following chapter on individuation, "NPS" takes up the absolute subject which is potentiated, but not articulated as such, in Schelling's 1815 *Ages*. Thus, one can see a Romantic encyclopedics emerging from "NPS"'s lectural architectonic, a theory of systems of knowledge coalescing from, and dynamised by, their unthought. Indeed, Wirth (*Conspiracy* 120) points out that "NPS" is an assemblage composed from several of Schelling's Erlangen lectures, and the very form of the lecture is extemporaneous, which underscores the possibility within the spoken event of "[following] the particular wherever it might lead, regardless of its consistency with a larger whole" (Rajan, "First Outline" 315). Thus it is possible to see "NPS" as a textual "ego" that emerged from a dissociative heterogeneity of speaking events and/or editorial "voices"; its textual history reflects Schelling's argument that no one system (or lecture) can assume final epistemological authority.

The core *experience* of Romantic metasubjectivity and its blueprint of *individuation* can be discerned from the baroque folds (and unfoldings) of "NPS," which Schelling wrote roughly 20 years after the 1800 *System* in part as an attempt to decrypt and work through the encounter between the *System* and the *First Outline*; Schelling ironically meant the *System* to fuse with the *Naturphilosophie* into an overarching "system," but Nature traumatises the *System*'s self-consciousness, unworking its pretense to sovereignty and presenting an unsolvable dilemma for cognition of which Schelling was acutely aware. The Schelling of "NPS" is a consummately Romantic philosopher of intensity, of potentiation, of the *écriture* (de)composing systems of knowledge according to the inscrutable rhythms of a grammatology of Being which Jung later supplies with an experiential therapeutics. Indeed, Bowie sees "NPS" as not only the inauguration of Schelling's positive philosophy but also the intellectual foundation of his critique of Hegel ("Translator's Introduction" 25), and Michael Forster recognises the specifically Romantic intensity of Schelling's lecture, which carries over into the positive philosophy (43ff). If, as Schelling writes in the 1815 *Ages*, evolution proceeds from involution (*Ages* 83), then the 1821 "NPS" is evolution, the extension of *Ages'* involutive cosmology. *Ages'* potentiation suggests a psychology taken up later by Jung, but "NPS" outlines an *aetiology* of systemic knowledge nascent in Schelling's thought since the *Freedom* essay, presented here as a philosophical psychology of "ecstasy." Indeed, this aetiology has its ultimate source in the derangement of natural production which Schelling develops in the *Naturphilosophie*. Moreover, "NPS" explains the trajectory by which this aetiology creates a *subject-ed* knowledge – that is, knowledge produced in the wake of the absolute subject's sublime happening, left in the hands of the individuating person. This knowledge exists as the purposive unfolding of an individuative *Trieb* which articulates the motility of Romantic metasubjectivity. We can express this in Deleuzian terms as the subject which emerges from the (un) folding of analytical psychology and Schellingian philosophy and their disciplinary "subjects" under the "law of curvilinearity," the "law of folds or changes of direction" which articulate a liquidity of inside and outside determined by the elusive force of an individuating unity (Deleuze, *The Fold* 14).

"NPS" lies on the cusp of Schelling's later "positive philosophy," which

> seeks to get beyond [Hegel's] 'negative philosophy' [which] explicates the forms of pure thought that determine what things are, to *a conception which comes to terms both with the fact that things are and with the real historical emergence and movement of consciousness.* [...] The positivity of the positive philosophy lies in the demand for an explanation [...] of the fact that there can be self-contained a priori systems of necessity. Such systems cannot [...] explain their own possibility: [for example,] whilst geometry maps the structure of space, it does not account for the existence of space. (Bowie, *Schelling* 13–14, 144; my second italics)

History's sheer facticity, which Jung represents as the "extremely historical organism" emerging from an inscrutable matrix of material and organic processes, has concerned Schelling since *Naturphilosophie*'s central (and unresolved) question of why Nature creates things in the first place. It is also at the core of Schlegel's "progressive universal poetry," whose progress lies precisely in its losing itself in this unfolding history as an uncanny othering in an endless approximation to the "circumambient world" (*AF* #116). "NPS" thinks this laterally unfolding historicity as a uniquely Romantic aetiology: knowledge unfolds through history as an illness of incommensurability, vitiated only through philosophy as a "free act of the spirit" (227). Thus, philosophy in "NPS" is a *pharmakon* hoping to "cure" freedom through freedom. And it is Novalis who specifically takes up this aetiological poetics of human freedom as a "poetics of affliction" that conducts a path to a "higher synthesis" in this illness of incommensurability. This path is a cultivated love of one's melancholy which does not end in transcendental perfection, but rather unfolds according to a gradient of sado-masochistic harmony – increasing grades of "terrible pain" and "hidden in dwelling pleasure" (Novalis, *Notes* #653).

As a retrospective Schellingian analysis of *Naturphilosophie*'s tenuous alignment with the *System*'s transcendental philosophy, "NPS" is a consciously paradoxical attempt to systematise this aetiology of difference that gives rise to system, the intellectual intuition meant to achieve its experience, and the absolute subject as organising principle of the systems emerging from the differentiation at the core of Being. For this reason, I read the "Nature" in the title contrary to its status as dead metaphor ("the *nature of* philosophy as science"), as an intensive marker alongside "philosophy" and "science." That is, "Nature" harbours an unnamed vitality in "NPS" which serves as the backdrop for the disunity between systems giving rise to knowledge; it is the stage upon which the encounter with the absolute subject occurs. Thus, suspended between "Nature" and "science," "philosophy" is possessed (in the possessive sense; the nature *of* philosophy) by a quasi-theosophical ecstasy which puts the *System*'s intellectual intuition under analysis. In this way, a philosophical psychology emerges in "NPS" from within the determinations of "philosophy as science."

Schelling begins "NPS" by asserting that human knowledge emerges from a primordial *asystasy*, a differential economy of nonknowledge[4] resembling the primal fluidity of the *First Outline*:

> The idea or the endeavour of finding a system of human knowledge, or [...] of contemplating human knowledge within a system [...] presupposes, of course, that originally and of itself it does not exist in a system, hence that it is an [asystaton] [...] something that is in inner conflict. In order to recognize this *asystasy*, this non-existence,

this disunity […] in human knowledge (for this inner conflict must become apparent), the human spirit must already have searched in every possible direction. […] The need for harmony arises first of all in disharmony. (210)

The quest for an absolute knowledge, whose erasure and lack must be brought to light through a rhizomatic "searching in every possible direction," discloses the (non-)ground of knowledge itself as a *failure* of disclosure, the inner conflict of asystasy as the disunity grounding all knowledge. Schelling attempts to articulate a "true system" of knowledge which fuses system with the indeterminacy that constitutes and paradoxically completes it in a "unity of unity and opposition" (210). Developing the 1815 *Ages*' conception of knowledge as "a living, actual being" (xxxv), Schelling's interdisciplinary organicism here implies a transference of knowledge between different "systems" of organs. But the threat of disease attending the organic – the risk that one organ "which has its freedom or life only so that it may remain in the whole *strives to be for itself*" (*Freedom* 35; my italics) – *sickens* this absolute subject with the incommensurability between system and freedom that suspends them relative to one another. Hence philosophy as a *pharmakon* "free act of the spirit."

But such a system can only form around "a subject of movement and of progress," a subject "*proceeding through everything and not being anything*" ("NPS" 215). This purposive force organises the system, constellating its aleatory energies while remaining uninhibited by its particulars. This organising principle, implicit for Schelling since the *Naturphilosophie* (Peterson xxviii), is the absolute subject – a purposive current through the unconditioned, a liminal force which touches and does not touch existence. This subject is "not indefinable in such a way that it could not also become definable, not infinite in such a way that it could not also become finite, and not ungraspable in such a way that it could not also become graspable" ("NPS" 219). It is a sylleptic subject which traverses its contradictory aspects while remaining immune to its predicates; in one and the same moment it both "adopts" and "divests" a given form (219). Such change underpins all thought: thought cannot be an underlying principle, "since if knowledge is constantly changing it cannot finally know itself *as* itself because the fact of its identity […] depends on an other that it cannot encompass within itself: namely, the principle of *change*, 'eternal freedom', the absolute subject" (Bowie, *Schelling* 137). Insofar as it is the motor force of the productive unconscious, the absolute subject, "inhabiting the subject position, overturns the workings and pretensions of the subject position" as its "immanent critique" (Wirth, *Conspiracy* 37). Its anteriority to reflexive thought and its purposive Thanatopoietic movement through knowledge put it outside the personalist economy of psychoanalysis, just as it establishes a futurity which anticipates the positive philosophy.

Thus, Schelling's move away from a negative philosophy of the Concept in "NPS" consists of a certain revocation of knowledge, a negative capability for the Socratic dictum of knowing only that one does not know, which brings the absolute subject into view as knowledge's receding origin ("NPS" 228). But "NPS" also promises a return of knowledge to the "ignorant" knowing subject through a movement which is essentially countertransference *avant la lettre*, a movement in which absolute subject and "ignorant" subject move through each other, touching and not touching. In movements very similar to Bataille's description of inner experience,[5] this psychology's tripartite movement (which amounts to a "moment," or *event* of knowledge) begins with absolute subject and consciousness (as "ignorant knowledge," knowledge ignorant of its interiority in "absolute outwardness") at opposite poles. In the second, counter-transferential stage, the absolute subject "becomes object" just as "absolute ignorance makes the transition to knowledge," and "the transition from subject to object is reflected in the transition from object to subject" (230). The third and final stage effects a "restoration" in which the absolute subject returns to its inwardness but leaves a trace of itself in consciousness as a *knowing* ignorance, an "internalization" of the absolute subject as a remembrance of the eternal freedom of which it is a part: "now [consciousness] knows this freedom, knows it indeed immediately, namely as that which itself is the interior of it, of ignorance" (231). And while this movement may seem rather Hegelian, it is precisely this ignorance and lack, as the object of cognition, which constitutes knowledge while making its terminus impossible; this ignorance ensures that knowledge can never fully return to itself.

But what is the *experience* of this asystasy in "NPS"'s philosophical psychology? To articulate the encounter with this absolute subject, Schelling retrofits the *System*'s concept of intellectual intuition with a history and a nature resisted by his earlier work. Schelling subjects intellectual intuition to a scrutiny absent from his previous account, deconstructing its "intellectual" quality to imbue it with a materiality repressed in the *System*'s aesthetic economy. Here, Schelling tells us that the "intellectual" in "intellectual intuition" means that "the subject is not lost in sensory perception, i.e., in a real object, but that it is lost in, or gives itself up in, something that *cannot* be an *object*" (228). For this reason, he drops "intellectual" because it neglects the sense-aspect of such an encounter (228). Instead, Schelling describes this encounter as *ecstasy,* an affective experience where

> our ego, namely, is placed *outside* itself, i.e. outside its role. [...] Confronted with the absolute subject, it cannot remain a subject, for the absolute subject cannot behave like an object. It must, then, give up its *place,* it must be placed outside itself, *as something that no longer exists.* Only in this state of having abandoned itself can the absolute subject appear to [the ego] in its state of self-abandonment, and so we also behold it in *amazement.* (228; my third italics)

The central question of "NPS" evokes the text's deconstructive turn: the question of the "true" system of knowledge becomes the question of how man can "be brought to this ecstasy – a question that is synonymous with: *how can man be brought to his senses?*" (229; my italics). Schelling's original German reads: "*wie wird der Mensch zur Besinnung gebracht?*" (*Sämtliche Werke* I.9.230), but Schelling's use of *Besinnung* (root *Sinn*) goes beyond its already multivalent translation as "meaning," "sense" or "signification." Discussing Schelling on character [*Gesinnung*], Wirth writes that *Sinn* also means "to sense, [to become] 'sensitized' to the life of that which one cannot understand in advance" (*Conspiracy* 28). More specifically to the point of intellectual intuition, Wirth aligns *Sinn* with sensation [*Empfindung*], "sensation or sensory experience" – in a word, "direct experience" (91). Thus, the transition here from intellectual intuition to ecstasy involves a return of the repressed object(ive), and Deleuze and Guattari take this further to describe the "being of sensation" as "not the flesh but the compound of nonhuman forces of the cosmos, of man's nonhuman becomings" (*What is Philosophy?* 183).

So with Schelling's notion of ecstasy, the sensory aspect of nature and materiality supplements the otherwise philosophical exercise of intellectual intuition. And with this return of the object(ive) in the countertransference between the absolute subject and consciousness, we discover the territory in which Deleuze later maps out *sense* as the relation of forces constituting an object:

> We will never find the sense of something (of a human, a biological or even a physical phenomenon) if we do not know the force which appropriates the thing, which exploits it, which takes possession of it or is expressed in it. [...] All force is appropriation, domination, exploitation of a quantity of reality. Even perception, in its divers aspects, is the expression of forces which appropriate nature. That is to say that *nature itself has a history. The history of a thing, in general, is the succession of forces which take possession of it and the co-existence of the forces which struggle for possession.* The same object, the same phenomenon, changes sense depending on the force which appropriates it. *History is the variation of senses.* [...] Sense is therefore a complex notion; there is always a plurality of senses, a constellation, a complex of successions but also of coexistences. (*Nietzsche and Philosophy* 3–4; my italics)

Deleuze reads *history*, as the "variation of sense," away from its disciplinary formations and toward Romantic *historicity* as the play of forces (actant, archetype) which constitutes history and the changes these forms undergo as they unfold stepwise through time. Moreover, because Deleuze is a thinker "interested primarily in experiences that defeat the conditions of representation and threaten to dissolve the subject in a becoming" (Welchman 247), the Deleuzian *event* is "paradoxically [what] *both* has already happened and is about to happen; a way of thinking the past and future within the present. In short, sense explains what *is*" (Young 278–79). Brought to our senses, we are brought to a confrontation with nature and materiality as egoity is "dislodged" in and by historicity ("NPS" 229).

Thus Schelling's ecstasy opens consciousness up to the matrix of nonmolar forces that constitute historicity, the energies which congeal into the vicissitudes of history. We are brought forward to Deleuze's thinking of sense but also to the distinctly Jungian conception of quantitative libido which, as we have seen, which is not bound by a specific *quality* (or qualities) but is rather hypothesised through the quantity, or *intensity* of libido and the "relations of movement" informing its manifestation in natural objects (Jung, "On Psychic Energy" para. 3). Apropos of Deleuzian intensity, Claire Colebrook writes:

> Against the idea of representation – that there are persons or things that we come to know through qualities – we can say that there is a world of perceptions, intensities or varying qualities from which we produce extended things or an underlying human nature. This means that cultural or artistic works do not represent an already given human nature so much as produce general interests from intensities. (88)

Bearing the mark of Jungian libido but exploring its ontological implications further, Deleuze's intensity is the differential measure of a univocal being irreducible to analogy or hierarchy (lecture on *Anti-Oedipus* and *1000 Plateaus*). And in "NPS," "being brought to one's senses" is nothing less than the cultivation, in the properly "philosophical" subject, of an awareness of the differential, asystemic (libidinal) transferences between systems of knowledge. And in observing that "[e]ven the most individual systems are not absolutely unique, but offer striking and unmistakable analogies with other systems" ("On Psychological Understanding" para. 413), Jung minds the gap, so to speak, between knowledges marked by ecstasy as the limit-experience of sheer materiality – something already come into being but nevertheless carrying the weight of an event, a *happening* of absolute subjectivity. Precisely this sublime ecstasy marks the happening of the "Self of one's self."

Yet it is also intellectual intuition's displacement as ecstasy which unworks the "consciousness of eternal freedom" at the core of "NPS"'s philosophical psychology. "NPS"'s epistemology insists on a double movement of restoration and restitution. As we saw in the transferential moment, the absolute subject is "restored from" the ignorance of consciousness just as consciousness "remembers" its connection with eternal freedom. But "NPS" displaces intellectual intuition into an ecstasy which *experiences* but cannot definitively *know* its knowledge: the ego of Schelling's philosophical-psychological subject, as the focal point of systemic knowledge, is cancelled out in the very moment of apprehension, dissociated from itself as something that no longer exists. The hopeful idealist question at the introspective centre of Schelling's text – "what if we ourselves were eternal freedom restored as subject after being the object?" (226) – is in fact hopeless, invoking a knowing subject which can never know the dissociative difference at its core. The materiality of sense which marks this dissociative difference articulates Romantic metasubjectivity's fundamentally ambivalent experience of selfhood. Romantic metasubjectivity furnishes this limit-experience of absence with an experiencing psyche which allows it to be written into a futurity to come. With this in mind, let us move forward by looking behind – by turning to the 1800 *System* to examine intellectual intuition's first ambivalent formulation in an equally mutagenic text which straddles Idealism and Romanticism as a primal site for the philosophical psychology of "NPS."

The *System of Transcendental Idealism*: self-consciousness and its discontent

The 1800 *System* is, to use the words of Schelling in the *First Outline*, a "misbegotten attempt" (35) that is quickly set aside and never taken up again; indeed, Andrew Bowie suggests that by *On the True Concept of Naturphilosophie* (1801) Schelling, unencumbered by transcendental philosophy, returns to the *Naturphilosophie*'s epistemology for the rest of his philosophical career (*Schelling* 57). The *System* is both a repetition and a surpassing of Fichtean subjectivism, staging a break which Dalia Nassar describes as "one of the most significant moments in the development of German Idealism" (159). Indeed, Schelling would later reflect on the *System* as a mere "exposition of Fichtean Idealism" which nevertheless contained a "new system" that "sooner or later had to break through" (*On the History* 111). Against the hegemony of its own Idealism, the *System* lays the groundwork for a psychological dissociationism important to the middle Schelling and which Jung develops in analytical psychology. Indeed, the *System* emerges from the ambivalence toward Nature's energies present in the Introduction to the *First Outline*: as an attempt to "make a nature out of intelligence" the *System* attempts to bond with the *Naturphilosophie*, which was meant to discern the intelligence in nature (*STI* 7). In other words, the *System*'s transcendental philosophy "*materializes the laws of mind into laws of nature*, or annexes the material to the formal" (*STI* 14).

In the *System*'s nascent psychology, intellectual intuition defines an encounter between self-consciousness and a productive unconscious at the heart of Nature, an unconscious which is unavailable to philosophy. It is the problematic index of the *System*'s emergent self and the locus of the text's neurosis, marking the persistence and resistance of material

Nature against the *System*'s drive to fold intuition into an idealist economy of self-consciousness.[6] Already in the *First Outline* Schelling refers to *Naturphilosophie*'s need to break out of conceptual confines by finding "corresponding intuitions" to give its ideas materiality, and intuition is further described as an "infinite becoming," an endless progression of moments of apprehension which surpasses both reason and the powers of the imagination (*FO* 15 & n). As Snow puts it, in the *System* "the irrational becomes a source of movement and life within the system, yet does not become entirely subsumed into the rational" (123). But contrary to Snow's somewhat optimistic assertion that this irrationality "[expands] the limits of the idealistic understanding of consciousness" (121), I argue that Romantic metasubjectivity marks this Idealism's limit-experience with an unconscious materiality which determines it, but which this Idealism cannot know. Put differently, the ontopoietic experience of Romantic metasubjectivity emerges from within the *System*'s aesthetic scene of "infinite contradiction" based in an "unconscious infinity" (*STI* 225), but against the will of the aesthetic in Schelling's text. This tension between "conscious and unconscious activities" (225) is represented in the aesthetic as the "organon" of philosophy (14) – an *organ* which Schelling's Idealism cannot control, but instead attempts to sublate in a repressive drive to complete itself as a system. The *System* does this by using art to lead its circle of knowledge "back to its starting point" in a process which fuses art and philosophy as objective and subjective (232).[7]

Bowie writes that in the *System* "the conceptual structures of the *Naturphilosophie* recur, but as descriptions of the I" (*Schelling* 46). Yet in itself this does not account for the dialogic tension between the *First Outline* and the *System*, or the way in which the *System*'s aesthetics attempts to close down these structures. Indeed, the *System* does not complete Schelling's "system" of knowledge but rather recontextualises its aporiae, which is why the *System* is "more ambitious and comprehensive, but also more precarious, than any other work Schelling ever published" (White 55), and, for all its confidence and presuppositions, the *System* seems to "obscure rather than illuminate" (one could read "repress" for "obscure") the problems of *Naturphilosophie* (Krell, *Contagion* 23). In Schelling's words, the transition from *Naturphilosophie* to transcendental Idealism is meant to form a "system" of knowledge, "a whole which is self-supporting and internally consistent with itself" (*STI* 15). But what kind of system is composed of two entities which "must forever be opposed to one another, and can never merge into one" (2)? Hence, the *First Outline* and the *System*'s convergence marks a countertransference that recognises, even as it seeks to repress, Nature's materiality.

Schelling's vision of philosophy in the *System* is "a progressive history of self-consciousness" with "an internal coherence which time cannot touch [in the form of a] *graduated sequence [Stufenfolge]* of intuitions whereby the self raises itself to the highest power of consciousness" (*STI* 2). But in a dilemma already encountered by Schelling in the *First Outline*, this *Stufenfolge* is always already troubled by Nature's incommensurability with its own products. Quite apart from Schelling's later descriptions of art's unification of real and ideal as "bliss" and "tranquillity" (*STI* 221), here we have mind and Nature in sublime suspension, their contagious incommensurability seeping through the disciplinary boundaries of Schelling's project. We shall begin by examining the *System*'s analytic determination of self-consciousness, its problematic propositional relationship between the "I think" of the represented, determined self and the "I am" of a sylleptic self immune to final predication, which opens up a space for considering intellectual intuition as a first outline of ecstasy as the experience of the absolute subject in "NPS." The *System* insists on the systemic drive later deconstructed in "NPS"; the compulsive repetition of the self's grounding *in thought*, as the *System*'s pleasure principle, is a drive to annul the absolute subject nascent in Schelling's thought since the *First Outline*. But despite this repetition of the self's essence as thought, the *System*'s neurotic Idealism, driven to abject what falls outside the boundary of consciousness, cannot manage or economise the metonymy of natural objects constellated by the "I am." Elaborating on Schelling's conception of intellectual intuition we will then turn to the *System*'s closing pages, in which the aesthetic is invoked as a means of harmonising its discordant energies in the work of art.

The genesis of self-consciousness in the *System* is described in terms analogous to the inhibition of Nature in the *First Outline*. The self is pure process, "*infinite activity* [...] originally a pure producing out towards infinity" which, through the act of self-consciousness, becomes inhibited as an object to itself amidst other objects (*STI* 36). Through an act as inexplicable as Nature's inhibition in the *First Outline*, the being of the self in the *System* is always already displaced into its concept: "the concept of the self arises through the act of self-consciousness, and thus *apart* from this act the self is nothing; its whole reality depends solely on this act, and *it is itself nothing other than this act.* [The self] has no other predicate than that of self-consciousness" (25–26). It is "pure act, a pure doing" (27) which must be nonobjective precisely because it is the "*principle* of all knowledge" (26). Schelling's idealist self is paradoxically indistinct from its conceptual thinking *and* irreducible to this reflexive thinking as its anterior organising principle. But let us dwell for a moment on this paradox, which reflects the baroque curvature of his thinking on the self. Emphasising the *System*'s more overtly psychological implications, Alan White suggests that the *System* – a text implicitly *about* the unconscious – is infected with its subject, unaware of many of its own insights (71ff). White gets to the heart of the matter: for Schelling's "I think"/"I am" distinction marks precisely the gap between the self of intellect, which freely reconciles contradiction in an idealist aesthetic, and the self of Being, of intellectual intuition and connection with the productive unconscious. In Schelling's words, the "I think" "accompanies all presentations and preserves the continuity of consciousness between" concepts and thoughts; the "I am" is a return to infinite productivity, an irrepresentable "*original* self-awareness" (*STI* 26). Schelling asserts this syllepsis as "beyond doubt a higher proposition" (26), but self-consciousness, as a kind of *knowing* and not a kind of *being* (16), amplifies the gap between transcendental Idealism and the materiality of Schelling's Nature. Despite this gap between knowing and Being, the *System*'s founding principle of a science of knowledge – the "Principle of Transcendental Idealism" – is absolute identity (A = A), which needs to exist in *Being*. For this reason, the principle of transcendental Idealism is split into *identical* and *synthetic* propositions. Identical propositions (A = A) are contentless; as a statement of the unconditioned as a purely logical proposition, A = A asserts the identity of A apart from contingency or materiality. A *is* A *in essence*; A is A and can *only* be A.

However, Schelling also writes that

> In all knowledge an *objective* is thought of as coinciding with the subjective. In the proposition $A = A$, however, no such coincidence occurs. Thus all fundamental knowledge advances beyond the *identity* of thinking, and the proposition $A = A$ must itself presuppose such knowledge. Having thought A, I admittedly think of it as A; but how, then, do I come to think A in the first place? If it is a concept freely engendered, it begets no knowledge; if it is one that arises with the feeling of necessity, it must have objective reality. (22)

This "objective reality" comes with the synthetic proposition (A = B), which links all subject-predicate statements to "*something alien to the thought*, and distinct from it" (22; my italics). If A is, it is some*thing*. But in the following section entitled "Elucidations," which disavows more than it elucidates, Schelling nevertheless attempts to fold this materiality into the principle of identity as "an act of thinking which *immediately becomes its own object*" occurring only in self-consciousness as *thought*. The *System* wants to establish an "identity between being-in-thought and coming-to-be" (25), between identical and synthetic propositions. And indeed it is *selfhood*, in the form of "the proposition *self = self*," which "converts the proposition $A = A$ into a synthetic proposition" as "the point at which identical knowledge springs immediately from synthetic, and synthetic from identical" (30).

But what can be made of this new "alien" proposition, this objectivity in the subjective *thought*-project of the *System*? In an oft-quoted passage, Schelling writes that "self-consciousness is the lamp of the whole system of knowledge, but it casts its light ahead only, not behind" (18). As a rejoinder to Schelling's Idealism, White points out that "much later, the light of self-consciousness nevertheless does shine backward, at least in that it reveals that the pure ego is not the highest ground; that ground is absolute identity, which becomes ego by dividing itself in the primal act of self-consciousness" (71). But this absolute identity, A = A, is always already conditioned by the alien proposition of self = self – indeed, the former is "only possible though the act expressed in the proposition *self = self*. [...] Did not *self = self*, then nor could $A = A$" (30). Thus, the idealist economy of "thought" and "consciousness" in the *System* becomes infected with a materiality it cannot contain within the "circle of knowledge" to which the *System* belongs, a circle which *excludes* the facticity of Being (18). In other words, the *System* gestures to that which is "behind" knowledge as its precondition – the "autonomy" of knowledge apart from its reflexiveness (18–19). Schelling awkwardly conjugates "pure consciousness" and "self-consciousness" into "pure self-consciousness" (as a timeless act constituting time), which he sets against an empirical consciousness "[arising] merely in time and the succession of presentations" (32). This conjugation suggests a consciousness which cannot work through the traumatic materiality that constitutes it. In McGrath's words, "the 'I think' becomes a subject, distinct from the object and other subjects, at the price of the fullness of the intuition 'I am'" (*Dark Ground* 98).

Thus the *System*'s overarching trajectory is that of an introverted analytic scene, the unfolding of a depth-psychological encounter with the unconscious as thought is troubled by its outside. The self begins as "nothing distinct from its thinking" (*STI* 26), but in the final pages of the *System* the Schellingian unconscious manifests itself as the "intervention of a hidden necessity into human freedom" (204), a productivity tainting the operations of the intellect's conceptual freedom. In the *System*'s "assumed relationship between freedom and a hidden necessity,"

> necessity is nothing else but the unconscious. [Through freedom] something I do not intend is brought about unconsciously, *i.e.*, without my consent; [consciousness] is to be confronted with an unconscious, whereby out of the most inhibited expression there arises unawares something wholly involuntary. (204)

This encounter with an unconscious that brings about unintended thoughts or actions is Schelling's way of expressing the paradox of freedom and necessity (which assumes special importance in the *Freedom* essay): to be free is *necessarily* to be open to the indeterminate, the "necessity" and compulsion of that which lies outside the purview of consciousness. And although here Schelling displaces this unconscious into an "unconscious lawfulness" geared toward a "*moral* world-order" in the service of the human species (206), without this zero-point where ideal and real, identical and synthetic touch and do not touch, "one can will nothing aright; [...] the disposition to act quite regardless of consequences as duty enjoins us, could never inspire a man's mind" (204). It is also the *System*'s only path to a science of knowledge, as "a knowing that has its object outside itself" (22). This zero-point is intellectual intuition: a hinge between ideal and real that ruptures the autoerotism of the *System*'s self-consciousness. For Schelling, the self *is* intellectual intuition, which is "the organ of all transcendental thinking" (27).

Describing intellectual intuition, Jason Wirth pithily writes:

> What is intellectual intuition if not creativity, if not remarkable, unexpected births? [It is] the overthrow of the tyranny of the ego [...] an intimation, an *Ahnung*, of the abyss of freedom. It is a percept of death as akin to the unfathomable depths of the past as they re-intimate

themselves as the future. [...] The intellectual intuition, quite simply, is the indispensable birth of philosophy. (*Conspiracy* 106, 108, 114, 115)

Intellectual intuition is the site of a paradoxical materiality. As "the instantiation within what is there of what is not there" (111), of what is *im*material in terms of a metaphysics of presence, it recalls Nature's radical productivity from which all material comes. It is, as Michael Vater puts it, an *unconscious* principle of consciousness," a "knot of pure fact" (xxiii, xxx) which is not as beholden to consciousness as the *System*'s Fichtean pedigree would have it. Indeed, in *Ideas for a Philosophy of Nature* (1803) Schelling thinks the pretext for intellectual intuition through Nature, writing that to pursue the soul-body/mind-matter antithesis means to ultimately confront a point "where mind and matter are one [...] where the great leap we have so long sought to avoid becomes inevitable; and in this all theories are alike" (40). Philosophy is now "*a natural history of* [the human] *mind*" (30), which anticipates Jung's "extremely historical organism" in its proposal of Nature's "absolute *purposiveness*" as a critique of theoretical dualism (41; my italics). Philosophy becomes a dissociative, *genetic* force which "allows the whole necessary series of our ideas to rise and take its course, as it were, before our eyes" in a manner which consciousness cannot control (30).

In intellectual intuition, Schelling is working through the materiality of what Jung, via Janet, takes up as analytical psychology's dissociationist topography. In a poignant critique of the Cartesian *cogito*, Schelling writes:

The 'I think' is [...] in no way something immediate, it only emerges via the reflection which directs itself at the thinking in me. [...] Indeed, *true thinking must even be objectively independent of that subject that reflects upon it*; in other words, it will think all the more truly the less the subject interferes with it. [Therefore,] because there is *an objective thinking which is independent of me*, it follows that that which reflects might deceive itself about that supposed unity, or, by attributing the original thinking to itself, it might be precisely this attribution about which it is deceived, and the 'I think' could have no more significance than expressions I also use, such as 'I digest', 'I make juices', 'I walk' or 'I ride'; for it is not really the thinking being that walks or rides. *It thinks in me, thinking goes on in me, is the pure fact*, in the same way as I can say with equal justification: 'I dreamed', and 'It dreamed in me'. (*On the History* 47–48; my italics)

Compare Jung in 1937:

We have got accustomed to saying apotropaically, '*I have* such and such a tendency or habit or feeling of resentment,' instead of the more veracious 'Such and such a tendency or habit or feeling of resentment *has me.*' [...] The truth is that [...] we are continually threatened by psychic factors which, in the guise of 'natural phenomena,' may take possession of us" (*Psychology and Religion* para. 143; trans. mod.)

Intellectual intuition, in other words, is knowledge always already imbricated with its object and thus displaced into its own incompletion. That the self *is* intellectual intuition marks the *System*'s Romantic turn away from the text's Idealism, even as the *System* retains the form of an analytic treatise.

As a transcendental philosophy based in the subjective as "the *first* and only ground of all reality" and "the sole principle of explanation for everything else," the *System*'s knowledge begins as an analytic of epochs of consciousness and ends as a *poetic* "odyssey of the spirit," what Schelling would have us believe is interminable aesthetic progress toward "that world of fantasy which gleams but imperfectly through the real" (*STI* 232). Nature is now an "imperfect reflection" of the inner world of consciousness (232). For the *System*, the Idealism of aesthetic production begins with consciousness and the unconscious divided for the sake of the production of art – its "becoming-objective" (220). But for the work of art to be a "complete manifestation of [their] identity" (220), it ends its production "unconsciously" – in the domain of the objective, of being in the world. But in this objective domain "there must be a point at which the two [once again] merge into one" (220), and thus this artistic production is no longer "free," no longer in the domain of the subjective. For this reason, Schelling insists on the reconciliation of conflicting conscious and unconscious activity *in consciousness*: "[t]he intelligence will therefore end with a complete recognition of the identity expressed in the product as an identity *whose principle lies in the intelligence itself*; it will end, that is, in a complete intuiting of itself" ending in "infinite tranquillity" (221). And while the conscious "intelligence" cannot claim this unity of conscious and unconscious as something entirely of its own making, in a passage evocative of reason's privileging in the Kantian sublime Schelling ends by saying that the intelligence "will feel itself astonished and *blessed* by this union, will regard it, that is, in the light of a bounty freely granted by a higher nature" (221). Consciousness ultimately harmonises what was all along "the preestablished harmony between the conscious and the unconscious" (221).

Finally, in his closing "General Observation on the Whole System," Schelling writes that his "system" is split between the two "extremes" of intellectual and aesthetic intuition (233). But where before the self *was* intellectual intuition, here it has no provenance in everyday consciousness; it only attends to "the fraction of a man," where art "brings the *whole man*" to a "knowledge of the highest" (233). Aesthetic intuition is that faculty which works to resolve the conflict of the sublime experience "which threatens our whole intellectual existence," whereby "a magnitude is admitted by the unconscious activity which it is impossible to accept into the conscious one" (226). But one wonders how great this threat really is, since aesthetic intuition is the inevitable result of this conflict which once again brings about, in another ventriloquism of Kant, an "unexpected harmony" (226) which establishes aesthetic intuition as the highest power of consciousness (233). Thus, Schelling's previous desire to synonymise intellectual and aesthetic intuition (the aesthetic intuition is "simply the intellectual intuition become objective" [229]) masks the profound neurosis which separates them, driving the materiality of intellectual intuition and its sublime limit-experience into the background as aesthetic intuition becomes the alibi for a missed encounter with the energies of the productive unconscious. The *System* ends up eliciting an analysis of philosophy itself in the form of intellectual intuition as philosophy's "indispensable birth," but the aesthetic reinscribes this within the economy of consciousness as the neurosis of the *System*'s thought-project. The *System* avers that "the self itself is an object that exists by knowing of itself" (28) but represses the facticity of this "knowing" as Nature *itself*, the "producing and reproducing" that has claimed reason as early as the *First Outline* (*FO* 195). We will see in the following section that Jung is caught in an analogous dilemma with synchronicity, which articulates a psychic materiality that fuses psyche and Nature and which both constitutes the experience of Romantic metasubjectivity and imperils its experiencing subject.

Jung and synchronicity

Jung recollects the following experience in a session with an analysand, who relates a dream in which she was given a golden scarab:

> While she was still telling me this dream, I heard something behind me gently tapping on the window. I turned round and saw that it was a fairly large flying insect that was knocking against the window-pane from outside in the obvious effort to get into the dark room. This seemed to me very strange. I opened the window immediately and caught the insect in the air as it flew in. It was a scarabaeid beetle, or common rose-chafer [...] whose gold-green colour most nearly resembles that of a golden scarab. I handed the beetle to my patient with the words, 'Here is your scarab.' This experience punctured the desired hole in her rationalism and broke the ice of her intellectual resistance. (*Synchronicity* para. 982)

Here, an event in the natural world which cannot possibly be anticipated (the beetle's appearance) and the current condition of a human psyche (the analysand relating the scarab dream) converge in an event for which causality cannot be rationally established and which has a profound effect on the therapeutic moment. This is the essence of synchronicity – the affective and momentous experience of the psychoid archetypal as it touches and does not touch consciousness beyond the normal threshold of awareness.

The germination of some 20 years of thought,[8] synchronicity is a late concept in Jung's oeuvre and the culmination of an individuative gradient in his thinking which leads away from the restricted economy of Kantian epistemology and toward the characteristically Schellingian question of Being as an excess to conceptual logic. Jung's writing on synchronicity is concentrated in two essays: "On Synchronicity" (1951), a shorter and more popularised version of *Synchronicity: An Acausal Connecting Principle* (1952). The latter is Jung's central statement of the concept which emerged from his collaboration with Wolfgang Pauli, the Nobel Prize–winning quantum physicist who, like Jung, sought to articulate the relationship between the particular and the universal and the known and unknown, but from within physics as opposed to psychology.[9] But where Schelling's intellectual intuition is a uniquely human capacity, synchronicity is a universal phenomenon which Jung ultimately cannot confine to the human mind. Yet as we will see, Jung's attempt to articulate synchronicity within the rubric of the scientific experiment (perhaps in an effort, following Pauli, to scientise the concept) at times obscures synchronicity's specifically Romantic potency. Indeed, just as the Idealism of the *System*'s thought-project elides intellectual intuition's Romantic materiality, Jung's ambivalence about thinking synchronicity outside the human psyche leads at times to a missed encounter with the full import of synchronicity as analytical psychology's experiential cornerstone; the derangement of Nature is ranged, demarcated in a questioning where answers are suppressed.

In his correspondence with Pauli, Jung describes synchronicity as

> a *formation* by means of which "similar" things coincide, without there being any apparent "cause." […] Insofar as for me synchronicity represents first and foremost sheer being, I am inclined to subsume any instance of causally inconceivable states of being into the category of synchronicity. [Such states] represent a "so-ness" [*So-sein*] or a unique formation or a "creative act." (letter to Wolfgang Pauli, 30 Nov 1950, 60; trans. mod.)

Jung later defines synchronicity as an acausal connecting principle which articulates "the simultaneous occurrence of two analogous but not causally connected events […] of a certain psychic state with *one or more external events* which appear as analogous parallels to the momentary subjective state—and, possibly, vice versa" (*Synchronicity* pars. 849–50; trans. mod.; my italics). Synchronicity *is* the experience of the archetypal – it marks a fleeting encounter with the unconditioned plenitude of Being, the primitive metaphoricity, the "hot liquid stream" Nietzsche ("On Truth and Lying" 148) sees flowing from both the human imagination and the "indestructibly mighty and pleasurable" "eternal life of that core of being [persisting] despite the constant destruction of the phenomenal world" (*The Birth of Tragedy* 39, 41). Synchronicity is a parabolic alignment of real and ideal whose outcome is undecided. If meaning comes, its origins are in the inscrutable third, that unknown = X to which real and ideal gesture without defining – the selfhood of Romantic metasubjectivity.

Synchronicity is translated in the English *Collected Works* as "meaningful coincidence" [*sinnvolle Koinzidenz*], an experience that creates meaning and thus one which might suggest an external agency. This mistranslation has skewed synchronicity's reception in English scholarship and diluted its intrinsic aleatorism; as a result, some clarifying remarks on this crucial Jungian concept are apropos as it relates to both analytical psychology and Romantic metasubjectivity. Giegerich makes the important observation that Jung's original German almost exclusively describes synchronicity as *sinngemäße Koinzidenz*. *Sinngemäße* means "analogous to;" thus, *sinngemäße Koinzidenz* is the coincidence of things that mean *roughly* the same thing but are not identical (Giegerich, "A Serious Misunderstanding" 501–2). This crucially emphasises that in synchronicity one is confronted not with the fusion of two events in an experience always already replete with meaning but with the gravitation of two events towards each other which does not culminate in a direct subject-object experience. Meaning is not guaranteed. Therefore, in almost every case I translate "meaningful" as "analogous." However, Giegerich uses this to argue unconvincingly that synchronicity has nothing to do with "Meaning with a capital M, with human *experiences* of meaning, with what is meaningful *for us* and makes existence meaningful" (502). This argument depends on Giegerich's insistence on a stringent inside/outside distinction at all costs as well as the denigration of nonrational psychological states, which the concept of Romantic metasubjectivity contests *tout court*. Indeed Jung acknowledges this dilemma, writing that "[i]n view of the possibility that synchronicity is not only a psychophysical phenomenon but *might also occur without the participation of the human psyche*, […] in this case we should have to speak not of *meaning* [*Sinn*] but of similarity [*Gleichartigkeit*] or conformity" (*Synchronicity* para. 942 n. 71; trans. mod.; my first italics). And Jung will complicate things further by collapsing this meaning/similarity distinction, writing that "For the connection of psychic states to each other or to nonpsychic events, I use the term 'meaning' as a psychically appropriate paraphrasing of the term 'similarity'" (letter to Pauli, 30 Nov 1950, 60), and in 1953 further writing that synchronicity is predicated on the idea that Being is itself "endowed with meaning [*Sinnbegabtheit des Seienden*]" (letter to Pauli, 7 March 1953, 98). Where Giegerich's Hegelian reading of Jung leads him to dismiss synchronicity's *Romantic* ramifications (in fact synchronicity itself) out of hand ("A Serious Misunderstanding" 506), we will see that this metaphoricity is rescued by Schelling's copular logic, which situates it as the constellation of two factors by and through an "unknown = X" which recedes from the purview of consciousness. The possibility and *potentiation* of meaning suggested by Jung's language, and not its relegation to either a strictly subjective or objective point of origin, is key for Romantic metasubjectivity.

Let us return to synchronicity proper, as a marker of the affectivity of the psychoid archetypal as Jung's zero-point of suspension between mind and Nature. But as a "psychically conditioned relativity of time and space" (*Synchronicity* para. 840; trans. mod.), this affectivity cannot be a direct experience of the atemporal and unconditioned in human consciousness. Rather, it is the *limit-experience* of that consciousness when confronted by "the necessary deformity belonging to the truth of an *unprethinkable* existence" (Warnek 53), the "incomprehensible base of reality" in "the indivisible remainder" which (un)grounds Being (*Freedom* 29). It is

> a factor which bridges the apparent incommensurability of body and psyche, giving matter a kind of 'psychic' capacity and the psyche a kind of 'materiality,' by means of which the one can act on the other. [This would mean that] being [*Sein*] would be grounded in an as yet unknown Being [*Wesenheit*] which possesses both material and psychic qualities. (Jung, *Flying Saucers* para. 780)

As contact with an "unknown Being," which Jung elsewhere describes in terms of the libidinal energy that underlies changes in phenomena ("On Psychic Energy" para. 3), synchronicity marks the tangential moment of an inscrutable unfolding which degenerates the teleological apperceptions of consciousness into purposiveness in defiance of the operations of reason. In the specifically Romantic sense I use here, the concept of "degeneration" had a unique meaning in late-eighteenth/early-nineteenth century moral, political, and natural-historical discourses. Joan Stiegerwald explains that while degeneration in the early eighteenth century meant "a decline from a noble birth or pure form" with all its political, moral, and biological implications, by the end of the century "degeneration continued to mean a deviation from an ideal type and lineage, but it was no longer confined to negative notions of decline. The term marked the effects of the material world on organic forms, but also the capacities of living forms to respond variously to alterations in their physical living conditions" (270). This "degenerate" nature of Jung's archetype is reflected in the influence of Baldwin over Lamarck (Hogenson).

But Jung's attempt to contain synchronicity in the genre of the scientific experiment also foregrounds a strange tension informing synchronicity's centrality to analytical psychology. As the final phase of Jung's long goodbye to Kantian epistemology, synchronicity forms a strange knot in Jung's late thinking, and indeed a strange chiasmus in relation to Schelling's *System*-period thinking on intellectual intuition. Where in the *System* the aesthetic sublates intellectual intuition, Jung estranges synchronicity from the mythopoesis he uses elsewhere to discuss the experience of the archetypes and the collective unconscious. Here there is no dragon guarding the "treasure hard to attain," no contact with the "mists of time," no mythopoetic descriptions of self-realisation. Instead, in *Synchronicity* Jung writes with a forensic voice reminiscent of his early writings on dementia praecox, in which he analysed the presence of complexes in word-association charts with stimulus-words, reaction words, and response times. At the argumentative core of the essay is an eclectic astrological experiment, replete with statistics and charts meant to explore connections between individual character and marriage choice. Here as elsewhere, Jung marginalises the influence of philosophy and religion on what he wants to establish as "not a philosophical view but an empirical concept which postulates an intellectually necessary principle [which] cannot be called either materialism or metaphysics" (para. 960).

And just as Schelling responds to the insoluble dilemma of Nature by attempting to fold intellectual intuition back into a restricted economy of self-consciousness, in a strange *peripeteia* Jung attempts to reinscribe synchronistic events within a psyche distinct from Nature's indeterminacy, an idealist self-consciousness akin to that of the *System*. The relativisation of space and time characteristic of synchronicity's "timelessness" now becomes possible "when the psyche observes, not external bodies, but *itself*" (para. 840). And yet later in the essay Jung writes emphatically that synchronicity is *wholly* within the realm of the psychic, being "the *simultaneity of two different psychic states*" (para. 855; trans. mod) – a strange ambivalence, given that Jung had all but synonymised psyche and Nature as far back as the 1931 "Weltanschauung" essay. Indeed, in privileging the human psyche here in 1952, Jung resists what he more radically asserts later in 1957, namely that in the experiment Nature experiments with the doctor. Here, the experiment is an *interrogation of* Nature:

> [The experiment] consists in formulating a definite question which excludes as far as possible *anything disturbing and irrelevant* [*alles Störende und Nichtzugehörige*]. It sets conditions, imposes them on

Nature, and in this way forces her to give an answer to a human question. She is thus denied the opportunity to answer out of the fullness of her possibilities since the latter are restricted as far as possible. For this purpose there is created in the laboratory a situation which is artificially restricted to the question and which compels Nature to give as unequivocal an answer as possible. The workings of Nature in her unrestricted wholeness are completely excluded. (*Synchronicity* para. 864; trans. mod.; my italics)

Indeed, one might wonder if, by experimenting in this way, Jung is asking (or responding) in the right language. For the experiment closes down precisely the derangement [*Störung*] of Nature in "the fullness of her possibilities" that Jung elsewhere articulates as the psychoid archetype, which is precisely the source of synchronicity's experiential charge. We shall see this derangement recrudesce in the following chapter on individuation and the Self.

Yet *Synchronicity*'s penultimate chapter, "Forerunners of the Idea of Synchronicity," dramatically unworks the repression of Nature's "unrestricted wholeness" in the experiment. Pushed to the end of the essay as an appendix of sorts, it nevertheless infects the hermetically sealed laboratory scene Jung previously constructed: now, the Western mindset responsible for the genre of the his experiment is "not the only possible one and is not all-embracing, but is in many ways a prejudice and a bias that ought perhaps to be corrected" (para. 916). This "appendix" continues to inscribe synchronicity in a history including the Chinese concept of Tao, Italian Renaissance philosopher Pico della Mirandola, Hippocrates, Leibniz, and others. But remarkable for our purposes here is its turn from the forensicality of the previous chapters to the rubric of German Idealism and Romanticism. To be sure, Jung's resistance to analytical psychology's specifically Romantic intensity is troubled by his alignment of synchronicity with Romantic-era "magnetism" (Mesmer's magnetic crisis and sleep) even as he dismisses it as a "causal" science (para. 850). And this turn to the philosophy Jung previously disavows ironically opens up a space for considering the aporiae in Jung's conceptualisation of synchronicity. These aporiae mirror Schelling's attempts to elucidate self-consciousness through Nature's unruly materiality and from which Romantic metasubjectivity emerges as a contestation of the idealist thought-project. More significantly for Romantic metasubjectivity, this "appendix" links synchronicity directly to "absolute knowledge" as "causeless arrangement, or rather, of meaningful arrangement [...] a knowledge not mediated by the sense organs" (para. 948; trans. mod). Here Jung completes his epistemological break with the Kantianism he previously claimed as foundational to his thinking on the archetype, even as he tries to cast this absolute knowledge as *disembodied*, "not mediated by the sense organs" (while relating a story about hearing a beetle knocking against the window, capturing it, and showing it to an analysand). Jung again seems to resist the materiality his formulation of synchronicity demands, even as, again contra Kant (who insisted that that intellectual intuition – and, *mutatis mutandis*, synchronicity – "forms no part whatsoever of our faculty of knowledge" because it goes beyond the objects of experience [*Critique of Pure Reason* 270]), Jung argues that synchronicity "postulates a meaning [*Sinn*] which is *a priori* in relation to human consciousness and apparently exists outside man" (*Synchronicity* para. 942).

And in another *peripeteia* Jung goes further: in a bold assertion resonating with Schelling's intellectual intuition, synchronicity reflects "some possibility of eliminating the incommensurability between the observed and the observer" (para. 960), which would effectively close the epistemological gap between scientist and object that Jung attempts to keep open in the experiment. Paul Bishop argues (with some hyperbole) that the overarching structure of Jung's psychology is marked by "a desire for the Absolute and a yearning for 'intellectual intuition'. [...] Even if Jung never used the term [...] the concept of synchronicity only makes sense in terms of it" (*Synchronicity* 2). But what this Absolute *is* emerges only through the analysis which the concept of synchronicity seems to demand of *Jung*: the working-through of the psyche-Nature connection that is part of Jung's own individuation, a process which resonates throughout his oeuvre as Schelling's philosophical individuation resonates throughout his. Indeed, nearing the end of his life in 1959 Jung writes: "[A]ll of the books that I have written are but by-products of an intimate process of individuation, even when they are connected by hermetic links to the past and, in all probability, to the future" ("Talks with Miguel Serrano" 395). Tina Keller, a member of Jung's early circle, recalls: "I remember how I said: 'But what you say today is just the contrary of what you said last week,' and he answered: 'That may be so, but this is true, and the other was also true; life is paradox'" (qtd. in Chodorow 3).

As a twentieth-century differentiation of intellectual intuition, synchronicity opens up a space for considering the proximity of experience to knowledge in a way irreducible to the labour of the Concept or other teleological constructs such as the *Stufenfolge*. Jung makes two claims for synchronicity, analogous to Schelling's claims of intellectual intuition: 1) that real and ideal converge in a limit-experience of thought and 2) that knowledge (as "meaning") can emerge from this experience. These claims show Jung's "true Romanticism" in his desire to move beyond Kantian boundaries and establishes synchronicity as arguably Jung's most consummately Romantic concept (Bishop, *Synchronicity* 185, 348). To this end Jung states, again contra Kant, that "it is necessary for science to know how things are 'in themselves' " ("On Psychic Energy" para. 45), and thus synchronicity is a necessary postulate of scientific reasoning (*Synchronicity* para. 960). But "even science cannot escape the psychological conditions of knowledge," and this is precisely what opens a space for "the symbolic conception of causes by means of the energic standpoint" ("On Psychic Energy" pars. 46; trans. mod.) by which phenomena are interpreted purposively. Jung goes further, writing that "psychic finality [i.e. the energic view of libido] rests on a 'pre-existent' meaning [*Sinn*] which becomes problematical only when it is an unconscious arrangement. In that case we have to suppose *a 'knowledge' prior to all consciousness*" (*Synchronicity* para. 843 n. 38 my italics). Jung's scare quotes emphasise his tentative encroachment on the philosophy he elsewhere seeks to hold at arm's length.

Even though Schelling writes in the *System* that "*Nature is purposive, without being purposively explicable*" (*STI* 12), purposiveness remains ultimately bound by the teleology of the *Stufenfolge* – indeed, Schelling makes no distinction here. But the tension between the two is more acute in synchronicity, where the predeterminations of teleology (in the form of Jung's therapeutics of presence) are undermined by purposive unfolding in an encounter without guarantees.

It is in precisely this purposiveness that we must situate the experience of the Self both emerging and receding in this limit-experience of reason. The terminology describing this experience circles the phenomena, just like Jung's attempts to define the archetype and Schelling's attempts to define the actant. We can use "irruption," "sublime," "suspension," or "limit-experience" to conceptualise this affect-charged encounter with the unknowable, but the ineffability of this experience is ultimately the receding silence of the self-organising principle. Synchronicity is Jung's way of thinking this difference, even if he at times represses its darker outcomes and ramifications for the sake of an individuative image of thought, an interiority through which the psyche, as self-consciousness, wants to observe itself. Nevertheless, this image of thought does not square with the more radical implications of Jungian metapsychology. If "Jung's system drives relentlessly towards a psychic monism which proclaims a unity or Absolute" (Bishop, *Synchronicity* 182), then seen through the lens of Romantic metasubjectivity this "Jungian Absolute" is not teleological, nor is it a circumscription of psyche by self-consciousness. Outside the tenuous boundaries of the experiment, synchronicity remains a Romantic absolute without Idealism, a revelation of the asystemic space between knowledges which inherits the dark materiality of Schelling's intellectual intuition. Indeed, here *Jung* seems to withdraw before the darker, more indeterminate implications of synchronicity as "the hiding-places of Man's power."

The limit-experience of Romantic metasubjectivity is thus marked by a materiality named by intellectual intuition and synchronicity, the derangement of Nature across which systems and organisations of knowledge range. We have seen how the experience of this derangement has been theorised by Bataille's "non-knowledge," but its important place in contemporary philosophy is reflected in Deleuze's "dark precursor" – his term for the strange self-identity of difference which makes difference possible. Jung's metonymy of terms for synchronicity – "ordering system," "so-ness," "creative act" – describes its differential core as a psychological analogue of the dark precursor as an ontological knot, an abstract term for the excess of Being:

> When we speak of communication between heterogeneous systems […] does this not imply a minimum of resemblance between the series, and an identity in the agent which brings about the communication? […] *Are we not condemned to rediscover a privileged point at which difference can be understood only by virtue of a resemblance between the things which differ and the identity of a third party?* […] Thunderbolts explode between different intensities, but they are preceded by an invisible, imperceptible *dark precursor,* which determines their path in advance but in reverse […] Likewise, every system contains its dark precursor which ensures the communication of peripheral series. […] The question is to know in any given case how the precursor fulfils this role. […] *There is* an identity belonging to the precursor, and a

resemblance between the series which it causes to communicate. This 'there is', however, remains perfectly indeterminate. Are identity and resemblance here the preconditions of the functioning of this dark precursor, or are they, on the contrary, its effects? [Thus the dark precursor represents] the in-itself of difference [...] the self-different which relates different to different by itself. (*DR* 119; my first italics)

The dark precursor, as "object = x" (123), is Deleuze's expression of the constellation of subject and predicate through the differential energy of Jungian libido, here as a magnetic force which allows "peripheral series" to communicate as their common un-ground. The dark precursor "does not relate two fields of individuation according to a resemblance between them, but rather because it finds expression in both simultaneously, while resembling neither" (Somers-Hall 82). Similarly, for James Williams the dark precursor "[works] away behind the scenes of a well-determined subject and self [to make] them individual [while undermining] any claims to full self-knowledge or to absolute freedom as a subject" (205).

Like the archetype's paradoxical relationship to representation, Deleuze leaves as indeterminate whether the dark precursor is cause or effect of "identity and resemblance." In the absence of apparent cause, object-systems or sense-events are nevertheless constellated in a relation of difference and sameness in a spontaneous act of creation, a thunderbolt explosion with a *poiesis* which, as we will see, approaches the cosmological trauma inaugurating time and history in Schelling's *Ages*. Put simply the dark precursor, as the "self-different which relates different to different by itself," is Deleuze's attempt to reach the bottom of the abyss, to sound beyond the mere repetition of the Same and find "the real subject of repetition [...] the Self of repetition, the singularity within that which repeats" (*DR* 23). Jung of course conceives of "Self" as the goal of the development of personality; hypostatised at times within his therapeutics of presence, his metapsychology nevertheless casts this Self as a nonmolar force which energises a purposive individuation process crucial to some of Schelling's most important works. Indeed, the derangement which is all but stifled in Jung's experiment in/on synchronicity recrudesces in his conception of individuation and the Self. This is the focus of the following chapter, which begins with Schelling's 1809 *Freedom* essay and the 1815 *Ages of the World* as core texts for the concept of individuation in Romantic metasubjectivity.

Notes

1. While *Anschauung* is typically translated as "intuition," Marcus Weigelt translates it as "perception," which reads a physicality into this experience against Schelling's (and perhaps his other translators') desire to idealise this experience in the *System*'s cognitive sphere.
2. In 1827, Schelling disparages the mystical as "the *hatred* of clear insight – of understanding, [and] of science in general" (*On the History* 185; trans. mod). However, Schelling also argues that it is not the insights themselves, but the *way* they are asserted which makes them "mystical" or "scientific": arguing simply from an "inner light" or from sheer "feeling" makes an insight mystical, but the same insight developed "from the depths of science" is scientific (184–85). This "quasi-mystical element" of ecstasy, while it marks a profoundly non-rational experience, is developed from within the framework of Schelling's critique of systemic knowledge and not immediate revelation.
3. The English Romantic poet John Keats, who never read *The Prelude*, used the term "egotistical sublime" to describe what he saw as Wordsworth's overweening emphasis on his own mind, as opposed to the "Poetical Character" which "is not itself—it has no self—it is everything and nothing— It has no character—it enjoys light and shade; it lives in gusto, be it foul or fair, high or low, rich or poor, mean or elevated" (letter to Richard Wodehouse, 27 Oct 1818, 194–95).
4. This term is from Bataille, who went further than Schelling in exploring the relationship between ecstasy and knowledge (although Schelling can certainly be seen as a precursor). Bataille's nonknowledge is "that which results from every proposition when we are looking to go to the fundamental depths of its content, and which makes us uneasy" ("The Consequences" 112). Bataille elaborates on nonknowledge in *Inner Experience* (1943/1954): "NONKNOWLEDGE LAYS BARE. [. . .] This proposition is the summit, but should be understood in this way: lays bare, therefore I see what knowledge was hiding up to there, but if I see I know. In effect, I know, but what I knew, nonknowledge again lays bare. If nonsense is sense, the sense that is nonsense loses itself, becomes nonsense once again (without possible end). [. . .] NON-KNOWLEDGE COMMUNICATES ECSTASY. Nonknowledge is first of all ANGUISH. In anguish appears nudity, which leads to ecstasy. But ecstasy itself (nudity, communication) slips away if anguish slips away. Thus ecstasy only remains possible in the anguish of ecstasy, in the fact that it cannot be satisfaction, *grasped knowledge*" (57).
5. Although Schelling may well have seen Bataille's ecstasy as *Schwärmerei*, or religious (over)enthusiasm (one wonders if Schelling would have countenanced a nonknowledge "beyond absolute knowledge" [57]), Bataille nevertheless outlines an experience of nonknowledge (as "pure experience") strikingly similar to Schelling's understanding. The *ipse* (subject), wanting to be everything by appropriating the world for its projections, comes to anguish

as "the nonsense of the will to knowledge arises, nonsense of every possible, making the *ipse* know that it is going to lose itself and knowledge along with it. Insofar as the *ipse* perseveres in its will to know and to be *ipse* anguish lasts, but if the *ipse* abandons itself [and] gives itself to nonknowledge in this abandonment, rapture begins. In rapture, my existence recovers a meaning, but the meaning immediately [becomes] a rapture that I ipse possess, giving satisfaction to my will to be everything. As soon as I return there, [. . .] the loss of my self ceases, I have ceased to abandon myself, I remain there, *but with a new knowledge*" (58; my last italics). Bataille's ecstasy cannot be folded back into a science as its knowledge collapses in on itself with a joyful masochism absent in Schelling's conception of philosophy, but Schelling's philosophical subject also "wants to be everything" through "searching in every possible direction" (as the following discussion shows).

6. Already in the *First Outline* Schelling refers to *Naturphilosophie*'s need to break out of the confines of the merely conceptual by finding "corresponding intuitions" to give its ideas materiality, and intuition is further described as an "infinite becoming," an endless progression of moments of apprehension which surpasses both reason and the powers of the imagination (*FO* 15 & n).

7. Yet there is the faintest glimmer, within the *System*'s Idealism, of the indeterminacy which Schelling would tacitly give to art in his later thought. Schelling very briefly pushes art further into *mythology* as the medium for art's "return to science," and in ways which look back to pre-1800 work on mythology but also forward to Schelling's Philosophy of Mythology (*STI* 232–33).

8. *Synchronicity* para. 816. See also Bishop, *Synchronicity* 28f. for a brief summary of this preoccupation. Jung's first mention of "synchronism" occurs in 1928 seminar on dream analysis (*Dream Analysis* 44–45).

9. Pauli's correspondence with Jung began circa 1933 and continued for over 20 years. They collaborated on a volume (translated in English as *The Interpretation of Nature and the Psyche* [1952]) featuring complementary articles: Jung's "On Synchronicity" and Pauli's "The Influence of Archetypal Ideas on the Scientific Theories of Kepler." While Pauli never entered analysis directly with Jung, Jung analysed more than 400 of Pauli's dreams in his alchemical studies. For a detailed account of their collaboration, see Zabriskie.

Chapter 4

Romantic metasubjectivity: individuation

The problem of individuation – how individual entities come into being and how they exist in the world – has concerned Schelling since the *Naturphilosophie* of the *First Outline* where, as we have seen, it is framed as the emergence of natural products from the deadlock between infinite productivity and infinite inhibition. This concern is also central to the *Freedom* essay, the 1815 *Ages*, and the positive philosophy. But what is the nature of this individuation? Often in Schelling there is a persistent tension between a teleological drive to resolve contradiction and difference in an ultimate horizon of unity, and a purposive drive which defies a final endpoint in the unfolding of its own internal logic. And indeed, the rhythms of purposive unfolding in texts like the *Freedom* essay and the 1815 *Ages* ultimately destabilise the pretence to linearity in Schellingian individuation. Schelling does not use the idea of rhythm *per se* to describe the dynamism in the *Freedom* essay or *Ages*, but Hölderlinian rhythm nevertheless names the unfolding of a purposive order which has regularity without closure, a regularity which is not the compulsive repetition of the Same. As we will see, while this understanding of rhythm and caesura may at times suggest regularity it rests upon a radically indeterminate tragic ontology, a "living sense which cannot be computed" (Hölderlin, "Notes on the *Oedipus*" 317). Thus, these two texts of Schelling's can be read as responses to Hegel's *Phenomenology of Spirit*; they do not dismiss dialectic, but rather decouple it from the teleology of absolute spirit and the conception of knowledge which ultimately returns to itself. In 1815 Schelling writes that "all knowledge must pass through the dialectic" (*Ages* xxxix), and Jung, too, conceives dialectic as central to the analyst-analysand encounter (*The Relations* para. 339). But where this dialectic *leads* is another matter entirely.

Not that Idealism is absent from these two texts: central to the *Freedom* essay's theodicy is a recasting of the *First Outline*'s *Stufenfolge* as God's progression toward an ultimate apocatastasis, a "final, total separation" reminiscent of *The Book of Revelation* wherein "everything true and good" is "raised into bright consciousness" and the "eternally dark ground of selfhood" is locked away in a resolution where everything is "subordinate to spirit" and temporality and contingency are gathered up into an idealist regime (*Freedom* 70). The Introduction which accompanies all three versions of the *Ages of the World* also looks to the horizon of a "golden age of truth and fable" where *logos* and *mythos* are united in a visionary refrain, a "great heroic poem" meant to manage the unruly abyss of the past. For the Schelling of the 1815 *Ages*, the way to this golden age is through the *Potenzenlehre*, a triad of endlessly circulating forces (contractive, expansive, and the force of their synthesis), unfolding stepwise through time. But these forces can never be inhibited, and thus this golden age is always to come. It consists not in the recovery of either history or knowledge but in their interminable analysis, a mutual transparency between contractive and expansive forces as questioning and answering beings in a "future objective presentation of science" (*Ages* xl). And this futurity paradoxically (un)grounds knowledge in its own historicity and experience; the three potencies are forever in an "irresolvable concatenation" (*Ages* 12).

Thus, authentic knowledge restlessly reverberates with the melancholic "indestructibly mighty core of being" Nietzsche later saw so clearly as the birth of tragedy. Likewise, the *Freedom* essay's bright horizon of spirit is clouded by the "anarchy" of a dark ground which can always break through to existence (*Freedom* 29), and this is humanity's "propensity" [*Hang*] for evil as the energy of personality in time and history (47). Thus Schelling writes: "mere Idealism does not reach far enough [to] show the specific difference [*Differenz*], that is, precisely what is the distinctiveness, of human freedom. [...] Idealism, if it does not have as its basis a living realism, becomes [an] empty and abstract [system]. [...] Idealism is the soul of philosophy; realism is the body; only both together can constitute a living whole" (*Freedom* 22, 26). What later becomes the absolute subject which traverses and organises knowledge in "NPS" is given a history and a nature in *Freedom* as "absolute *personality*" (62) with the possibility of evil. And the absolute subject's centripetal self-organisational force now runs the risk, as human personality, of being sidetracked or mutated by one organisation being for-itself in a repetition of what *Ages* calls the first potency's rotating movement, its "self-lacerating rage" (91), the energy driving individuation.

When we turn to the question of the experiencing and individuating psyche which marks Romantic metasubjectivity, the question becomes: what is the nature of an individuation that is both constituted and destabilised by its limit-experience? The tension between teleology and purposiveness that dogs Schelling's metaphysics is reiterated in the tension between Jung's therapeutics of presence and the metapsychology which often destabilises the linearity Jung at times imposes on the analytic encounter. This is to say that experience and individuation are mutually entangled: the anxiogenic experiences of connection with the grammatology of Being, with Jung's collective unconscious, are precisely what bear the traumatic freight of purposiveness which marks an *a*teleological individuation. To this end Jung writes that "[t]eleology says there is an aim toward which everything is tending, but such an aim could not exist without presupposing a mind that is leading us to a definite goal, an untenable viewpoint for us. However, *processes can show purposive character without having to do with a preconceived goal, and all biological processes are purposive*" (*Introduction* 93; my italics). The encounter with this purposive force is anxious because the experience of individuation can be intuited, but never made a full object of knowledge; certainty recedes with the experience to leave the trace Schelling describes in "NPS" as "knowing ignorance" left in the wake of the absolute subject. The gap in consciousness left by this limit-experience is suspensive, both courting and resisting interpretation. For Jung, this is the synchronistic experience of the individuation process as "the process of life itself" (*Visions* 2: 758), and this tension likewise constitutes the individuation process of Romantic metasubjectivity.

This chapter, then, elaborates this Romantic metasubjective individuation. I begin with the *Freedom* essay, which I read as a case study of the purposive energic rhythms of individuation which underwrite a uniquely Romantic ontology. This ontology informs the *Freedom* essay's theodicy – the dramatisation of both the inscrutable beginnings of time and history and the individual's rhythmic move toward and away from what Schelling, using a term from Böhme, calls the *centrum* as the basis of personality. It also informs the (meta)physics of the work of the three potencies [*Potenzenlehre*] at the core of the 1815 *Ages*. Indeed, *Ages'* cosmology develops a (meta)physics of potentiation which complements the *Freedom* essay, narrating the same impenetrable abyss of the past, supplementing the drama of man's relationship to the dark ground of his existence with the anxiogenic "rotatory motion," the unremitting movement without differentiation Schelling sees as intrinsic to Being. But *Ages'* work of individuation also makes more explicit the psychology nascent in the *Freedom* essay: the potencies' intrinsic and necessary "madness," harking back to the *First Outline*'s deranged Nature, reflects the aetiology of Romantic illness which is carried forward to discussions of magnetic sleep and alchemy. And just as intellectual intuition prefigures synchronicity in Romantic metasubjectivity's intellectual history, I will argue that the dramaturgy of the *Freedom* essay and the (meta)physics of the 1815 *Ages* are theoretical precursors of Jung's concepts of *inflation* (where consciousness is overwhelmed by archetypal energies) and the *transcendent function* (the analytic moment where a new state of awareness and being emerges), both of which are crucial to articulating individuation in analytical psychology. But despite Jung's efforts to align individuation with a linear sequence of alchemical stages, inflation and the transcendent function both serve a darker, more purposive unfolding of individuation than teleology can articulate.

We have seen that in "NPS"'s philosophical psychology, systems of knowledge emerge from that which is anterior to knowledge: the absolute subject travels through these spheres, organising them in its wake in a manner unique to its circumstance in time and history. But while "NPS" articulates a dialectical experience of the absolute subject unbeholden to Hegelian teleology, it does not explain *how* this experience, or the knowledge systems to which it gives rise, is organised in lived experience; its focus is not individuation proper. However, the question of the person's relation to the absolute subject *is* inextricably bound up with the questions of freedom, necessity, and evil which preoccupy the earlier *Freedom* essay. As I will illustrate below, "NPS"'s guiding question of how systems of knowledge emerge from asystasy is cast in the *Freedom* essay as the problem of God's emergence into time and history not as a system, but as a *life* which must thus unfold in Nature. And with this we return to the *Naturphilosophie*, whose ambivalent Nature watermarks God's individuation in the *Freedom* essay and which is in turn recapitulated in the individuation of the person; to this end, Schelling writes that *Naturphilosophie* is the only project adequate to the task of human freedom (*Freedom* 26–27). In the *Freedom* essay's more eschatological register Schelling conceives individuation as a *telos*, guided by the unifying power of love, leading to an apocatastasis marked by the "complete actualization of God" and a "final separation of good from evil" (67). But evil is also a positive, productive force which drives this *telos* while making its achievement impossible. The Nature and historicity which drive the individuation of both God and man also ensure its interminable incompletion. Indeed, such an infinite process can only be accompanied by an unbeginning, an un-*grounding* – thus we turn to Schelling's formulation of the *Ungrund* as the abyss from which all things inexplicably emerge.

Schelling's *Freedom* essay: the *Ungrund* and the emergence of personality

The *Freedom* essay returns to the graduated sequence of stages [*Stufenfolge*] of the *First Outline*'s *Naturphilosophie*, but casts it as the series of stages through which God himself must proceed. In other words, where the *First Outline*'s speculative physics theorised the emergence of products in Nature as part of Nature's individuation toward the absolute product, the *Freedom* essay turns to God, who is "not a system, but rather a life" that must also individuate (*Freedom* 62). As Alan White explains:

> In the *Freedom* essay, the ground as such is said to have all content within it and to resist being grasped or explained by the power of understanding, to resist revealing itself in actual existence; at every stage of dialectical development, the ground is forced to expose more of itself than the power of understanding has previously grasped. In the *Freedom* essay, the source of content is obscurity and darkness rather than clarity and light. (119)

This "obscurity and darkness" which recedes from knowledge is what Schelling calls "the original ground or the *non-ground*" [*Ungrund*], "a being before all ground and before all that exists [and] before any duality," indeed before God (*Freedom* 68). The *Ungrund* is a state of "absolute *indifference*" (68) between opposites which does not nullify them (it is not what Hegel famously called "the night where all cows are black") but rather suspends them as what Jeff Love and Johannes Schmidt describe as "a point of indifference between oppositions where they are in balance, where they are indifferent the one to the other" (168 n. 95). Thus, Schelling writes that even though the *Ungrund* is before all opposites and duality, it is "neutral" towards them, which is precisely why opposites and polarities can "[break] forth immediately from the Neither-Nor" of its indifference (69). It is no surprise, then, that Schelling begins the *Freedom* essay, as he will begin *Ages*, with a discussion of copular logic. For following this logic, the *Ungrund* is the unknown $= X$ without which subject-predicate relationships could not be conceived and from which existence emerges.

For Schelling, the *Ungrund* provides a resolution to the problem of how things emerge from a God that is "infinitely" different to the world of things (28). This resolution is also momentous for Romantic metasubjectivity, as the *Ungrund* marks the dark ground of spirit, the receding origin of Being and becoming analogous to Jung'scollective unconscious. The world of becoming, of time and history, can only emerge from God; but how can things separate from a God which always already encompasses all things? Schelling's answer is that things are ultimately grounded in "that which in God himself is not *He Himself,* that is, in that which is the ground of his existence" (28) – the *Ungrund*, which marks the *not-God within God*, that within God which God cannot know and which always already implicates God in the history of Nature. In other words, the *Ungrund* is God's unconscious; it harbours "the yearning [*Sehnsucht*] the eternal One feels to give birth to itself" (28),[1] the drive to individuation in and through Nature's materiality. But we have seen from the *Naturphilosophie* that this materiality is deranged, ambivalent toward its own existence. As life, then, God's yearning is driven by unknown forces, and in this God is like man; both God and man are confronted with their un-grounding Other which becomes an existential *pharmakon*, both the cause of and cure for melancholic desire and the endless approximation to wholeness. Both God and man are consigned to "the deep indestructible melancholy of all life" (63).

Melancholy [*Melancholie*] is only mentioned once in the *Freedom* essay, but it is pervasive throughout the broader individuative economy of the text. This tension between futurity (a desire for love that unites all) and melancholy (the acknowledgement that this desire must find and re-find itself) is central to the text's complexity. After all, as Schelling writes: "the good *should* be raised out of the darkness […] whereas evil *should* be separated from the good in order to be cast out eternally into non-Being" (*Freedom* 67; my italics). The optative tone here should not be overlooked. Thus, this melancholy does not throw up its hands in despair but instead marks the medium of personality which ultimately fuels the *Freedom* essay's futurity. It is the basis for the analogy Schelling draws between

God's relationship to the not-God of the *Ungrund* and the human being's relationship with the *centrum*, "the undivided power of the initial ground" as it exists in the person (44). Through the freedom of the not-God within God, "a fundamentally unlimited power is asserted next to and outside of divine power" which is conceptually unthinkable and which inaugurates a divine individuation marking Schelling's radical turn from the notions of emanationism and theodicy prevailing in his time. This not-God within God marks the (un)beginning of all things as a difference always already operating in Being, and this (un)beginning's human equivalent is in Schelling's formulation of personality.

In contrast to Hegel's assertion that dialectical progression is always already embedded in Being, the *Freedom* essay emphasises the emergence of personality in an unprethinkable "moment" of creation analogous to God's entry into time and history, a non-egoic "free act" from the abyss of the unconditioned:

> Man is in the initial creation [...] an undecided being – [...] only man himself can decide. But this decision cannot occur within time; it occurs outside of all time and, hence, together with the first creation (though as a deed distinct from creation). [...] The act, whereby his life is determined in time [belongs] to eternity [and] goes through time (unhampered by it) as an act which is eternal by nature. (51)

"Decision" [*Entscheidung*] cannot be an act of conscious volition, since it precedes ego. Rather, it is a primordial separation [*scheidung*], a scission which inaugurates becoming. This paradoxically free and necessary act makes freedom *the freedom to exist as one must*, and this free necessity is the kernel of Schelling's philosophy of freedom. For Schelling this free necessity, as personality, is "the connection between a self-determining being and a basis [*centrum*] independent of him" (*Freedom* 59). And crucially for the *Freedom* essay's protopsychological dimension, this act leaves in each individual a residual correspondent *feeling* of personality in time and history, as the mark of both what one has always been and what one *must also be*. This feeling is "a feeling in accord with [this act] as if he had been what he is already from all eternity and had by no means become so first in time. [Thus this act] cannot appear in consciousness to the degree the latter is self-awareness and only ideal, since it precedes consciousness just as it precedes essence, indeed, first *produces* it"

(*Freedom* 51). Thus, the act of decision which marks personality is explicitly unconscious: "the fundamental force of all initial and original creating must be an unconscious and necessary force since no personality actually leaves its mark" (*Ages* 102).[2] To be sure, this force conjugates the grammatology of Being – but it is always a "future *tense*," endlessly deferred, wrought with anxiety over its eternal self-incommensurability, caught from the beginning in perpetual melancholy, the quest for a lost, impossible object. But while we have seen how Schelling conceives the *Ungrund* and its human analogue, we must now turn to how Schelling articulates this conjugation dynamically, as well as the crucial role evil plays in the *Freedom* essay's theodicean drama.

Evil and the dialectic of production

While the *Freedom* essay's Idealism wants to recast the *Stufenfolge* as the progressive individuation of both God and man, its disclosure of the *Ungrund* as God's unconscious, and the *centrum* as its human iteration, articulates a dark kernel of indeterminacy which frustrates this *telos*. It should be noted that idealist teleology was taken up by Samuel Taylor Coleridge, the aspiring system-philosopher of the English Romantics, and specifically as a retort to the darkening of Being that the *Naturphilosophie* transfers to the *Freedom* essay. Coleridge's *Theory of Life* (1816) is a prolonged engagement with Schelling's *Naturphilosophie* unique in English Romanticism, and provides Coleridge's most systematic account of individuation as idealist teleology as "the power which unites a given *all* into a *whole* that is presupposed by all its parts" (510). In terms recalling the *Stufenfolge*, Coleridge conceives individuation as "an ascending series of intermediate classes, and of analogous gradations in its class" as part of "the great scale of ascent and expansion," culminating in man as individuation "perfected in its corporeal sense [and beginning] a new series beyond the appropriate limits of physiology" (516). Individuation is "a tendency to the ultimate production of the highest and most comprehensive individuality [as] the one great end of Nature [...] which bears to a final cause the same relation that Nature herself bears to the Supreme Intelligence" (517–18). Taking to heart what Schelling expresses more wistfully, Coleridge's God ultimately dispels the strife of Nature in his theory of life. Indeed, theology is a dangerous supplement in the *Theory*, simultaneously adding to and (ultimately) repressing the darker, more inscrutable aspects of physiology and epigenesis. This leads Coleridge to write a year later that Schelling's fatal mistake in the *Naturphilosophie* is putting "objective and unconscious nature" before "intelligence" (*Biographia* 1: 255) and that "the highest perfection of natural philosophy would consist in the perfect spiritualization of all the laws of nature into laws of intuition and intellect" (1: 256).

But against Coleridge's efforts to ultimately Christianise Nature, for both Schelling and Jung the rhythm of unfolding in Being is unpredictable: individuation can go awry and the power of the *centrum* can always be falsely appropriated by the ego's being-for-itself, which Schelling will describe as the basis of evil. Freedom is the necessary introduction of the anarchy of the *Ungrund* into time and history, a fracturing of Idealism in the *Freedom* essay and the 1815 *Ages* which reflects Schelling's turn away from a teleological explanation of Being (Bowie, *Schelling* 129). Evil is the energic force of movement without which existence would founder and congeal, unable to move. But how do we conceive this dialectical yet purposive dynamic?

Edward Beach offers a useful distinction which highlights Schelling's critique of Hegel's labour of the Concept.[3] Hegel's *dialectic of sublation* [*Aufhebungsdialektik*] operates through a continuous "thought-experiment," testing the truth of concepts in a way which implicates Being in an existing *telos*, however inchoately it may present itself in philosophy or (natural) history. Conversely, Schelling's *dialectic of production* [*Erzeugungsdialektik*] reaches behind reason, so to speak, "so as to be capable of recovering the willing that allegedly precedes rational thought itself," the unthought anterior to and constitutive of reason (85). As a recapitulation of the unprethinkable act by which the cosmos came into being, the dialectic of production's "procreative causality" demands both logical understanding and corroboration in "direct historical experience" (85), which implicates this dialectic in the uniquely Romantic historicity described by Pfau. To connect with this causality is to connect with the *will*, and for Beach the *Freedom* essay's crucial importance lies in this emphasis on "volition" (his word for Schelling's will) at the heart of ontology (84). Schelling writes:

> In the final and highest judgment, there is no other Being than will. Will is primal Being to which alone all predicates of Being apply: groundlessness, eternality, independence from time, self-affirmation. All of philosophy strives only to find this highest expression. (*Freedom* 21)

As the desire for "self-affirmation," will designates philosophy *itself* as a protracted individuation process which, on account of its groundlessness, can never complete itself. This "willing" also correlates to Jung's conception of the energy which underlies libidinal development, which suggests a broadly analytical-psychological component to this dialectic. Thus, Schelling's dialectic of production allows for the irruption of new ideas that are not bound by the labour of the Concept.

Schelling's account of freedom both diagnoses creaturely existence as what the *First Outline* called a "misbegotten attempt" – here, a miscomprehension of the proper relation to "universal will" – and prognoses a transfiguration by which the person (as creature) unites with "the primal will" of understanding:

> [The dark principle of] self-will of creatures[,] to the extent that it has not yet been raised to (does not grasp) complete unity with the light (as principle of understanding), is pure addiction [*Sucht*] or desire, that is, blind will. The understanding as universal will stands against this self-will of creatures, using and subordinating the latter to itself as a mere instrument. But, if through advancing mutation and division of all forces, the deepest and most inner point of initial darkness in a being is finally transfigured wholly into the light, then the will of this same being is indeed, to the extent it is individual, also a truly particular will, yet, in itself or as the *centrum* of all other particular wills, one with the primal will or the understanding, so that now from both a single whole comes into being. (*Freedom* 32; trans. mod.)

Here, individuation is the dramatisation of the blind individual will's elevation into something more than it was, as part of the universal will. Personality is "selfhood raised to spirit" (38), both a cision in the individual and a connection with the ideal, as "a relatively independent principle" (32), "will that beholds itself in complete freedom [as] above and outside of all nature" (33). In Schelling's drama of freedom, individuation is not driven by a process of identification or the unfolding of something preformed. Rather, the "mutation and division of all forces" drives self-will from its darkness into a transfiguration where it paradoxically becomes particular and universal as "selfhood," just as for Jung individuation "does not shut one out from the world, but gathers the world to oneself" to make one paradoxically both individual and collective ("On the Nature of the

Psyche" para. 432). Yet this prognosis is nevertheless one of a *completed* individuation, of final transfiguration. So if will is groundless Being, what does it mean to unify with the *centrum*, the primal will? Is it not to unite with the groundlessness of primal Being, just as to "gather the world to oneself" is to imperil oneself with exposure to Nature's derangement, a dissociative matrix whose experience puts one *outside* oneself? In the *Freedom* essay, this imperilment is the evil nature of the world – the *inevitable* suspension of this transfiguration as the condition for time and history. This positive force of evil persists in spite of Schelling's efforts to fold individuation's *Erzeugungsdialektik* back into an idealist economy through the *Freedom* essay's scriptural traces of "darkness" and "light," like Jung's more optimistic moments in which he suggests that individuation can be "achieved."

In the *Freedom* essay, Schelling closely aligns evil with disease. Evil results from the self's estrangement, as the "dark principle of self-will," from the *centrum* (44). In this human, all too human estrangement, the will "steps out from its being beyond nature" to "elevate the ground over the cause, to use the spirit that it obtained only for the sake of the *centrum* outside the *centrum* and against creatures; from this results collapse within the will itself and outside it" (34). In other words, self-will attempts to bend the *centrum* to its own designs. Outside the harmony of the *centrum*'s "divine measure and balance" self-will, as "a bond of living forces," can no longer rule the rebellious dominion of forces as "addictions and appetites," which leads to a "peculiar life [of] mendacity, a growth of restlessness and decay" (34). As a disruption of cosmic harmony which thereby shows this harmony's constitutive self-difference, evil is the force whereby "things feverishly move away from their nonthingly center" (Wirth, *Conspiracy* 170).

But this evil is *productive*, and in precisely the same way as Nature's ambivalence toward its products in the *First Outline. Erzeugungsdialektik*'s connection with historicity and materiality risks the individual's annihilation or subsumption in "restlessness and decay" as the ego proclaims: *I am the centrum*. But it is also a connection with the purposive movement toward what the *Freedom* essay calls transfiguration and is thus essential to the individual's existence in the world. Jung takes up precisely this purposiveness in the energic view of libido which, as we have seen, conceives the transformation of phenomena in terms of an underlying energy. Indeed, it is ironic that in a discussion of alchemy, Jung explicitly casts individuation as an *a*teleological process which unworks the "logical" alignment of alchemical stages and individuation. That is, transformation cannot be simply guaranteed through the exertions of self-consciousness or underwritten by a logically ordered Being:

> I have often seen people simply outgrow a problem which had completely shipwrecked others. This "outgrowing," as I called it earlier, turned out to be an increase in the level of consciousness. Some higher and further interest appeared on the horizon, and through this broadening of the horizon the insoluble problem lost its urgency. *It was not solved logically in its own terms*, but faded when life adopted a newer and stronger course. It was not repressed and made unconscious, but merely appeared in a different light and so became different. ("Commentary" para. 17; trans. mod.; my italics)

In contrast to Giegerich's "psychology of interiority," which privileges alchemical teleology and the logical movements of "soul," Jung insists that "*what really exists as such cannot be alchemically sublimated*, and whatever appears sublimated was never what a false interpretation made it seem to be" ("The Practical Use of Dream-Analysis" para. 328; trans. mod.; my italics), which distances Jung from even his own inclination to equate individuation with alchemical stages. While Jung elsewhere bids to re-idealise alchemical individuation into an apocatastatic vision similar to the one Schelling had previously incorporated into the *Freedom* essay as the discussion of love (Jung, *Aion* 169; "The Archetypes and the Collective Unconscious" para. 550), Jung's metapsychology ultimately casts teleological individuation as a sublime moment in a larger purposive economy. That is, teleological "moments" of system (where order manifests itself in epiphany) circulate in a fluid freedom according to inscrutable laws and indiscernible (but intuitable) connections; these moments are corpuscular, circulating in a larger current.

So what Jung describes as the "outgrowing" of a problem is a fundamental shift in libidinal *intensity* – libido's "will" as it were – and not this energy's manifestation as teleological movement. Indeed, Jung ultimately casts Schelling's philosophical "will" of *Erzeugungsdialektik* as the differential movement of a *libidinal gradient* [*Gefälle*]:

> It is not in our hands to arbitrarily transfer [libido's] "disposable" energy to a rationally chosen object. [This energy can] at best be [so]

applied for a short time. But for the most part it refuses to take hold of rational possibilities given to it for any length of time. Psychic energy is simply a fastidious thing which wants to fulfil its own conditions. However much energy is present, we cannot make it useable until the correct gradient is discovered. [In the favourable case] when this disposable energy, this so-called libido, takes hold of a rational object, one thinks one has brought it about through conscious effort. But this is misleading, for the greatest effort would not have sufficed had there not also been an existing gradient in the same direction. [...] *Only there, where the gradient lies, can the path of life be pursued.* But there is no energy where there is no tension between opposites; therefore, the opposite of the conscious attitude must be found. (*On the Psychology* pars. 76–78; trans. mod.; my italics)[4]

Measured by the intensity invested in "rational objects," the Thanatopoietic movement of the libidinal gradient in and through the "tension between opposites" pre-exists the metonymies of its possible objects. And like Schelling's absolute subject, which moves through everything without being anything, the libidinal gradient is the constellating force of individuation; the "Self of one's self." This process cannot be based on the causal processes of consciousness insofar as conscious direction of this energy is either purely phantastic or ill-advised. In the Introduction, we saw how Jung articulates this as the energic view of libido, a "final" concept of energy "abstracted from relations of movement" which "underlies the changes in phenomena [with] a definite direction (goal) by unalterably (irreversibly) following the potential gradient" ("On Psychic Energy" para. 3; trans. mod). In the previous chapter, we saw that the tragic-melancholic *experiencing* of this gradient is an encounter with the derangement of Nature's materiality; as such, this encounter expresses the (im)possibility of individuation's completion, *Trieb* without consummation. And while this tragic element is certainly present in the *Freedom* essay as the melancholy of all finite life, the *Freedom* essay cannot be simply labelled a tragic work. It is in fact Hölderlin whose theory of tragedy is an early articulation of the tragic potential of the self-*centrum* relationship, the *Ungrund*'s potential to irrupt and disrupt the person's relation to the *centrum*. Indeed, Hölderlin's theory of rhythm and caesura in tragedy informs Schelling's pivotal turn from an early aesthetic Idealism to the darkened powers of the *Freedom* essay. Let us turn briefly then to Hölderlin, who was more willing than the young Schelling to see the ontological implications of a tragic aesthetics.

Excursus: Hölderlin and the rhythm of Romantic ontology

Krell argues compellingly that of all the German Idealist and Romantic thinkers, it is the German Romantic poet and philosopher Friedrich Hölderlin (1770–1843) who took tragedy to its farthest-reaching conclusions.[5] Before Schelling, "Hölderlin is […] already engaged in a life-long confrontation with tragedy; Schelling will come to such a confrontation later, and more traumatically" with the death of his wife Caroline Schelling in 1809, a loss from which he never fully recovered (*The Tragic Absolute* 41). Where the early Schelling's repressive thinking about intellectual intuition darkened only much later into "NPS"'s ecstatic experience of absolute subjectivity, Hölderlin famously writes circa 1800 that the tragic "is the metaphor of an intellectual intuition" ("The Lyric" 302). As Krell writes, "intellectual intuition *is* in Hölderlin's view *tragic* thinking" (*The Tragic Absolute* 302) because it marks an always already fractured absolute anticipating what the *Freedom* essay will elaborate essentially as God's unconscious. Hölderlin's intellectual intuition is the simultaneous, paradoxical experience of embodiment and separation, attraction and repulsion:

> The unity present in the intellectual intuition embodies itself in the very same degree in which it departs from itself, in which the division of its parts takes place, which only separate themselves, because they feel themselves to be too unified, when in the whole they are closer to the centre, or because they do not feel themselves to be united enough according to their completeness, if they are secondary parts, lying further from the centre, or, according to their liveliness, if they are neither secondary parts, in the given sense, nor essential parts, in the given sense, but because they are not yet actualized, because they are still only divisible parts. (Hölderlin, "The Lyric" 305)

In an eternally moving One which "must not remain always in the same closer and further relation, so that all encounters all, and each [part] receives its entire right, its entire measure of life" (304), how can such an intuition *not* suspend, indeed shatter the ego's frail categories, leaving a gap which cannot be assimilated but must be minded by the nobler souls

Hölderlin addresses? A far cry, to be sure, from the self-consciousness of Schelling's 1800 *System*. Hölderlin's most significant statements on tragedy are his "Notes on the *Oedipus*" (1803) and "Notes on the *Antigone*" (1803), which offer a theory of rhythm and caesura that articulates, in the aesthetic register of tragedy, the systolic-diastolic dynamic which underpins Romantic metasubjective individuation – a dynamic which Schelling later figures differently as the *Freedom* essay's self-*centrum* rhythm.

In "Notes on the *Antigone*," Hölderlin develops the "calculable law" of tragedy not as a structuralist formula to be applied to a work of art, but rather as a means of tracking the development of "idea and feeling and reflection" according to the logic of a poem or drama. Hölderlin writes:

> For just as philosophy always treats only one faculty of the soul, so that the representation of this *one* faculty makes a whole, and the mere connection between the *parts* of this faculty is called logic: so poetry treats the various faculties of a human being, so that the representation of these different faculties makes a whole, and the connection between *the more independent parts* of the different faculties can be called the rhythm, taken in a higher sense, or the calculable law. ("Notes on the *Antigone*" 325)

Hölderlin is describing how Greek tragic plots unfold, but also what they point to beyond their textual margins: namely, a "calculus for holding on to the incalculable and dangerous totality of life, which manifests itself at its purest in tragedy" (Adler and Louth lii). And this "higher sense" of rhythm is not a philosophical exercise directed at the human faculties *themselves*, but at the human faculties as *divided forces* – connections between their "independent parts" that by definition are for-themselves to varying degrees in a denial of unity and indifference. To properly discern tragedy, one must observe

> how the particular content relates to the general calculation *within a continuum which, though endless, is yet determined throughout*, and how the development and the intended statement, the living sense which cannot be computed, may be related to the calculable law. [...] Hence the rhythmic succession of ideas wherein the *transport* [*i.e.*, metaphor] manifests itself demands a counter-rhythmic interruption, a pure word, *that which in metrics is called a caesura,* in order to confront the speeding alternation of ideas at its climax, so that not

the alternation of the idea, but the idea itself appears. ("Notes on the *Oedipus*" 317–18; my first italics)

This "continuum" ensures that the rhythm in question cannot be the mere repetition of the Same. It is the incalculable derangement of Nature within which the tragic plot unfolds; as such, it is the tragic gradient of Jungian libido, whose purposive movement can only be fleetingly glimpsed as Hölderlin's "idea" through the traumatic rupture of continuity. It is a substrate for the relation between tragedy's calculable law and that "living sense" of tragedy which forever remains irreducible to it.

Just as for Jung blocked libido regresses to a state of undifferentiated polyvalency to enable possibilities for transformation, *caesurae* cause "the idea itself" to manifest in the tragic metaphor ("transport") of intellectual intuition in a moment of potential epiphany. Krell writes: "[E]ven though the term caesura is borrowed from versification, Hölderlin applies it to the faculties of human knowing and feeling as well as to the events of the tragic plot. [The caesura is] a protracted instant or elongated point within which we can see how and why matters are tearing ahead so relentlessly and so perilously" (*The Tragic Absolute* 294, 203). The tragic interplay of rhythm and the caesural transport of intellectual intuition depend on the wayward "independent parts" of the faculties in the tragic individual – the dissociationist paradigm of melancholy in which our faculties are no more "themselves" than we are when we say "I." The eternal possibility of caesura, of the *Ungrund*'s anarchy breaking into existence, is the basis of both personality and the traumatic historicity which Pfau sees as intrinsically Romantic. In psychoanalytical terms, "it is the subject's experience of the 'real' that opens the caesura and illuminates the (contingent) subject's glimpse into the elusiveness, the caesura, of Being" (Gosetti-Ferencei 132).

Building on Hölderlin's ideas in a specifically Romantic ontology, Arkady Plotnitsky places intellectual intuition's confluence of real and ideal specifically within a tragic-melancholic paradigm. He sees Hölderlinian rhythm as a confluence of "the inaccessible efficacity of all events, the incalculable emergence of individual events, [and] rhythmic effects and counter-rhythmic movement, giving rise to caesuras" ("The Calculable Law" 135). In this interplay of rhythm and caesura,

The rhythm of any life can radically alter at any point, revealing this underlying 'caesured' discontinuity, rarely completely random, even if not always manifesting a tragic fate, and hence making this caesura belong to the structure of [tragic] representation. [...] A caesura opens a possibility of another, different – "erratic" [...] "caesured" history, and [...] reveals a different, rhythmic temporality, which is the *condition* of all history. (132, 133)

More specifically, Plotnitsky takes up Hölderlinian rhythm and caesura and contemporary quantum theory to describe Romantic ontology as an ontology of the unprethinkable, a "scepticism concerning the possibility of capturing the ultimate workings of matter or thought by thought [which makes] the ultimate workings of matter or thought inconceivable, *un*thinkable, ultimately unthinkable even as unthinkable" (125). Despite Kantian epistemological limits on knowing and thinking the unconditioned, there are nevertheless "collectivities" of events which manifest order and rhythm without closure: "The overall structure of such collectivities is not random, even though *any two events* still cannot be connected by any law" (130).

Jung both courts and resists this Romantic structuring of tragedy. On the one hand, his fourfold Aristotelian account of the dream-work: (1) statements of place, protagonist, and temporality; (2) plot development; (3) a "culmination or peripeteia" in which "something decisive happens or something changes"; and (4) the *lysis*, or "solution or result produced by the dream-work" ("On the Nature of Dreams" pars. 561ff) is meant to gather up Romantic ontology's discontinuity into a linear structure formalising dream-works, as "separate acts of compensation," into individuation's "planned and orderly process of development" (para. 550). But on the other hand, rhythm and caesura mark the purposiveness in Jungian metapsychology which does not always fit Jung's compensatory psychic economy; not all dreams are faithfully tied to the conscious attitude, and indeed dreams without *lysis* mark the "fated" nature of the dissociationist psyche in which "we do not dream, but rather we *are dreamt*" (Schelling's "it thinks in me"). Such dreams are "anticipated fate" and, at least in his seminars on children's dreams, seen as catastrophic (*Children's Dreams* 158–59). So in spite of Jung's resistances, Jungian libido – hence individuation itself – belongs to the existential melancholy of Romantic ontology, assuming the characteristics of Hölderlinian rhythm and unworking this teleological imperative (all the more interesting that Jung relies heavily on Hölderlin's poetry in *Symbols* to articulate the movements of libido).

Jung writes: "Libido blocked by an obstacle does not necessarily regress to earlier sexual applications, but rather to infantile rhythmic activities, which serve as the original basis for both the nutritional and sexual acts. [...] [I]t is not impossible that the invention of fire-making in fact came about in this way, through the regressive reawakening of rhythm" (*Symbols* 154). Encountering the existential caesura of an obstacle, libido regresses, switches tracks, canalises ("awakens") into a different rhythmic temporality. Indeed rhythm, taken somewhat more literally here as a "classic device for impressing certain ideas or activities on the mind" (154), is responsible for the materiality of the archetypes as both producers and products of repeated experiences and activities. "The rhythmic tendency [...] is a peculiarity of emotional processes in general. *Any excitation, no matter in what phase of life, has a tendency to rhythmic manifestations, that is, to perseverative repetitions*" (155; trans. mod.; my italics). But within this "rhythm" are encrypted evolutionary caesurae, the kernels of differentiation which permeate the development of world processes in Jung's "extremely historical organism." For Jung, it is affect and "emotional processes" which deconstruct the faculties into their "independent parts" under the melancholic regime of rhythm and caesura.

Thus, Hölderlin's development of rhythm and caesura articulates a specifically Romantic ontology for the progressive-regressive movement of Jungian libido and the *Freedom* essay's self-*centrum* drama. But from within this interplay of rhythm and caesura, Romantic ontology marks an emergent order always on the cusp of Being, within "the irreducible, rhizomatic multiplicity of temporal effects" which, by way of "structural isomorphism" (Plotnitsky, "The Calculable Law" 136), is iterated in tragedy, history, and their confluence in Jung's historical psyche. The potential order within what Plotnitsky calls "collectivities" of events (130) organises the "living realism" of Schelling's *Freedom* essay (*Freedom* 26), which he intended as the antidote to an Idealism characterised by "the abhorrence of everything real" (26). But in theorising what Schelling dramatises as the self-*centrum* relation, Hölderlinian tragedy puts this relation under analysis to reveal its incommensurability with the apocatastatic "love conquers all" narrative which ends Schelling's text. In this sense, Hölderlin's positing of rhythm and caesurae as nonmolar forces anticipates the dissociationist cosmogony of Schelling's 1815 *Ages*. Indeed, one can read *Ages* as a sort of retroactive metapsychology for the *Freedom* essay: where the *Freedom* essay develops the self-*centrum* relationship within a theodicean framework, *Ages* disperses this drama across multiple energic centres; psyches meeting in Mesmeric crisis, individual potencies, and even celestial bodies are now implicated in individuation's cosmological work of yearning.

Schelling's *Ages of the World* (1815): the work of yearning

In *Ages*, yearning [*Sehnsucht*] is the beginning of the end – and of the beginning again. For here, Schelling writes of first Nature that "Since it did not begin sometime but began since all eternity in order never (veritably) to end, and ended since all eternity, in order always to begin again, it is clear that that first nature was since all eternity and hence, equiprimordially a movement circulating within itself; and that this is its true, living concept" (*Ages* 20). In the *Freedom* essay, yearning is God's desire for self-understanding – "the yearning the eternal One feels to give birth to itself" (28). In *Ages*, yearning and desire cause the "inner cision" in eternal nature, the unprethinkable moment which releases the endless movement of the potencies into time and history; yearning begins with cision (56, 28). And it is the lack marked by yearning that distinguishes the *Trieb* of Romantic metasubjectivity from a merely mechanistic process. For in poeticising the sublime beginning of a moment of yearning – a moment over before (and *as*) it has begun – Schelling makes *Trieb* something more than endless mechanism or the perfect rhythm and symmetry of a divine Newton's Cradle in perpetual motion on God's office desk. With yearning, *Trieb desires* itself. "Aware" of itself – rather, of that which it is *not* – *Trieb* "now" (to speak in time) wants to find itself and can only do so by stepping into time and history, finding itself *in* time, but never finding itself in *time*. Yearning separates *Trieb* from the stasis of the unconditioned to give it the endlessly unfolding ground of its self-comprehension. Yearning is the personality of *Trieb*. As Jung says, personality is a "happening," and this development of "personality" informs Jung's earliest thinking about instinct and archetype. Instincts (as "typical modes of action") and archetypes codetermine each other; indeed, the archetype is "*the instinct's perception* [Anschauung] *of itself* [...] the self-figuration [*Selbstabbildung*] of the instinct," that which determines instinct's "form and direction" as instinct strives to become aware of itself ("Instinct" para. 277; trans. mod). In other words, for Jung the instinct yearns for knowledge and self-apprehension through the archetype; *Trieb*'s purposive nature is endlessly recapitulated through psyche, archetype, instinct, and world. Schelling "disciplines" this yearning as the philosophical psychology of "NPS," which articulates the movements of the absolute subject as it travels through paradigms and systems of knowledge without arresting its motion in any one thing. But it is not until the *Freedom* essay and the 1815 *Ages* that Schelling puts *Trieb* under analysis to articulate the dynamics of its desire.

The 1815 *Ages* is the third of a series of attempts by Schelling to write the history of the past, but it also blueprints the futurity which marks Schelling's later positive philosophy.[6] Indeed, *Ages*' textual history can be read as a microcosm of the trajectory of Schelling's oeuvre as a whole, from transcendental Idealism to the dark, indeterminate forces of Being and their operations in time and history. The first (1811) version is a work of Idealism, suffused with Christian teleology and promising a completed futurity underwritten by the Trinity; it is a work of "ontotheology as anthropology, [a] complete work that Schelling later unworked" (Rajan, "First Outline" 321). Less theological, the second version (1813) nevertheless retains a visionary teleological horizon of completion and has a tranquillity absent in 1815. Here, the powers of generation are contained within spirit as its consummate creation, lacking the potentiated rhythm of the third version but retaining a religious rhetoric of "joy" and "bliss" (Schelling, *The Ages of the World [1813]* 144–45). In 1813, philosophy is the alibi for 1815's nascent psychology. Rajan points out that the interminable dynamism of the third version is absent and, as a result, individuation is more of a visionary ascension to a completed future Coleridge would no doubt have appreciated ("Abyss" para. 8). To reach this visionary futurity, the philosopher must dissociate ("separate") from himself, but in a "distancing from the present [and] an *abandonment to the past*" ultimately serving a "great heroic poem" of true opinion "indubitable, rooted for all time" (*The Ages of the World [1813]* 115–16, 119–20; my italics).

The 1815 *Ages* turns from an "anthropogenesis" in 1813 (shared with the 1800 *System*), which represses a primordial, traumatic rotatory motion, to a radical "psychoanalysis" whose disciplinary counter-transferences displace this philosophical history into interminable analysis: "[*Ages*] returns to the theory of history (and its three ages or periods) sketched at the end of the *System* to provide a psychoanalysis of this history: to disclose that history cannot begin without a psychoanalysis that may well make history impossible, in the Hegelian sense of a transition from nature to spirit and from spirit to freedom" (Rajan, "Abyss" para. 2). But while *Ages* certainly serves as "a laboratory for a psychoanalysis *avant la lettre*" (para. 1), to articulate this "psychoanalysis" means understanding the term, with Rajan, as something broader than Freudian thought, which cannot decode the visionary futurity of "that future objective presentation of science" to come, a "great heroic poem" optimistically projected into a future without guarantees, meant to *narrate* what can only be *explored* (*Ages* xl). If *Ages* is a "laboratory," Schelling's abortive experiments, his "misbegotten attempts" to write the past, try to answer (to) the impossible objects of Nature. And this narrative experimentation is part of a philosophical continuum leading Schelling forward to "NPS"'s philosophical psychology, the philosophical religion of the positive philosophy and the Philosophy of Mythology. Failing to write *history*, *Ages* enacts *historicity* through (meta) physics.

Schelling emphasises that *Ages* is a work of imagination, but it has little to do with the rhapsodic tenor which marks later moments in the 1800 *System*'s discussion of art. As a narrative which we must *imagine* "although this cannot be conceived as actually having happened in this way" (77), the text's engagement with the unprethinkable cision which inaugurates time and history is closer to a working-through of the "crisis of consciousness" which Schelling later attributes to the first mythological poets (Homer, Hesiod) in the 1842 Philosophy of Mythology (*HCI* 18), which we will discuss in the next chapter. *Ages* carries forward the project of the *Naturphilosophie* by putting under analysis the account of the actants in the *First Outline*. Where the *First Outline* articulated Nature's productivity in terms of the (de)composability of the actants relative to each other, *Ages*' cosmogony narrates the inauguration of Nature itself as the eternal "moment" of potentiation. Indeed, as McGrath puts it, the potencies are "a metaphysics of God which is indissolubly linked to a metaphysics of Nature" (*Dark Ground* 141). The *Potenzenlehre* deconstructs the actants themselves into what Jung would call their *complexio oppositorum*, their dynamic of opposing contractive/expansive forces.

Although its beginning seeks a "golden age of truth and fable" uniting myth and science, *Ages* nevertheless breaks with the *Freedom* essay's idealist narrative wherein the work of yearning's lysis into "bright consciousness" leads to the locking away of the "dark ground of selfhood" (*Freedom* 47, 70). In doing this, *Ages* moves closer to the evil of the *Freedom* essay in describing the first potency's endless motion and restlessness, the drive to be for-itself which impels movement away from the *centrum* and which in *Ages* is now fundamental to knowledge. The *Potenzenlehre* ultimately conceives this motion as the scene of mesmeric crisis, and thus a crypto-psychology emerges from a text which Snow aptly describes as "a guided tour of the limits of philosophy" (Snow 184). This derangement of the margins of philosophy drives *Ages* to "[reconstitute] history (and also ontology) around [...] geology" (Rajan, "Abyss" para. 5) as part of the text's interdisciplinary individuation, an uncanny repetition of its cosmogony whereby a "particular nature" separates from the whole to assume its own anxiogenic rotation about its own axis in "self-lacerating rage" (*Ages* 91). Yearning degenerates from history to the materiality of historicity as a generative physics of potentiation (indeed, individuation recapitulates compulsively, rhizomatically in *Ages*: potencies and particular natures are for themselves and imbricated with their others, as potentiation and creation spin and swirl through each other).

Jung also thinks the psyche geologically, but as a sedimentation of individuals, families, clans, nations, anthropological groupings, and primates through to an underlying "central fire" at the earth's core from which the previous strata derive, and which, like a dormant volcano, can erupt through these sedimentary layers to the surface (*Introduction* 142–43). Some have read this Jungian geohistory of the psyche as a "mystical geological vision," a turn to theosophical-emanationist "völkisch mysticism" casting analysis as a teleological journey toward the molten core of the personality (Noll 99ff). Yet the affinity between Jung's geological map and the disciplinary unfoldings of its Schellingian territory unworks any pretence to *telos* or terminable analysis; in this model the sedimentary rhythms of history are always vulnerable to eruption from, and disruption *by*, historicity's molten core. Indeed, reading Jung's geohistory through Schelling opens up a space for considering the historical psyche as the logical extension of a Romantic geohistory which, in Schelling's time, "turned out to be as contingent, as unrepeated, and as unpredictable (even in retrospect) as human history itself" (Rudwick 6). This contingency begins in the *Naturphilosophie* as Nature's ambivalence toward its own products – the Thanatopoietic drive of Romantic metasubjectivity which Jung later recasts as the ambitendency of Jungian libido. The 1815 *Ages*' cosmogony, through the dynamic of the three potencies, metaphysically dramatises Jungian individuation, which in turn retrofits *Ages*' outer limits of metaphysics with a therapeutics and mode of being in the world. But in order to understand how *Ages* conceives this dynamic, we must examine Schelling's *Potenzenlehre* in more detail.

The movement of the potencies

Writing the *Ages* drafts, Schelling both refers to a higher, "intimated" knowledge based on symbolic meaning *and* turns away from the symbolic *per se* to the theory of the three potencies [*Potenzenlehre*] that would figure in his later work on mythology (see Beach 36). These three potencies articulate the yearning of *Trieb* in *Ages* as nonmolar forces which, in a state of "irresolvable concatenation" with each other, define primordial being as contradiction (*Ages* 12), difference within unity always already bursting forth into Being as movement and yearning. As McGrath writes, they are predicated on a Böhmian distinction between a principle of dark, violent contraction and a principle of light, love, and expansion analogous to the *Freedom* essay's distinction between "Ground" and "Existence" (*Dark Ground* 45). As such, "contingency (not necessity, reason, or 'the notion') grounds the Schellingian dialectic. Although the movement from one potency to the other is logical, the whole sequence itself is not. [...] The contingency, anarchy, and spontaneity of the actualization of first potency undergirds the logical necessity of each of the successive potencies" (146). In a similar vein, Jung is the great psychologist of the *complexio oppositorum*, which informs both his exposition of the archetypes (in their "light"/"dark" aspects) and his thinking of libido as "ambitendency." But while Jung's individuation process is predicated upon this ambitendent conception of the archetypes, Schelling's *Potenzenlehre* thinks the dynamism of the potencies through a (meta)physics which narrates a cosmology of the archetypes, but also articulates the laws of expansion and contraction by which the tension of opposites manifests and unfolds. We will see that this (meta)physics also prefigures what Jung later psychologises as the transcendent function, the intersubjective unfolding of libido according to the same dynamic of potentiation.

Schelling begins *Ages*' work of yearning with the first potency (A^1), the negation from which all else comes:

> That God negates itself, restricts its being, and withdraws into itself, is the eternal force and might of God. In this manner, the negating force

is that which is singularly revealing of God. But the actual being of God is that which is concealed. The whole therefore stands as A that from the outside is B and hence, the whole = (A = B). (15)

Here, God's power is self-withdrawal and contraction. Harking back to the sex-hating Nature of the *First Outline*'s *Naturphilosophie*, this withdrawal is for-itself and antipathetic to prehension. But unlike the *Naturphilosophie*, the potencies of *Ages* now possess a psychology, existing in "rotatory motions" of contradiction, "loathing and anxiety [*Widerwärtigkeit und Angst*]" (32). In this sense, time and history are inaugurated by a *dissociative* act whereby the first potency must "dislocate [*sondern*] itself from itself in order to be, so to speak, its own complete being" (9). Yearning is the paradoxical uplifting through a "pulling downward" by eternal nature reverberating through the chain of potencies. Thus the second potency (A^2), as "Being to the second power," forms a "primordial antithesis" with A^1 which is not mutually exclusive but rather "an opposed relationship" (18). A^2 is thus "the savior and liberator of nature […] outside and above this nature and thereby comport[ing] to it as the spiritual comports to the corporeal; yet only as something spiritual to which nature is the next echelon and that is again capable of an immediate relationship to it" (34).

In his discussion of first nature (A^1), Schelling describes the primary decisionary movement whereby the break into the potencies is followed by new movement and "each subordinate potency attracts the potency immediately higher in it" (56). In this process each potency, realising its higher counterpart as that which it is capable of, attracts it through a "bewitching," numinous force: as A^2 is pulled down (bewitched) to A^1, A^3, as the posited unity of A^1 and A^2, becomes visible to itself as counter-projection in A^2 (59). In other words, A^1's involution, its being "inwardly posited" through its encounter with A^2 (35), leads to the evolution of A^3. A^3 is spirit in nature, an animating force which places the affirmative force of A^2 in a free relationship with the negating force of A^1 (36). A^3 is

that universal soul by which the cosmos is ensouled, the soul which through the immediate relationship to the Godhead is now levelheaded and in control of itself. It is the eternal link between nature and the spiritual world as well as between the world and God. It is the immediate tool through which alone God is active in nature and the spiritual world. (37)

But A^3 does not remain ascendant, for this movement, "having arrived at its peak [...] retreats back into its beginning" in an eternal return (*Ages* 19). Thus Schelling's *Potenzenlehre* articulates, on the level of cosmology, an interminable analysis where even God's "levelheadedness" is but a moment within this universal unfolding. Momentarily equalised between Nature and spirit, even God is inevitably deranged once again in the next moment and movement of potentiation. "Evolution presupposes involution" (83) as "from time to time, every physical and moral whole needs, for its preservation, the reduction to its innermost beginning" (xxxviii). *Telos* is supplanted by a rhythmic pulsation with no discernible beginning or end, but which nevertheless retains a promissory horizon of the new age to come, a purposive and *potentiated* way forward. Just as the highest comes into view only as potencies are pulled down towards eternal nature in the primordial antithesis, so the unconscious strives to express itself through both its lower (instinctual) *and* higher (spiritual) qualities in the "organic relationship" required between negating and affirming potencies (34). Where depth psychology limits Jung to speaking hypothetically from the standpoint of consciousness, *Ages'* (meta)physics invites us to imagine the obverse standpoint of God entering Being as the Negative through the incomprehensible primordial act, engendering time and the figural through which God can operate in Being (37). And yet even this distinction is an illusion, an elision: for Jungian analytical psychology and Schelling's *Potenzenlehre* can only hypothesise and narrate this abyss of the unconditional upon which the figural conscious rests.

Jung's collective unconscious, as primordial fluidity ("beginning," "end," and neither), flows through and encompasses this complex of opposites while being articulated by it through the eternal movement of ascension and descent that Schelling outlines in *Ages* (19). In this way, the primordial interplay of contracting unconscious and affirming conscious, of the Eternal No and Eternal Yes (A^1 and A^2), is recapitulated, through the bridge of the symbol, in (counter)transference, within which is replicated the dual (light/dark) aspect of the archetypes in the analyst-analysand encounter. Schelling's primordial antithesis and Jungian individuation thus converge as a self-organising pattern which repeats itself in different modalities in the eternal attempt to comprehend itself. As we shall see, the Self, as centripetal force of psychic self-organisation and paradoxical emblem of the "uncertainty relationship" between opposites in the necessary freedom of God (*Aion* 226), exists as the outer limit of the psychic archive. In the universe model we have seen, the archetypes, as ambitendent forces, constitute the outcome of the "self-lacerating rage" of spiritualised contradiction engendering matter as "individual and independent centres that, because they are also still held and driven by averse forces, likewise move about their own axes" (*Ages* 91). The 1815 *Ages*' shift in emphasis to a proto depth-psychological dynamic as an analogue for cosmic movements makes its discussion of questioning and answering beings, and its specific focus on Mesmerism and magnetic sleep, a crucial facet of *Ages*' crypto-psychology and its continuity with analytical psychology.

Ages' cosmogonic yearning begins in a drama of anamnesis and transference. The text's Introduction establishes the self-organisation of the universe as a "primordial life" produced by and through the confluence of freedom and necessity – a life which is "a nature in the most complete understanding of the word, just as the person is a nature regardless of freedom, nay, precisely because of it" (*Ages* xxxv). Indeed, to answer the question of how to bring about the "golden age" of truth and fable Schelling turns to a proto-Jungian analysis of the *individual*, who must catachrestically "*climb up* to the *beginning* of the ages" toward realising a principle "outside and above the world" contained within itself (xxxv–xxxvi). Here as in the *Freedom* essay, personality means something more than ego. In personality, an "unknowing and dark" principle containing the "archetype of things" as a rhizomatic "recollection of all things, of their original relationships, of their becoming, of their meaning" is bound to the "supramundane principle" of Being and the person (xxxvi).[7] *Ages* figures this lower principle's yearning as the "intimation and longing for knowledge" realised through questioning and answering beings in an allegorical countertransference:

> In the higher principle everything lies without differentiation and as one. But in the Other it can differentiate, express, and set apart what in it is one. Hence there is in the person that which must again be brought back to memory, and an Other that brings it to memory; one in which the answer to every research question lies and the Other which brings the answer out of it. This Other is free from everything and is capable of thinking everything, but it is bound by this innermost witness and cannot hold anything for true without the agreement of this witness. On the other hand, the innermost is originally bound and cannot unfurl itself; but through the Other it becomes free and

reveals itself to the same. Therefore, both yearn with equal intensity for the cision. [...] This cision, this doubling of ourselves, this secret circulation in which there are two beings, a questioning being and an answering being, an unknowing being that seeks knowledge and an unknowing being that does not know its knowledge, this silent dialogue, this inner art of conversation, is the authentic mystery of the philosopher. (xxxvi)

The "unity of unity and difference" which constitutes the absolute in Schelling's *Ages* is thus unfolded through the countertransference between consciousness (as "witness") and its unconscious Other. Put in Jungian terms, the productive unconscious, "free from everything and capable of thinking everything," needs the witness of consciousness to create knowledge in time and history as its eternal attempt at self-comprehension. In this witnessing, consciousness and the unconscious assume aspects of each other. But nevertheless, here the "silence" of this dialogue reflects its nature as a conversation in the *mind* of the philosopher, an interiorised conversation which is opened to a dangerous Outside in Mesmerism.

Unique to the 1815 *Ages* and fatal to the pervasive Idealism of former drafts (Rajan, "Abyss" para. 10 n. 10), Mesmerism,[8] and specifically the mesmeric *crisis* in the psychodynamic between hypnotist and hypnotised, is deployed by Schelling as an analogue of the primordial cision in Being leading to time and history, the very occasion for the "entrance of yearning into the eternal nature" (*Ages* 28–29). For Mesmer, *crisis* is an "illness," or division, an intermediate state of suspension "between wakefulness and perfect sleep" ("Dissertation by F.A. Mesmer" 124). This crisis was the goal of every hypnotism session, as "beneficial crises" had healing power ("Dissertation on the Discovery" 48). In the state of crisis, those hypnotised can "foresee the future and bring the most remote past into the present. Their senses can extend to any distance and in all directions, without being checked by any obstacles. In short, it seems that all Nature is present to them. Will itself is communicated to them apart from conventional means" (112) in a state analogous to both "NPS"'s "ecstatic" contact with the absolute subject and Jungian synchronicity. In *Ages*, Schelling sees mesmeric crisis as an intrapsychic *Potenzenlehre*: it awakens the "seed" of "soul-like essence" in the lower potency, whose "irresistible magic" (*Ages* 57) attracts the higher potency to it. Crisis begins individuation in Being, and Schelling specifically connects Nature's individuative crisis with the crisis seen in magnetic sleep (57), which is meant to remedy the "sick" condition of "interrupted guidance between the higher and lower principles" (69, 70).

However, by extending the dynamic of magnetic sleep to sleep in general Schelling goes further than Mesmer, and in fact moves significantly closer to the dissociationist model of the psyche. Schelling argues that while in waking life the human being is governed by an "externally binding unity" (*Ages* 68). But in sleep, the copular link which unifies these forces is severed, and "each force retreats back into itself and each tool now seems to be active for itself and in its own world. [...] [W]hile the whole is outwardly as if dead and inactive, inwardly the freest play and circulation of forces seems to unfold" (68). This free circulation of forces is analogous to psychological derangement; it is now coterminous with the primordial productivity of Nature, what in analytical psychology is the anarchy of the collective unconscious. It is the psyche's experience of the intellectual intuition repressed in the 1800 *System*. But this "most fully voluptuous inner unfolding of all forces" (67) does not amount to a full dissolution of the copula – indeed, without the unknown = X to express the unity of subject and predicate/object, existence would dissolve into a plenitude of forces with no means of binding them into knowledge – in a word, psychosis. There is instead a "voluntary sympathy" governing this free circulation of forces (67), but Schelling leaves the nature of this voluntarism unexplored.

Significantly, Schelling also delineates three degrees of "inner life" which are possible in magnetic sleep. In the first stage the soul, liberated from the "material of human nature," engages in "free circulation" with a salubrious, higher "spiritual being" (*Ages* 69). Schelling rather optimistically writes that in this first stage magnetic sleep always restores, "at least for awhile," the previously "interrupted guidance between the higher and the lower principles" (*Ages* 69, 70). But he also aligns the dissolution of the copula and the being-for-themselves of forces in crisis with precisely what the *Freedom* essay develops as sickness and evil. So with this dissolution of the copula

something terrible becomes manifest [previously] held down by the magic of life. And what was once an object of adoration or love becomes an object of fear and the most terrible abjection. For when the abysses of the human heart open up in evil and that terrible thought comes to the fore that should have been buried eternally in night and darkness, we first know what lies in the human in accordance with its possibility and how human nature, for itself or left to itself, is actually constituted. (*Ages* 48)

Thus *what restores balance and guidance also imperils the organism*, and this is also true of the "terrible thoughts" of the unconscious (Jung would say that dreams do not always "guide" but can also traumatise the conscious attitude). In other words, *Ages* recapitulates the dissociationist topography of forces and the cisionary *pharmakon* which confront the Nature of the *First Outline*, whose derangement of actantial forces ensures its purposive individuation while making its consummation impossible. In the second stage (the highest stage of magnetic sleep) this spiritual aspect of the person puts soul under analysis, drawing soul to it "in order to show it, as if in a mirror, the things hidden in the soul's interior and what lies still wrapped up in the soul itself (pertaining to what is future and eternal in the person)" (70). Schelling writes rather cryptically of the third and final stage, which lies "in the relationships that lie utterly outside customarily human relationships," that "it is better to be silent about them than to speak of them" (70).

While Jung recognises the importance of Mesmerism in the *historical* development of analytical psychology, this strictly historical concern leads him to see it as largely predicated on "suggestion" ("Fundamental Questions" para. 231; see also "Review of Waldstein" para. 797). However, Schelling's naturalisation and cosmologisation of magnetic sleep, through its relation to Nature's actantial dynamic and the *Potenzenlehre*, bring it much closer to analytical psychology's human *and* preterhuman dimensions. Seen in this light, the mesmeric principle forms the basis of the profoundly *transpersonal* aspect of Jungian countertransference, which Andrew Samuels describes as an "intensity of relational energy" greater than a merely intersubjective relationship – indeed, akin to a "simulacrum or reprise of a relation to the divine" (193). This countertransference articulates psychologically what Schelling calls those "unusual states" in which "the power is bestowed upon one person in relation to another such that the one has an unleashing and liberating effect on the other" (*Ages* 68), and yet it also gestures toward Mesmerism's third degree, the nonhuman dimension of which Schelling declines to speak. This preterhumanity takes the form of an excess which Deleuze later takes up in a Jungian tenor as the productive unconscious, where the question of Being has a persistent power which "always comes from somewhere else than the answers":

> Problems and questions thus belong to the unconscious, but as a result the unconscious is differential and iterative by nature; it is serial, problematic and questioning. […] It concerns problems and questions which can never be reduced to the great oppositions or the overall effects that are felt in consciousness. (*DR* 107–8)

As the embodied subject of an immanence and drive to transformation – "an attempt to locate, within an overarching system or structure, those points from or axes along which the system or structure can be transformed" (Mitchell and Broglio para. 1) – the Romantic metasubject is dramatised by the interplay of the *Freedom* essay and *Ages* as questioning and answering textual beings in Schelling's oeuvre, two texts which respond in different ways to the research question of the absolute subject which pervades Schelling's thought. Schelling's concern with this selfhood inevitably turns to *affect* – anxiety as "the governing affect that corresponds to the conflict of directions in Being" (*Ages* 101) and the melancholy which suffuses Being in the *Freedom* essay. In turn analytical psychology, as a counter-science of affect and experience, casts as therapeutic dynamic the dialectic between questioning and answering beings and the self-*centrum* rhythm which marks the individuation of Romantic metasubjectivity. But in translating these dynamisms into the analyst-analysand encounter, analytical psychology offers no more guarantees than Schelling's philosophy that personality will remain free from the irruption of the *Ungrund* or the destructive misrelation to Nature's derangement.

Jung, individuation and the self

As a text which never got past the past (so to speak) in its interdisciplinary account of the ages of the world, *Ages*' protopsychology questions itself in a textual anxiety and disavowal, but without finding a voice to proclaim its future, which remains spectral and promissory. So as a text whose "reversion to the beginnings of the world also puts under erasure its own originary moment" (Rajan, "Abyss" para. 1), *Ages* would seem to corroborate the death drive and interminable nostalgia of what would become psychoanalysis. But within the "primordial antithesis" of the first two potencies there is also "the structure for a future, inner unity in which each potency comes out for itself" (*Ages* 18). Indeed, one can read *Ages* as a crucial stage in an individuative *Erzeugungsdialektik* inhering in Schelling's oeuvre. Rajan observes that by putting other disciplines under analysis and constellating them around geohistory as a new discipline, *Ages* articulates "a countertransference wherein the earth's sedimented strata and the body's pathological interior and secret heredity summon man to a knowledge of history's unconscious" ("The Abyss of the Past" para. 5); in this sense *Ages* wants to move forward purposively, in a movement where previous forces (history, ontology, "the science of right") are "not sublimated but abiding" (*Ages* 17). But *Ages*' decentred unity in which "each potency comes out for itself" lacks a voice to answer (to) its own speculative methodology. The person *is* the world "writ small" (*Ages* 3), but while it gestures toward psychology with magnetic sleep *Ages* does not have the psychological tenor of the later mythology lectures, where mythology emerges as a way of working through a primordial crisis of mythological consciousness. In *Ages*, the purposive individuation process of Romantic metasubjectivity is still largely cosmological; it remains for analytical psychology to cast the cosmological forces of *Ages*, and the self-*centrum* drama of the *Freedom* essay, as a distinctly human encounter. And this encounter is one in which the preterhuman, cosmological dimensions of Schelling's thought are not sublimated but abide in a psyche with the fluidity of the Nature it engages (this profoundly Romantic fluidity between human and preterhuman will also inform the final chapter's discussion of Romantic poetry). With this in mind, we shall first briefly revisit Jung's formulation of individuation in order to amplify it in dialogue with its core concepts of inflation and the transcendent function which, I argue, therapeutise the *Freedom* essay's self-*centrum* drama and *Ages'* *Potenzenlehre* respectively. I conclude with some detailed discussion of Jung's concept of the Self, his version of Schelling's absolute subject and the empty centre toward which individuative *Trieb* strives.

Writing in 1921, some 25 years before his crucial turn in thinking about the archetypes, Jung describes individuation as "the process of formation [*Bildung*] and particularisation of individuals, especially the psychological individual as something distinct from the general, collective psychology. Thus individuation is a process of differentiation whose goal is the development of the individual personality" in a dialectic of production between individual and collective ("Definitions" pars. 757; trans. mod). Jung describes individuation in terms of a paradox he elsewhere reserves for the archetype, as "the *a priori* existence of potential wholeness [...] as if something already existent were being put together" ("The Psychology of the Child Archetype" para. 278). In the Introduction, we saw Jung describe individuation as a paradoxical "building up of the particular" which is "already ingrained in the psychic constitution" ("Definitions" para. 761). But we have seen that Jung's psyche is ultimately definable only in terms of a fluidity which un-defines and dissociates it into nodal points of intensity, aligned and entwined with the derangement of Schelling's Nature, traumatic *historicity* in its specifically Romantic sense, the grammatology of Being which underwrites all attempts at *history*. In *Ages*, individuation is the "highest science" of the person as the living being within knowledge, a movement toward the confluence of truth and fable. Thus, the individual's libidinal gradient can never be reduced to the *Stufenfolge* of Jung's therapeutics of presence; it is eventually blocked by involutive turns which reflect the primordial difference within Nature. Jung often describes individuation optimistically in terms of wholeness, but this blockage is always imperilling; the cuts and breaks of caesurae always risk infection. Indeed, this blockage is figured in the *Freedom* essay as evil's "turgor, turgescence, tumescence, the swelling that comes from the isolation of the part from the general economy of forces" (Wirth, *Conspiracy* 170).

Jung figures this tumescence in remarkably similar terms as the *inflation* of the personality: in inflation, the ego is overwhelmed by archetypal forces in an "identification with the collective psyche" (*The Relations* para. 260) as it attempts to assume control over the entire personality, which typically leads to the destructive identification with a single archetypal force or symbol. "In such a state one fills a space which normally one cannot fill. One can only do this by appropriating to oneself contents and qualities which exist for themselves alone and should be considered outside our bounds" (*The Relations* para. 227; trans. mod). Inflation is psychic cancer – archetypal life that grows out of control and pushes an always already precarious ego further away from equilibrium in a "weakening of consciousness" (Jung, *A Study* para. 621). Put in Schellingian terms, the person is overwhelmed by the *Ungrund*. When this happens,

the more forceful and accordingly the more dangerous become the unconscious contents that are struggling to restore the balance. This leads ultimately to a dissociation: on the one hand, ego-consciousness makes convulsive efforts to shake off an invisible opponent [...] while on the other hand it increasingly falls victim to the tyrannical will [...] which displays all the characteristics of a daemonic subman and superman combined. (Jung, *The Psychology of the Transference* para. 394)

Jung's classic example of inflation is Adolf Hitler who, as a prophetic "medicine man" ("Diagnosing the Dictators" 115), was inflated by the God archetype in the form of his "Voice." "His Voice is nothing other than his own unconscious, into which the German people have projected their own selves; that is, the unconscious of 78 million Germans" ("Diagnosing the Dictators" 119–20). "Hitler has sacrificed his individuality, or else does not possess one in any real sense, to this almost complete subordination to collective unconscious forces" ("Jung Diagnoses the Dictators" 139).

In a word, inflation is psychosis: and in a statement strikingly similar to Schelling's critique of the Cartesian *cogito*, Jung writes that in this state "*he* no longer thinks and speaks, but *it* thinks and speaks within him. He hears voices" (*The Relations* para. 229).[9] Inflation is, at bottom, the foolhardy attempt of consciousness to close the gap separating mind and Nature, to appropriate for the ego the deranging powers of Nature opened to the individual in magnetic crisis. But just as in the *Freedom* essay man neither can nor should attain an impossible homology with God, so ego can never attain Self, can never reign like Jupiter over an infinite pantheon of archetypal energies. No drive can ever be fully realised. Yet even this is beside the point; thoughts have *us*, Jung writes, with some necessary inhibition from a healthy consciousness. We are in no small way lived *by* personality, but it is evil, as the power of the *Ungrund* in Nature (*Freedom* 44), which powers the inscrutable rhythms by which we move toward and away from the *centrum*. And just as evil is necessary for Schellingian individuation, for Jung the risk of inflation is *necessary* for the individuation process, a by-product of the work of analysis (*The Relations* para. 243). Inflation, then, is a caesura in the rhythm of individuation, a tumescent blockage which can catalyse either compensation or destruction – the vantage point of Krell's "protracted instant" which offers a fleeting glimpse of the whole that can either enlighten or overwhelm.

Thus freedom, necessity, and evil are inseparable in the *pharmakon* unfolding of Romantic metasubjectivity, in which individuation is powered by its "failure." But how is one to "treat" this melancholic existence? How does one "individuate through" it, so to speak? In the *Freedom* essay, humanity's perennial propensity to do evil by appropriating the ground is powered by self-will, which in turn catalyses the "will of love" (47), a process which ultimately "consists in the reconstruction of the relation of the periphery to the *centrum*" (34–35), the projected restoration of Jung's point of equilibrium. Jung more specifically develops a potential antidote as the transcendent function, which harks back to Schelling's suggestive remarks on magnetic sleep's point of contact with the "free circulation of forces." Yet where magnetic sleep treats the inner life of the individual in a somnambulist state, the transcendent function marks a potentiated encounter between analyst and analysand as Jungian questioning and answering beings, but energised in ways which surpass Jung's efforts to contain these energies in the therapeutic dynamic.

For Jung, the transcendent function is a product of the counter-transferential dynamic of the analytic encounter; it addresses the question of the proper "mental-moral attitude [*geistig-moralische Einstellung*]" to adopt toward the manifestation of unconscious material to the analysand ("The Transcendent Function" para. 144; trans. mod). The transcendent function marks the convergence of two positions in a third position or state of awareness:

> The to and fro of arguments and affects represents the transcendent function of opposites. The confrontation intrinsic to this position [*die Gegenüberstellung der Position*] denotes an energetic tension which generates living things, a third which is not a logical stillbirth [...] but a movement out of the suspension between opposites, a living birth which brings about a new stage of being, a new situation. The transcendent function manifests itself as *a quality of approximated opposites.* (para. 189; trans. mod.; my italics)

This third thing, this "new level of being" created by consciousness and the unconscious as questioning and answering beings, comes to be through a dialectic between analyst and analysand as conspirators in a rhythm of "approximation [*Angleichung*] and differentiation [*Unterscheidung*]" (Jung, "Foreword to Michael Fordham" para. 1172). The energic tension in such a moment constellates conscious and unconscious in conditions much like those of a synchronistic experience (although not every meaningful event is accompanied by ecstatic awareness or synchronistic occurrences like Jung's account of the scarab beetle) to provide a theoretical blueprint for the intensive variation of intellectual apprehension of new attitudes synthesising conscious and unconscious energies. Jung's essay casts the analyst-analysand relationship in terms similar to that of Schelling's "higher principle" (as second potency or A^2) guiding the soul emerging from consciousness (*Ages* 59), or a waking equivalent of the "guidance" restored in the first stage of magnetic sleep outlined by Schelling. However, Jung is ultimately ambivalent about the dynamics which (un) ground the transcendent function. On the one hand, he wants to contain the transcendent function within the analysand, so to speak; the analyst "mediates the transcendent function for the patient [to] help bring conscious and unconscious together and so arrive at a new attitude" as part of managing the analysand's transference on to the analyst ("The Transcendent Function" para. 146). But on the other hand, Jung elsewhere writes of the productive and unpredictable aspects of countertransference: "For two personalities to meet is like mixing two different chemical substances: *if there is any combination at all, both are transformed*" ("Problems of Modern Psychotherapy" para. 163; my italics).

There is, then, a risk of *contagion* in the analytic scene of the transcendent function, where both analyst and analysand are dissociative matrices of archetypal forces and nodal intensities. With the transcendent function, Jung may ultimately desire what Rodolphe Gasché calls an ethics of *Auseinandersetzung* ["confrontation"], a situation in which "the critic comes face to face in a direct confrontation with the thought of an Other" in which "real and concrete issues come to word, while the debate itself mobilizes energies that themselves testify to the urgency [...] of the problems in question" ("Toward an Ethics" 315). However, this scene is fundamentally the site of a rhizomatic convergence wherein, exchanging insights and ideas on the conscious level, each also affects the other's unconscious and any number of connections and counter-transferences[10] between forces can be made. Thus on one level, the analyst can "guide" the analysand to greater awareness, but beyond this rubric of "higher guidance" the counter-transferential encounter activates a fluidity whose ripples can be neither anticipated nor measured. Analyst and analysand can project on to each other in imperceptible ways; both can be transformed (for better or worse). Indeed, seen through the lens of Schelling's copular logic, the transcendent function's particular energic charge consists in the awareness of *both* analyst and analysand as *predicates* before the absolute subject, which manifests here as knowledge of a new state or configuration of experience which travels through analyst and analysand without originating in either. This is why Jung insists that this function's "transcendence" is not the apprehension of a sublated ideality but instead denotes *"the transition from one attitude to another organically,* that is, without loss of the unconscious" ("The Transcendent Function" para. 145; trans. mod.; my italics). In other words, the transcendent function marks the copula of Being through a libidinal economy where the unconscious is not depotentiated with new conscious awareness. Yet this persistent unconscious valency not only resists the orthodox Freudian psychoanalytic project of depotentiating the unconscious in service to consciousness; it also constitutes a contagious excess which permeates and imperils the Jungian analytic encounter.

Ages' Potenzenlehre is nothing less than a cosmological parable for the transcendent function, which reciprocates its dynamism on the level of the psyche. Let us recall the work of yearning in the movement of the potencies: in the eternal moment of creation, the expansive potency (A^2) is "bewitched" and pulled down to the first, contractive principle (A^1) because A^1 sees its futurity in A^2, something it is capable of. This process makes A^3 visible as spirit in nature, the freedom underwriting A^1's relationship with A^2. In the orthodox counter-transferential dynamic of the analytic scene, the analysand projects their unconscious content on to the analyst; the analysand, as A^1, confronts the analyst's psyche (A^2), "bewitching" it, pulling its archetypal material to itself. Schelling writes in *Ages* that the first potency's "self-lacerating madness," which is now "innermost in all things" as the eternal beginning of Being, must be "verified by the light of a higher intellect" (103). That is, the unconscious material needs consciousness to witness and express it in the exchange, and thus it is here that A^3, the force of the Self as freedom, can manifest, can touch and not touch consciousness, opening up opportunities for a new attitude and new knowledge – a recapitulation of this eternal beginning of Being *in* Being. But the third thing created from this free flow is, like Schelling's A^3, re-implicated in eternal unfolding in an individuation process without guarantees. Because there is no loss of unconscious valency, the third thing's non-rational nature drives the process forward as an undecidable force.

Yet "The Transcendent Function" harbours an indeterminacy at its textual core which recapitulates Jung's problematic attempts to contain counter-transferential contagion in the analyst-analysand encounter, and thus troubles the essay's capacity as a manual for the analysand's "guidance."

The middle of Jung's essay (pars. 166–75) is occupied by a detailed discussion of *active imagination*: a therapeutic method of stimulating fantasy production in the analysand in order to articulate the affectivity of the present emotional state as the "beginning" of the transcendent function (para. 167). Jung would later write that active imagination is in fact the transcendent function's theoretical core, "the indispensable second part of any analysis that is really meant to go to the roots" (letter to Mr. O., 2 May 1947, 459). In the state of active imagination, the analysand "must make himself as conscious as possible" of the current emotional state and record "fantasies" and "associations" which manifest: "Fantasy must be allowed the freest possible play, yet not in such a manner that it leaves the orbit of its object, namely the affect" (para. 167). From this comes "a more or less complete expression of the mood" or, more precisely, "a picture of the contents and tendencies of the unconscious that were contained together in globo" in the crisis (para. 167; trans. mod). Jung positions active imagination contrary to (Freudian) free association, which for him "leads away from the object to all sorts of complexes, and one can never be sure that they relate to the affect" (para. 167).

However, in outlining the procedure for the analysand's practice of active imagination, Jung takes up a Cartesian boundary between the mind and its object:

> Contemplate [the object] and carefully observe how the picture begins to unfold or to change. Don't try to make it into something, just do nothing but observe what its spontaneous changes are. Any mental picture you contemplate in this way will sooner or later change through a spontaneous association that causes a slight alteration of the picture. You must carefully avoid impatient jumping from one subject to another. Hold fast to the one image you have chosen and wait until it changes by itself. Note all these changes and eventually step into the picture yourself, and if it is a speaking figure at all then say what you have to say to that figure and listen to what he or she has to say. (letter to Mr. O., 2 May 1947, 460)

As the transcendent function's core, active imagination in fact recapitulates the transcendent function's analytic scene on the level of the individual psyche. Here the analysand assumes the role of "guide" to their own unconscious material, observing and scrutinising changes which *ostensibly* occur in the object as it changes "by itself." Indeed, the other appellation Jung gives to this process – "confrontation [*Auseinandersetzung*] with the unconscious" (letter to Mr. O., 30 April 1947, 459) – depends on this distinction. The ability to decide when to "step into the picture yourself" presumes a conscious control which resonates with the synchronicity experiment, in which the scientific observer demands answers from Nature. But the assumption that one can differentiate between changes in the object and changes created by consciousness is profoundly troubled by the Jungian psyche's intractable fluidity, its affinity with Schelling's deranged Nature. How does one know a train of associations leads *away* from the object unless (in Schellingian terms) one follows it "the particular wherever it might lead, regardless of its consistency with a larger whole" (Rajan, "First Outline" 315) so as to *intuit* that "whole"? Indeed, in spite of the tacit attempt to sublate this dilemma into a revelation of the object or affect, Jung duly notes the dangers this fluidity poses to not only the self-analytic experiment, but also the analysand in the form of psychosis (*Mysterium* 530–31). For active imagination is an encounter with archetypal forces, "images [which] have a life of their own and [...] symbolic events [which] develop according to their own logic" (*Tavistock* para. 397).

Ultimately, the untameable fluidity and contagion of the Jungian psyche is precisely what imperils the dialogic aspect of both the transcendent function and active imagination – that is, their *Auseinandersetzung* as a structured debate or dispute in which each side is given its due. Via Heidegger, Gasché takes up Nietzsche's understanding of *Auseinandersetzung* as "true philosophy," as "that which, in a thinker's thought, [...] obeys the law of thinking, thinking's own law" ("Toward an Ethics" 316). Jung attempts this *Auseinandersetzung* as psychology. But while the intersubjectivity of the transcendent function may make it more manageable, the Schellingian derangement intrinsic to active imagination effectively deconstructs this *Auseinandersetzung* and the ethics generated by the binding distance required to hold each side in place relative to the other and do justice to their particularities (317). If *Auseinandersetzung* marks what in thought is intrinsic to "thinking's own law" (316), what happens when these very "laws" collapse thinking into its Other (which is implied by Schelling's early equation of reason with the processes of Nature [*FO* 195])? When this "confrontation" becomes conflagration? All the more striking that Jung equated the teleology of alchemy with active imagination (*Mysterium* 526) when active imagination clearly has the potential to derange teleology.

Thus, *Auseinandersetzung* transpires on the shaky ground of Hölderlin's incalculable law, as that which can alter or annul the arbitrary contract between conscious and unconscious at any time. Here is where analytical psychology perhaps draws closest to Deleuze's transcendental-empirical "science of the sensible," an ontoaesthetics predicated on the sensing of difference, an acknowledgement of the elusive proximity of mind and Nature and the disruption of the Kantian faculties by sense:

> Empiricism truly becomes transcendental [...] only when we apprehend directly in the sensible that which can only be sensed, the very being *of* the sensible: difference, potential difference and difference in intensity as the reason behind qualitative diversity. [Transcendental empiricism's object is] the intense world of differences, in which we find the reason behind qualities and the being of the sensible [...] precisely the object of a superior empiricism. This empiricism teaches us a strange 'reason', that of the multiple, chaos and difference (nomadic distributions, crowned anarchies). (*DR* 56–57)

Deleuze's strange "reason" resists the dialectical ordering of Being along the lines of a logical endpoint of absolute knowledge; it marks the emergence of ideas from experience rather than Kantian categories. Similarly, the transcendent function apprehends the moment of system's declension from the datum of sense, a remembering and repeating of the moment where infinite productivity is conjugated into form. The "living tension of the universe" (Wirth, "Translator's Introduction" xxiii), inaugurated by Schelling's primary cision and recapitulated in the dynamic between questioning and answering beings in magnetic sleep, takes human form in a metapsychology allowing for the creation of new inflections of this tension in what Deleuze calls a reason of "the multiple, chaos and difference" (*DR* 57). Indeed, the specific energy and event of "transcendence," and its revelation of a sylleptic third, allow us to narrate the ineffable self-creation of the archetypes *themselves* as magnetised particles of creation, conjugations of Schelling's contractive (A^1) and expansive (A^2) potencies. To use Schelling's *Naturphilosophische* language: the archetype's "free transformation" drives it to repeat its own nature, its own pattern and potential, but at the same time it must expand in "universal prehension," entangling itself with other archetypes to form the rhizomatic fabric of Being. But it remains for us to examine the horizon of futurity which inheres in this matrix; the goal toward which this movement is driven – the Jungian Self.

It is not by accident that the copular bond returns in *Ages* as *character*, the emblem of personality which is not chosen but rather *happens* to one as the subject constellating all future predicates. Just as the X that is both "ball" and "blue" enables us to say "the ball is blue" without logical contradiction, so character is that which can be both "good" and "evil" without strictly being either (*Ages* 8–9). It thus assumes the role held by personality as the "nonthingly center" of the *centrum* in the *Freedom* essay (Wirth, *Conspiracy* 170), and in "NPS" this is, of course, the absolute subject. Analytical psychology conceives of this purposive organisational force as individuation's drive of "endless approximation" toward the "empty centre" of the Self. Jung writes:

> The goal of this approximation seems to be anticipated by archetypal symbols which represent something like the circumambulation of a centre. With increasing approximation to the centre there is a corresponding depotentiation of the ego in favour of the influence of the "empty" centre, which is certainly not identical with the archetype but what the archetype points to. [...] One can describe the "emptiness" of the centre as "God." Emptiness in this sense doesn't mean "lack" or "absence," but something unknowable of the highest intensity. If I call this unknowable the "self," [I have given] the effects of the unknowable [an] aggregate name, but without prejudicing its contents. [...] The self is therefore a *limit concept* [*Grenzbegriff*] by no means reducible to known psychic processes. (letter to Pastor Walter Bernet, 13 June 1955, 258; trans. mod.)[11]

Jung often associates the experience of the Self with an ultimately affirming process of centring, an affect-laden experience of "the timelessness of the unconscious which expresses itself in a feeling of eternity or immortality" (*Psychology of the Transference* para. 531). But we have seen that the depotentiation of the ego which attends the sublime experience of the Self is precisely the danger of the dissociationist psyche as inflation or Schelling's impossible homology between man and God – here, an identification with the Self as "God-image" ("A Psychological Approach" para. 231). And we have also seen that Jung elsewhere acknowledges the profound ambivalence of archetypal experience, and particularly the experience of the Self, of which only "antinomial statements" are possible (*Transformation Symbolism* pars. 399 n). The experience of Self thus points to a very real psychological peril that Jung occasionally (and perhaps grudgingly) accepts: sometimes individuation can "lead to a fatal outcome (predominance of destructive tendencies!), for example suicide or other abnormal acts 'predetermined' in the life plan of certain burdened individuals" ("On the Nature of Dreams" para. 547; trans. mod). Jung insists that in psychological reality "a proposition can only lay claim to significance if the obverse of its meaning can also be accepted as valid" ("Fundamental Questions" para. 236; trans. mod.), and this problematises an implicitly moral *telos* which assumes that such experiences are always positive. The "Janus-faced" aspect of the unconscious and the possibility of inflation mean that wrong advice can be given and right advice can be ignored; a Self-experience can come to the "wrong" person at the "wrong" time and result in death or catastrophe. One cannot calculate the incalculable law by which caesurae irrupt within the indiscernible rhythm of an individuative line of flight.

For Jung, the Self is a "virtual nucleus" (*Introduction* 129) reflecting personality's inscrutable emergence from the always already divided *Ungrund* of the Schelling of the *Freedom* essay and *Ages*, the God-and-not-God of the primordial cision. Indeed, just as *Trieb* desires itself, the Jungian Self figures the absolute subject, the pre-existent marker of personality, the badge of self-desire worn by Schelling's God. Like the archetypes it constellates, the Self's yearning to articulate itself means that it unfolds in time and history, in the grammatology of Being:

> The ego stands to the Self as sufferer [patiens] to agent [agens] or object to subject, because the determinations which emanate from the Self are extensive and therefore superior to the ego. Like the unconscious, the Self is an a priori existent from which the ego develops. It preforms the ego, so to speak. *I do not create myself, rather I happen to myself.* [But] an absolutely preformed consciousness and a totally dependent ego would be a futile spectacle, as everything would run just as well or even better unconsciously. The existence of ego-consciousness only has meaning if it is free and autonomous. (*Transformation Symbolism* para. 391; trans. mod.)

The "prefiguration," in freedom, of personality is the closest Jung gets to the paradox of system and freedom Schelling so painstakingly elaborates in the *Freedom* essay. But Jung also writes that the Self offers a provisional and paradoxical completion of the subject as its objective Other: it "*is felt empirically not as subject but as object*, and this by reason of its unconscious component, which can only come to consciousness indirectly, by way of projection. Because of its unconscious component [the Self] can only be partially expressed by human figures; the other part of it has to be expressed by objective, abstract symbols" ("The Psychological Aspects" para. 315). The Self *is* not Jesus; it *is* not Buddha, nor *is* it Mohammed, the Virgin Mary, or the Lamb of God. It is nothing in particular, but can be anything.

Jung's late thinking on the Self marks a final break with teleology. He writes of the Self shortly before his death in 1961:

> So far I have found no fixed or precisely determined center in the unconscious, and I do not believe such a thing exists. What I call the Self is a hypothetical center, equidistant from the ego and the unconscious. It probably corresponds to the most comprehensive natural expression of individuality in its state of fulfillment or totality. Like Nature, so man strives to express himself, and *the self fulfils this dream of wholeness*. It is therefore a purely ideal center, something created. ("Talks with Miguel Serrano: 1959" 394, trans. mod.; my italics)

In Schellingian terms, the Self is the equivalent of Nature returned to primordial stasis by paradoxically having created and travelled through all of its possible derangements. It is derangement at rest, having reached its "most comprehensive natural expression" – in a word, indifference. But like God's "level-headedness" in *Ages*, even this indifference is only a hypothetical moment, for as an equidistant point between an unconscious without beginning and a consciousness which can never fully know itself, the Self remains subject to the fluctuation of its poles. Indeed, Jung's late thinking on the ultimate goal of individuation radically *potentiates* it as a *complexio oppositorum* (*Answer to Job* para. 716), a magnetic constellation of energies evocative of the *Potenzenlehre* and the work of yearning in *Ages*. And in 1958 Jung goes even further to define the Self's most comprehensive expression as nothing less than "the whole range of psychic phenomena in man" ("Definitions" para. 789), a dissociative matrix of energic centres reminiscent of Schelling's description of celestial bodies in the construction of the cosmos (*Ages* 89ff). Archetypal energies now orbit a centripetal force which is itself imbricated and implicated in a matrix of nodal points. The Romantic metasubject, the "Self of one's self," *is* the plenitude, the excess of Being.

If the Self is "the whole range of psychic phenomena in man," and psyche is coterminous with Nature in all its derangement, then the intellectual partnership between Schelling's philosophy and Jung's psychology which articulates the *Trieb* of Romantic metasubjectivity reaches beyond the purview of the strictly human. And unlike Hegel, who conceives individuation as the immanent unfolding of absolute spirit in human history, or Freud, who sees individual development as a project of mastering the unconscious, neither Schelling nor Jung ultimately conceived individuation as exclusively focused on the human being. Schelling's copular logic is worth invoking here once again for its expression in the logic of the Jungian symbol. Jung's conception of the archetypal symbol is the vehicle of an aesthetics that surpasses the confines of Schelling's 1800 *System*, which represented the aesthetic as a series of idealist "odysseys of the spirit." This copular dynamic is expressed in the therapeutic encounter through the archetype's metaphoricity – its necessary embodiment in symbols and situations that gesture toward an excess within its own representation:

> An archetypal content always states itself first and foremost as a linguistic simile [*sprachliches Gleichnis*]. If it speaks of the sun and identifies it with the lion, the king, the dragon-guarded treasure or the life and health of man, it is neither the one nor the other but instead the unknown third, which is more or less adequately expressed in all these similes but which – and this will always offend the intellect – remains unknown and informulable. ("The Psychology of the Child Archetype" para. 267; trans. mod.)

A living symbol, then, contains an intensity which is expressed through a metonymy of predicates which can never reach the archetype's "unknown third," the energic continuum which flows through it. In the final chapter, we examine the workings of this metaphoricity in the Romantic poetry of Wordsworth and Shelley; although *The Prelude* and *Prometheus Unbound* ostensibly work within the domain of the human, we shall see that they also invoke the same fluidity which marks the individuative *Trieb* of Romantic metasubjectivity and the preterhuman domain through which it unfolds.

Notes

1. Love and Schmidt in the *Freedom* essay, and Wirth in *Ages*, translate *Sehnsucht* as "yearning." But *Sehnsucht* can also mean "craving," which arguably does more justice to the agitation, restlessness, and forward desire in both texts. Of course, in translation there is so often no one correct answer; both meanings bring out crucial aspects of Schelling's work which should be considered in tandem.
2. For more on the concept of personality developed in the *Freedom* essay, see Appendix A, "Disentangling Romantic Metasubjectivity."
3. For Schelling's critique of Hegel in his own words, see *On the History* 142–43.
4. *Gefälle* is a crucial Jungian concept whose full import is somewhat obfuscated in the English *Collected Works*. *Gefälle* typically means "gradient," "incline," "decline," or slope," but it also means "difference" as a difference in degree to which something rises or falls. In English, "gradient" can be defined more abstractly as "a continuous increase or decrease in the magnitude of any quantity or property along a line from one point to another" (*OED* 2a), which is much closer to Jung's formulation of libido, and *Gefälle* should be read in this light. Hull translates *Gefälle* variously as "slope" ("On Psychic Energy" para. 91), "pull"/"flow" (*The Psychology* pars. 423, 467), "current" (*Psychological Types* 249), and "potential" (*Answer to Job* para. 665 and throughout *Psychological Types*). The latter two definitions come closest to Jung's intent but do not fully capture Jungian libido's intensive differential. Significantly, Jung also equates *Gefälle* with *Drang*, "compulsion": while the unconscious resists becoming conscious, "it must also be emphasized that it has a kind of inclination [*Gefälle*] towards consciousness, which is to say a compulsion [*Drang*] to become conscious" (*A Study* para. 545 n. 55; trans. mod).
5. At the end of the eighteenth century Schelling, Hegel, and Hölderlin were all students (and roommates) in the Tübingen *Stift*, a theological seminary for gifted and/or prestigious students. Franz Nauen notes their close collaboration (VII), which led to the "Oldest System Programme of German Idealism" (1796). Adler and Louth write that they all shared a preoccupation with tragedy, particularly its "dialectic structure" and "the great, indeed religious, significance located in the tragic action," but that "both in philosophical reach and poetic conviction Hölderlin's thoughts go beyond anything in the work of his peers, and it is generally accepted that his thinking had a considerable influence on the others' " in their collaboration (xlv). Bowie suggests that Hölderlin's important critique of Fichtean subjectivism became the core of Schelling's critique of Hegel ("Translator's Introduction" 7), so Hölderlin quite possibly helped effectuate Schelling's transition from the strictly aesthetic thinking of tragedy in the *Philosophical Letters* (commonly understood as addressed to Hölderlin) to the *Freedom* essay's darker thinking on tragedy.
6. The compulsive nature of Schelling's attempts is made clearer by Horst Fuhrmans' 1944 discovery of 12 variants of the first book of *Ages* in the University of

Munich library cellar. Sadly, these drafts were lost when the Allies bombed Munich, destroying the library (Wirth, "Translator's Introduction" vii).

7. Schelling's use of "archetype" at times differs radically from Jung's. In the *Freedom* essay Schelling uses the term in a preformationist sense, referring to "the archetypical [*urbildlich*] and divine man who was with God in the beginning and in whom all other things and man himself are created" (44). He later argues that although the anarchy of the *Ungrund* suggests an infinity of possible worlds, "by no means is this [infinity] to be thought as if there were no archetype [*Urtypus*] in the ground containing the only possible world according to God's essence. [...] In the divine understanding itself, however, as in primeval [*uranfänglich*] wisdom in which God realizes himself ideally or as archetype [*urbildlich*], there is only one possible world as there is only one God" (62). In *Ages* the term is more ambivalent: in the present passage, the "archetype [*Ur-Bild*] of things" seems to cast archetype once again in a preformationist role. But later, archetypes, as "ideas," become something more aleatory, "precisely ideas in that they are something eternally becoming and in incessant movement and generation" (66–67). In *Ages*, then, the archetype is the domain of all knowledge, but as the following passage indicates, these ideas must also be brought up by the higher principle; in short, they must be *witnessed*.

8. Anton Mesmer (1734–1815) was a German physician who postulated an energic transference between organic and inorganic objects. On Mesmerism's role in the evolution of nineteenth-century dissociationist notions of the psyche leading forward to analytical psychology, see Faflak 38, 53, and Fulford 65.

9. This dissociative state recalls David Fincher's film *Fight Club* (1999), which can be read as a case study of the dissociationist psyche. In the derelict house on Paper Street, Jack discovers articles written in the first person from the perspective of organs aware enough to seriously consider striving to be for themselves: "Jack's *medulla oblongata*," "Jill's nipples," "Jack's colon," etc.

10. Jung's ambivalence regarding transference can be seen in the fourth *Tavistock Lecture*: transference here is "a priori," yet can and should be dissolved because it "is always a hindrance, never an advantage. You cure in spite of the transference, not because of it" (pars. 315, 349). But just as "we do not need transference just as we do not need projection," in the same breath Jung asserts that archetypal images "have to be projected, otherwise they inundate consciousness" (pars. 351, 361). We may chide Jung for remaining in a somewhat stagnant complex of opposites (here a stark tension between the "aetiology" and the "therapy" of the transference [pars. 328, 357]), but Jung nevertheless points to the rhythm of archetypal projection and recollection rendered more fluidly in Schelling. Jung's later *On the Psychology of the Transference* (1946) offers a more thoughtful and mitigated account. Warren Steinberg offers a useful (if somewhat psychologising) account of Jung's evolving thought on transference (29ff).

11. For a more detailed discussion of the relationship between Self and archetype see Appendix C, "Self and Archetype."

Chapter 5

Romantic myth-subjectivity
Wordsworth and Shelley

This chapter examines how the experience of Romantic metasubjectivity and its purposive model of individuation operate within the libidinal matrix of Romantic thought and poetry. More specifically, it explores the ways in which Romantic metasubjectivity amplifies Romanticism's focus on mythology through the existential imperative of both Schelling's positive philosophy and analytical psychology's focus on experience. For both Schelling and Jung, mythology conceptualises the potentiated, libidinal forces of Being; that is, mythology articulates the grammatology of Being in which Romantic metasubjectivity unfolds. This "mythology" is not simply a structuralist pantheon of, say, Christian or Greek origin, nor is it beholden to a Barthesian semiotics whereby cultural discourses attain the status of "mythologies." Rather, Schelling and Jung ultimately consider mythology as a matrix of nonmolar forces and potentiations, motile forces unfolding the traumatic historicity at the heart of Romanticism. Indeed, Jung collaborated with the Hungarian classicist Karl Kerényi in a joint publication entitled *Essays on a Science of Mythology* (1941), which draws directly from Schelling's Philosophy of Mythology (*Essays* 155). The text broadly adopts Schelling's conception of mythology as a matrix of theogonic forces: mythology is not simply narrative but the movement of forces ("mythologems"), something "solid and yet mobile, substantial and yet not static, capable of transformation" (2). Mythology has no guiding question or ideology; it is, in fact, nothing less than the "spontaneous regression to the 'ground'" (7).

In this sense, mythology organises both Romantic literature and philosophy. As early as his *Philosophy of Art* (1803–1804) Schelling argues that *Naturphilosophie* should ground a mythology of the future, relocating its nascent absolute subject in a mythology which individuates itself as "a collectivity that is an individual as *one* person" (§42). Taking up this project, Schelling's 1842 lectures on mythology (*HCI*) read the *Potenzenlehre* of the 1815 *Ages* into the origins of humanity, deconstructing the Christian myth of the Fall as a play of potencies to explain the origins of tribes, peoples, and mythological traditions as resulting from a cision from the primordial relationship to God. Arguing for a primal, poetical "crisis of mythological consciousness" from which mythologies emerge (*HCI* 18), Schelling deliberately conceives his Philosophy of Mythology as a *psychoanalysis* of mythology in the broadest non-Freudian sense: the scientific spirit does not colonise its object of inquiry, but instead "induces it to open the sources of knowledge that are hidden and still concealed in itself" (7). In this way, the spectator himself "take[s] active part in the continued formation of science" (7). Mythology becomes the disciplinary unconscious of the sciences and the location of the "absolute process" (151) which is philosophy.

This psychoanalytic "inducement" is an invitation to a counter-transferential encounter with *historicity itself* as a "system of the gods" (*HCI* 9). This "system" is not a pantheon but a nexus of potentiations which unfolds through history, an economy of autochthonous "pure matter" (14) which is represented in specific historical representations as "historical beings" (10) without being reducible to any one species of representation. In this sense mythology is the manifestation, in and through human consciousness and history, of the *Naturphilosophie*'s self-organising actants, cast here as "theogonic powers" (144). This distinctly psychological component of Schelling's lectures anticipates analytical psychology's emphasis on mythology as an indispensable organisational force of archetypal knowledge and experience for Jung's "extremely historical organism." Jung puts it simply: to individuate is to live one's own myth. Indeed, during his own confrontation with his unconscious after the traumatic break with Freud, Jung asks himself: "what is your myth – the myth in which you do live?" (*Memories* 171). While this use of "myth" in the singular might suggest a monocular view of myth as one overarching narrative, it is clear from his metapsychology that Jung equates "myth" here with the purposive individuation of a life. A myth and the archetypal forces a myth constellates are mutually entangled to the extent that it is the purposive *Trieb* of individuation that *decides* (in the Schellingian sense) on their organisation. As a result, Schelling's mythological potentiation and its role in humanity's ultimately Christian individuation is both corroborated and troubled in Jung, who radicalises this individuation on the level of the psyche and, in so doing, depotentiates Schelling's Christian eschatology. In turn, Schelling's deconstructive approach to mythology troubles Jung's tendency to personify mythical figures as archetypes in analytical psychology's therapeutics of presence.

This chapter examines two Romantic "myth-subjectivities" – William Wordsworth's *The Prelude* (1799/1805)[1] and Percy Bysshe Shelley's *Prometheus Unbound* (1820) – as two different Prometheanisms which articulate mythology's energic matrix. Both these instances of Romantic "mythmaking" at once inhibit and reinvoke Romantic metasubjectivity's radical productivity as purposive *Trieb* against the idealist teleology of individuation which both poems seek to preserve. The Promethean elements of both poems thus trouble the Hegelian promise of a final revelation of self-consciousness in history. In *The Excursion* (1814) Wordsworth writes of myths in general, and the myth of Prometheus in particular, that they are "Fictions in form, but in their substance truths,/Tremendous truths! familiar to the men/Of long-past times, nor obsolete in ours" (6.545–47); Prometheanism thus unfolds in *The Prelude* as personal experiences of the growth of a poet's mind. However, the poem's textual history from 1799 to 1850 reflects *Trieb*'s displacement into a philosophical *Bildungsroman* as mythology's play of forces is gradually interpellated into discourse; the philosophy of Wordsworth's "philosophical poem" gradually becomes an interiority absorbing Nature's phenomenology into its self-grounding, so that what begins in 1799 as "embryonic theogony" (Hartman, "'Was it for this…?'" 137) is overdetermined by poetic theology by 1850. This chapter stages focused incursions into Wordsworth's epic to discuss three scenes of Promethean thievery (the theft of woodcocks, raven's eggs, and the Shepherd's Boat) and their place in the rhythms and caesurae of *1799*'s Romantic metasubjective economy. These scenes constitute a gradual amplification of Promethean intensity in 1799, a staging of the Poet's libidinal gradient whose productive energies are inhibited in 1805. I then turn to the 1805 version to discuss the failed crossing of the Alps and the sublation of this traumatic failure in the Poet's experience on Mount Snowdon, where the Poet represses the more radically productive forces of Nature and its analogous unconscious. By reframing *1799*'s opening encounter, *1805* makes Nature a stage where its darker "under-powers" are subordinated to the mind and its reflection(s). Thus, I argue that *The Prelude* is *mythmaking* in a personal sense, in which Wordsworth expresses the growth of his poetic mind through a phenomenology removed from established literary or religious pantheons.

In contrast, *Prometheus Unbound* is a dramatisation of *myth making*, a psychic scene of emergence for Schelling's system of the gods. Here, metapsychology is *metamythology*, the paradoxical deployment of Biblical motifs of flood and plague and figures from Classical mythology (such as Jupiter, Mercury, and personifications of earth and moon) to dramatise the nonmolar movement of potentiation. The Prometheanism of Shelley's lyrical drama unbinds the energy of Prometheus from his brief lyrical presence in the poem, distributing it across planets, natural forces, and gods in what is ultimately a dissociative topography of the Romantic metasubjective psyche. In *Prometheus Unbound* Prometheus, hitherto considered mostly as a *megasubject* unifying disparate forces into a self-present One Mind, is unbound into *metasubjectivity*. Classical mythology – presumably less personal and more universal than individual narrative – is rethought in a topography of "operations of the human mind" (*Prometheus Unbound*, "Preface" l. 45) at once more radically universal *and* personal than the individual poet's relationship to their personal memories. In this sense Shelley is closer to the organisational force Schelling develops in his mythology lectures, where the purposiveness of the "Self of one's self" is not merely a personal force but is thought on the level of peoples, mythologies, and indeed humanity itself.

In psychoanalytic terms, we can say that *The Prelude* gradually represses Romantic metasubjectivity whereas Shelley's *Prometheus Unbound* negates it. For just as negation amounts to a lifting of repression but not intellectual acceptance of what was repressed (Freud, "Negation" 236), so Shelley's text gives a voice to Romantic metasubjective *Trieb* while offering the text *itself* as a means to intellectually bind its own purposive energies. That is, the end of *Prometheus Unbound* problematically superimposes political Idealism over its psychological insights, thereby suspending the full implications of Romantic metasubjectivity for the poem's implicit ethos. Read in this way, *The Prelude* is a phenomenological case study of the dissociative topography retroactively traced by *Prometheus Unbound*, a deployment of its energies on the personal level of childhood experience and later reflection. Both Wordsworth and Shelley exemplify the evolution of Schelling's mythological thinking from the early Idealism of the tenth *Letter* to Schelling's later Philosophy of Mythology: the trajectory of *The Prelude* wants to ultimately aestheticise the tragic element of Greek mythology; *Prometheus Unbound* ontologically asserts these terrors as the postlapsarian Babelic confusion of languages and peoples, even as it moves to inscribe them in an ultimate apocatastasis. In his tenth *Philosophical Letter on Dogmatism and Criticism* (1795) Schelling discusses the *"sublime* thought" of Greek tragedy, which is "to suffer punishment willingly even for an inevitable crime," to fight against "an objective power which threatens our freedom with annihilation" – the power of fate itself – and, in so doing, to be vanquished (192–93). This tragic narrative is not dissimilar to the narrative of Prometheus, who suffers for acting precisely according to his nature. But in the tenth *Letter* Schelling backs away from the phenomenological and psychological implications of this trauma: "Such a fight is thinkable only for the purpose of tragic art," for tragedy as a human mode of action "would presuppose a human race of titans" raging against the terrors of impossible objects, teetering on the brink of schizophrenic rupture, "tormented by the terrors of an invisible world" (194). *The Prelude*'s *Bildungsroman* phenomenologises this titanogeny which is disavowed by the young Schelling, and *Prometheus Unbound*'s poetic metapsychology casts Schelling's "terrors of an invisible world" as distinctly psychological forces. Thus *The Prelude* attempts to contain the libidinal energies of Romantic metasubjectivity in a promissory horizon of poetic individuation, but these energies remain dispersed in Shelley, unbound to the end in a poem whose hero remains spectral in spite of Shelley's desire to portray Prometheus as a megasubject symbolising political freedom.

The 1799 *Prelude*: potency, amplification

A narrative of "the growth of a poet's mind," *The Prelude* is nevertheless, like Schelling's *Ages*, a text wrapped up in its repeated attempts to tell the past.[2] In the 1814 "Preface to *The Excursion*" Wordsworth writes that he intended *The Prelude* as a "preparatory poem," an "ante-chapel" to the "gothic church" of *The Recluse*, Wordsworth's never-written great "philosophical poem" and *magnum opus* of reflections on the world by a retired poet ("Preface to *The Excursion*" 5). Indeed, Wordsworth often uses "preparatory" texts to equip the reader for potentially uncomfortable experiences of indeterminacy; in an earlier fragment on the sublime and the beautiful, Wordsworth writes that the sublime requires "preparatory intercourse" ("The Sublime and the Beautiful" 359). But this first outline of Wordsworth's masterwork is itself plagued by a dilemma of origins.

The Prelude begins – and remains – without a proper name. The title is posthumous: almost from its inception the project was understood by Wordsworth as "the poem to Coleridge," who functions as an absent answering being throughout the poem and whose life events catalysed different revisions and versions of *The Prelude*.[3] And where *Ages*' Idealism is gradually unbound as it is revised from 1811 to 1815, the opposite is the case with Wordsworth's epic: *1799* stages encounters with Romantic metasubjectivity's radical, productive unconscious in the form of Nature, and the intensity of these encounters is sublated (and sublimated) in subsequent revisions.

Nevertheless, *The Prelude*'s complicated textual history reflects a fluidity the text attempts to contain under the rubric of what Abrams has famously called its "crisis-autobiographical" movement, a Hegelian *Aufhebungsdialektik* whereby the Poet's experience is structured by poetic crises, followed by recoveries and reaffirmations of a stronger, more determined poetic will as part of a teleology of poetic progress (77, 177, 225ff). This drive to read *The Prelude* as a Hegelian phenomenology of spirit emphasises a progress of "self-consciousness" which often aligns with psychoanalytic interpretations of *The Prelude* inevitably predicated on the formative impact of childhood scenes on the maturation of the poet's mind (see Wilson, *The Romantic Dream* 8–9 and Ellis). Yet there remains an aleatory quality to *The Prelude* making it less of an ante-chapel and more of a Borgesian infinite library, an unruly psychic economy which the 1805 Thirteen-Book and 1850 Fourteen-Book versions attempt to mitigate under the rubric of the poetic mind's teleological progress. Despite Abrams' (now perhaps dated) belief that a work must be judged as "a finished and free-standing product" (76), the 1799 *Two-Part Prelude* is a Wordsworthian "under-presence" that troubles any understanding of *The Prelude* as such (Wordsworth uses "under-" compound nouns at significant moments to denote an unconscious process or drive, or a force which recedes from phenomenological view). Against Abrams' somewhat totalising hermeneutic, which argues in Hegelian fashion that *The Prelude*'s revisionary history from 1799 to 1805 was one of conscious revision, to reveal a poetic teleology "invisibly operative from the beginning" (76), Parrish's introduction to the Cornell Wordsworth edition of *1799* explains the poem's fluid textual history. *1799* exists in two MSS.: MS. JJ (Part One) and RV (Part Two). JJ is an incomplete notebook, composed in a strange back-to-front manner, with fragments of the same episode (the Boy of Winander) scattered throughout and with disconnected passages written in different inks. Parrish describes the Cornell reading text as a "plausible" reconstruction (5). In contrast, RV seems to have been assembled from lost working drafts (27), which makes definitive chronology impossible. The Cornell *Prelude* thus represents *1799* in its earliest stages, but as a reconstruction it is not absolutely authoritative.

Viewed through the lens of Romantic metasubjectivity, *The Prelude*'s revisionary history from *1799* to *1805* recapitulates, on the level of *Bildungsroman*, a Schellingian inhibition or cision inaugurating time, history and Nature, and what Jung narrates as the emergence of (poetic) consciousness from the inscrutable primordial past of the collective unconscious. What tries to emerge is a self-consciousness akin to that of Schelling's 1800 *System*, but it is a self-consciousness pursued by the shadow of a materiality inhering in both the poem's subject matter and its textual history. So if the poem is a *Bildungsroman*, the text's unfolding ultimately shows the (speculative) tension Beiser sees in the term *Bildung* (see Chapter 1, note 6). As Hartman writes, "Wordsworth [does not] discover nature as such but rather the reality of the *relation* between nature and mind" (*Wordsworth's Poetry* 170), and this relation is far more indeterminate than the Poet lets on. Put differently, *The Prelude*'s absent centre is a site of endless approximation; indeed, emanations from its body (such as "The Boy of Winander," "Vaudracour and Julia") were detached from it to become poetic centres of their own, yet always existing in tension with this ideal centre, this dream of totality which underwrites *The Prelude*.

1799 begins with past and present suspended in a moment of poetic blockage – the Poet's failure to write his great philosophical poem. This Two-Book primal site already reflects what in subsequent revisions becomes clearer as the Poet's "unsettling psychic ontology, his inability to master 'who he is'" (Faflak 99). Indeed, the Poet is not only a "split subject" but a subject to whom Nature synaesthetically speaks in a dissociative chorus ("strange utterances," "low breathings," "huge and mighty forms," the River Derwent, the huge Cliff) as part of his tragic-melancholic line of flight. But here, this lack of mastery takes the form of an infinitely productive Deleuzian question: in the beginning refrain to the River Derwent ("Was it for this?" [1.1, 6, 17]) the Poet questions, with the river as witness, his relation to his younger years. Interrogating his history, the Poet's indeterminate "this" places both past and present under erasure in a poetic suspension, a sublime blockage that recapitulates the "inhibitive sublimity" of Schelling's *Naturphilosophische* account of creation in the *First Outline* and *Ages* (Krell, *Contagion* 7).[4] Indeed, as a period which rethinks literary genres as philosophical modes of consciousness, Romanticism is also marked by an eighteenth-century "absorption of the rhetorical concept of difficulty into *the experiential notion of blockage*" (Hertz 48; my italics) which makes the natural and rhetorical registers of the sublime "mutually cognate" (Weiskel 11).

Put differently, *1799* begins enmeshed in the very "crisis of consciousness" that inaugurates mythology as historicity for Schelling. Where the *First Outline* and *Ages* begin from the perspective of the pre-subjective unconditioned, Schelling explains in the mythology lectures that "it is *history* to which the Philosophy of Mythology first has a relation" (*HCI* 159), and this history is comprised of mythology's very emergence through "the inner processes and movements of consciousness" that reach back to "pre-historical time" as "the time of the cision or crisis of the peoples" which gives rise to mythological systems (162). This crisis, and the individuation it inaugurates, means that we are confronted with a psyche working through its dispossession by its own purposiveness. As Carolyn Culbertson writes of Schelling, in the crisis of ecstasy and suspension "we are permitted another beginning. For Schelling, however, this other beginning is not a ground separate from Nature but *the potency of Nature itself*" (235; my italics). And in *1799* the Poet connects with this potency in ways that are elided and inhibited in *1805*. The poetic blockage that marks *1799*'s beginning is tied to a questioning of the river as perennial symbol of the flow of libido and emblem for the Poet's libidinal gradient. The Poet's symbolic return to the river marks an involutive turn, what Jung calls the regression of libido as part of a larger Thanatopoietic movement of poetic energy. Indeed, *1799* insists on the Poet's connection with the river as libidinal analogue, which "loved/To blend his murmurs with [the Poet's] Nurse's song,/And from his alder shades, and rocky falls,/And from his fords and shallows, sent a voice/ That flowed along [the Poet's] dreams" (1.2–6). But how is this involution, this suspension and blockage negotiated? The transition from the "Was it for this?" refrain to the following recollections take the form of a conjunctive "And afterwards," which bridges to the memory of woodcock stealing (1.27), followed by "Nor less, in spring-time" (1.50) which begins the theft of the raven's eggs. Neither of these episodes answers or dispels the question "Was it for this?" but instead work through this caesura in a Thanatopoietic shift to three crucial scenes which sustain the poem's enantiodromal rhythm.

In 1799, then, the theft of the woodcocks, the theft of eggs from the raven's nest (1.50–66), and the theft of the Shepherd's Boat (often called the "Stolen Boat" episode; 1.81–129) evoke a crucial Prometheanism that is mitigated in *1805*. Origins here take the form of recollected metaphors of Promethean cision and rebellion, an enacted difference which, as a *mise en abyme* within Wordsworth's poem, personalises the poem's reference back to itself as a *pharmakon* for its own blockage. Put differently, the overcoming of *1799*'s caesura and blockage does not provide a safe grounding for a stable subject but instead opens up into personalised sites of ungrounding. But this ungrounding, this contact with Romantic metasubjectivity's radical productivity, is precisely where the Poet's "stolen" gift of poetic consciousness resides.

With the Poet's recollection of the stolen woodcocks (1.27–49), *1799*'s questioning refrain is redirected to "Gentle Powers" (35) in an apostrophe absent from *1805*, giving the earlier version of the episode a mythic texture closer to the theogonic powers of Schelling's system of the gods than the reified concepts of *1805*. Indeed *1799*'s Poet, driven to the theft by a desire which "overpowers" his whole person (42–43), is more susceptible to the dissociative fabric of the episode, closer and more intimately entwined with its implicit Promethean *Trieb*. In *1805*, the poetic self of this episode is already "critiqued" in a quasi-Kantian sense: strong desire now overpowers "*better* reason" (*1805* 1.326; my italics), a reason now mandated as ruling faculty in a manner that removes the entire subject from Promethean desire. Following Freud, Onorato calls this scene a "sexual fantasy of the child's separation from the mother" (185), which corroborates an "Oedipal configuration" (186) in which the "Low breathings" and "sounds/Of undistinguishable motion" the Poet hears "when the deed was done" (*1799* 1.45, 47–48) represent a punitive superego. But the rhythm and caesurae of Promethean enantiodromia at work in the opening of *1799* interrogates this model of psychoanalytic guilt. While there is furtiveness in the Poet's "anxious visitation" and excitement about the theft (*1799* 1.38ff), the "low breathings" do not create penitence in the Poet's recollection; there is no primal scene of theft or transgression. Instead, these "sounds of indistinguishable motion" (47–48), which *as* indistinguishable mark aurality as an "organ of vision" for Wordsworth (Hartman, *The Unremarkable*

Wordsworth 23), hark back to the "Gentle Powers" to which the episode is addressed (*1799* 1.35–36).

The following episode in which the Poet steals raven's eggs (*1799* 1.50–66) fills out the broader rhythms and caesurae of the Poet's Promethean enantiodromia begun by the woodcock episode. The woodcock and raven's egg thefts are rhythmic, isocolonic, recapitulating subtle yet profound natural strife. On one level, there is a Promethean theft which catalyses a reflection on the dissociative matrix of the Romantic metasubjective psyche, one focused on Wordsworth's aural "organ of vision" ("low breathings" and "strange utterances"). But on another, more fundamental level, the Poet's actions unfold against the backdrop of Nature's auto-alterity, its characteristically Schellingian ambivalence toward its own products. Here this auto-alterity is represented in flowers: the woodcock episode begins when "the frost and breath of frosty wind had *snapped*/The last autumnal crocus" (*1799* 1.29–30; my italics), and the theft of raven's eggs unfolds when "The shining sun had from his knot of caves/*Decoyed* the primrose-flower" (*1799* 1.51–52; my italics). "Snapped" and "decoyed" reflect Nature's traumatisation of its own products through seasonal fluctuation; the crocus is broken by frost and the primrose is decoyed, *lured* into a process which should ostensibly be part of a harmonious natural cycle. Indeed, Nature's auto-alterity persists in the "strange utterance" the Poet hears as the dissociative vocalisation of Nature's generative powers, in a moment of sublime suspension where "the sky seemed not a sky/Of earth, and with what motion moved the clouds!" (1.65–66).

The "Stolen Boat" episode (*1799* 1.81–129) is the culmination of the Poet's Promethean mythologem, amplifying it into the human sphere: here the Poet steals not a "natural" object (woodcock, raven's egg) but a human product, a "Boat" whose movements resemble "a man who walks with stately step/Though bent on speed" (89–90). For this reason, "low breathings" and "strange utterances" are replaced by "the *voice*/Of mountain echoes" (91–92), a clearer sense of aural agency metonymically related to the "huge Cliff" that will traumatise the Poet's endeavours "as if with voluntary power instinct" (108–9). And with this the Poet begins to realise, within the phenomenology of his poetic reflection, the very essence of the tragic which the early Schelling of the tenth *Letter* wants to confine to art. Even here, the "voluntary power" with which the cliff pursues the Poet unfolds in "measured motions" in line with the counted beats of the Poet's oar-strokes ("twenty times/I dipped my oars into the silent lake") and the growing stature of the cliff as the Poet "struck, and struck again" with his oars (113, 103, 110). The Poet's furtive progression is still contained in the music of "meaningful differentiation." In a transference of Freud's conflict-model of the psyche on to *The Prelude*, David Ellis categorises the theft episodes under a "common pattern" as "some kind of assault on the environment which the environment ('Nature') resists" (41). Yet this does not do justice to the rhythms and caesurae that inform a Romantic-metasubjective reading of the poem: the Poet's anxiety, as caesurae within the finer, broader rhythm of his libidinal gradient, is not at odds with Nature but rather one moment of a larger mythological *Erzeugeungsdialektik*.

The Poet turns back with "trembling hands" when the cliff "Rose up between [him] and the stars, and still/With measured motion, like a living thing, strode after [him]" (111–14). Often read as an expression of societal guilt (which is behind Ellis' description of this scene as a Freudian "flight reaction" [71]), what begins as "an act of stealth/And troubled pleasure" (90–91) crucially does not end the Poet's "stealing" once he turns around. This reversal is still part of the episode's Promethean continuum; just as he stole across the lake in the Shepherd's Boat, so he "*stole* [his] way/Back to the cavern of the willow-tree" (115–16; my italics). The differential rhythm sustaining the entire episode expresses the Poet's libidinal gradient, which is amplified to its culmination in a convergence of ideal and real. This synchronicity is uncontained by parental imagos, released into the general economy of the collective unconscious and the theogonic forces from which Schelling's mythology emerges. The rhythm and "cadence" of the Poet's oar-strokes are matched exactly by the growing stature and "measured motions" of the predatory cliff which spontaneously, autochthonically assumes life. Ideal and real rhythms converge in a synchronistic moment where the Poet touches and does not touch the mythological forces animating Nature as they are reflected in the Poet's address to "ye Beings of the hills" (130–32). Put in Hölderlin's terms of rhythm and caesura, this synchronistic moment emphasises a crucial dynamic: namely, that *it is precisely the convergence of two symmetrical rhythms (Poet and cliff) which causes the caesura*. There can be no convergence of ideal and real; their identical polarity means that they are destined to push away from each other at the same time as they are brought together in a moment of magnetic attraction. Indeed, in the very act of rowing a boat the rower must face *away* from the path ahead in order to move forward – an exquisite ekphrasis of the Poet's fleeting connection with his libidinal gradient. Once the Poet turns, admonished by the Cliff, he sees what was *once* but *is no longer* the gradient and path of poetic growth, with which the Poet can never directly connect. And through precisely this contact with the mythological matrix of Romantic metasubjectivity the Poet ultimately leaves not admonished, but gifted with a Promethean intuition of the "hiding-places of [his] power" (*1805* 11.336), the libidinal-mythological matrix of Romantic metasubjectivity as "a dim and undetermined sense/Of unknown modes of being" (121–22). The caesura has allowed the Poet a fleeting glimpse of the whole. But this gift is less a "cure" for poetic indecision and more of a *pharmakon*: the Poet emphasises that the "solitude" and "blank desertion" in his mind after the episode have nothing to do with "familiar shapes/Of hourly objects, images of trees,/Of sea or sky, no colours of green fields" but instead with autochthonic, indeterminate potencies which hover on the edge of representation, "huge and mighty forms, that do not live/Like living men" (123–28). Joseph Sitterson sees this metaphoricity as the "primary metaphoric ability or power" repressed in both Freud and Lacan, an attribute of a "Wordsworthian subject" irreducible to entanglement in primal scenes or the psychoanalytic "incessant sliding of signifiers" (104).

In the Stolen Boat episode, then, the Poet touches and does not touch the asystasy anterior to all systems of (poetic) knowledge, and this is why the *pharmakon* of such synchronistic "absolute knowledge" can only be represented by indeterminacy, trauma and absence, the pervasive trauma of non-anthropomorphic forms "that moved slowly through [his] mind/By day, and were the trouble of [his] dreams" (128–29). If there is guilt in the beginning of the Stolen Boat episode, this guilt becomes something else by its end; just as for Jung patients often outgrow problems that cannot be solved logically, so the gradient of the Poet's individuative *Trieb* leads from the possibility of societal transgression to a broader awareness of the preterhumanity of Romantic metasubjectivity's mythological economy. These forms reflect "the symptomal force of Wordsworth's unconscious life" (Faflak 101) but are also the "terrors of an invisible world" of Schelling's Tenth *Letter*, the *pharmakon* gift of living tragically for one who now sees with Promethean eyes. From "low breathings" to "strange utterances" to "voices," the Poet's troubles are trebled into *Trieb*. Thus, the theft episodes unfold a rhythmic alternation between scenes of theft and glimpses of Promethean insight furnished by a dissociationist mythological matrix of "Powers," natural objects (cliffs, yew-trees, crags), "spirits," and "huge and mighty forms." These moments are rhythmic pulsations, alternations in the "strain of music" performed by the Poet in concord with "Gentle Powers," "Beings of the hills" and "eternal things" (1.130, 136). This rhythm, in turn, is gathered up into what Jung calls a "re-experiencing" (*Alchemical Studies* 162–63) of the Promethean mythologem, its amplification through the phenomenology of the Poet's memory and experience culminating in an intuition of the purposiveness of Romantic metasubjectivity.

The 1805 *Prelude*: the burden of the unnatural self

Hartman suggests that Wordsworth does not want "to see nature purely under the aspect of the human. The ultimate figure remains a borderer, at once natural and human" (*Wordsworth's Poetry* 202). But beginning with the "Glad Preamble," the inhibitive progression from *1799* to *1805* suggests that the Poet would prefer to shut these borders rather than entertain an uncomfortable liminality with Nature. *The Prelude* in general retains the aleatory nature of a working-through of Schelling's crisis of consciousness. Nevertheless, *1805* interpellates *1799*'s primal energies, locating them in a topology of name and place (Schelling's "tribes and peoples") to furnish a typically Wordsworthian "preparatory intercourse," an idealist economy of mind which binds, without dispelling, the energies of Romantic metasubjective *Trieb* unfolding through the Poet. The "rover" who steals raven's eggs is now moralised as a "plunderer," and the *1805* Poet retrospectively judges his *1799* "unnatural self" as "careless," through "meditative" eyes that will continue to circumscribe ecstasy in the Snowdon episode, which I will discuss below (*1799* 1.53; *1805* 1.337, 13.124, 126). Moreover, the libidinal territory of *1799* is mapped in *1805*; the River Derwent, which assumes so much importance as an emblem of the Poet's libidinal gradient, is now socialised as a "Playmate" tracked from "Mountains" to the "Towers of Cockermouth," passing "Behind my Father's House [...] Along the margin of our Terrace Walk" (*1805* 1.287–91). The Stolen Boat episode is now an event "by the Shores of Patterdale" involving a "Stranger [...] A School-boy traveller, at the Holidays." And the "unexpected chance" by which the boy Poet discovers the boat distances him from *1799*'s potentiated fate, accentuating the doubt lurking in the Poet's self-assuring "surely I was led by her," "her" now a gendered, personified "Nature" instead of *1799*'s "quiet Powers" whose guidance was unmistakable (*1805* 1.364–82; *1799* 1.81). Put mythologically, *1805* departs from the ecstatic "new beginnings" to which *1799* was closer; potentiation has now "fallen" into a postlapsarian poetics of time, locale, and history. The encounters with the mythological potentiation of the Romantic metasubjective unconscious are now displaced from the Poet's beginnings as "trances of thought" and "mountings of the mind" which must be "shaken off" as "that burthen of [his] own unnatural self" (1.20–23), a self once formed by "Powers of earth" and "Genii of the springs" that have now become "presences of Nature" (*1799* 1.186; *1805* 1.491).

Indeed, this division of natural and unnatural selves persists in a self-doubling that eclipses the *Erzeugungsdialektik* of the Poet's individuation with a profoundly Hegelian schematic of recognition. When the Poet reflects on "the calm existence that is mine when I/Am worthy of myself," it is after an idealisation of the paean to the "mind of man." Where *1799*'s ambitendent, ambivalent "spirits" and "quiet Powers" visited the Poet "as at the touch of lightning" (*1799* 1.69ff), here the emphasis is once more on the Christianised "breath" and "harmony" of music which serves a "dark/Invisible workmanship that reconciles/Discordant elements, and makes them move/In one society" (1.352–56). In the famous "Lordship and Bondage" section of Hegel's *Phenomenology of Spirit*, recognition is an intersubjective process, a discursive mirror-stage through which self-consciousness is constituted by mutual acknowledgement (¶178ff). This mutual "self-worthiness" occurs not within the strains, rhythms and caesurae of differential music or the dissociative matrix of powers, but within a "workmanship" reconciling elements in language moving away from *1799*'s mythic textures. Indeed, reading the struggle for recognition as that between the Poet's two "selves" (the interchangeable "I" and "myself"), the Poet's "calm existence," as the pleasure principle of his balanced psychological intersubjectivity (being "worthy of himself"), makes him a lord disconnected from Nature's "workmanship," which must necessarily remain "dark" and "invisible." In Hegel's terms, the lord remains "a consciousness that is for itself [...] mediated with itself" through both a phenomenological "thing" and the bondsman (slave), as "the consciousness for which thinghood is what is essential" (¶190). Alexandre Kojève offers some useful insights on what is here the Master-Poet's relationship with an inaccessible Nature through the workmanship of things: "The Master's superiority over Nature [...] is realized by the fact of the Slave's *Work*. This Work is placed between the Master and Nature. The Slave transforms the given conditions of existence so as to make them *conform* to the Master's demands" (42). "Nature" here is the mythological matrix inaccessible to the Poet, whose illusory "mastery" remains troubled by the dark invisible workmanship beyond his control. This entrance into a discursively grounded type of self-recognition is an overdetermination further marking the repression of Romantic metasubjectivity's radical, nonmolar productivity; here, the "Self of one's self" is the "self of one's self." With this, the music of differentiation that underscores the Poet's individuation is not dispelled, but alters its symbolic tenor. Where in *1799* the Derwent's music "blends" and "flows" with the Nurse's song and the Poet's dreams in "steady cadence," *1805*'s "gentle breeze," a "Messenger" and intermediary interjecting between the Poet and a river which once "composed" his thoughts, now "beats against" the Poet's cheek "And *seems* half conscious of the joy it brings" (3–4, my italics; *1799* 1.11). This conflictual rhythm displaces the Poet from the "knowledge" and "dim earnest of the calm/Which Nature breathes among the fields and groves" (*1799* 1.14–15).

1805 begins not with the libidinal symbolism of the "Was it for this?" refrain but the "Glad Preamble" (*1805* 1.1–54), where a gentle breeze provokes within the Poet a "corresponding mild creative breeze." As a "blueprint of the mind's *visionary* awakening" (Faflak 105; my italics), the Preamble reads *1799*'s Nature as spirit, releasing it into a poetic world interpellated by history and time in ways *1799* is not. But this "corresponding breeze," as a Christianised symbol removed from the mythological potentiation of *1799*'s ambivalent "Powers," nevertheless recapitulates, even as it represses, the "loathing and anxiety" of Schelling's rotatory motion and Jung's libidinal blockage as a "tempest, a redundant energy/Vexing its own creation," which is only uneasily balanced with the promissory "vernal promises" of "The holy life of music and of verse" (43–54). As we have seen, Schelling's first potency exists in "loathing and anxiety" because it "unites within it conflicting forces, of which one always craves the outside and of which the other is inwardly restrained [and] does [not] know whether to turn inward or outward and in this fashion falls prey to an arbitrary, revolving motion" (*Ages* 32). This vexation shapes the poetic economy of doubt and conflict in *1805*'s opening, and for which the Poet aims to compensate through re-idealising Nature into the life of the prophetic (visionary) mind. Doubting both his "consecrated joy" and the existence of the "corresponding mild creative breeze" (1.39, 41), the Poet of *1805* is left to unfold a musical individuation now in more "measured strains" and encased in the language of prophecy ("poetic numbers" from a spirit "cloth'd in priestly robe"), an idealised space of immediacy in which "the very words which I have here/Recorded" (1.57–59) are supposedly identical with Nature in what amounts to a messianism displacing the messianic.[5] Indeed, the Poet regains confidence not through the phenomenology of Nature but from the sound of his own voice, "and, far more, the mind's/ Internal echo of the imperfect sound" (64–65), an interiority which recalls the uneasy assertion of self-consciousness in Schelling's 1800 *System* against the *Naturphilosophie*.

What follows is a prolonged meditation on this "revolving motion" between the Poet and his "corresponding mild creative breeze," a meditation on the Poet's "unmanageable thoughts" (1.150) and a projection of the Poet's drama of self-consciousness on to a Nature which persists as an indeterminate remainder to this idealist economy. The Poet retires to sit beneath a tree, and his "being not unwilling now to give/A respite to [the] passion" of his autoerotic prophecy reflects Wordsworth's characteristic use of litotes to mark ambivalence and blockage, or, as Michael Cooke puts it, an incorporation of "potential resistance and rejection in a controlled innocuous form" (1.68–69; Cooke 198). For the Poet *does* continue his tenuous prophetic soliloquy, couched within a pleasure principle of "perfect stillness" wherein he "[passes] through many thoughts, yet mainly such/ As to [him]self pertained," (1.79–81). Indeed, his priestly belief that his words conjure up reality persists as he imagines his new home "And saw, methought, the very house and fields/Present before my eyes" (1.83–84). Just as Nature both supports and unworks the thought-economy of Schelling's 1800 *System*, so here Nature both enables and interrupts the Poet's soliloquy of self-consciousness, providing a "genial pillow of [earth] and "a sense of touch from the warm ground" (1.88, 90) and rupturing this internal drama with the startling sound of dropping acorns (1.94).[6] The "defrauded" Eolian harp and its resulting disavowal ("Be it so,/It is an injury […] to this day/To think of any thing but present joy" [1.104–110]) is amplified into "self-congratulation […] complete/Composure, and […] happiness entire" (1.122–23) which ironically reasserts the loathing and anxiety of Schelling's negative, contracting potency, for this "composure" comes at the cost of Wordsworth's own composition of the growth of the poet's mind. The failure of the Eolian harp is followed by *textual* caesurae in the poem's individuative rhythm – "What need of many words?" strangely represses, through abridgement, the Poet's travels to Dove Cottage in what is supposed to be, after all, a narrative of his own poetic development, and addressing Coleridge as answering being the Poet finds himself unwilling to communicate such an important feeling of self-congratulation: "I spare to speak, my Friend, of what ensued" (1.114, 117).

Working through these "unmanageable thoughts" – his conflicting forces of "sickness" and "wellness" (1.148) – the Poet's "rigorous inquisition," continuing his self-analysis, subverts *1799*'s potencies by making "Elements," "Agents," and "Under-Powers" into "Subordinate helpers of the living mind" (1.164–65). The "philosophic Song/Of Truth" on which the Poet decides releases him from the generic formalism of the epic catalogue of possible themes he rehearses (178ff), turning from primal historical *scenes* to his own primal phenomenological *site* of poetic creation. And in the end, all of "this" – the Glad Preamble, the Poet's preoccupation with his own voice, and "the mind's/Internal echo of the imperfect sound," and his "unmanageable thoughts" – now designate the indeterminate "this" which began *1799* (now *1805* 1.272ff). Staging an idealist soliloquy, the *Ungrund* to which *1799* was attuned is now grounded in the Poet's self-analysis, wherein Nature becomes a screen for the restricted play of self-consciousness in the creation of a "philosophic Song" in which poetry remains sutured to philosophy. In this "philosophic Song," the Promethean amplification is envisioned through the "Wisdom and Spirit of the Universe!/Thou Soul that art the Eternity of Thought!" that gives "a breath/And everlasting motion" to both "forms and images," constricting the "huge and mighty Forms" of the Stolen Boat episode within a universe overdetermined by mind and thought where Nature recedes quietly into the background (1.429–32). The binding of *1799*'s aleatorism culminates in the ascent of Mount Snowdon, which figures a climactic encounter with the *Ungrund* of the Romantic metasubjective psyche even as the Poet attempts to work through its trauma via a poetic metapsychology which both courts and resists its own "under presences."

The ascent of Mount Snowdon which opens the final Book of the 1805 *Prelude* is widely considered the apogee of the Poet's psychological growth. Sublating the trauma of a previously failed Alps crossing (6.452–648), Mount Snowdon is an emblematic binding, an ideation of *1799*'s spots of time and aleatory phenomenology. Where *1799*'s mythological texture is expressed by "Powers" and "Genii," the Snowdon episode congeals this energic matrix into the concepts of Imagination and Nature. The *Two-Part Prelude*'s purposive unfolding is refolded into a linear schema whose manifest content would seem to corroborate Abrams' crisis-autobiographical model. But just as Jung's metapsychology troubles the teleological drive of his therapeutics of presence, Romantic metasubjectivity opens up a poetic metapsychology in the Snowdon experience which unworks Wordsworth's drive to consolidate Nature into the "perfect image of a mighty mind" (13.69). Snowdon ends *1805* with a psyche whose unruly energies are nevertheless repressed, bound within the confines of the quasi-Kantian moral law Wordsworth habitually attaches to the concept of the sublime.[7] Nevertheless, inhibiting *1799*'s productive mythological energies, *1805* ends up uncannily reconnecting with these purposive energies *as psyche*, even as this sublime event is analogically recast in terms of spirit's unfolding as "intellectual love."

The trauma of the earlier failed Alps crossing and its visionary recuperation set the stage for the Poet's idealisation of the Snowdon episode. Here, the incommensurability between mind and unruly Nature manifests itself in poetic disappointment with the "soulless image" of Mont Blanc "Which had usurp'd upon a living thought/That never more could be" (6.454–56), a melancholy which privileges the death of a "living thought" for which Nature must make "rich amends" (6.460) with the Vale of Chamouny. Indeed, the Poet's literal bookishness reflects this missed encounter with Nature as its energies are inhibited into the economy of mind; the scenery is a prophetic "book" in which the Poet and his companion "could not chuse but read/A frequent lesson of sound tenderness,/The universal reason of mankind" (6.474–76). And in the Snowdon narrative, Wordsworth will try to (problematically) synonymise reason and imagination. This textual substitute-formation, in which Nature recedes as a mute stage for "dreams and fictions pensively composed," serves a "meditativeness" (6.481, 487) which, here and in the Snowdon episode (6.126), marks an interiority in which the idea of imagination is invoked against Nature's purposiveness, writing it into the drama of the Poet's self-consciousness as a mute subaltern where the Poet's natural surroundings are fitted to his "unripe state/Of intellect and heart" (6.470–71).

The trauma of the failed Alps crossing is remembered and recollected through the rhythms of *Thanatopoiesis*, the progression-regression dynamic characterising the libidinal movement of Romantic metasubjectivity. But the anxiogenic aspect of this rhythm is that it leads *nowhere*, or only to a state of blockage that resists the linear teleology of the Poet's self-narrative and is unable to guarantee the ultimate unfolding of poetic spirit. The narrative is prompted by "something of stern mood, an *under thirst/*

Of vigour, never utterly asleep" (6.489–90; my italics) which interrupts the pleasure principle of meditation and the formalism of genre through which the Poet screens Nature. One of several "under-" compound nouns Wordsworth uses throughout *The Prelude* to denote unconscious processes, "under thirst" here catalyses the traumatic recollection and the sublation of Imagination. But it also leads to the Poet's encounter with the "Characters of the great Apocalyps" (6.570) which traumatise, in turn, the imagination's pretense to teleological sublimation. As a natural phenomenology of the "faded mythology" Schelling sees in language (*HCI* 40), these "characters" are even more powerfully figured in the Poet's experience at Snowdon. In the Poet's retelling, he and his companion "[descend] by the beaten road that led/Right to a rivulet's edge, and there broke off" (6.502–3) to cross and start up the other side. Missing their comrades and doubting their way, they meet a Peasant who tells them to go back the way they came and "find the road/Which in the stony channel of the Stream/Lay a few steps, and then along its Banks," learning that their course lay "downwards, with the current of that Stream" (6.514–19). This confusion recapitulates the movement of Romantic metasubjective libido, whose blockage or inhibition leads to regression and a change of form (Jung, *Symbols* 158). They cross the stream, going against its flow, and they must retrace their steps and return ("regress") to find the right path which follows its flow and current. Not having done this, and not having (re)connected with the perennial emblem of Romantic metasubjective libido as part of an authentic rhythm of poetic individuation, the Alps experience was forfeit.

The following recuperatory apostrophe to the "unfather'd vapour" of imagination, which "lift[s] up itself/Before the eye and progress of my Song" as a "usurper" (6.525–26, 533), transpires in the poetic present, an effusion from the Poet in 1805, whose recollection of past (1790) trauma and existential blockage has brought a moment of sublation: "I was lost as in a cloud,/Halted without a struggle to break through,/And now recovering to my Soul I say/I recognize thy glory" (6.529–32). Here Wordsworth echoes Kant's argument that sublime trauma catalyses both imagination's failure before awe-inspiring magnitude (here the lack of the Alps) and a "simultaneously awakened pleasure" stimulated *by* this trauma which clears the way for triumphant "ideas of reason" (Kant, *Critique of Judgment* §27). Bringing with it "thoughts/That are their own perfection and reward" (6.545–46), Imagination becomes Wordsworth's substitute for Kantian reason, and indeed Wordsworth will merge the two in the

Snowdon episode where imagination is "but another name for [...] reason in her most exalted mood" (13.167–70).

But *does* Wordsworth's imagination simply restore the teleological growth of a poet's mind? Does the sublime only exist for an Idealism where thoughts need not touch Nature's contagion? The significance of the failed Alps crossing for the Snowdon ascent lies not only in both episodes' participation in the Poet's *Aufhebungsdialektik*, but also in what is repressed in this sublation. Both episodes figure experiences of radical productivity, the *Ungrund* of Romantic metasubjectivity which touches and does not touch the Poet as he both courts and resists the traumatic kernel of sublime experience. After the apostrophe to Imagination and its working through of the Alps trauma, it becomes difficult to say whether what follows – the "recuperated" sublime of the "Characters of the great Apocalyps" (6.549–72) – is part of the retelling (part of circumstances "relate[d]/Even as they were" [6.493–94]) or if it is imagination tainting a narrative of things past with the working-through of the poetic present. The Poet returns to the Alps narrative where he and his companion have "entered with the road which [they] had missed/Into a narrow chasm" (6.553), following the libidinal dynamism of Romantic metasubjectivity. The libidinal regression which the Poet and his companion perform by turning back in confusion has changed form and now bears the aegis of imagination – which, as "unfather'd vapour" (527), lacks the (paternal) origins which could otherwise place it within a Freudian economy of *Nachträglichkeit* and primal phantasy. They descend into the chasm and follow once more the libidinal gradient emblematised by the stream. The following experience is worth quoting at length:

> The immeasurable height
> Of woods decaying, never to be decay'd,
> The stationary blasts of waterfalls,
> And every where along the hollow rent
> Winds thwarting winds, bewilder'd and forlorn,
> The torrents shooting from the clear blue sky,
> The rocks that mutter'd close upon our ears,
> Black drizzling crags that spake by the way-side
> As if a voice were in them, the sick sight
> And giddy prospect of the raving stream,
> The unfetter'd clouds, and region of the heavens,

Tumult and peace, the darkness and the light
Were all like workings of one mind, the features
Of the same face, blossoms upon one tree,
Characters of the great Apocalyps,
The types and symbols of Eternity,
Of first and last, and midst, and without end. (6.556–72)

What imagination brings, then, at the behest of this "stern under thirst," is something that cannot be entirely bound within the economy of reason. Here as in the Snowdon ascent, the 1805 *Prelude* unfolds a poetic metapsychology of the radically productive psyche; it is a poetic territory of the "one mind," but one that is also "sick," "giddy," a dissociationist chorus of muttering rocks, speaking crags, and raving streams which reveals Wordsworth's imagination as a speculative term like Hegel's *Aufhebung*, one which enantiodromally shifts into its opposite.[8] Far from the stage of self-consciousness, we have now returned to the loathing and anxiety of *Ages*' potencies and the ambivalence of Nature in the *Naturphilosophie*. The sublime suspension of "woods decaying, never to be decay'd" and "stationary blasts of waterfalls" reflect a Nature once again in conflict with itself, its products unwilling to comply with the physics of their existence.

Yet all of these are "Characters of the great Apocalyps,/The types and symbols of Eternity,/Of first and last, and midst, and without end." As "charactered," or inscribed (*OED* 1), Wordsworth's "great Apocalyps" clearly harks back to the Biblical deluge. But read as contact with the *Ungrund* of Romantic metasubjectivity, the general economy of archetypal grammatology's infinite productivity, there is nevertheless an "under presence" of Schelling's primordial cision and mythological beginnings that Schelling, too, associates with the apocalyptic Flood and the (archetypal) role of water in the involutive (libidinal) turn that stimulates further development. Indeed, in his discussion of the Flood as cisionary moment Schelling fuses mythology and geology: "water has [a crucial role] in all transitions from a *dominant* principle to a second, to which it yields, not merely in the history of the earth but rather also in mythology. [Noah's Flood was the] great turning point of mythology [which] was later followed by the unceasing transition itself, the confusion of the languages […] along with the various systems of the gods, and the separation of humanity into peoples and states" (*HCI* 108), the "characters" of the Apocalypse. Thus, these inscribed "characters" are not of Biblical experience but rather impressed archetypal experiences from Nature's mythological phenomenology. We are here at the mythological wellspring, a site of Nature's auto-alterity and the seethe of autochthonic archetypal forces which we cannot with certainty determine as past narrative or present effusion. Indeed, it is a "stern under thirst of vigor," a *Trieb* which drives the Poet to recollect the trauma, interject a paean to imagination, and follow it with an experience of the *Ungrund* of Romantic metasubjectivity. This experience leads to sleep "close upon the confluence of two streams" (6.576) which suggests a unification of libidinal purposiveness, amplifying into "a lordly River, broad and deep" (6.583). But their rest in a "Mansion [...] deafen'd and stunn'd/By noise of waters" (6.577–79) does not allow for an untroubled resolution; the dissociative vocality of the water abides as an under-presence even as the Poet and his companion reach Lake Locarno.

This tension between the purposiveness of the *Ungrund* and the Poet's visionary self-consciousness reaches its apogee in the paradoxically chasmal ascent of Mount Snowdon. Here, Snowdon's poetic metapsychology amplifies the "Characters of the great Apocalyps," releasing its grammatological metaphor into the unbound phenomenology of Nature. In the Alps, the "narrow chasm" leads to the sublime encounter with natural products suspended in (geological) time, but nevertheless inscribed, both Biblically and Miltonically, as "characters" of the Apocalpyse, overdetermining their infinite productivity with a rhetorical appropriation of *Paradise Lost* ("Of first and last, and midst, without end" [6.572]; see *Paradise Lost* 5.165). In contrast, the Snowdon episode takes place within a Nature that unworks the sovereignty of mind so often attributed to Wordsworth's "spots of time," sublime moments of "deepest feeling that the mind/Is lord and master, and that outward sense/Is but the obedient servant of her will" (11.271–73). The poetic metapsychology here figures a Schellingian Nature that

> [dominates] the outward face of things,
> So molds them and endues, abstracts, combines
> Or by abrupt and unhabitual influence
> Doth make one object so impress itself
> Upon all others, and pervade them so
> That even the grossest minds must see and hear
> and cannot chuse but feel. (13.78–84)

Nature's autochthonic qualities here trouble the mind's Idealism, at times overpowering its egoity through "abrupt influence" so as to (dis)possess the mind. Just as for Jung the archetypes simply *happen* to one, and for Schelling thoughts autonomously "think within" the person (Schelling, *On the History* 48), so natural objects can traverse the porous boundary between mind and Nature, irrupting within egoity in an imaginative process Wordsworth both courts and resists.

Unlike the Alps crossing, where the Poet and his companion are symbolised as two streams ultimately uniting in one purpose into a "lordly River," the ascent of Mount Snowdon begins with an interiorised preparatory intercourse in which the Poet's silence is broken only by encounters with the anxiety and conflict intrinsic to Nature's products as part of its auto-alterity and self-differentiation. In this sense, the "barking turbulent" with which the shepherd's dog unearths a hedgehog aligns with the Poet's own agon with Nature, proceeding "With forehead bent/Earthward, as if in opposition set/Against an enemy" (13.18–31). Indeed, in a Romantic metasubjective chain of Being, Nature's auto-alterity proceeds from animal (dog-hedgehog) and human (Poet-Earth) not to the theological or preterhuman, but to the geological: a "huge sea of mist," a "still Ocean" whose "vapours shot themselves,/In hedlands, tongues, and promontory shapes/[into] the real Sea, that seem'd/To dwindle and give up its majesty,/Usurp'd upon as far as sight could reach" (13.43, 46–51). This geological figuration of Nature's self-usurpation unfolds in what both Schelling and Wordsworth (here and in Book Six) see as a mythological space, where the archetypal grammatology of Nature's auto-alterity represents the "first poesy" of mythology, "a poesy *originally* preceding all plastic and compositional art, namely, one originally inventing and producing the raw material" (*HCI* 167).

Where Book Six presents us with "types and symbols of Eternity," here archetypal grammatology is represented through Nature's auto-alterity as the curious symmetry of the *breach*. The Poet's visuals lead us from "positive" breaches of phenomenological presence, the "hundred hills" which "their dusky backs upheaved/All over this still Ocean" (13.45–46), to their supplementation by a "negative" breach of phenomenological lack, an ekphrasis eclipsed by the aural, Wordsworth's recrudescent "organ of vision" in the dissociationist "voice" of "streams/Innumerable":

A blue chasm, a fracture in the vapour,
A deep and gloomy breathing-place thro' which

Mounted the roar of waters, torrents, streams
Innumerable, roaring with one voice. (13.56–59)

This phenomenological lack is privileged by the Poet as the authentic site of both "Soul" and "Imagination," now synonymous, recasting Imagination as "under presence":

The universal spectacle throughout
Was shaped for admiration and delight,
Grand in itself alone, *but* in that breach
Through which the homeless voice of waters rose,
That dark deep thorough-fare had Nature lodg'd
The Soul, the Imagination of the whole. (13.60–65; my italics)

The Poet's sight is trained first on the "meek and silent" spectacle of the positive breaches which "rested at [his] feet" (13.44) – a passive scene of Nature's auto-alterity – then to the blue chasm in a visual movement back in figural time to the *Ungrund* of origins. In "Freud and the Scene of Writing," Derrida takes up Freud's theorisation of the breach in *Beyond* (71–72) as marker of the trace and the opening of an absence which has always been "present" in presence, as part of a project to discover, in psychoanalysis, "condensed and sedimented" elements of deconstruction that "can only uneasily be contained within logocentric closure" (198). For Derrida, from the earliest days of psychoanalysis (e.g. Freud's *Project*), the psychoanalytic breach (*Bahnung*) is Freud's metaphor for the creation of memory in the psyche as a movement of difference, designating memory *itself* as the essence of the Freudian psyche through a "metaphorics of the written trace": "Breaching, the tracing of a trail, opens up a conducting path [presupposing] a certain violence" (200). As "the first representation, the first staging of memory," this constitution of memory is "the very essence of the psyche: resistance, and precisely, thereby, an opening to the effraction of the trace" within a psyche which is "neither the transparency of meaning nor the opacity of force but *the difference within the exertion of forces*" (201; my italics).

The blue chasm represents a Romantic metasubjective scene of writing, the formation of (poetic) memory as the play of differential forces, but one which Freudian metapsychology can only do justice to, ironically, through repression. In this sense, read through Romantic metasubjectivity, the metaphoricity of the blue chasm's breach puts Derrida's *fort/da* with psychoanalysis under analysis. In this light the blue chasm is not a "first staging of memory," a scene for the (dis)appearance of the trace and a following *repression* of first memories; it does not amount to the "erasure of selfhood" (230), although the "homeless voice of waters" amounts to a sublime suspension of presence before the "dark deep thorough-fare" of the blue chasm (13.63, 65). Rather, the chasm is a *staging of first memory*, an epigenetic site where the Poet is confronted with a "weave of traces" at the creation of a memory which is not bound to Freud's representative unconscious. The chasm is a limit-experience of the archetypal-grammatological site of historicity *itself*, the "dark foundry, the first forging place of mythology" (*HCI* 17) from which emerge Schelling's system of the gods and Jung's collective unconscious. Instead of repression, one must speak here of Schellingian inhibition: for where repression marks the conflict-model of the Freudian psyche (where one can, at best, come to an uneasy truce with one's infantile past), we have seen that inhibition inaugurates Nature's Thanatopoietic bidirectionality, which ungrounds nostalgia with a futurity that cannot be folded back into Freud's "short-circuits" on the return to inorganicity, or a *Nachträglichkeit* ultimately bound to the spectre of primal phantasy. If *The Prelude* is an epic of "soul-making" (Hartman, *Wordsworth's Poetry* 220), this soul is now the unruly imagination which, as "under presence," will resist the Poet's efforts to inscribe it within the project of showing "how the mind of man becomes/A thousand times more beautiful than the earth/On which he dwells [...] as it is itself/Of substance and of fabric more divine" (13.446–52). In other words, "soul" is now the soul of *Ages*, an interiority that opens on to its Outside, an opening which "commences with the arousal of that internal bifurcation that spreads throughout all of nature" (*Ages* 58). As Wirth puts it, soul is "the deformative force indwelling within all form [...] the excess of the form within the form, its animistic life" ("Translator's Introduction" xii).

Book Eleven of *1805* captures the fundamental dynamic of Thanatopoietic movement: "the hiding-places of my power/Seem open; I approach, and then they close" (11.336–37). What closes these "hiding-places" of radical productivity to the Poet is the "meditation" (13.66ff) occurring after he encounters Snowdon's "breaches." Like the "meditativeness" of Book Six, this meditation remembers and works through the experience of the *Ungrund* at Snowdon, binding it under the visionary rubric of Imagination, sublimating the indeterminate purposiveness of the "dark deep thorough-fare" into a teleology which, in working through sublime trauma, appropriates the symbol of the stream as a condensation of potencies to dilute their synchronistic charge. In effect, *The Prelude*'s teleological therapeutics put the ecstasy of this encounter under erasure. The Poet figures the scene atop Snowdon as

> The perfect image of a mighty Mind,
> Of one that feeds upon infinity,
> That is exalted by an underpresence,
> The sense of God, or whatsoe'er is dim
> Or vast in its own being. (13.69–73)

The poetic metapsychology here once again both courts and resists the potency of the original sublime event at Snowdon. The "underpresence" so consanguineous with the "under thirst" driving the Poet in Book Six paradoxically "exalts" a "perfect image," but the "sense of God" is *also* equated with this underpresence and whatever is "dim or vast" in itself. God is thus supplanted through analogy even as *1799*'s language of potentiation (retrospectively judged as "careless" [13.124]) is now transcendentalised: the "higher minds" which now monopolise an obedient imagination are now "Powers" emanating "from the Deity" (13.106–7).

But the Poet's triumphant reassertion of teleology now equates Snowdon's unruly imagination with "reason in her most exalted mood" (13.170) as it poeticises the emergence of consciousness from the depths of the unconscious. *The Prelude* now becomes a Hegelian phenomenology of spirit, a project "[tracing] the stream/From darkness, and the very place of birth in its blind cavern" to its paths "Among the ways of Nature" only to lose and find it once more "reflecting in its solemn breast/The works of man and face of human life" (13.172–81). This human, all too human teleology represses the geo-mythological *Ungrund* encountered at Snowdon. Ironically, it is the very figure of God – here both "Deity" and "underpresence" – that marks a persistent unruliness, a purposive energy underwriting the Poet's sublimation of these powers just as the Poet's "History" is "brought/To its appointed close" (13.269–70). The consummated "Poet's mind" takes a bow while Nature, as "softening mirror of the moral world" (13.271, 288), recedes. *The Prelude* manages to retain some semblance of lyric voice through its constitutive tension between Nature's purposive energies and the mind's teleological impetus.

But turning to *Prometheus Unbound*'s dissociative topography of the Romantic metasubjective psyche we find – paradoxically, in a lyrical drama written years after *The Prelude* – a dark precursor to Wordsworth's poetic voice where the lyric voice is almost completely subsumed by the chorus of Romantic metasubjectivity's inscrutable beginnings.

Prometheus Unbound: the traumatic awakening of Romantic metasubjectivity

In "To Wordsworth" (1816), Shelley criticises what he sees as a conservative turn in Wordsworth's political thinking. "In honoured poverty thy voice did weave/Songs consecrate to truth and liberty, –/Deserting these, thou leavest me to grieve,/Thus having been, that thou shouldst cease to be" (11–14). The "Songs consecrate to truth and liberty" are ostensibly political, but Shelley's connection of poetry with the "moral improvement of man" and view of the imagination as "the great instrument of moral good" ("Defence" 517) clearly align poetry and moral action; inhibition of poetic energy brings with it inhibition of political freedom (the rhyme structure of Shelley's sonnet [*ababcdcdeefgfg*] is neither Petrarchan nor Shakespearean – almost as if Shelley wants to *poetically* liberate Wordsworth through his poem's irregular structure). Shelley's desire in this poem to emancipate Wordsworth from the shackles of a perceived conservatism reflects a sentiment that persists in *Prometheus Unbound* (1820) which, as Shelley wrote to Thomas Peacock in 1819, is "a drama, with characters & a mechanism of a kind yet unattempted" (*Poems of Shelley* 2: 458). But the unfoldings of Shelley's lyrical drama problematise the political Idealism he deploys to bind its dramatism. In his essays "On Life" and the "Defence of Poetry," both conceived and published contemporaneously with *Prometheus Unbound*, Shelley insists that things only exist as they are perceived ("On Life" 508; "Defence" 533). In the Preface to *Prometheus Unbound*, however, Shelley tells us the poem's imagery is meant to show "the operations of the human mind, or [...] those external actions by which they are expressed" (l. 45).[9] As we will see, it is the problematic transferential imagery of the poem, whereby *dramatis personae* adopt each other's characteristics and (at times) thoughts, that make perception something less than the dependable arbiter of existence Shelley wants.

This transferential fluidity also resists a critical orthodoxy surrounding *Prometheus Unbound* which constellates its dynamisms around the mind of Prometheus as a self-present being. And if psychoanalytic criticism of *Prometheus Unbound* has tended to focus on the personalist Oedipal agon between Prometheus and Jupiter as tyrannical father, the poem has also been subject to the orthodox Jungian archetypal taxonomy of Shadow, Anima/Animus, Wise Old Man/Woman, and so forth. In both approaches the focus is on a character conspicuously *absent* from much of the text (and significantly the entire final act), and this problematises the arbitrary centring of Shelley's "lyrical drama" on a single "lyric" voice – indeed, one doubts if such a single voice can be found in a text whose diachrony exceeds the purview of Prometheus. For example, Earl Wasserman's highly influential study of *Prometheus Unbound* claims that

> the human revolution and the history of human perfection [...] have here been transposed to the level of total Existence, the metaphysical reality here named "Prometheus." [...] [E]xcept for Demogorgon, Prometheus is the only reality actually present in the play, and it would be short of the truth even to say that the drama takes place *in* his mind; he *is* the One Mind. [As opposed to unknowable Being,] the limited domain of *Prometheus Unbound* is that unitary *mode* of Being that appears in thought-constituted existence. (257)

Like many psychoanalytic readings of the poem, Wasserman tacitly privileges consciousness in the form of Prometheus as both dramatic figure and mythological emblem. He thus elides the degree to which the poem's psychic topography intuits a profoundly *pre*conscious, *pre*discursive Romantic dynamism, a dramatic unfolding of the emergence of the personal from the nexus of nonmolar forces which constitute its outside. This hypostatisation is shared by Thomas Frosch, who argues that "Shelley tells the story of both Prometheus and Asia emerging from parental figures into their own maturity" (128). Frosch also suggests a pantheon of stable lyrical unities in *Prometheus Unbound*'s unfolding individuative movement: "from a Jungian perspective, we might read act 1 as a confrontation with the shadow, or dark side of Prometheus, and act 2 as a confrontation with the anima, or his female side" (316 n. 2). Also dutifully applying an orthodox Jungian taxonomy, William Hildebrand adopts the language of "Jungian romance" to describe Asia as Prometheus' "anima" and Demogorgon as the "dragon guarding the treasure-hard-to-find" (195). These figures ultimately turn back to the personalised figure of Prometheus;

the transition from Acts One to Two is a Romantic reverie involving "an inner dialectic among figures that are aspects of [Prometheus'] self" (194). Similarly, Thomas Simons views the poem as "being played out against a mental/mythic, terrene/cosmic subjectively shifting backdrop where everything that arises has its source in the various aspects of, and conflicts in, the mind of Prometheus" (2–3).

A reading through the lens of Romantic metasubjectivity rescues *Prometheus Unbound* from these personalistic trappings and casts the text (specifically Prometheus' curse and Demogorgon's proclamation at the end of the poem) in its properly Romantic dimensions, as something irreducible to Oedipal dynamics or Jungian structuralism. As Rajan writes,

> The interdiscursive nature of the Romantic lyric problematizes the mode by revealing the traces of another voice within the seemingly autonomous lyric voice. [In *Prometheus Unbound*, while] the lyrics bear the freight of the play's idealistic vision, [...] their insertion into a dramatic context radically decentres this vision, potentiating the traces of its differences from itself. [Lyric] is associated with a logocentrism that mutes the difference between language and what it signifies, whereas drama makes explicit the dialogic nature of language, because the presence of more than one speaker makes the text as a whole and even the individual speeches within it a perpetually shifting intersection of textual surfaces rather than something fixed. ("Romanticism" 195, 203)

Indeed, Rajan's critique of the lyric sheds light on an unresolved contradiction in Frosch's account, perhaps typical of efforts to centre *Prometheus Unbound*'s poetic energies solely on Prometheus. Frosch writes that "to change the world, Prometheus must change his words," but "words are like things or physical forces" (134). The ego-centricity of the former is undermined by the suprapersonal nature of the latter; the performative aspect of Romantic language offers a productive way of thinking this contradiction but leads away from Frosch's personalist account.

In a lyrical drama about the *unbinding* of Prometheus, the rubric of potency and trace is entirely apropos. Reading Prometheus' curse and the protean figure of Demogorgon through the lens of Romantic metasubjectivity, I want to show how *Prometheus Unbound* offers a topography of the productive, differential unconscious emerging through this dissociative fault-line between lyric and drama. Structured by the differential of archetypal grammatology, the *dramatis personae* (Jung's complexes) both differ from and meld into each other in a play of intensities, coming forth, speaking, and receding in a dramatic unfolding which figures Prometheus not as epic centre (or epicentre), but as a Schellingian natural product neither fixed nor stable within the poetic economy of Shelley's lyrical drama. Through *Prometheus Unbound* Shelley does not figure the operations of the Idealist mind, but unfolds the moments of individuative *Trieb* and the dissociative psyche from which they emerge, even as the tension between lyric and drama leads him to attempt to re-bind this psyche's indeterminacy in his own troubled Idealism.

Thus, *Prometheus Unbound* dramatises the dissociative psyche in a traumatic double-bind which marks Romantic metasubjectivity's epigenesis. That is, this topography is informed by two narratives which touch and do not touch each other: Prometheus' revolution against Jupiter's tyranny and the emergence of consciousness from the unconscious. The inability of these narratives to tell each other allegorises Jung's dissociationist historical psyche as the motor force of Romantic metasubjectivity. The traumatic and dissociative substructure of Shelley's poem is evident from the beginning: *Prometheus Unbound* opens with Prometheus chained to a rock in the Caucasus, unable to remember the words of the momentous curse which precipitated his imprisonment. This inability catalyses his dialogue with "voices" of Nature and ultimately the Earth, who brings forth the phantasm (who is and is not Prometheus) to utter the curse's cisionary words which impel the poem's unfolding through a fluid economy of *dramatis personae* who at times synaesthetically adopt each other's attributes. Shelley's classical framework thus dramatises Schelling's unprethinkable cisionary moment, the *Naturphilosophische* economy to which it gives rise, and the purposive drive of a Romantic metasubjective individuation which is not confined to Prometheus himself. Away from (or perhaps "beneath") *Prometheus Unbound*'s political allegory, Schelling's "drama of a struggle between form and the formless" becomes the dramatic emergence of consciousness from an infinite productivity emblematised by gods, spirits, and chorea. Through their own fluid dramaturgy, and thus their problems with identity akin to the problems of type shared with actant and archetype, these Shelleyan forces write Schelling's alignment of language with mythology as psychic topography. I thus read the complex nature of Prometheus' curse of Jupiter, the dramaturgic (counter)transferences between the text's characters, and Demogorgon's significance as focal points in the dissociative topography of the Romantic metasubjective psyche.

The emergence of consciousness from the productive unconscious in *Prometheus Unbound* is conditioned by its unfolding within a history allegorised by Shelley's political Idealism, but also troubled by the metapsychology *avant la lettre* which makes this history possible. This "impossible and necessary double-telling," "the inextricability of the story of one's life from the story of one's death" (Caruth 8), marks the traumatic nature of *Prometheus Unbound* and its double-telling of both the "life" of (political) consciousness and the "death," the cision into time and history, which represent the poem's diachronic and synchronic elements. Cathy Caruth sees trauma as "a fundamental enigma concerning the psyche's relation to reality. [...] Traumatic experience, beyond [psychological suffering], suggests a certain paradox: that *the most direct seeing of a violent event may occur as an absolute inability to know it*; that immediacy, paradoxically, may take the form of belatedness" (91–92; my italics). Trauma thus involves a fundamental bifurcation of two stories: the latent, "originary" trauma whose origins are lost in their very emergence and a more manifest narrative of repetition-compulsion whose trauma is redoubled in its own melancholy, its quest for the dis-appeared trauma of its beginning. Trauma is a failed exorcism, or rather an exorcism aware of its own traumatic origins – exorcism haunted by its archaic meaning of "to conjure up" as well as to dispel (*OED* 3). Put differently, if the history of trauma (or the trauma of history) means that "it is referential precisely to the extent that it is not fully perceived as it occurs [...] that a history can be grasped only in the very inaccessibility of its occurrence" (18), the incommensurability between these two stories bespeaks the trauma of Romantic metasubjectivity's historical psyche.

What for Jung recedes into the inchoate "mists of time" is encrypted here in the hieroglyphics of myth. As Rajan puts it, *Prometheus Unbound*'s action "takes place in a space outside the space of history: a mental space that risks implication in the ambiguities of the historical process if it seeks to embody itself in fact and event, and accepts a certain abstraction if it does not achieve such embodment" (*Dark Interpreter* 91). But *Prometheus Unbound*'s dual narrative of trauma, in fact, suggests that this risk has already been taken. Through the lens of Romantic metasubjectivity, the transferential dynamic running through the lyrical drama marks the movements of a dissociative psyche without conceivable origin – always already placed in history. Even as Shelley's rewriting of Aeschylus resists reconciliation between Jupiter and Prometheus, the end of the poem (exemplified by Demogorgon's warning: we are free, but tyranny can always return) both courts and resists this tyrannical return to stasis in a Thanatopoietic rhythm. Without naming *Thanatopoiesis*, the transference Jerrold Hogle sees at the heart of Shelley's poetry is described in Freudian terms as a "*thanatos*, the fading of [whose] past moments is simultaneously an *eros* seeking another relation" (22). For Shelley, this transference has an ontological charge; "language itself is poetry" (Shelley, "Defence" 512), and as such this transference becomes "the force moving through all writings and readings" of literature and culture (Hogle 5). Thus, one can read *Prometheus Unbound*'s dual narratives of emancipation and emergence as the robust exposition of a Romantic hermeneutics which, as "a process with consequences for the intellectual life of the interpreter," risks a productive transference with the reader (Rajan, *Supplement* 70–71). Shelley's troubled Idealism leads him to attempt to gather up the transferential dynamic of *Prometheus Unbound* into a *Trieb* toward freedom in the guise of "Necessity." But the figure of Demogorgon, as the poetic force of Schelling's "No that resists the Yes, [the] darkening that resists the light, this obliquity that resists the straight" (*Ages* 6), persists as an indeterminate remainder in the text's economy, a dark figure whose presence eternally frustrates this idealist thrust even as it guarantees its persistence. Indeed the final act of *Prometheus Unbound*, as "a polyphonic hymn in which different voices are part of a single harmony" from which Prometheus himself is conspicuously absent (Rajan, *Dark Interpreter* 93), has an indeterminate, metapsychologically dissociative horizon that resists Shelley's Idealism. Let us turn, then, to *Prometheus Unbound*'s compulsive beginnings.

In *Prometheus Unbound* the drama of dissociation presents us with the paradox of a prediscursive discourse – metadrama and metadialogue, words spoken about a state of time and history which both has yet to come into being and has somehow already transpired (Prometheus is, after all, bound for a reason). The poem thus marks a Romantic yearning for the *Ungrund*, the quest for erased origins. Across its mythological, political, and metapsychological determinations, the trauma of *Prometheus Unbound* is thus Shelley's staging of the erasure of beginnings already present in the actants' mutual derangement in the *First Outline* and which also informs *Ages*' rotatory motion. It is the liminal state of Jung's archetypes and the collective unconscious, the unprethinkable beginnings of the "operations of the human mind." Indeed, like *Ages* and *The Prelude*, *Prometheus Unbound* begins and begins again in a cyclic motion. In this, it emulates the willingness to repeat that drives the Jungian archetype as a force on the cusp of Being and its own differentiation in time and history. Like the archetypes and the collective unconscious, it *has happened* (the *there is* of the unconscious) and *has yet to happen* (insofar as this *there is* only *comes to be* in time and history, in specific manifestations). Act One begins in an unconscious virtual space of "the shadows of all forms that think and live" (1.195ff), with Prometheus' confrontation with his curse as *écriture*, as deep "imageless truth" (2.4.116), followed by his torment at the hands of the Furies as traumatic affect, motile forces which, like Jupiter's phantasm, do not "know" in the conscious sense, "execrable shapes" at which Prometheus stares in "loathsome sympathy" because they emerge from himself (1.463, 451, 470–72). Act Two compulsively re-begins on the other side (so to speak) of *Prometheus Unbound*'s psyche. Here, Asia and Panthea awake from sleep, both recollecting and repressing knowledge of Prometheus' trauma in Act One (one dream can simply not be remembered) through a visionary ekphrasis that congeals its play of forces into a perfect analytic scene in which one can "read" not only the other, but Prometheus' "soul" (2.1.61ff). Act Three recapitulates Act One's traumatic beginnings: in Jupiter's court, Thetis is congealed into an image of thought ("bright Image of Eternity!" [3.1.36]), a representation concealing her traumatic rape by Jupiter which begets "a third/Mightier than either [of them], which, unbodied now/Between us, floats, felt although unbeheld, Waiting the incarnation, which ascends [...] from Demogorgon's throne" (3.1.43–48). This repressed trauma leads to Demogorgon's appearance as "fatal child." His conquest of Jupiter (3.1.53ff) recapitulates the cosmogony of Prometheus' curse on the level of history, which inaugurates historicity itself as the contracting force (A^1) of tyranny exploded by Demogorgon as the indeterminate, infinite expansion of A^2.

The final Act, like Act One, is a primal site which contains no scenes. It opens in a visionary mode, replete with spirits and choruses whose rhyming songs now supplant the more disjunctive, traumatic rhythm of the curse. In other words, these beginnings play out the differentiating economy of the collective unconscious. But the Act closes with Demogorgon's warning of tyranny's return, invoking the text of *Prometheus Unbound* itself as "spell" (4.568), an interminable rotatory motion meant to assert the purposiveness of historicity (as Necessity) against any efforts to congeal it into a hegemony of the Same – even the tyranny of Shelley's troubled Idealism. The text compulsively repeats itself as a circle of knowledge without circumference. In this sense, read as what Jung calls an archetypal situation (birth, coming into consciousness but also the struggle for freedom), the entirety of *Prometheus Unbound* is a deconstruction of the archetype into its unmanageable and potentially infinite forces. The transferential dynamic between *dramatis personae* in Shelley's lyrical drama emblematises the impossibility reflected in Jung's "as if" regarding the archetype. Of course, the drama unfolds in the sequence of events Shelley consciously intends, but Demogorgon's reference back to the text of the play at the end (reminiscent of James Joyce's *Finnegans Wake*) reflects a compulsive repetition which invites the reader to revisiting the text again (and again?) to re-experience the act of reading, even as every reading is different. This compulsive self-referentiality – *Prometheus Unbound*'s archetypally repetitive pattern – ensures the repetition of difference within the Same in precisely the same way the archetype is experienced. Like Prometheus' curse, *Prometheus Unbound* is language beside itself in precisely the same sense as mythology when Schelling writes that "*every* meaning in mythology is merely potential, like in chaos, but without therefore allowing itself to be limited or particularized" (*HCI* 14).

Thus the text aptly begins with a cosmic view of "bright and rolling worlds" whose ever-present activity, visible only to Prometheus and Jupiter, is unavailable to Asia's desire for truth's visionary disclosure in Act Two. In response to Asia's desire for proper names and presence, Demogorgon replies: "a voice/Is wanting, the deep truth is imageless;/ For what would it avail to bid thee gaze/On the revolving world?" (1.2, 2.4.115–18). And Earth, as the first Act's rotatory motion of the "revolving world," is anxiogenic for Prometheus. Like Asia's demand for visionary presence in Act Two, Prometheus asks Earth for the proper words of the curse. As a dissociative force both itself (Earth) and a chorus of "Voices," the Earth cannot give *an* answer, but gives *answers* dispersed across the four elements and traumatic events in natural history (1.74ff). The Earth's following account of the Magus Zoroaster's vision (1.191ff) might seem to promise a Shelleyan version of Wordsworth's "preparatory intercourse" to the sublime convergence of real and ideal. Zoroaster's vision is synchronistic, revealing a continuity between ostensibly Promethean consciousness and its shadowy Other in "two worlds of life and death," a world of the living and a Demogorgonian world inhabited by Gods, "Powers," "The shadows of all forms that think and live" which are uncannily consubstantial with the products of the imagination (195–202). The curse is known by all of these powers ("Son, one of these shall utter/ The curse which all remember" [1.209–10]), and the Earth tells Prometheus to "Call at will/Thine own ghost, or the ghost of Jupiter,/Hades, or Typhon, or what mightier Gods/From all-prolific evil" (1.210–13). But repressing this traumatic revelation, Prometheus admonishes his mother Earth to "let not aught/Of that which may be evil, pass again/My lips, or those of aught resembling me" (1.218–20), calling forth Jupiter's phantasm which, in his infatuation with an idealist self-consciousness, he mistakenly understands as absolutely different from himself.[10]

Prometheus asks for the curse and instead receives accounts of its effects in Nature from the four Voices, whose lines of unified rhyme paradoxically express scenes of natural cataclysm. This makes Prometheus lament his maternal Earth as Other, as a chorus and not an answering being: "I hear a sound of voices: not the voice/Which I gave forth. [...] Know ye not me,/ The Titan? he who made his agony/The barrier to your else all-conquering foe?" (1.112–13, 117–18). This stands in stark contrast with the second beginning, the perfect transference Asia enjoys with Panthea as questioning and answering beings (2.1.35ff), but it also ironically points to *Prometheus Unbound*'s entanglement in early nineteenth-century discourses. These "operations of the human mind" – particularly throughout Act Four and the encounter with Demogorgon – are written through and between geology, astronomy, and evolution in a proliferation of scientific discourses arguably unprecedented in English Romantic poetry (*The Poems of Shelley* 2: 469). This disciplinary transference resists a metaphysically privileged reading or an idealist personalism that asserts, for example, that "Jupiter has been created and sustained in being by the actions and attitudes of Prometheus himself" (Wasserman 467). In this intertextual sense, *Prometheus Unbound* establishes constitutive metaphors of natural processes and phenomena for its psychic topography in precisely the spirit in which Jung writes that "*the unconscious is Nature*" (*Symbols* 62). In this spirit, Hogle argues that a density of textual transferences in the opening of the poem informs the dynamic of Promethean "disruption and reconstitution" from Aeschylus to Milton to the Jesus of Thomas Paine (174).

Within this dissociative topography, Prometheus' curse exists as both *ideology* and *aetiology* – as the political declaration of freedom from Jupiter's political tyranny but also a locution of the Schellingian cision into time and history, a curse pronounced in Shelley's version of Wordsworth's "characters of the Apocalyps." The curse is a poetic locution of Jung's archetypes and Schelling's actants, whose origins in language and Nature, respectively, are crystallised in the pronunciations of a Being which has begun *and* has yet to begin. *Prometheus Unbound*'s first beginning is thus one of cision and separation: Prometheus is chained to the precipice and, pitted as he is against Jupiter, they are both nonetheless the sole witnesses to the rotatory motion of the planets. Already they are linked in the transference, the separation and combination that persists throughout the poem to its ambivalent ending. They are witness to the imbrication of forces at the heart of the cosmos. We are already in an anxious psychic topography.

While Everest and Matthews point to the strangely (and significantly) contrived turning point in Prometheus' wish for vengeance on Jupiter (1.53–59),[11] the curse itself is subject to several levels of determination. "The Curse/Once breathed on thee I would recall" (1.58–59): the significant ambiguity of "recall," which can mean either "remember" or "revoke," has been the focus of much debate (481 n. 59). But within the framework of Romantic metasubjectivity's dissociative topography, the terms in fact converge to punctuate the curse's cisionary status. Prometheus' curse is always already unthinkable apart from its phantasmic nature: alien to Prometheus himself, it is "breathed" as language beside itself, Schlegel's arche-poetry in its enigmatic density, an utterance eluding its own nature as "language" while retaining its cisionary performativity. As a trope of the grammatology of Being, trauma is the curse's *arche*. With one exception, the curse is the only language "breathed" and not "spoken" or "told"; the other instance, fittingly, is in the Spirit of the Hour's post-liberation vision, where nymphs synaesthetically "look" the love "felt" by Prometheus, Asia, and the Earth, and no hollow talk "makes the heart deny the *yes* it breathes" (3.4.150). Shelley would doubtless be attuned to the significance of breath as spirit, *afflatus*. This liberated "yes," read as a terrestrialisation of the loving *yes* of Schelling's God and the impetus of creation (*Ages* 73, 65), forms the obverse of the curse, which, as a declaration of political separation but also of *binding* transference, can be seen as Schelling's No.

Schelling writes: "There is no dawning of consciousness [...] without positing something past [...] something that is at the same time excluded and contracted" (*Ages* 44). The curse signifies a Schellingian apostrophe to/of the lightning flash, the indeterminate birth of both language and poetry for Shelley ("Defence" 520, 528) and Schelling's "incomprehensible primordial act" which both "decides" human freedom and marks the beginning of time and history (*Ages* 77–78). Thus, to remember the curse would be *precisely* to revoke it, to bring it into the purview of the thinkable – to speak it in a discourse which has not yet come into being. And yet, this past is "posited," with no conceivable beginning. The curse, then, is language beside itself, language whose performativity is always already written into Nature in the guise of the reactions of the four spirits to the event, as well as the "many-voicèd Echoes" of Mountains which can only echo the curse, iterate it in the discourses of natural science and geology (1.60 & ff) as manifestations of archetype and actant. Mind can only express itself in Nature – indeed, one wonders how porous the boundary is between them.

When the curse of Prometheus finally manifests, it is through the phantasm of Jupiter summoned by the Earth; it is not spoken, but emerges ventriloquised through a transferential dynamic. In terms of a Jungian therapeutics of presence, Prometheus is a stubborn analysand who both disavows (as "evil" [1.218–21]) and invokes Jupiter as his "shadow" (Wasserman's "moral opposite" [259]) – a figure of the tyranny of which Prometheus himself is capable. But the relationship between Prometheus and the phantasm of Jupiter exceeds the orthodoxy of self-present archetypes such as Shadow, Anima, and Animus, just as it exceeds Wasserman's taking Prometheus at his word to reductively judge the curse as an "evil" (259).[12] Rather, the mesh of dissociation and transference surrounding the curse amplifies its status as cisionary signature, a marker of the unthinkable beginnings of the productive unconscious to which *Prometheus Unbound*'s dramaturgy attests. To be sure, the curse's profound statement of egoity ironically enunciates the dissociative transference between Prometheus and Jupiter: Jupiter's phantasm, ventriloquising Prometheus, proclaims: "O'er all things but *thyself I* gave *thee* power,/And *my* own will" (1.273–74; my italics). Indeed, when the phantasm speaks under the influence of this spirit, "the heaven/Darkens above" in a re-manifestation of the natural events attending the original curse, seemingly in contradistinction to the undifferentiated underworld of "shadows of all forms that think and live/

Till death unite them and they part no more" (1.198–99; see also 1.101–2, 1.256–57). Dissociations upon dissociations; the overdeterminations of this statement pile up to make these words less intersubjective locution and more impersonal dynamism. The first line, "O'er all things but thyself I gave thee power," recognises the fundamental dissociation in both dramatic figures of this encounter, who are both given power by their respective Other (through the floating signifiers "thyself," "thee," and "my") and yet *lack* the idealised self-consciousness which never materialises in the polyphonic hymn which ends the drama. After all, Prometheus cannot remember/revoke the curse which catalyses his liberation, or "self-dawning" as consciousness of freedom, and the curse is spoken here by a phantasm whose words are not "informed by thought" (1.249), a phantasm itself "seized" and "torn" by a "spirit" even from the inhabitants of the "world of death" to which Prometheus must turn to remember the curse (1.254). This Promethean "analysis" at the dynamic core of *Prometheus Unbound* is an anamnesis, in effect a schizoanalysis with a pantheon of forces (Earth, Voices, and Echoes) symbolising the indeterminate forces of Schellingian actant and Jungian archetype.

We have seen that actant and archetype are both attended by the same epistemological difficulties: Schelling can no more set down the laws by which actants (de)compose than Jung can move beyond the "as if" of archetypal typology. Even though for Schelling each "decombined" individual actant follows a trajectory of "free transformation" when left to its own devices (*FO* 33), it is only when they are combined that they approach the "*most original fluidity*" from which all products come, a body without organs liminal in itself, held tense against the moment of its very dissolution and reconstitution. This is Schelling's *Naturphilosophische* statement of the paradoxical relationship between freedom and necessity which, we have seen, figures so importantly in the later *Freedom* essay as a theory of personality. Complementing Schelling's metaphysics, however, Jung's focus on the interplay of opposites informs his ideas on the transference as "a special form of projection," a "carrying over from one form into another," a "dynamic relationship between subject and object" which Jung equates with translation (*Tavistock* pars. 311f, 317). Indeed, Hogle sees Prometheus *himself* as transferentially constructed: "each point of departure [...] finds itself at least half-repeating shapes in the repository of older forms that is the 'ground' of the new figure [...] and, whatever happens, cannot be left entirely for dead. Hence *the Titan is this drama*" (176; my italics). This is the only sense in which we can talk about *Prometheus Unbound* as a "personalised" drama – through the transferences between *dramatis personae*, analogous to the dance of (de)composition in Schelling's actants and the general economy of the archetypes which articulate the dissociative topography of Romantic metasubjectivity. Shelley's text even shares Jung's ambivalence over the phenomena of the transference: on the one hand, embodying the very interplay of freedom and necessity, the transferences in *Prometheus Unbound* serve Shelley's troubled Idealism in the form of characters who can read each other perfectly and synaesthetically share experiences. On the other hand, the confluence of Prometheus and Demogorgon in the poem's opening and (as we will see) in the curse unsettle the integrity of the boundaries which make this Idealism possible.

"Lift up thine eyes/And let me read thy dream" (2.1.55–56): thus begins the second beginning, the idealised analytical scene between Asia and Panthea. What Panthea brings to Asia – "music" of "wordless converse; since dissolved/Into the sense with which love talks" (2.1.51–3) – ventriloquises Prometheus, yet this "sense" of love synaesthetically combines seeing, reading, and hearing. What follows in the exchange between Asia and Panthea is not merely the analysis of a subject presumed to know. Panthea not only "knows" her first dream and can communicate it to Asia in a perfect scene of counter-transference; Asia can also read the dream Panthea *cannot* recall (2.1.127ff) – a dream of pure *Trieb* whose "follow! follow!" impels them toward Demogorgon's Cave just as it serves as the occasion for Panthea's recalled dream, in turn, to "Fill, pause by pause, [Asia's] own forgotten sleep/With shapes" (2.1.142–43). Both dreams of vivid imagery, signed with "methought" as uncertainty and a troubling of the ekphrastic containment both seek to impose, uncannily mirror each other as they gesture toward a *Trieb* which can only be a formless imperative. Both are accompanied by a wind with ill portent ("unwilling" or "frost-wrinkling" [2.1.137, 147]), and in both dreams this imperative is "stamped" and narrated in the forms of the natural world, bringing together the dark imperative of poetic language with the stamp, or type, of archetypal forms themselves saturated with the Nature they "typify" (2.1.139–40, 152, 155).[13]

The utterance of the curse, however, points to a darker confluence which does not eclipse the transference between Asia and Panthea, but is rather the focal point of *Prometheus Unbound*'s dramatic *telos*. The confluence between Prometheus and Demogorgon, allusively embedded in the fabric of the curse ("One being only you shall not subdue" [1.265]), is rendered more obscurely than Asia's and Panthea's idealised commingling. Written outside any phantasy of commensurability, the suggestiveness of this "One" points to an "other," darker side of transference *not* predicated on an anamnestic desire to (as Paul de Man would say) "intentionally forget" Prometheus as object of desire through the reminiscence of dreams.[14] Rather, in its erasure of metaphoricity the allusiveness of this "One" asserts ontological difference – the "imageless" deep truth – *against* intentional structure; indeed, both instances of allusive transference between Prometheus and Demogorgon (1.2, 265) mark "One" as an absent image – a bodying-forth of One which is always already many. And insofar as across these two key passages "One" refers variously to Prometheus, Jupiter, and Demogorgon, this Shelleyan "One" can be read as a depth-psychologisation *avant la lettre* of Schelling's Godhead in the *Ages of the World*. That is, the "One" is the "No" (Jupiter as "consuming No, an eternally wrathful force that tolerates no Being outside itself" [*Ages* 73]), the "Yes" (Prometheus as Love, "an eternal outstretching, giving, and communicating of […] being" [*Ages* 11]), and the third term, or (in)compossibility of the Yes and No (Demogorgon as Necessity, born from Jupiter/the unconscious, who frees Prometheus by claiming Jupiter [3.1.52ff] while averring that Jupiter/the unconscious can always return). Put differently: just as consciousness emerges from the unconscious through some inscrutable historical process for Jung, and for Schelling the cisionary break into time and history *must* have happened (through precisely the Necessity Shelley here imputes to mythological-historical processes), so Shelley's Promethean narrative of the "operations of the human mind" posits this emergence in a narrative of political revolt which cannot narrate its own topography. Indeed, the transferences between characters and their variations in intensity and determinacy figure Schelling's assertion that Yes or No can be dominant and recessive at different times, depending on "the simultaneity among the different forms being sublimated and transformed into a succession" (*Ages* 77).

Demogorgon's "appearance" is thus heralded by the *Trieb* of *follow!* (2.1.132 & ff), which moves away from the phenomenological object even as it compulsively repeats its own refrain (indeed, Panthea's and Asia's blank verse is increasingly punctured by hyphenated caesurae with the waxing of the Song of Spirits [2.3.22ff]). Yet as evinced in Asia's and Panthea's encounter in Demogorgon's cave, there is something more to Demogorgon than a symbol for the power of language to posit *things* or "do things," as Frosch avers (135). To be sure Demogorgon is, in one sense, "a name for a beginning or a name by which a beginning is made, a mystification that both clears the way for new forward developments and stops things from developing backward in an infinite regression" (Frosch 167). But this is only one of *Prometheus Unbound*'s narratives – a linear narrative of (for Shelley, political) progress which, as I have said, cannot account for the traumatic conditions of its emergence. For in another more significant sense Demogorgon resists the very idea of origins, as "a basic silence at the heart of things which refuses to be defined and yields no ultimate assurances" (Rajan, *Dark Interpreter* 89). And it is this un-beginning, this absence of origins and unwriting of finality that constitutes Demogorgon as the essence of Romantic metasubjective *Trieb*. Indeed Demogorgon's dual aspect, as both before beginning and time *and* an historical entity which overthrows Jupiter, makes him an emblem of the problem of Schellingian beginnings; Demogorgon embodies the paradoxical, erasural act of beginning in a lyrical drama which ends without ever having truly *begun*. This un-beginning, in Schelling's mythological terms, is a crisis of consciousness which narrates the transferences between the theogonic forces which engender it.

It is precisely in Demogorgon[15] as the figure of Necessity – *Trieb* itself – that we find the Thanatopoietic drive of Romantic metasubjectivity which systolic-diastolically regresses and progresses toward the horizon of "Self"hood. It is tempting to see Prometheus, retired with Asia in their timeless cave and idly bantering about time and change, as an emblem of the "Self of one's self" in Shelley's poem. But it is precisely their depotentiated language that removes them from the fundamental historicity of Romantic metasubjectivity's grammatology of Being, making Demogorgon the force of purposive individuation as the "absent center" of the Self. Asia and Panthea are led to Demogorgon's cave by the same "echoes music-tongued" which exist in a liminal suspension between the mimetic and the epigenetic. These echoes[16] do not simply mimic Asia's recounting of her dream ("*follow! follow!*" [2.1.162]); they speak, as it were, with the strange utterance of *Trieb*'s necessity, and in sustained rhyme reserved almost exclusively for Voices (1.74ff), the Furies (1.95ff), the Chorus (1.539ff), and the Song of Spirits (2.3.54ff). The echoes speak a rather odd epigenesis – the imperative to *follow!* is expressed as an epistemological shift away from de Man's intentional Romantic image and toward abstractions of lack and phenomenological absence. "Dew-stars" which "fade away" (2.1.168–69); a pursuit "Where the wild bee never flew" (180); "Through [...] darkness" and "By" the synaesthetic "odour-breathing sleep" of flowers; and finally, "To the rents, and gulfs, and chasms,/Where the Earth reposed from spasms/On the day when He and thou/Parted" (202–5). These negations accompany the refrain "O follow, follow" (2.1.173ff) under the governance of "Demogorgon's mighty law," which "draws" spirits forward, even as these same spirits are affectively "impelled" through "soft emotion" in the paradox of freedom and necessity characterising both actant and archetype (2.2.43–44, 50–51).

It is no accident that Asia and Panthea's final passage to Demogorgon's cave is through "rents, and gulfs, and chasms" – figurations of the *Ungrund* which uncannily mirror the 1805 *Prelude*'s chasmal Promethean phenomenology in Wordsworth's own "perfect image of a mighty mind." Demogorgon is not one of the poem's mythic personae: described as "Power," "velèd form," and "mighty Darkness," Asia and Panthea nevertheless *feel* Demogorgon affectively as "living Spirit" (2.3.11; 2.4.1, 2, 7). In response to Asia's autoerotic wish for commensurability between the "discourse of her heart" and revelation from this "living Spirit," Demogorgon instead

> refers her to the intentionality rather than the autonomy of the transforming imagination. In his equivocal and indirect answers he allows [Asia's discourse] to come up against a wall of silence which allows it to hope, but only in solitude and monologue, and without the support of dialogue with a transcendental source. (Rajan, *Dark Interpreter* 89)

Asia's encounter with Demogorgon is the exact obverse of her earlier, perfect analytical transference with Panthea. Asia asks Demogorgon for a proper name (2.4.9ff), a transcendental signified behind "the living world," the human psyche's faculties of "thought, passion, reason, will,/Imagination" and indeed the yearning essence of imaginative drive itself: "that sense which [...] Fills the faint eyes with falling tears which dim/The radiant looks of unbewailing flowers,/And leaves this peopled earth a solitude/When it returns no more" (2.4.12–18). Her response to Demogorgon's enigmas is to supply her own theogony – yet another beginning in Shelley's poem that establishes Demogorgon as *Ungrund* at the origins of mythology itself. Asia's theogony (2.4.32ff) is a cosmogonic screen memory, eliding the nonmolar (Demogorgonian) origins of the universe to make the cause of Nature's auto-alterity (the "unseasonable seasons" [52]) Jove and not the Promethean curse in a primal scene of Saturn's overthrow (49–58). In this vision's categorical imperative man receives the gift of speech, and "speech created thought/Which is the measure of the universe" (72–73) as well as the "harmonious mind," whose "all-prophetic song" (76–77) takes the form of love as binding force for the "disunited tendrils" of history (63–65). But this harmony is resisted by the polyphonic hymn at the poem's end, and the repressed element of the curse returns to reveal her theogony as a working-through that does not quite manage to measure the universe. For prophecy lays claim to a Necessity that remains indeterminate at the end of the theogony. The latent question beneath the manifest narrative is: who – significantly not *what*, but still *who* – underwrites the curse? (108–9). Asia's theogony adopts what Schelling calls the "poetic view" of mythology, mythology as merely poetic fabrication without truth (*HCI* 12ff). Schelling does not dismiss this view of mythology as false, but it must be sublated, thought to a higher potential by recognising the power (truth) of its generative ground.

Asia's theogony is a history which she, as subject presumed to know, relates to *herself* in the face of Demogorgon's refusal to do anything other than refer her to her own transformative energies (2.4.111–12). As actant or archetype in this dramatic topography Asia does not "bind," and is forced by Demogorgon, as *Trieb* of Necessity, to undergo her own "free transformation" prior to her later "recombination" with Prometheus in Act 3, Scene 3 (see *FO* 33). Indeed, only after this transformation can Asia retire with Prometheus to participate in the imaginative activity of making "Strange combinations out of common things,/Like human babes in their brief innocence" and "[weaving] harmonies divine, yet ever new,/ From difference sweet where discord cannot be" (3.3.32–33, 38–39). But the analytic encounter between Asia and Demogorgon in fact mirrors the movements of Jung's transcendent function, whereby new knowledge is created – here, a Thanatopoietic third which supplants Asia's poetic theogony. Only when Asia demands that Demogorgon answer "As my own soul would answer, did it know/That which I ask" (2.4.125–26) is that intentional representation reinstated in a vision of the cars of the "immortal Hours" which embody the Thanatopoietic progression-regression dynamic of Jungian libido considerably more abstracted in the figure of Demogorgon, who ventriloquises Asia's "soul" as answering being. Here, in the vision "demanded" by Asia (2.4.141), the Hours which ostensibly measure the progress of Promethean revolution, but more fundamentally the "operations of the human mind," look both "behind, as fiends pursued them there," and lean forth, and drink/With eager lips the wind of their own speed,/As if the thing they loved fled on before,/And now, even now, they clasped it" (2.4.133, 135–38).

But even here, in the seeming recrudescence of Shelley's troubled Idealism as Jupiter's inevitable downfall, the similes "as" and "as if" mark the indeterminacy of this very movement. The vision of the Hours is a product of the encounter between Asia and Demogorgon as questioning and answering beings: Demogorgon pulls the vision, so to speak, from Asia's soul (a soul Asia does not know), and in this vision is a "spirit with a dreadful countenance," a "shadow of a destiny" (2.4.142ff) emblematic of the nonmolar mythological forces beyond the merely poetic view of Asia's theogony. This vision is the third of Jung's transcendent function, except that where the transcendent function transpires between the human psyches of analyst and analysand, here it is between Asia and Demogorgon as the force of the *Ungrund itself.* This is why, in the reinstated intentionality of Asia's poetic imagery, *Thanatopoiesis* is not quite "real" – indeed, it only acquires real formative force with the unbinding of Prometheus and its proclamation by Demogorgon as *Ungrund*, or the *Trieb* of Necessity. Thus Asia's theogony remains imaginary, incommensurable with the mythological historicity represented by Demogorgon as "absent force."

With a phantasmal liminality mirroring Prometheus' cisionary curse, Demogorgon's final speeches are marked by "words that are not words." They unfold dramatically, on the level of language, across apostrophes and invocations to Earth, Moon, "Daemons and Gods,/Etherial Dominations," "Ye happy Dead," "Ye elemental Genii" and Voices (4.519ff). As "a mighty Power [...] rising out of Earth, and from the sky [...] showered like night, and from within the air/Burst[ing]" (4.510–13), Demogorgon's address manifests itself first as "a sense of words" and "an universal sound like words" which disrupts Ione's and Panthea's exclamations with caesurae (4.517–18). His address only gradually coalesces into proclamatory "words" once it turns to invoke forces tied more to Earth's temporal sphere – "elemental Genii," "Spirits whose home are flesh," and the various phenomena of the natural world (539ff). Demogorgon's final invocation, as linguistic and supralinguistic force, opens the horizon of futurity commensurate with Prometheus' unbinding, heralded by the blowing of a "many-folded shell" (3.3.80).

But if the shell's "mighty music" heralds futurity, its "thunder mixed with clear echoes" (3.3.82) nevertheless marks a remainder troubling any idealist conception of Demogorgonian Necessity as unbridled progression or the unmitigated dawning of Promethean consciousness. So what is at the heart of this futurity, this poetry of the shell? What are "the spells by which to re-assume/An empire over the disentangled Doom" (4.568–69)?[17] Do these spells refer to Demogorgon's final proclamations, or to the fraught "moment" of *Prometheus Unbound itself* as a dramatisation of the unaccountable beginnings of Romantic metasubjective *Trieb*? Either way we are confronted with the enigmatic density of poetic language which offers no guarantees, and the "Self of one's self," the provisional totality of Romantic metasubjectivity, is not figured as Prometheus (who is nowhere to be seen). Rather, it is the deep imageless truth of Demogorgon-as-Necessity, an individuative drive irreducible to its embodiment in any single personalised form. Demogorgon proclaims that what is "alone Life, Joy, Empire, and Victory" is when "Hope creates/from its own wreck the thing it contemplates" – a poetic figuration of analytical psychology's project of becoming its own object, and the fusion of real and ideal at the heart of Schelling's philosophical project (4.574ff). But this is not the Promethean. This victory is "like" Promethean glory, but this similitude nevertheless encrypts a difference which folds Shelley's hopeful Idealism back into the dissociative grammatology which engenders it. Demogorgon is not simply a force of "good" or "freedom": the dubious "empire" of his final speech signals the negation of Romantic metasubjectivity's purposiveness, which is no longer repressed yet lacks recognition in the discursive register of the poem's political Idealism. This "empire" reminds the reader that "past time is not sublimated time. What has past certainly cannot be *as something present*, but it must be as something past *at the same time with the present*" (*Ages* 76; my italics). The self-referential reflection of Demogorgon's language – which also makes *Prometheus Unbound*'s dissociative trajectory *itself* the "spell" and antidote to the hegemony of the One or the Same – positions Demogorgon as the centripetal force of a narrative *Trieb*, a transferential contagion.

With both *The Prelude* and *Prometheus Unbound*, the psyche of Romantic metasubjectivity unfolds in an anxiogenic topography in which its purposive individuation exists in tension with idealist teleology. Determined by the Promethean mythologem, *The Prelude* inscribes this individuation within a *Bildungsroman* whereby the poetic mind's maturation ostensibly contains the indeterminate energies of primal sites of contact with the productive unconscious. *Prometheus Unbound* stages a retroanalysis of Wordsworth's poetic psyche, mirroring the cursive writing of Romantic metasubjectivity's trauma with a similarly idealistic political narrative of emancipation that also fails to contain the radical, nonmolar energies of its psyche. In other words, the Promethean in these two poems is far less an idealist epic of the "one mind" and far more the seething entanglement of the freedom of unconscious productivity with self-consciousness as a systemic emblem of political discourse or the imperative of the moral sublime. Both poems seek to elide this tension on some level by suggesting, through poetry's equivocal fluidity, ways in which the poetic can nevertheless lead to a moral human existence. This perennial tension between art and morality – one not always acknowledged by the Romantics, who often attempt to synonymise them – leads us to a crucial question which I ask by way of concluding: is there, or can there be an *ethics* of Romantic metasubjectivity?

Notes

1. *1799* includes what Stephen Parrish calls the poem's "final form," from a MSS that "Wordsworth appears to have been closer to" (41). Interestingly, the differences in punctuation separating this text from others (notably the Norton edition) present a two-part *Prelude* more unbound than its Norton counterpart, published only two years later. For *1805*, I use the AB-Stage reading text from *The Thirteen-Book Prelude*. Although aside from the rare citation (as 1850 *Prelude*) I do not deal with the 1850 *Fourteen-Book Prelude* here, it should be mentioned that this final edition, published only a few months after Wordsworth's death in 1850, inhibits much of 1805's aleatory energy. Subject to several posthumous revisions, the ambivalent natural powers of *1799* and *1805* are thoroughly Christianised and harmonised into a paean to what at the poem's close is "a mind sustained/By recognitions of transcendent power/In sense, conducting to ideal form" (*1850 Prelude* 14.74–76). All other references to Wordsworth's poetry are from *The Poems*, 2 vols.
2. In one of the few studies focusing on Wordsworth and Schelling, E.D. Hirsch argues that they "developed independently [the] identical Weltanschauung" (4) of Enthusiasm, "a constant and sober way of confronting reality" somehow akin to being "possessed by a god," yet different from the religious *Schwärmerei* Schelling criticises elsewhere (15). Beyond a certain reductive optimism, in limiting his study to periods where both writers'

"outlook remained stable and constant" (7) Hirsch misses the fluidity of their oeuvres.

3. The *Five-Book Prelude* Wordsworth created for Coleridge's convalescence in Malta can be seen as a transitional text that begins to narrativise the aleatory energies of *The Prelude* as a whole. Where in *1799* the Poet invokes Coleridge only at the end as somewhat of an afterthought (2.496ff), like *1805* the *Five-Book Prelude* begins with the Glad Preamble, in which Coleridge is very much present as poetic answering being, and continues with the Poet's rumination on what subject matter to use in his poetic vocation, interpolating some 270 lines before the beginning of 1799 ("Was it for this?") and the scenes of Promethean theft. While the *Five-Book Prelude* contains several of *The Prelude*'s potentiated episodes (the Discharged Soldier, the Drowned Man, the Boy of Winander), they are pushed forward to the final two books, deferred by Book Three as a prolonged narrative about the Poet's studies at King's College.

4. As a suspension or checking of the rational understanding, an encounter with indeterminacy in the face of something vast and uncontainable (a raging storm, a towering mountain, an endless landscape, or certain alterations of perception, or even powerful rhetoric), the sublime is analogous with, but not identical to, Schelling's idea of ecstasy in "NPS." Mitchell has shown how Romantic poets, engaging with the science of their day, sought to create a sense of suspension or suspended animation in their own writing. While a fuller treatment of the sublime is beyond my scope here, I suggest that Romantic metasubjectivity involves the anamnesis of a darker, more indeterminate element in the sublime which is elided in most Romantic thinking, which tends to follow Kant in seeing the sublime as an occasion for reasserting the dominance of reason.

5. In *Archive Fever* (1996), Derrida defines the *messianic* as a future to come which cannot be placed within any order of knowledge; *messianism*, on the other hand, contains and limits the heterogeneity of the messianic (72).

6. Nature's ambivalence toward the Poet's recumbence is reflected in the text's revisionary process as well. The Norton *Prelude* follows *1805* MS. A 1.88ff., in which the Poet is "Cheared by the genial pillow of the earth/Beneath [his] head, soothed by a sense of touch/From the warm ground, that balanced me, else lost/Entirely, seeing nought, nought hearing, save" acorns falling. The Cornell *Prelude*'s A-B Stage text (109 n. 90) notes the hypometric nature of this line with a pencilled caret marking the omission, substituting "*though* lost/Entirely" from MS. M, the fair copy sent to Coleridge in 1804. "Else lost/Entirely" adds a beat to the Poet's ambivalent rhythm with Nature; Nature's balancing "warm ground" seems to save the Poet from complete mental entropy, only to interrupt this "balancing" with falling acorns. Nature's (im)balance surrounds (balances?) the Poet's merely rhetorical, chiastic balance of "seeing nought, nought hearing." "*Though* lost/Entirely" suggests the independence of the Poet's mind from Nature, even as Nature both fosters and interrupts his rhetorical pleasure principle.

7. The extent of Wordsworth's direct engagement with Kant remains a matter of debate, but Duncan Wu suggests that he was reading Kant's *Critique of Judgment* around the time *1799* was composed (80–81). Thus, Kant may have directly informed Wordsworth's understanding of the sublime.

8. Sublation [*Aufhebung*] is typically understood as the transformation a state into a new, higher state of being and an essential movement to the ultimate revelation of absolute spirit in history. Yet in the *Science of Logic* (1813–1832) Hegel is clear about sublation's bivalent nature: "The German '*aufheben*' has a twofold meaning in the language: it equally means '*to keep*,' 'to "preserve",' and 'to cause to cease,' '*to put an end to*.' Even 'to preserve' already includes a negative note, namely that something, in order to be retained, is removed from its immediacy and hence from an existence which is open to external influences. – That which is sublated is thus something at the same time preserved, something that has lost its immediacy but has not come to nothing for that. [. . .] But it must strike one as remarkable that a language has come to use one and the same word for two opposite meanings. For speculative thought it is gratifying to find words that have in themselves a speculative meaning" (81–82).

9. Shelley's ambiguity here is intriguing; the enigmatic conjunctive "or" can be read either as substitutive ("external actions" are what the "operations" of the mind are really all about) or inclusive (the poem depicts the mind's operations *as well as* its external actions, which are not necessarily commensurate with these operations).

10. This trauma is precisely why Prometheus, once freed, seeks to recuperate an illusion of himself as "one mind" without an unconscious, retiring with Asia outside of history where they "will sit and talk of time and change,/As the world ebbs and flows, ourselves unchanged" (3.3.23–24). But even as the cisionary power of the curse now seems to be mere banter, the Titans' preoccupation with "time and change" reflects the persistence of historicity as something which can irrupt again; Demogorgon's warning at the poem's close extends even here.

11. Here (*The Poems of Shelley* 2: 480 n. 53–9), Everest and Matthews touch on Stuart Sperry's significant observation that Prometheus' change of heart from disdain to pity is perhaps less Promethean waffling and more representative of the vicissitudes of universal change. But seen through a depth psychological lens these two positions converge: Prometheus, marking the emergence of consciousness out of the unconscious and the dawn of freedom over tyranny, *himself* experiences enantiodromal shifts of flux and change. Thus his "liberation" into consciousness and freedom redoubles the dissociative unconscious which engenders it.

12. Wasserman acknowledges the mirroring of Prometheus and Jupiter but maintains that Prometheus "has dispelled these evils from himself now that he no longer hates but pities." However, this argument sidesteps Ione's reassurances, after Prometheus "doth repent" the curse, that "'tis

but some passing spasm,/The Titan is unvanquished still" (1.314–15). The indeterminacy underwriting the polyphonic hymn at the poem's end persists in spite of Wasserman's insistent Idealism (see Wasserman 260).

13. Everest and Matthews catalogue the extent to which this imperative is "written in nature and humanity" (*The Poems of Shelley* 2: 535 n. 141)

14. De Man writes: "[Romantic imagery's] nostalgia for the natural object, expanding to become nostalgia for the origin of this object [. . .] can only exist when the transcendental presence is forgotten" (6).

15. Everest and Matthews suggest along political lines that Demogorgon's name represents a play on the Greek for something like "the terrible people," referring to the power of the "unrepresented multitude" (*The Poems of Shelley* 2: 468–69). Given the traumatic narrative bifurcation of *Prometheus Unbound* as a metapsychology showing the "operations of the mind," however, this more significantly denotes the "terrible multitude" of nonmolar forces and indefinite forms represented by Demogorgon in the poem's dissociative fabric.

16. Significantly, Everest and Matthews (*The Poems of Shelley* 2: 537 n. 166ff) observe that in an earlier fair copy (*Notebook* 8) Shelley specifically cancelled out "V" for speaker identification and replaced it with *Echoes*. This further corroborates a reading of Shelley's lyrical drama which resists egoic personalism in favour of the dynamics of Necessity.

17. "Empire" has various meanings in *Prometheus Unbound*, but the *OED*, apart from a definition (possibly obsolete in Shelley's time) simply as "independent nation" (3), overwhelmingly defines "empire" in terms of absolute rule by a sovereign figure. Thus, this "re-assumed empire" retains the possibility of tyranny's return (or the recrudescence of unconscious forces) despite the final association of empire with the "Good, great and joyous, beautiful, and free" (4.577–78).

Chapter 6

Conclusion

Romantic meth-subjectivity

Let us crystallise the concept of Romantic metasubjectivity whose domain we have mapped in the previous chapters. Nourished by the tributaries of Schelling's philosophy and Jung's analytical psychology, Romantic metasubjectivity is a model of personhood which describes more of the true compass of Romantic thinking on the person than the accepted amalgamation of psychoanalysis and deconstruction prevailing in Romantic criticism. Unbound by economies of nostalgia or endless difference, Romantic metasubjectivity unfolds in the world according to a rhythmic ontology of progression and regression and introversion and extraversion, traversing traditional metaphors of height and depth, darkness and light without remaining bound to these metaphors as transcendental signifying matrices. What Novalis calls the "Self of one's self," as the unique organising force of knowledge and experience in the individual, is not the preformed endpoint of an inevitable teleological drive toward absolute knowledge; nor is it a final plateau of consciousness to be reached by an individual or the species, or a mode of transcendence removed from the indeterminacy of the natural world. Rather, this nonmolar force marks the epigenetic, purposive unfolding of a self-organising personality, and this is precisely what is figured by Schelling as the absolute subject and by Jung, in a more explicitly psychological framework, as the Self. This unfolding – Schelling's absolute subject moving through everything without *being* anything – is what Jung puts at the heart of analytical psychology as the individuation process, around which Jung's core concepts are constellated.

When we turn to the question of an ethics – the question of how Romantic metasubjectivity can inform a way of living in the world – we are faced with a troubling question: how can one derive an ethics from an individuation process so intimately connected with the indeterminate productive energies of Nature and the unconscious? *Must* we derive an ethics from this, and is an *ethics* the only viable human outcome for Romantic metasubjectivity's being in the world? We have seen that for Schelling, personality is inextricably linked with the *Ungrund* of existence and that the person is "the world writ small," and that for Jung consciousness is always already implicated with the unconscious, which *is* a Nature that can never be sublated into consciousness or spirit. Thus, the very coextensivity between mind and Nature intrinsic to Romantic metasubjectivity makes discursive ethics at best provisional, nullifying its claims to universality. While this need not mean jettisoning ethics altogether, it *does* demand the bracketing of its universality in favour of the experiences which make such discourses possible in the first place – experiences which cannot be reduced to or contained by the "thou shalt"s of the ethical. In other words, Romantic metasubjectivity does not promulgate ethical discourse, but instead unfolds as what John Caputo, in his *Against Ethics* (1993), has called a poetics of obligation, a species of morality which "happens" in events unbound by the discursive confines of ethics (4–5). In a word, this happening is *morality as obligation*, which contains an undecidability that destabilises ethics as its dangerous supplement even as it insists on *decision*, albeit decision freed from the guarantee of the ethical. If there is an "ethics" to come from this, it can only be ethics as non-system, an ethics on the cusp of system but which is attuned to its own historicity and evolutionary flux, unwilling to complete itself with the pleasure principles of universal equality and transcendental justice.

We can state the issue in terms of the tension between the system of ethics and the freedom of obligation, the freedom to be bound by obligation's inscrutable magnetic pull, a pull which follows the purposive energies of the "Self of one's self." While Caputo does not go so far as an organising purposiveness, he nevertheless sees this obligation as fundamentally *religious*, and in a manner which resonates with Schelling's positive philosophy and Jung's conception of analytical psychology as a fundamentally religious enterprise. Caputo writes: "The impossible is the religious, the *re-ligare*, which means the one-on-one bond of the existing individual with the Absolute, the absolute relation to the Absolute. The *re-ligare* is the *ob-ligare*, the absolute bond, the obligation, but without the shelter afforded by the universal, the rational, the eternal" (18). And Jung: "Analytical psychology helps us to recognize our religious potentialities [and] teaches us that attitude which meets a transcendent reality halfway" (letter to Hélène Keiner, 15 June 1955, *Letters* 2.265). To articulate this "religious" nonethics I will first briefly examine Jung's *Answer to Job* (1952), a controversial commentary on the *Book of Job* which presents Jung's view of evil as energic in a manner closely resembling Schelling's *Freedom* essay and which uncannily mirrors the emergence of time and history in *Ages*. Indeed, *Answer to Job* occupies a unique place in Jung's oeuvre: while it was often harshly condemned (see Bishop, *Jung's* Answer to Job 44ff), Jung saw it as an integral part of his own individuation process, coming from "an increasingly urgent feeling of responsibility which in the end I could no longer withstand" (letter to Pastor Walter Uhsadel, 6 Feb 1952; *Letters* 2.39). We will then turn from Job's Yahweh to the more specifically nonhuman conceptions of the archetypes and individuation as rather remarkable extensions of the crystallogeny which informs Romantic thinking about both the organic and inorganic. This profoundly nonethical and nonhumanist dimension to individuation grounds Caputo's critique of ethics, even as Romantic metasubjectivity goes further by presenting the specifically nonmolar dynamics of this ontology. I will then end with an all too brief analysis of Walter White, the antihero of the hit TV series *Breaking Bad* (2008–2013), who provides us with an uncannily resonant case study of Romantic metasubjectivity in contemporary culture.

Answer to Job: even God must individuate

The *Book of Job* is an Old Testament book concerned with the issue of divine justice and the problem of human suffering. *Job* opens with Yahweh praising the righteous, God-fearing nature of his worshipper Job, and Satan, who is strangely part of God's court,[1] bets Yahweh that Job would curse God were he deprived of his material possessions and health. To very generally summarise the narrative of this complicated text: *Job* is structured by a beginning Prologue, the speeches by Job and his friends in which they debate divine justice and Job's complaints, and the climactic exchange between Job and Yahweh where Yahweh justifies his treatment of Job in a series of speeches invoking the creation of the universe and Nature (*Job* 38: 1 ff) – speeches which do not, however, address Job's specific complaint. The remarkably ambivalent ending of *Job*, which concerns us here, has generated a great deal of commentary. But what is salient for us here is how Jung reads *Job* as a crucial cisionary point in a larger Biblical individuation process culminating in Christ as a figure of totality, and what this means for morality in analytical psychology as it informs Romantic metasubjectivity. Jung's basic argument in *Answer to Job* is that the Holy Trinity of Father, Son, and Holy Spirit must be supplemented by Satan as the dark side of God to make it a quaternity and authentic expression of totality. Of interest for our discussion of Romantic metasubjectivity is that Jung reads *Job* far from its orthodox grain, as an analytic scene where Yahweh's encounter with Job reveals a "divine darkness" (*Answer to Job* para. 561) at the heart of God. Indeed, it is because Yahweh is "too unconscious to be 'moral'" (para. 574; trans. mod.) that Job is *a catalyst for Yahweh's own individuation process*: the final encounter in *Job* effectively inaugurates Yahweh's own individuation which, for Jung, culminates in Christ as the fulfilment of Yahweh's "intention to become man" (para. 648). The very reason for God's becoming man, Jung writes, is encrypted in Yahweh's encounter with Job (*Answer to Job* para. 624). We have seen that there is little evidence that Jung read any of Schelling's work first-hand before the mythology lectures. But seen through the lens of Romantic metasubjectivity, *Answer to Job* is Jung's ontopsychological response to the cosmological concerns of *Ages*, irrespective of the moral superiority Jung attributes to Job over Yahweh in a bid to inhibit the text's cosmological potency into a personalised encounter (para. 640). Paul Bishop describes *Answer to Job* as "a miniature exercise in cultural history" (*Jung's* Answer to Job 26), but this misses the point of *Answer to Job*'s distinctly preterhuman dimensions and their significance for the moral implications of Romantic metasubjectivity. Indeed, in articulating the preterhuman aspects of Jung's reading of *Job*, I argue that Jung recapitulates the cisionary drama of God's coming to be in time and history of Schelling's *Ages*, recasting this drama in contemporary terms of the problem of evil and the genesis of morality. The nonhuman aspects of individuation in *Answer to Job* also make this text a corroboration of Jung's mature thinking on the archetypes and individuation, connecting this thought to contemporary critiques of discursive ethics. Let us then briefly trace the contours of Jung's reading of the Job-Yahweh encounter.

"The archetype, as a natural phenomenon, [...] possesses no moral quality in itself but is amoral, like the Yahwistic God-image fundamentally is, and acquires moral qualities only through the act of cognition. Thus Yahweh is both just and unjust, kindly and cruel, truthful and deceitful" ("A Psychological View" para. 845; trans. mod). Thus Jung links the

Janus-faced collective unconscious and its archetypes to the ambivalence of the Old Testament God. Just as Schelling insists that God is "not a system, but rather a life" (*Freedom* 62), Jung insists that individuation is "*the life in God*" ("Jung and Religious Belief" para. 1624), and thus the cosmogony informing Jung's reading of Yahweh is marked not only by a yearning for time, history, and individuation, but also by the not-God within God Schelling discerns in the *Freedom* essay. Thus, in turning to focus on the exchange between Yahweh and Job, Jung writes: "the inner instability of Yahweh is the precondition not only of the creation of the world, but also of the pleromatic drama whose tragic chorus comprises humanity" (*Answer to Job* para. 686; trans. mod). This "inner instability" amounts to a lack of reflection, an unconsciousness on the part of Yahweh as a God who, omnipotent and (we are led to believe) omniscient, nevertheless takes Satan's cynical bets regarding Job's loyalty. As emblem of the not-God within God (the accuser in Yahweh's attendance), *Job*'s Satan, consanguineous with the questioning Job, catalyses *Job*'s repetition of the cision into time and history as Yahweh's creation of the world. But at the same time, Jung notes that in Yahweh's display of power there is a projection on to Job of something "we would not ascribe to him but to God [...] Yahweh projects on to Job a sceptic's face which is hateful to him because it is his own, and which gazes at him with an uncanny and critical eye. [...] *Job is challenged as though he himself were a god*" (*Answer to Job* pars. 591, 594; my italics).

Jung thus conceives of Yahweh and Job as questioning and answering beings in an analytic scene. But they are also *potentiated* in a way that reveals something more than a personalised encounter. Viewed in this light, Yahweh's first speech to Job (*Job* 38:1 ff) begins with a certain transferential ambiguity not dissimilar to the curse in Shelley's *Prometheus Unbound*; indeed, "Who is this that darkens counsel [the divine principles of creation] by words without knowledge?" (38:2), spoken to Job, also speaks to Yahweh's lack of reflection as undifferentiated unconsciousness. Jung writes:

> In view of the subsequent words of Yahweh, one must really ask oneself: Who is darkening what counsel? The only dark thing here is how Yahweh ever came to make a bet with Satan. It is certainly not Job who has darkened anything and least of all a counsel [...] Naturally this development was foreseen in omniscience, and it may be that the word

"counsel" refers to this eternal and absolute knowledge. If so, Yahweh's attitude seems the more inconsistent and incomprehensible [...] [So] Whose words are without insight? [...] The answer to Yahweh's question is therefore: it is Yahweh himself who darkens his own counsel and who has no insight. (*Answer to Job* pars. 585–87; trans. mod.)

For Jung, Yahweh's unconsciousness establishes him as the equivalent of Schelling's contractive potency,[2] the A^1 of self-withdrawal whose anxiogenic rotatory motion is expressed as rage and indignation. But what follows as part of this anxiogenesis is nothing less than what *Ages* calls an involution preceding evolution, a recapitulation of the creation of the world: the laying of the foundation of the earth and the measuring of its dimensions, light and darkness, and the elements and the constellations (*Job* 38: 4–38) are followed by a narrative of the creation of the animals (38: 39–39: 30). Although Yahweh is ostensibly questioning Job ("I will question you, and you shall declare to me" [*Job* 38: 3]), Job, as one who "induces" Yahweh "to open the sources of knowledge that are hidden and still concealed in itself" (*HCI* 7), holds his tongue (*Job* 40: 3–5) as Yahweh continues his narrative.

Thus, like Yahweh, Job is also both a questioning and answering being in this transferential dynamic, Schelling's A^2 which calls the first potency to expansion into time and history – here, as Yahweh's anamnesis, in the world, of the world's creation. Job's final response preserves the ambivalence of the encounter: he mirrors Yahweh's initial questions (42: 2–3) with profound irony, and when he says that "therefore I have uttered what I did not understand, things too wonderful for me, which I did not know" (42: 3), Job is reflecting on the nature of the God which he *did* not know, but has now metaphorically "seen" (42: 5) – a God of which God himself is not fully aware – in an experience which causes him to take comfort in "dust and ashes,"[3] the materiality of the world in which even God must individuate. In this sense, Jung describes Job in the Prefatory Note to *Answer to Job* as he "who expected help from God against God" – in other words, he who provokes the yearning of God for Being in a way which leads to Yahweh's recapitulation, *in time and history*, of the coming into being of time and history. Indeed, the idea of needing God's help against God encapsulates the moment and movement of potentiation in *Ages*: Job's complaint speaks directly to the not-God within God, Yahweh's lack of reflection and universal justice but also the yearning for time and history as individuation which, for Jung, leads to God's ultimately becoming man as Christ.[4] In other words, this "help" is the beginning of Yahweh's coming-to-consciousness which, for Jung, reaches its climax in Christ as the figure combining "heterogeneous natures" of Yahweh and Job "in a single personality" (*Answer to Job* para. 648). To this end, Jung points out that after his encounter with Job Yahweh loses his specifically contractive potentiation, and there is a shift to "apocalyptic communications" which gesture toward a futurity:

> After Job, we hear nothing further about new covenants. Proverbs and gnomic utterances seem to be the order of the day, and a real *novum* now appears on the scene, namely apocalyptic communications. This points to metaphysical acts of cognition, that is, to "constellated" unconscious contents which are ready to irrupt into consciousness. (para. 637)

God has been displaced from his specifically contractive potency; Job, as the expansive potency, has (to use Schelling's word) bewitched Yahweh into the time and history always already present as Satan, who "[goes] to and fro on the earth, and [walks] up and down on it" (*Job* 1: 7, 2: 2). As representative of the world's materiality and the suffering in it which challenges faith, Satan raises the doubt which catalyses Yahweh's individuation.

Thus Jung argues – like Schelling, who writes that the absolute subject exists above God ("NPS" 217) – that even God must individuate. Indeed, in the final paragraphs of *Answer to Job* Jung thinks the incommensurability between mind and Nature in terms of different modalities of individuation. On the one hand, there is a nonpsychic, "unconscious" individuation approaching a preformationist understanding of the organism, which "means no more than that the acorn becomes an oak, the calf a cow, and the child an adult" (*Answer to Job* para. 755) in which "consciousness nowhere intervenes [and] the end remains as dark as the beginning" (para. 756). On the other hand, there is individuation as "a process of differentiation of human consciousness" more closely aligned with the dynamic evolution in Schelling's *First Outline* (para. 758). Leaving aside for a moment Jung's fluid conception of the psyche, which he at times identifies with Nature itself, the crucial point here is that *individuation is not exclusively, and perhaps not even primarily a psychic process*: "You can never say with certainty whether what appears to be going on in the collective unconscious of a single individual is not also happening in other individuals or organisms or things or situations" (*Synchronicity* para. 912). This idea of individuation as the recapitulation of the difference between psyche and Nature summarises their uncanny affinity in Romantic metasubjectivity.[5] With this, let us turn one last time to the archetypes which Jung's later thinking describes in profoundly nonhuman terms. Indeed, as Jung's guiding image for describing the archetype's self-organisational nature, the crystal invokes a wider tradition of what Novalis called Romantic "crystallogeny" which reads the crystal's epigenesis as a trope for Being.

Schelling writes in the *First Outline* that life is "nothing other than an intensified condition of common natural forces [...] life is not anything in itself, it is only the phenomenon of a transition of certain forces from [this] intensified condition into the usual condition of the universal" (*FO* 68). Indeed, Eric Wilson writes that in his *On the World-Soul* (1798), Schelling

> maintains that *all* nature is a vast crystal. Rock or ice crystals are primitive organizations of life that will one day evolve into more conscious geometries – plants, animals, and humans. Crystallization is a primary phenomenon. It is the archetypal organization of the absolute. Crystals are early humans. Humans are advanced crystals. (28)

Jung writes in 1948 that the archetype's organisational potency can be "compared to the invisible, potential presence of the crystal lattice in mother liquor. [...] Empirically considered, [...] the archetype never emerged as a phenomenon of organic life, but appeared on the scene with life itself" ("A Psychological Approach" para. 222 n. 2, trans. mod.).[6] This metaphor represents Jung's shift in thinking about the archetype from its "merely psychic" operations to its psychoid basis in both mind and organic substrate. Let us dwell briefly on this jarring passage, which returns analytical psychology to the quasi-subjective space of Schelling's *Naturphilosophie*. Jung makes two remarkable claims about the archetypes: first, that they are coterminous with life *before* human instinct. Second, he suggests a difference between "organic life" and "life itself," emphasised by the archetype's comparison to a "crystal lattice" which establishes an ordering principle in *in*organic Nature analogous to that of organic Nature. In chemistry, the crystal lattice [*Kristallgitter*] is an integrated network of atoms whose intrinsic nature impels them to unfold regular, symmetrical patterns in an interwoven structure (the square shape of salt crystals being the most obvious example). We have already seen how Schelling's Nature "forms itself" around the "seed" of the actant in an analogous manner (*FO* 21 n. 1), and indeed Schelling also sees the organic as a "higher species of crystallization" in Nature's propensity to produce regular forms (*FO* 194).

Crystallisation also determines individuation in Jung's alchemical studies, where individuation is the process of an unknowable centre acting "like a magnet on the disparate materials and processes of the unconscious and gradually captures them as in a crystal lattice. [...] Indeed, it seems as if all the personal entanglements and dramatic peripeteia that make up life in its full intensity were [...] almost like petty complications and meticulous pretexts to the finality of this strange and uncanny process of crystallization" (*Psychology and Alchemy* 217–18; trans. mod). This conception of the crystal returns in 1954, when Jung writes that the archetype's form

> might perhaps be compared to the axial system of a crystal, which, as it were, preforms the crystal formation in the mother liquid without having a material existence of its own. [The individual crystal's concrete form] may be either large or small, or vary endlessly by reason of the different size of its planes or by the growing together of two crystals. Only the axial system, in its invariable geometric relations, remains constant. ("Psychological Aspects of the Mother Archetype" para. 155; trans. mod.)

Archetype as crystallogeny: the *OED* lists the first English use of "crystallogeny" in 1837, but the term is Novalis' – one can expect no less from a student of mineralogy and geology (*Notes* 160). This Romantic crystallogeny has its roots in Paracelsus and Swedenborg, both of whom heavily influenced Jung, who rethinks the crystal's epigenesis through the archetype as organising principle of human knowledge and life itself. Hegel's *Naturphilosophie* also makes extensive use of the crystal trope, referring to the "archetypal crystal," in its "abstract identity" and "transparency," as "the diamond of the Earth [...] the first-born son of light and gravity" (*Philosophy of Nature* 184). For Hegel, "crystallinity was both the culmination of the inorganic process, and foreshadowed the organization of life. It provided a conceptual entry into a consideration of the geological process, and of the structural composition and life of the earth" (Levere 110). But Novalis also sees crystallisation as a master trope of both geological and human history. The earth's development is governed by the waxing and waning of "states of flux" which cause "new, necessary mixtures" of natural forces and the "new, purer crystallization" of "new, beautiful forms" ("Faith and Love" #21). Growing in volume and mass, man is seen as a unity of "external, superficial" development and internal "formation in the depths" – "man is like a crystal of such a mass – capable of bringing forth infinite crystals. The perfect crystal, as it were, must consist of an innumerable number of *similar* smaller *crystals*" (*Notes* 72). Indeed, in this *Brouillon* entry Novalis continues to poeticise the general economy of both actant and archetype. These rhizomatic lines of "infinite crystals" articulate the "fundamental form" of the "seed of the human being," where all differences and "imperfections" in the "raw" system "must be brought into balance through the life of the system" in a way which preserves previous syntheses – "just as through the non-ego, the developed and perfected ego is the synthesis, as it were, of the raw ego and its infinite alterations" (72). In this way, Novalis approaches the ontological "poetics of self-organization" (Wilson, *The Spiritual History of Ice* 61) unfolded in crystalline structures central to both the dynamism of Schelling's Nature and the organisation of knowledge in the metasubjective psyche that emerges *from* this Nature. Crystallogeny, then, is the emblem of the purposive self-organisation marking Romantic metasubjectivity.

The darkness of obligation

What, then, happens to ethics if Being is always already implicated in individuative processes with no final endpoint? We live in a century marked by a recycled Kantian morality which presumes to create a globalised ethics and kingdom of ends in the form of universal proclamations of human rights. Indeed, one could argue – as Schelling does of the European philosophy of his time – that for the United Nations and the global neoliberalist enterprise it serves, "nature does not exist for it [...] it lacks a living ground" (*Freedom* 26; trans. mod). More than this: Nature exists for this neoliberalist regime as a dual phantasy – both an infinite resource and an infinite garbage dump, when in reality it is neither. This post-Kantian morality further decrees that Nature's sole purpose is to provide the opportunity for the teleological unfolding of human freedom as a "systematic union of human ends" (Guyer 412). This morality has been projected negatively on to analytical psychology by Paul Bishop, who faults Jung for what he sees as "the potentially devastating moral deficit at the heart of analytical psychology," its "failure to develop any ethical standpoint, particularly in the political sphere" (*Synchronicity* 163 & n. 43) – a critique which assumes (mistakenly) that analytical psychology is conducive to an ethics in the first place. And there are some who do want to give Schelling's Nature the ethical stamp of political activism: for example, Bruce Matthews argues that Schelling's mythology of nature harbours a "utopian potential" with "an emancipatory power capable of liberating an engaged hope from its bondage to the ideology of irony that currently emasculates transformative political action" ("The New Mythology" 203). To be sure, Matthews points to the interminable "chaotic rhythm" that is the *Ungrund* of Romantic metasubjectivity we have explored in Chapter 4 – in Matthews' terms, "an organic, and thus partially chaotic, process of self-differentiation that generates increasingly complex iterative systems" (207–8). But he nevertheless gathers up this imbrication of freedom and necessity into an idealist project of "balanced relationship [and] reciprocity with nature's nexus of living forces" in the name of "redemptive harmony" (212). Matthews ends up resuscitating an anthropocentric fantasy of "realizing a unity with nature" (213) which, in an ideological sleight-of-hand, reinstates human freedom in its idealist intensity as an ethical future which "offers unseen possibilities and thus an open-ended orientation to *what should be*" (215). In other words, Matthews acknowledges the aleatory energy of this self-differentiation but asserts transformative political action as an unproblematic possibility within this stochastic matrix, insisting on a "subversive and emancipatory power" (216) in Schelling's "mythology of nature" which cannot be corroborated *by* this Nature. Attempting to cast Schelling's Nature as a platform for a neo-Kantian kingdom of ends, Matthews ultimately eclipses Nature's radical productivity by tacitly assuming that humanity can and will one day control Nature as part of his desire for a transformative politics.

Romantic metasubjectivity is fundamentally counterposed to the specifically humanist activism Matthews sees in Schelling's "mythology of Nature" and Bishop sees in analytical psychology, implicitly arguing that both of these approaches critically misunderstand the potent nonhumanism which underwrites in both oeuvres. For while there is little reasonable doubt that humanity is damaging its environment to a degree which imperils the future of the species, we have seen that Schelling's mythology, like the actants in the *First Outline*, precedes humanity; it is tied to geology and the history of the Earth, thus resting on Nature's purposiveness, which is bound to neither anthropocentric teleology nor an interested preservation of our species. It was Carl Kielmeyer (1765–1844), the comparative anatomist who in Schelling's words opened "a completely new epoch in natural history," who situated Nature against transcendental philosophy, emphasising their incommensurability to the extent that the latter's conditions of possible experience can only exist "against the backdrop of a natural history full of extinction events" (qtd. in Grant, *Philosophies* 120–1).[7] In other words, "if transcendental philosophy reaches its limit with a merely possible nature, actual NATURE confronts merely transcendental necessities with the stark inevitability of the eventual elimination of species whose experience is conditioned by them" (121). Nature is indifferent to Idealism's coveted species, humanity. And while it is clichéd these days to talk about the death of metanarrative, it is less so to argue that human discourses are castles built upon the fluid, shifting sands of indeterminacy. We have seen clearly idealist moments in both Schelling's and Jung's oeuvres: Schelling wants to retain a promissory confluence of truth and fable in *Ages* that surpasses primordial indeterminacy, even as he criticises Idealism as "denial and nonacknowledgement" of the same (7). At times Jung, too, speaks of human individuation as something achievable through a teleological progression through the analytic encounter, even as his metapsychology makes this impossible. But as a psychologist who survived two World Wars and lived in an age marked by the wholesale destruction of Hiroshima and Nagasaki, Jung's understanding was conditioned by an unprecedented loss of life and the dawning of the nuclear age which for us is now a fact of life. Thus, Jung's writing is more ominous than Schelling's in several ways with respect to the destructive potential of the human psyche. And why should this not be the case? Given that Jung, it is said, had an hour-long precognitive vision of the First World War in the form of floods, drowned bodies, and a sea of blood (*Memories* 175–76), one can understand why analytical psychology, for all its futurity, harbours a pessimism far beyond that of psychoanalysis' split subject. Thus, if humanity, Nature, and even God must run the risks of individuation, there can be no overarching ethics without disavowing and repressing the prediscursive drives and imperatives of individuation.

In response to the dubious project of a neo-Kantian universal ethics and its "merely possible" Nature as an object of human consumption, the concept of Romantic metasubjectivity insists on the dangerous supplementation of ethics with a purposive, decentred model which authentically represents the rhizomatic, aleatory dynamisms of actant and archetype, of the energic matrices represented for both Schelling and Jung by mythology, but which for Jung is also figured psychically as the collective unconscious and its entanglement with Nature. John Caputo conceives this as a *poetics of obligation*, the outcome of a deconstruction of ethics which preserves a connectedness with both human and nonhuman others. For Caputo, this obligation is

> the feeling that comes over us when others need our help, when they call out for help, or support, or freedom, or whatever they need, a feeling that grows in strength directly in proportion to the desperateness of the situation of the other. *The power of obligation varies directly with the powerlessness of the one who calls for help, which is the power of powerlessness.* (5; my italics)

This obligation is displaced from all epistemes, ideologies, or moral codes as a sublime event cutting through discourses: like the archetype, "obligation happens" (6). Obligation is a chemical binding, a magnetic pull between the person and "the Other" in its most general sense, as "a deep anonymity in things, in the world, in the stars as in ourselves," the uncanny force within ethics that ethics cannot contain (18) – in the language of Romantic metasubjectivity, we may even call it the ethical's purposive unconscious. "The natural flow of libido, this same middle path, means complete obedience to the fundamental laws of human nature, and there is absolutely no higher moral principle than harmony with natural laws that guide the libido in the direction of life's optimum[, which] can be reached only through obedience to the fluid laws of the libido" (Jung, "The Type Problem" para. 356; trans. mod). Far from a Hegelian sociohistorical embodiment of ethics [*Sittlichkeit*], as "a spontaneous causality, a cause without antecedent that breaks in upon the unbroken regularity of phenomenal succession" (12) we may also say with Schelling that obligation dissociatively "thinks in me."

As a dissolution of the guarantees of the ethical, the poetics of obligation always risks what others will inevitably call obscenity: the risk that Yahweh's command to Abraham that he sacrifice Isaac stands on the same footing as the commands given to Nazi soldiers to kill Jews (10). To be sure, this obligation, this magnetic pull between an entity and its other, leads us into dark waters whose undertows remain opaque to the gaze of discourse. But this magnetism is precisely the energy of the individuation process, the power that draws together entities as complexes of opposites to create new iterations of Being: new products in Nature or new knowledge and experience in the human sphere. To this end, Schelling writes: "[c]haracter is the fundamental condition for all morality. Lack of character is in itself immorality" (*Ages* 85). Pursuing the "Self of one's self" leads away from the "thou shalt" of the ethical, because it always and everywhere *predates* the ethical (predate: to come before, but also to pursue, consume, to hunt for one's own needs). And while one's line of flight may intersect with, or at times run parallel to, the rigid trajectories of ethical paradigms, the individuation marking Romantic metasubjectivity is destined for moments of collision, rupture with the ethical – de-cisions away from its security and comfort. This obligation which underwrites Romantic metasubjectivity does not annul what we traditionally call "human rights." Rather, it brackets their naïve pretense to universality in order to interrogate the anthropocentrism grounding the discursive interiority which makes Nature merely possible in service to the human, rather than the actual in its indeterminacy, as the *there is* of Being. So when Bataille writes that "there is no need to entangle oneself with strictly moral considerations, but to entangle morality with intensity" ("The Consequences" 116), he is expressing the impotence of the merely ethical before the purposive magnetism of obligation. In other words, what is "right" is always implicated with the intensity of nonknowledge, the ecstatic, traumatic encounter with what I have articulated as the Romantic metasubject. All the more compelling that this interrogation of ethics has informed some of the most acclaimed works of recent fiction in contemporary culture, and there is no more poignant contemporary example of Romantic metasubjectivity than Walter White.

Breaking Bad: crystal clear morality

Breaking Bad (2008–2013) is one of several recent TV series which explore a pressing contemporary ethical issue: what happens when the evil one hunts is in one's own ranks – in the case of *Breaking Bad*, when a methamphetamine (crystal meth) kingpin is brother-in-law to a taskforce leader for the Drug Enforcement Administration (DEA)?[8] Moreover,

Breaking Bad focuses on a question directly relevant to everyone struggling in a twenty-first-century neoliberalist economy marked by ever-widening wealth gaps between rich and poor: is it immoral or unethical to break the law (in this case, manufacture crystal meth) to pay skyrocketing medical bills and support your family, even if what you do could ruin the lives of others? Indeed, this question strikes at the heart of the social contract: (when) is it moral to put one's family before the State? In dealing with such questions, *Breaking Bad* is uniquely connected with a specifically Romantic matrix of ideas, making it a powerfully resonant example of how the concept of Romantic metasubjectivity can inform contemporary insights about who one is and how one should act. Against the backdrop of modern science and chemistry, *Breaking Bad* presents us with a fictional case study of an antihero's libidinal *Trieb*, a purposive unfolding which is far from "ethical" but which nevertheless unfolds a line of flight traversing obligations to society, family, and self. In my limited space here I will follow the most basic contours of the series, which, I hope, will provide an example of what Romantic metasubjectivity can offer contemporary criticism.

Walter White is a vastly overqualified high-school chemistry teacher and former chemist specialising in x-ray crystallography. He is middle-aged, married, and father to a son with cerebral palsy and an unplanned baby on the way. As a graduate student he co-founded Grey Matter Technologies with colleague Elliott Schwartz, only to sell his shares years ago for several thousand dollars. The company is now worth billions, and Walter's damaged pride leads him to harbour resentment over this mistake for the rest of his life. Struggling to make ends meet for his family, he moonlights at a car wash where he is at times ridiculed by the high school students he teaches. Very early in the series, Walter collapses and is taken to hospital, where he discovers that he has terminal lung cancer. Walter's brother-in-law Hank Schrader is an Albuquerque DEA agent who takes him on a ride-along to a meth bust, where he spots a former high-school student of his turned meth cook (Jesse Pinkman) escaping the scene. After deliberation, Walter confronts Jesse with an ultimatum: help him cook crystal meth or be turned in to the police. At this point begins Walter's rise to become international meth kingpin, alias "Heisenberg," with a never-before-seen drug purity of nearly 100%. The signifier "Heisenberg" evokes both authoritarianism (Werner Heisenberg, the German physicist who developed nuclear fission for the Third Reich) and Heisenberg as the pioneer of quantum mechanics, which concerns itself with nonmolar quanta beyond the purview of classical physics. The latter reading may also include Heisenberg's uncertainty principle, which basically states that we can know a particle's *position* only in inverse proportion to knowing its *momentum* (and vice versa). Thus "Heisenberg" can be read in terms of both White's growing authoritarian narcissism as he consolidates his drug empire and what I will describe below as the purposive (and literal) *crystallisation* of his metasubjective *Trieb* as crystal meth cook, which unfolds in a continuum in which position and direction cannot be judged with absolute certainty.

"No matter how one looks at it," the eighteenth-century aphorist Georg Lichtenberg writes, "philosophy is always chemistry" (qtd. in Chaouli 38). And when Schelling writes in 1815 that his time is one "when all similes and metaphors are gotten from chemistry" (*Ages* 96), he is harking back to the *First Outline*'s emphasis on chemical processes as "the first rudiments of all organization" and insistence that "Nature and chemistry are related to one another like language and grammar" (*FO* 57–58). Chemistry is nothing less than a general economy of catalysis and reaction which articulates Nature's *écriture*, the grammatology of Being. Indeed, Chouli argues that the concept of early nineteenth-century chemistry is a significant cultural influence on Schlegel's experimental poetry, which is "reticulated with ideas of auto-formation, open-endedness, and uncontrollable contingency," a work consisting "of an open-ended *process* of combinatorial formation and deformation, a process, furthermore, over which the artist by no means retains full control" (5). Perhaps it is no surprise, then, that Schlegel describes Schelling's "real vocation" as that of articulating the "chemical process of philosophizing, to isolate, wherever possible, its dynamic laws and to separate philosophy – which always must organize and disorganize itself anew – into its living, fundamental forces, and trace these back to their origins" (*AF* #304).

All the more significant that Romantic chemistry is *Breaking Bad*'s guiding trope. At various points the series insists on the isocolon between Walter White and the American Romantic poet Walt Whitman – in fact, this connection is at the heart of Hank Schrader's eventual discovery of Walter's identity as Heisenberg (in the form of an inscribed copy of Whitman's *Leaves of Grass*, addressed to Walter by a fellow meth cook and admirer). More to the point for Romantic metasubjectivity, however, the dynamic heart of *Breaking Bad*, and Walter's metasubjective *Trieb*, is in chemistry.

In the pilot episode Walter describes chemistry to an apathetic high-school class as the study of matter, change, dissolution, and transformation. This description establishes the self-organising, purposive rhythms of change and differentiation in the chemistry behind Walter's production of crystal meth. But meth also crystallises a "meth-subjectivity" as Walter's line of flight, combining a Promethean antiheroism (Walter's "breaking bad," his break from the rigid trajectory of ethics into the possibilities of post-ethical consciousness as he transgresses to give humanity a "gift" which only benefits himself) with the "meta" of meth as inorganic emblem of the self-organising "Self of one's self," Walter's individuation following the inscrutable affinities of chemistry. Myth, meta, meth – a conjugation, in the grammatology of Being, of Romantic metasubjectivity's operations in the antiheroic narrative of *Breaking Bad*. But just as Shelley's dual narratives of psychic epigenesis and political Idealism can never successfully tell each other, so the melancholic incommensurability between psyche and Nature at the heart of Being permeates *Breaking Bad*'s dual narratives, which touch and do not touch. Walter's *scientific* narrative of creating the perfect crystal, as a projection of his own purposive *Trieb*, underscores his unconsciousness of the latter in his *personal* narrative, which is marked by egotism and an ultimate failure to understand the natural processes at work in his life. What he *objectivises* as crystal meth he never fully *subjectivises* as the crystalline unfolding of purposive individuation.

Walter has just found out he has terminal cancer. In the early morning hours he sits in his backyard in front of his swimming pool, alone, lighting matches and throwing them into the water, pondering his fate. An image of suburban despondency, to be sure. But it is also the symbolically charged scene of Walter's decision to "break bad" and accompany Hank on the ride-along to learn what is involved in creating a meth lab. Walter sits before a pool as a perennial symbol of the unconscious, and his repetitive act of lighting a flame and extinguishing it in the water – a rhythmic process of growth and decay of flame as a perennial symbol of consciousness – is the insistence of an archetypal scene of (dark) Promethean awakening. Cooking crystal meth emerges as a means to fund Walter's cancer treatment and provide for his family after his death, but it is also a scientific process whose symbolic import he never fully comprehends – a misunderstanding reflected in Walter's and Jesse's different approaches to the meth process (for Jesse, cooking is art; for Walter, it is basic chemistry). Indeed, the crystalline becomes a master trope for Walter's connection with his line of flight, even as this connection is often only intimated negatively in the chemical discourse of meth manufacture.

Cancer, as we all know, is the uncontrollable growth and proliferation of cells in the body; it is radical productivity out of bounds. By the end of the first season Walter has grudgingly agreed to chemotherapy; in the second season of *Breaking Bad* Walter's cancer is in remission, and while the chemotherapy may have had a role to play in Walter's improvement there is a more profound relationship between Walter's decision to cook meth and the shrinking of his tumours. Indeed, in the final season Walter stops cooking meth permanently, which is followed by the return of his cancer (and his chemotherapy) until his death in the final episode. Viewed through the lens of Romantic metasubjectivity, the purposive emblem of the crystal constitutes a new beginning for Walter. What in Jungian terms is the emergence of a new awareness in a state of proximate individuation (which "invariably has a healing effect" [Jung, *Symbols* 433]) is also, quite literally, a Schellingian *inhibition* of cancer's radical productivity into a new life, a self-organising libidinal gradient which guides Walter through the slings, arrows, and bullets of face-offs with Mexican cartels, White Power gangs, and rival drug dealers. And while Walter objectifies this process as the *science* of meth, he remains relatively unaware of its existential import: at a post-remission party, he cryptically remarks that he asked "why me?" not only when he was diagnosed with cancer, but also when he was told he was in remission.

In stepping away from the ethical to establish a meth empire, Walter continually maintains that he is doing what he does for his family – to secure their financial security after his death. And while it might seem as if *Breaking Bad* recapitulates a contemporary distinction between the needs of the State and the needs of one's family, Walter's relationship with his crystalline individuation cuts across discourses of State, family, and self with the fluidity of a poetics of obligation that is irreducible to any single interpellation. Indeed, in the final episode Walter White breaks from the family discourse he has held to throughout the series. In this reckoning, having irrevocably damaged the lives of his wife and son, and with his ex-partner Jesse working with the DEA for his downfall, Walter's final words to his wife reflect his own personal involvement in his individuative line: his meth empire was ostensibly for his family, but he did it for himself, which made him feel alive. But the poetics of obligation is not annulled on this account; rather, the magnetic intensities of his obligations shift and fluctuate. For the series ends with Walter coercing his former partners from Grey Matter Technologies into laundering his last nine million dollars into a trust fund for his son and daughter. Walter's final moments unfold in an encounter at the White Power camp which has enslaved Jesse as permanent meth cook, to which Walter travels for revenge against the men who stole his fortune. In an elaborate plan, Walter triggers a heavy machine gun in the trunk of his car which massacres the gang; Walter catches a stray bullet which will take his life. Thus, in a consummate act of individuation Walter kills himself unintentionally, un-consciously; like his life, his death follows the crystallised unfolding of his vocative line of flight. Significantly, Walter is *not* caught by the police – he collapses as they close in, dying with a Mona Lisa smile on his face, surrounded by laboratory equipment.

The clichéd pop-cultural appeal of Walter White as antihero – his pop-cultural mythology – lies in the temptation for us all to "break bad," to live the meth kingpin fantasy of money and power without concern for anything else. But this predictable antiheroism misses what Romantic metasubjectivity can offer a reading of *Breaking Bad*. The obligation at the heart of Romantic metasubjectivity's purposive unfolding points precisely to a magnetism between self and Other with meaning outside the interiority of the ethical and its "thou shalt/not"s. This does not involve jettisoning ethics altogether (even if such a thing were possible); there will always be ethical paradigms and norms, and most of us will abide by them (with some deviations). What Louis Althusser famously called the individual's interpellation by Ideological State Apparatuses is a crucial aspect of human identity. But Romantic metasubjectivity points us, finally, to the fact that these ethics are inventions, idealist constructs superimposed on an unruly Being, which, as Nature, can never be naturalised as one ethos or another. In Romantic metasubjectivity, the poetics of obligation is always the dangerous supplement to ethics, the freedom antagonising the margins of system. In Schelling's words, it is the realisation and experience of the fact that "God is something more real than a merely moral world order" (*Freedom* 26). In Denise Gigante's words, Romantic metasubjectivity demands that we "think of living forms as stubborn particulars, resisting logical abstraction and preserving (however partially) their freedom, [and in doing so] better understand the critical problem facing [...] Romantic natural philosophers" (28–29). Romantic metasubjectivity reminds us that ethics is not Nature, and that Nature can never be ethical; that Being will never conform to the discursive logics with which we make limited sense of the world; that there is nevertheless a purposive organisation with which we can make fleeting connection (sometimes at our own peril); and that the trajectory of the human life as it negotiates psyche and Nature, reason and ecstasy, suspended in doubt before the fleeting glimpse of Self or absolute subject, must always remain undecided.

Notes

1. David Clines makes the important observation that here, Satan is "not the 'devil' of later Jewish and Christian literature. [...] Here he acts as God's eyes and ears on earth" (*The Book of Job* 727 n). This point brings Satan closer to being an aspect of Yahweh, an organ of sensation, a way of perceiving the materiality of his created world. This understanding is sympathetic to Jung's psycho-ontological reading of the *Book of Job*. Here as elsewhere in my citations of *Job*, I rely on Cline's annotations.

2. This can also be measured in terms of Yahweh's proclivity to make binding contracts (covenants) with humanity (the Noahic Covenant; *Gen.* 12–17), the Israelites (the Mosaic Covenant; *Ex.* 19–24, the Davidic Covenant; *Jer.* 33:17–22), to name a few.

3. Clines notes that "therefore I despise myself, and repent in dust and ashes" (*Job* 42: 6) most likely means "I yield" or "I am discouraged," which could be read as an acknowledgement of the failure of transcendental justice in the face of the melancholy of Being.

4. To this end Tod Linafelt points out the profound ambivalence of the word "bless" (ברך) in *Job*, noting the ways in which it harbours Derridean traces of its opposite, "curse." Thus, Yahweh's "blessing" of Job (and vice versa) is a hermeneutical "faultline" which "evinc[es] a fundamental ambivalence about the character of YHWH" (156).

5. Thus Jung anticipates the work of Gilbert Simondon (1924–1989), French philosopher best known for his sophisticated work on the concept of individuation. Individuation is "true ontogenesis" insofar as it "designate[s] the character of becoming of being, that by which being becomes, insofar as it is, as being" (5). Simondon thinks individuation in terms of what he calls a *metastable equilibrium* – a system which includes *becoming* and is thus outside the restricted economy of the stable equilibrium ("Position" 10). Simondon distinguishes between three different modes of individuation: in *physical* individuation, the metastable system individuates and "resolves" into stable natural or "manufactured" objects (e.g., molecules). *Living* individuation pertains to the living organism, which "*conserves within itself a permanent activity of individuation*" as "*a system of individuation, an individuating system and a system individuating itself*" (7). Unique to the human subject, *psychic* individuation is "*the continuation of the vital*

individuation in a being that, in order to resolve its own problematic, must itself intervene as an element of the problem by its own action, as a *subject*" (8). Simondon read Jung and credited him with discovering, among other things, the "affective emotional regime" [*le régime affectivo-émotif*] in which psychic individuation operates (*L'individuation* 99–100).

6. "Mother liquor" (or "bittern") is a term in chemistry referring to the solution remaining after the process of crystallisation.

7. For another engaging discussion of Schelling's view of Nature relative to the early nineteenth-century discovery of fossilised evidence of mass species extinction, see Chapter One of Wirth, *Schelling's Practice of the Wild*.

8. This theme is also taken up in two other TV series: *Dexter* (2006–2013), the story of Dexter Morgan, a blood spatter analyst for Miami Metro Police Dept. who moonlights as a serial killer, and *Hannibal* (2013–2015), the story of Hannibal Lecter, serial killer and cannibal who is also a criminal psychiatrist for the police.

Appendix A: Disentangling Romantic metasubjectivity

Between Romantic poets and writers such as Novalis and Schlegel, a protean philosopher such as Schelling, and a depth psychologist like Jung, there are many words used to describe the human being. Because I make reference to several terms which are different from the "subject" (understood here as the human subject-ed to, and interpellated by, cultural, economic, and political discourses), I want to provide some provisional definitions of these different terms which, I hope, will aid the reader in tracking their differences.

The Romantic metasubject/Romantic metasubjectivity: the opening Novalis epigraph refers to the "Self of one's self," a term I use as a refrain throughout as synonymous with the Romantic metasubject as the "subject of the subject." The "meta" quality of this subjectivity refers to what Novalis calls a "transcendental Self," which points to an organising factor in the human psyche that is not identical with egoity. In the epigraph the "Self" also has a collective quality to it, linking the individual to both knowledge of their own ignorance as well as a "feeling for others," a sympathy which entwines the egoic "self" with a broader substrate common to humanity. This entwinement reflects the concern with uniting the ideal and real, mind and Nature, which preoccupied the major philosophers at the beginning of the nineteenth century. Indeed, the epigraph emphasises that only by understanding oneself in this way (i.e. as an entwinement of individual and collective) can one understand others.

Self: where Novalis' "Self of one's self" gestures to the collective substrate to the egoic "self," Jung uses the capitalised term "Self" in a similar yet palpably different manner. Where for Novalis the Self is a transcendental quality enabling sympathy and opening the way for knowledge, Jung more actively theorises the Self as an absent centre, a centripetal organising force that makes knowledge possible by organising archetypal energies in a way unique to the human individual. But where the epigraph from Novalis seems to insist on "seizing the mastery" of one's Self to make it available to the "self" as consciousness, analytical psychology emphasises that the Self is the goal of an "endless approximation," the striving of an individuation process that can never ultimately reach its goal. So while "self" and "subject" both signify the human being as it exists in time, history, and discourse, the Self is the self's unprethinkable substratum.[1]

Personality: in the manuscript of Coleridge's unfinished masterwork *Opus Maximum*, Coleridge differentiates "personeity" from "personality," stating that "we have proved that the perfection of person is in God, and that personeity, differing from personality only as rejecting all commixture of imperfection associated with the latter, is an essential constituent in the Idea of God" (177). But both Schelling and Jung conceive personality as something categorically different from what the ego presents to others – something which retains the "transcendent" nature of Coleridge's "personeity" without the latter's idea of perfection. In the *Freedom* essay, personality is the link between man as selfish, particular being and man as spirit – indeed, it is "selfhood raised to spirit," the human being's connection with the (un)ground paradoxically responsible for both man's unity with *and* separation from God (33, 38). Personality includes the egoic, but is not reducible to it: "Only in personality is there life, and all personality rests on a dark ground that indeed must therefore be the ground of cognition as well. But it is only the understanding that develops what is hidden and contained in this ground" (*Freedom* 75). For Schelling, personality is ultimately the expression of one's *character* – the preexistent yet unknowable stamp of uniqueness which sculpts each individual's unfolding.

Jung defines personality as "a well-rounded psychic whole that is capable of resistance and abounding in energy […] The achievement of personality means nothing less than the optimum development of the whole individual human being [in its] innate idiosyncrasy" ("The Development of Personality" pars. 286, 289). In other words, for Jung personality is the expression of the whole person through the process of individuation – the unfolding of the Self. But while Jung sometimes suggests "achievement" is a realisable goal, with characteristic ambivalence he goes on to state that "it is impossible to foresee the endless variety of conditions that have to be fulfilled" (para. 289). Thus, when I refer to "personality," I use it in Jung's latter sense as a process of unfolding, the goal of the endless approximation of the individuation process. I occasionally refer to "the person," which should be understood as a general locutionary mark. Jung will later extend individuation to the inorganic and preterhuman, which I take up in Chapter 4 and the Conclusion.

Note

1. Jung writes that the Self can be symbolised by human or animal figures, as well images of symmetry or order (e.g. a mandala, squares, circles, cubes). But following Lyotard, any symmetrical properties of the Self's figure-image, as part of "the order of the visible," should not be confused with attributes of the *figure-matrix*, whose unconscious origins instantly recede before the "schema of intelligibility" imposed on it from without (Lyotard 268). That is, symmetrical figures of totality can still be attended by experiences of profound difference and disjunction. See Chapter 2, note 19.

Appendix B: Situating Romantic metasubjectivity

Romantic metasubjectivity enters a debate on the subject which is roughly polarised by the so-called "reflection theory" on the one side, and on the other the "Heidelberg school" (begun with the work of Dieter Henrich, with Manfred Frank as its most notable thinker). Undoubtedly more familiar at present, the reflection theory of the subject sees self-consciousness as a "subject supposed to know" emerging from the mirror-stage (Lacan), as an epiphenomenon of signifying play (Derrida), or as discursive entanglement (Foucault). Thus, it rejects any prediscursive or prereflective aspect of self-consciousness. The Heidelberg school, on the other hand, draws more explicitly on early German Romantic thinking. Manfred Frank maintains that discursivity is crucial for the formation of "subjectivity," but preserves "individuality" against a "pathogenic" Enlightenment reason by revealing this reason's fantasy of universality: "individuals are subjects (although not all subjects are individuals) [who] are immediately self-conscious in the sense that they disclose their world in the light of interpretations that would remain unintelligible without consciousness. [While] this does not exempt individuality from the linguistic context [...] words do not mean by themselves, or by force of some anonymous institution; they [mean] only through hypothetical interpretations whose carriers are individuals" ("Subjectivity and Individuality" 23). The fantasy of rationality is thus founded on irreducible individuals who contest its impetus to closure, "who [make] possible the intersubjectivity of meanings exchanged in communicative acts, while at the same time [preventing] the given communicative system from becoming truly universal, in the sense that all meanings would become strictly determined and exhaustively definable. Thus reason opens out to history, and no *terme final* can be envisaged" ("Two Centuries" 75).

Robert Pippin's "On Not Being a Neostructuralist" (2005) is sympathetic toward Frank's critique of "neostructuralism" (which for Frank denotes the reflection theory, including deconstructionist and poststructuralist positions on subjectivity) but remains sceptical of Frank's "Schellingean-romantic" position's ability to establish a "positive philosophical project" (180, 169). Clearly stating his Hegelian position regarding "claims about the ineffable, the irreducible, the simply and eternally unrepresentable" (170), Pippin argues for considering intentionality within a matrix of "possible inferences" without a Platonic or "transcendental" basis (183). He concludes that thinking

> cannot involve the "internalization" of some "universal" by an individual consciousness: "[Thinking] must be a subscribing to a norm, not any private internalization, and if a norm is to be a norm, it must be backed by reasons, implications, and commitments [...] understood as the results of social interactions within communities over time, collectively self-constituted norms. [...] The important point here is that these are engagements with public matters not realizations in private" (185).

As a more pointed critique of Frank's position, Slavoj Žižek's "The Cartesian Subject Versus the Cartesian Theater" (1998) is one of the more fundamentalist expressions of the reflection theory. In this quizzical, neurotic text, Žižek frames Henrich's school as an "enemy" and, "instead of engaging in a direct dialogue with Henrich's school" (248), offers the insights of cognitive science as a screen for the deconstructive position he wants to defend against Frank, while at the same time conceding an unbridgeable gap between cognitive science and the "deconstructionist 'metatranscendental' probing into the conditions of (im)possibility of the philosophical discourse" it is meant to defend (249). Without meaningful citation of Henrich (and no citation whatsoever of Frank), Žižek raises straw men (e.g. the endorsement of "direct experience," which is nowhere mentioned) to knock them down in the name of (Lacanian) psychoanalysis. Ironically, Žižek's exposition of Daniel Dennett's cognitive science articulates a psyche more Jungian than Freudian (an insight which would no doubt appal Žižek), despite the attempt in Žižek's essay to smuggle a phylogenetic unconscious into psychoanalysis via Hegel.

While Romantic metasubjectivity is clearly more sympathetic toward Frank and the Heidelberg school, the *psyche* of this metasubject (which does not concern Frank) resists the more formalist and teleological tendencies in some of Frank's writing, where the language of normativity (but one contra Habermas) tends to cast the individual as monadic agent in the progression toward an idealised community of individuals under the auspices of the Kantian Idea ("Two Centuries" 83–84). By definition, Romantic metasubjectivity also cuts across the public/private, internal/external boundaries assumed by Pippin's critique of Frank. And insofar as Frank's discussion in "Two Centuries" leaves out the question (or even the existence) of Nature, Romantic metasubjectivity also vigorously questions the idealised *ethics* such a community might assume, which I discuss in the Conclusion.

Appendix C: Self and archetype

In his (in)famous proclivity for imprecise language, Jung often refers to the Self as an archetype (the best-known example being his statement that *"Christ exemplifies the archetype of the self"* [*Aion* 37]) – a designation which has been far too uncritically picked up by a good deal of writing (Jungian and otherwise) about individuation and the Self. Yet his late definition of Self as "borderline concept" (letter to Pastor Walter Bernet, 13 June 1955, 258) points not only to Jung's ambivalence over just how to define the "empty centre" of the Self but also to the underexplored yet critical theoretical problems with seeing the Self as an "archetype of wholeness."

The Self is Jung's name for the horizon of totality toward which the forward movement of individuation strives; it *organises* archetypal images, affects, and experiences. But Jung's hazy language leads us to the crucial question: can the Self, as that which constellates archetypes, *be* an archetype? On the one hand, Jung's own theory strongly suggests that the Self cannot be an archetype, for setting an archetype as the goal of development is the very essence of inflation – the overwhelming of the ego by unconscious energies which is by definition disastrous. But Jung's ambivalent language invites a more detailed analysis: in effect, we are presented with a dilemma similar to Russell's Paradox in set theory. Briefly, Russell's Paradox is as follows: given a multitude of sets in the world (of screwdrivers, concepts, nuclear warheads, vegetables, etc.), the question is: can there be a set (X) which contains all sets? Herein lies the paradox: if X contains all sets, it must also contain itself as a set. But if X contains itself, it thus becomes a *member* of all sets and is then not the set which contains all sets. Thus, in becoming the set of all sets, X also does *not* become the set of all sets. The result is that the "set of all sets" *cannot be determined* – it does not exist insofar as it cannot be definitely posited. Russell's ultimate resolution of this dilemma was to posit something outside sets, which is tantamount to stating that sets cannot contain and define everything. In other words, the complete system must paradoxically recognise that which is outside of itself – in effect, "completing" itself by recognising its incompletion. But this also brings us back to Schelling's critique of Hegel: Hegel's system proposed itself as a "set of all sets" which explained Being dialectically as the unfolding of Absolute Spirit. Schelling's critique, as we have seen, is that this system cannot explain its own facticity in Being.

To bring this back to the question of Jung's Self, it means that *the Self cannot be determined as an archetype*. The language here is important: the Self can certainly be *experienced* archetypally (as an experience of rebirth, transition, or wholeness in which the entire human race shares), but this is not the same as determining the Self *as* an archetype, which would pose the problem of how the archetypal matrix determines all of Being from entirely within itself. It is perhaps most useful to see the borderline concept of the Self as copular, as *liminal* with the archetypal, something which touches but does not touch the archetypal. If the Self had no connection whatsoever with the archetypes, it would have no constellating power. Yet it is also something else, that which is not-archetype – that which falls outside the set "archetype." Indeed, Jung says as much when he writes of the Self: "If I assert, 'The self exists,' I must supplement this by saying, 'But it seems not to exist'" (*Transformation Symbolism* para. 399n). Romantic metasubjectivity falls on the Schellingian side of the Continental-philosophical version of this debate by conceiving the Self as *Trieb*, which moves through archetypal energies without *being* any one configuration.

Bibliography

Abrams, M. H. *Natural Supernaturalism: Tradition and Revolution in Romantic Literature*. New York and London: Norton, 1971.

Adler, J. and C. Louth. "Introduction." *Friedrich Hölderlin, Essays and Letters*. Trans. and Ed. Jeremy Adler and Charlie Louth. London and New York: Penguin, 2009. xv–lv.

Bair, D. *Jung: A Biography*. New York: Back Bay Books, 2003.

Barentsen, G. "Freud, Jung, and the Dangerous Supplement to Psychoanalysis." *Mosaic* 44(4); 2011: 195–211.

Bataille, G. *The Accursed Share*. Trans. Robert Hurley. 3 vols. New York: Zone Books, 1991–1993.

Bataille, G. "The Consequences of Nonknowledge." *The Unfinished System of Nonknowledge*. Trans. Michelle Kendall and Stuart Kendall. Minneapolis and London: U of Minnesota P, 2001. 111–118.

Bataille, G. *Inner Experience*. Trans. Stuart Kendall. Albany: State U of New York P, 2014.

Battersby, C. *The Sublime, Terror and Human Difference*. London and New York: Routledge, 2007.

Beach, E. *The Potencies of God(s): Schelling's Philosophy of Mythology*. Albany: State U of New York P, 1994.

Behler, E. *German Romantic Literary Theory*. Cambridge: Cambridge UP, 1993.

Beiser, F. *German Idealism: The Struggle Against Subjectivism, 1781-1801*. Cambridge: Harvard UP, 2002.

Beiser, F. *The Romantic Imperative: The Concept of Early German Romanticism*. Cambridge and London: Harvard UP, 2003.

Beiser, F. *Hegel*. New York and London: Routledge, 2005.

Bishop, P. "The Use of Kant in Jung's Early Psychological Works." *Journal of European Studies* 26; 1996: 107–140.

Bishop, P. *Synchronicity and Intellectual Intuition in Kant, Swedenborg and Jung*. Lewiston, NY: Edwin Mellen P, 2000.

Bishop, P. *Jung's* Answer to Job*: A Commentary*. New York: Brunner-Routledge, 2002.

Bishop, P. "Jung's *Red Book* and its Relation to Aspects of German Idealism." *Journal of Analytical Psychology* 57(3); 2012: 335–363.

Blanchot, M. "The Athenaeum." Trans. Deborah Esch and Ian Balfour. *Studies in Romanticism* 22(2); 1983: 163–172.

Boundas, C. "Subjectivity." *The Deleuze Dictionary, Revised Edition*. Ed. A. Parr. Edinburgh: Edinburgh UP, 2010. 274–275.

Bowie, A. *Schelling and Modern European Philosophy: An Introduction*. London and New York: Routledge, 1993.

Bowie, A. "Translator's Introduction." *On the History of Modern Philosophy*. F. Schelling. Trans. Andrew Bowie. Cambridge: Cambridge UP, 1994. 1–37.

Bowie, A. *Aesthetics and Subjectivity: From Kant to Nietzsche*. 2nd ed. Manchester and New York: Manchester UP, 2003.

Broadhurst, J. Ed. *Deleuze & the Transcendental Unconscious*. *PLI* 4.1-2; 1992.

Brooks, P. "Freud's Masterplot: Questions of Narrative." *Literature and Psychoanalysis: The Question of Reading: Otherwise*. Ed. S. Felman. Baltimore and London: Johns Hopkins UP, 1982. 280–300.

Brown, R. *The Later Philosophy of Schelling: The Influence of Boehme on the Works of 1809-1815*. Lewisburg, PA: Bucknell University Press, 1977.

Caputo, J. *Against Ethics: Contributions to a Poetics of Obligation with Constant Reference to Deconstruction*. Bloomington and Indianapolis: Indiana UP, 1993.

Caruth, C. *Unclaimed Experience: Trauma, Narrative, and History*. Baltimore: Johns Hopkins UP, 1996.

Casey, E. "Jung and the Postmodern Condition." *C.G. Jung and the Humanities: Towards a Hermeneutics of Culture*. Eds. K. Barnaby and P. d'Acierno. Princeton: Princeton UP, 1990. 320–323.

Chaouli, M. *The Laboratory of Poetry: Chemistry and Poetics in the Work of Friedrich Schlegel*. Baltimore and London: Johns Hopkins UP, 2002.

Chodorow, J. "Introduction." *Jung on Active Imagination*. Ed. J. Chodorow. Princeton: Princeton UP, 1997. 1–20.

Clark, D. "Lost and Found in Translation: Romanticism and the Legacies of Jacques Derrida." *Studies in Romanticism* 46(2); 2007: 161–182.

Clines, D. "The Book of Job." *The New Oxford Annotated Bible: New Revised Standard Version With The Apocrypha. Fully Revised Fourth Edition*. Eds. M. Coogan, M. Brettler, C. Newsom and P. Perkins. New York: Oxford UP, 2010. 726–771.

Coleridge, S. T. *Biographia Literaria*. Eds. J. Engell and W. J. Bate. Princeton: Princeton UP, 1983.

Coleridge, S. T. "Essays on the Principles of Genial Criticism." *Shorter Works and Fragments*. Vol. 1. Eds. H. J. Jackson and J. R. de J. Jackson. Princeton: Princeton UP, 1995.

Coleridge, S. T. *Theory of Life. Shorter Works and Fragments 1*. Eds. H. J. Jackson and J. R. de J. Jackson. Princeton: Princeton UP, 1995. 481–557.

Coleridge, S. T. *Opus Maximum*. Ed. T. McFarland. Princeton: Princeton UP, 2002.

Comay, R. "Resistance and Repetition: Freud and Hegel." *Research in Phenomenology* 45(2); 2015: 237–266.

Cooke, M. *Acts of Inclusion: Studies Bearing on an Elementary Theory of Romanticism*. New Haven: Yale UP, 1979.

Craciun, A. *Fatal Women of Romanticism*. Cambridge: Cambridge UP, 2003.

Culbertson, C. "Nature and Self-Knowledge: On Schelling's Ambiguous Role in Merleau-Ponty's *The Concept of Nature*." *The Barbarian Principle: Merleau-Ponty, Schelling, and the Question of Nature*. Eds. J. Wirth and P. Burke. Albany: State U of New York P, 2013. 225–240.

D'Acierno, P. and K. Barnaby. *Preface. C.G. Jung and the Humanities: Towards a Hermeneutics of Culture*. Eds. K. Barnaby and P. d'Acierno. Princeton: Princeton UP, 1990. xv–xxix.

De Man, P. "The Intentional Structure of the Romantic Image." *The Rhetoric of Romanticism*. New York: Columbia UP, 1984. 1–17.

Deleuze, G. and F. Guattari. *Anti-Oedipus: Capitalism and Schizophrenia*. 1972. Minnesota: U of Minnesota P, 1983.

Deleuze, G. *Nietzsche and Philosophy*. 1962. Trans. Hugh Tomlinson. New York: Columbia UP, 1983.

Deleuze, G. and F. Guattari. *A Thousand Plateaus: Capitalism and Schizophrenia*. Trans. Brian Massumi. Minneapolis: U of Minnesota P, 1987.

Deleuze, G. and L. von Sacher-Masoch. "Coldness and Cruelty." *Masochism*. Trans. Jean McNeil. New York: Zone Books, 1991.

Deleuze, G. and F. Guattari. *What is Philosophy?* 1991. Trans. Hugh Tomlinson and Graham Burchell. New York: Columbia UP, 1994.

Deleuze, G. *Difference and Repetition*. Trans. Paul Patton. New York: Columbia UP, 1994.

Deleuze, G. "From Sacher-Masoch to Masochism." Trans. Christian Kerslake. *Angelaki* 9(1); 2004: 125–133.

Deleuze, G. *The Fold: Leibniz and the Baroque*. 1988. Trans. Tom Conley. New York: Continuum, 2006.

Derrida, J. "Différance." *Speech and Phenomena and Other Essays on Husserl's Theory of Signs*. Trans. David Allison. Evanston, IL: Northwestern UP, 1973. 129–160.

Derrida, J. "Freud and the Scene of Writing." *Writing and Difference*. Trans. Alan Bass. Chicago: U of Chicago P, 1978. 196–231.

Derrida, J. *Positions*. Trans. Alan Bass. Chicago: U of Chicago P, 1981.

Derrida, J. *Archive Fever: A Freudian Impression*. Trans. Eric Prenowitz. Chicago and London: U of Chicago P, 1996.

Derrida, J. *Of Grammatology*. 1976. Corr. Ed. Trans. Gayatri Spivak. Baltimore and London: Johns Hopkins UP, 1997.

Derrida, J. "In Praise of Psychoanalysis." *For What Tomorrow... A Dialogue*. Trans. Jeff Fort. Stanford: Stanford UP, 2004. 166–196.

Derrida, J. "The Transcendental 'Stupidity' ('Bêtise') of Man and the Becoming-Animal According to Deleuze." *Derrida, Deleuze, Psychoanalysis*. Ed. G. Schwab. New York: Columbia UP, 2007. 35–60.

Dourley, J. *Jung and His Mystics: In the End it All Comes to Nothing.* London and New York: Routledge, 2014.

Dufresne, T. *Tales from the Freudian Crypt: The Death Drive in Text and Context.* Stanford: Stanford UP, 2000.

Dufresne, T. "Introduction." *Beyond the Pleasure Principle.* S. Freud. Trans. Gregory Richter, Peterborough, Ont.: Broadview, 2011. 13–29.

Dufresne, T. *The Late Sigmund Freud: Or, The Last Word on Psychoanalysis, Society, and All the Riddles of Life.* Cambridge: Cambridge UP, 2017.

Ellenberger, H. *The Discovery of the Unconscious: The History and Evolution of Dynamic Psychiatry.* Basic Books, 1970.

Ellis, D. *Wordsworth, Freud and the Spots of Time: Interpretation in* The Prelude. Cambridge: Cambridge UP, 1985.

Faflak, J. *Romantic Psychoanalysis: The Burden of the Mystery.* Albany: State U of New York P, 2008.

Ferris, D. "Introduction – Tragic Freedom: Romanticism and the Question of Schelling." *Schelling and Romanticism.* 2000. Romantic Circles Praxis Series (RCPS) http://www.rc.umd.edu/praxis/schelling/. Accessed 16 June 2019.

Ffytche, M. *The Foundation of the Unconscious: Schelling, Freud and the Birth of the Modern Psyche.* Cambridge: Cambridge UP, 2012.

Forster, M. "Schelling and Skepticism." *Interpreting Schelling: Critical Essays.* Ed. L. Ostaric. Cambridge: Cambridge UP, 2014. 32–47.

Foucault, M. *The Archaeology of Knowledge and the Discourse on Language.* Trans. A.M. Sheridan Smith. New York: Pantheon, 1972.

Foucault, M. "Theatricum Philosophicum." *Language, Counter-Memory, Practice: Selected Essays and Interviews.* Trans. Donald Bouchard and Sherry Simon. Ithaca: Cornell UP, 1977. 165–196.

Foucault, M. *The Order of Things: An Archaeology of the Human Sciences.* 1966. New York: Vintage, 1994.

Frank, M. *What is Neostructuralism?* Trans. Sabine Wilke and Richard Gray. Minneapolis: U of Minnesota P, 1989.

Frank, M. "Two Centuries of Philosophical Critique of Reason and Its 'Postmodern' Radicalization." Trans. Dieter Freundlieb and Wayne Hudson. *Reason and Its Others: Rationality in Modern German Philosophy and Culture.* Eds. D. Freundlieb and W. Hudson. Oxford: Berg, 1993. 67–85.

Frank, M. "Subjectivity and Individuality: Survey of a Problem." Trans. Gunter Zöller. *Figuring the Self: Subject, Absolute and Others in Classical German Philosophy.* Eds. D. Klemm and G. Zöller. Albany: State U of New York P, 1997. 3–30.

Frank, M. "What Is Early German Romanticism?" *The Relevance of Romanticism: Essays on German Romantic Philosophy.* Ed. D. Nassar. New York: Oxford, 2014. 15–29.

Freud, S. *Gesammelte Werke.* Heraus. von Anna Freud, E. Bibring, W. Hoffer, E. Kris, und O. Iskower. 17 Bänden. Frankfurt am Main and London: S. Fischer Verlag/ Imago Publishing, 1940–1950.

Freud, S. *The Standard Edition of the Complete Psychological Works of Sigmund Freud.* Ed. and trans. James Strachey. 24 vols. London: Hogarth Press, 1953–1974.

Freud, S. "To C.G. Jung." 12 Nov. 1911. *The Freud-Jung Letters: The Correspondence Between Sigmund Freud and C.G. Jung.* Ed. W. McGuire. Trans. Ralph Manheim and R.F.C. Hull. 1974. Cambridge, MA: Harvard UP, 1979. 457–459.

Freud, S. *A Phylogenetic Fantasy: Overview of the Transference Neurosis.* Trans. Alex Hoffer and Peter Hoffer. Cambridge and London: Harvard UP, 1987.

Freud, S. *The Psychopathology of Everyday Life.* Trans. Anthea Bell. London and New York: Penguin, 2002.

Freud, S. *Moses the Man and Monotheistic Religion. Mass Psychology and Other Writings.* Trans. J.A. Underwood. New York: Penguin, 2004. 167–299.

Freud, S. *Beyond the Pleasure Principle.* Trans. Gregory Richter. Peterborough, Ont.: Broadview, 2011.

Freud, S. *Project for a Scientific Psychology. Standard Edition,* vol. 1.

Freud, S. *The Interpretation of Dreams. Standard Edition,* vols. 4–5.

Freud, S. *Totem and Taboo. Standard Edition,* vol. 13.

Freud, S. *Introductory Lectures on Psycho-Analysis. Standard Edition,* vol. 15.

Freud, S. *The Ego and the Id. Standard Edition,* vol. 19.

Freud, S. *An Outline of Psycho-Analysis. Standard Edition,* vol. 23.

Freud S./Jung C.G. *Briefwechsel.* Heraus. von William McGuire und Wolfgang Sauerländer. Ungekürzte Lizenzausgabe für den Buchclub Ex Libris Zürich. 1976.

Frosch, T. *Shelley and the Romantic Imagination: A Psychological Study.* Newark: U of Delaware P, 2007.

Fulford, T. "Conducting the Vital Fluid: The Politics and Poetics of Mesmerism in the 1790s." *Studies in Romanticism* 43; 2004: 57–78.

Gasché, R. "Foreword: Ideality in Fragmentation." *Philosophical Fragments.* F. Schlegel. Trans. Peter Firchow. Minneapolis: U of Minnesota P, 1991. vii–xxxii.

Gasché, R. "Toward an Ethics of *Auseinandersetzung.*" *American Continental Philosophy: A Reader.* Eds. W. Brogan and J. Risser. Bloomington: Indiana UP, 2000. 314–332.

Giegerich, W. *The Soul's Logical Life: Towards a Rigorous Notion of Psychology.* 1998. Frankfurt am Main: Peter Lang, 2008.

Giegerich, W. "'The Unassimilable Remnant': What is at Stake? A Dispute with Stanton Marlan." *The Soul Always Thinks: Collected English Papers.* vol. 4. New Orleans: Spring Journal Books, 2010. 443–474.

Giegerich, W. "Is the Soul 'Deep'? Entering and Following the Logical Movement of Heraclitus' Fragment 45 (Diels)." *The Soul Always Thinks: Collected English Papers, vol. 4.* New Orleans: Spring Journal Books, 2010. 131–163.

Giegerich, W. "Love the Questions Themselves." *Living With Jung: "Enterviews" with Jungian Analysts.* Vol. 3. New Orleans, LO: Spring Journal, 2010. 256–296.

Giegerich, W. "A Serious Misunderstanding: Synchronicity and the Generation of Meaning." *Journal of Analytical Psychology* 57(4); 2012: 500–511.

Giegerich, W. "Jungian Psychology as Metaphysics? A Response to Sean McGrath." *International Journal of Jungian Studies* 7(3); 2015: 242–250.

Gigante, D. *Life: Organic Form and Romanticism.* New Haven and London: Yale UP, 2009.

Gosetti-Ferencei, J. *Heidegger, Hölderlin, and the Subject of Poetic Language: Toward a New Poetics of Dasein.* New York: Fordham UP, 2004.

Grant, I. "Philosophy Become Genetic: The Physics of the World Soul." *The New Schelling.* Eds. J. Norman and A. Welchman. London and New York: Continuum, 2004. 128–150.

Grant, I. *Philosophies of Nature After Schelling.* London and New York: Continuum, 2006.

Guyer, P. *Kant.* 2nd ed. London and New York: Routledge, 2014.

Harman, G. *The Quadruple Object.* Winchester: Zero Books, 2011.

Hartman, G. "Romanticism and Anti-Self-Consciousness." *Romanticism and Consciousness: Essays in Criticism.* New York: Norton, 1970. 46–56.

Hartman, G. *Wordsworth's Poetry: 1787-1814.* New Haven and London: Yale UP, 1971.

Hartman, G. *The Unremarkable Wordsworth.* Minneapolis: U of Minnesota P, 1987.

Hartman, G. "'Was it for this…?': Wordsworth and the Birth of the Gods." *William Wordsworth.* Ed. H. Bloom. Updated ed. New York: Chelsea House, 2007. 131–146.

Hartmann, E. *Philosophy of the Unconscious.* 1868. Trans. William Coupland. 1932. 3 vols. New York: Routledge, 2010.

Haule, J. "From Somnambulism to the Archetypes: The French Roots of Jung's Split With Freud." *Jung in Contexts: A Reader.* Ed. P. Bishop. London and New York: Routledge, 1999. 242–264.

Hegel, G. W. F. *Philosophy of Nature.* Trans. A.V. Miller. London: Oxford UP, 1970.

Hegel, G. W. F. *The Science of Logic.* Trans. George di Giovanni. Cambridge: Cambridge UP, 2010.

Hegel, G. W. F. *Phenomenology of Spirit.* Trans. Michael Inwood. Oxford: Oxford UP, 2018.

Henderson, A. *Romantic Identities: Varieties of Subjectivity, 1774-1830.* Cambridge: Cambridge UP, 1996.

Hertz, N. "The Notion of Blockage in the Literature of the Sublime." *The End of the Line: Essays on Psychoanalysis and the Sublime.* New York: Columbia UP, 1985. 40–60.

Hildebrand, W. "Naming-Day in Asia's Vale." *Keats-Shelley Journal* 32; 1983: 190–203.

Hirsch, E. D. *Wordsworth and Schelling: A Typological Study of Romanticism.* New Haven: Yale UP, 1960.

Hoffer, P. "The Concept of Phylogenetic Inheritance in Freud and Jung." *Journal of the American Psychoanalytical Association* 40(2); 1992: 517–530.

Hogenson, G. "The Baldwin Effect: A Neglected Influence on C.G. Jung's Evolutionary Thinking." *Journal of Analytical Psychology* 46; 2001: 591–611.

Hogle, J. *Shelley's Process: Radical Transference and the Development of His Major Works.* New York and Oxford: Oxford UP, 1988.

Hölderlin, F. "Notes on the *Antigone.*" *Essays and Letters.* Trans. and ed. Jeremy Adler and Charlie Louth. London and New York: Penguin, 2009. 325–332.

Hölderlin, F. "Notes on the *Oedipus.*" *Essays and Letters.* Trans. and ed. Jeremy Adler and Charlie Louth. London and New York: Penguin, 2009. 317–324.

Hölderlin, F. "The Lyric, In Appearance Idealic Poem...." *Essays and Letters.* Trans. and ed. Jeremy Adler and Charlie Louth. London and New York: Penguin, 2009. 302–306.

Hölderlin, F. *Essays and Letters.* Trans. and ed. Jeremy Adler and Charlie Louth. London and New York: Penguin, 2009.

Johnston, A. *Time Driven: Metapsychology and the Splitting of the Drive.* Evanston, IL: Northwestern UP, 2005.

Jung, C. G. *Two Essays on Analytical Psychology.* Trans. H.G. and C.F. Baynes. London: Baillière, Tindall and Cox, 1928.

Jung, C. G. *The Collected Works of C.G. Jung.* Eds. H. Read, M. Fordham and G. Adler. Trans. R.F.C. Hull. 20 vols. Princeton: Princeton UP, 1953–1971.

Jung, C. G. *Bibliothek-Katalog.* Küsnacht-Zürich, 1967.

Jung, C. G. and C. Kerényi. *Essays on a Science of Mythology: The Myth of the Divine Child and the Mysteries of Eleusis.* Trans. R.F.C. Hull. Princeton: Princeton UP, 1969.

Jung, C. G. "Letter to Hélène Keiner." 15 June 1955. *Letters.* 2 vols. Vol. 2. Trans. R.F.C. Hull. Ed. G. Adler. Princeton: Princeton UP, 1973–1975. 265.

Jung, C. G. "Letter to Mr. O." 2 May 1947. *Letters.* 2 vols. Vol. 1. Trans. R.F.C. Hull. Ed. G. Adler. Princeton: Princeton UP, 1973–1975. 459–460.

Jung, C. G. "Letter to Pastor Walter Bernet." 13 June 1955. *Letters.* 2 vols. Vol. 2. Trans. R.F.C. Hull. Ed. G. Adler. Princeton: Princeton UP, 1973–1975. 257–264.

Jung, C. G. "Letter to Pastor Walter Uhsadel." 6 February 1952. *Letters.* 2 vols. Vol. 2. Trans. R.F.C. Hull. Ed. G. Adler. Princeton: Princeton UP, 1973–1975. 39–40.

Jung, C. G. "Letter to Zvi Werblowsky." 17 June 1952. *Letters.* 2 vols. Vol. 2. Trans. R.F.C. Hull. Ed. G. Adler. Princeton: Princeton UP, 1973–1975. 69–71.

Jung, C. G. "To Herr N." 9 May 1959. *Letters.* 2 vols. Vol. 2. Trans. R.F.C. Hull. Ed. G. Adler. Princeton: Princeton UP, 1975. 504–506.

Jung, C. G. "Diagnosing the Dictators." *C.G. Jung Speaking: Interviews and Encounters.* Eds. W. McGuire and R. F. C. Hull. Princeton: Princeton UP, 1977. 115–135.

Jung, C. G. "Talks with Miguel Serrano: 1959." *C.G. Jung Speaking: Interviews and Encounters.* Eds. W. McGuire and R. F. C. Hull. Princeton: Princeton UP, 1977. 392–405.

Jung, C. G. "Jung Diagnoses the Dictators." *C.G. Jung Speaking: Interviews and Encounters.* Eds. W. McGuire and R. F. C. Hull. Princeton: Princeton UP, 1977. 136–140.

Jung, C. G. "Letter to Sigmund Freud." 14 Nov. 1911. *The Freud-Jung Letters: The Correspondence Between Sigmund Freud and C.G. Jung.* Trans. Ralph Manheim and R.F.C. Hull. Ed. W. McGuire. Cambridge, MA: Harvard UP, 1979. 460–461.

Jung, C. G. "The Border Zones of Exact Science." *The Zofingia Lectures.* Trans. Jan van Jeurck. Princeton: Princeton UP, 1983. 1–19.

Jung, C. G. "Thoughts on the Nature and Value of Speculative Inquiry." *The Zofingia Lectures.* Trans. Jan van Jeurck. Princeton: Princeton UP, 1983. 57–88.

Jung, C. G. *Dream Analysis: Notes of the Seminar Given in 1928-1930.* Ed. W. McGuire. Princeton: Princeton UP, 1984.

Jung, C. G. *Memories, Dreams, Reflections.* Ed. A. Jaffé. Trans. Richard and Clara Winston. 1963. New York: Vintage, 1989.

Jung, C. G. *Visions: Notes of the Seminar Given in 1930-1934 by C.G. Jung.* 2 vols. Ed. C. Douglas. Princeton: Princeton UP, 1997.

Jung, C. G. *Zofingia-Vorträge 1896-1899.* Heraus. H. Egner. Zürich und Düsseldorf: Walter Verlag, 1997.

Jung, C. G. "Letter to Wolfgang Pauli." 30 Nov. 1950. *Atom and Archetype: The Pauli-Jung Letters, 1932-1958.* Trans. David Roscoe. Ed. C.A. Meier. London and New York: Routledge, 2001. 59–63.

Jung, C. G. *Children's Dreams: Notes from the Seminar Given in 1936-1940.* Trans. Ernst Falzeder. Eds. L. Jung and M. Meyer-Grass. Princeton and Oxford: Princeton UP, 2008.

Jung, C. G. *The Red Book (Liber Novus): A Reader's Edition.* Trans. Mark Kyburz, John Peck, and Sonu Shamdasani. Ed. S. Shamdasani. New York: Norton, 2009.

Jung, C. G. *Gesammelte Werke.* Heraus. L. Hurwitz-Eisner, L. Jung-Merker, M. Niehus-Jung, F. Riklin, E. Rüf and L. Zander. 24 Bänden. Ostfildern: Patmos Verlag, 2011.

Jung, C. G. *Introduction to Jungian Psychology: Notes of the Seminar on Analytical Psychology Given in 1925.* Rev. ed. Ed. S. Shamdasani. Princeton: Princeton UP, 2012.

Jung, C. G. *Dream Interpretation Ancient and Modern: Notes from the Seminar Given in 1936-1941.* Trans. Ernst Falzeder. Eds. J. Peck, L. Jung and M. Meyer-Grass. Princeton and Oxford: Princeton UP, 2014.

Jung, C. G. "The Psychology of Dementia Praecox." *Collected Works,* vol. 3.

Jung, C. G. "On Psychological Understanding." *Collected Works,* vol. 3.

Jung, C. G. "On the Doctrine of Complexes." *Collected Works,* vol. 4.

Jung, C. G. "Symbols of Transformation." *Collected Works,* vol. 5.

Jung, C. G. "Definitions." *Collected Works,* vol. 6.

Jung, C. G. "Psychological Types." *Collected Works,* vol. 6.

Jung, C. G. "The Type Problem in Poetry." *Collected Works,* vol. 6.

Jung, C. G. "On the Psychology of the Unconscious." *Collected Works,* vol. 7.

Jung, C. G. "The Relations Between the Ego and the Unconscious." *Collected Works,* vol. 7.

Jung, C. G. "On Psychic Energy." *Collected Works*, vol. 8.

Jung, C. G. "On Synchronicity." *Collected Works*, vol. 8.

Jung, C. G. "On the Nature of Dreams." *Collected Works*, vol. 8.

Jung, C. G. "On the Nature of the Psyche." *Collected Works*, vol. 8.

Jung, C. G. "A Review of the Complex Theory." *Collected Works*, vol. 8.

Jung, C. G. "Basic Postulates of Analytical Psychology." *Collected Works*, vol. 8.

Jung, C. G. "Instinct and the Unconscious." *Collected Works*, vol. 8.

Jung, C. G. "The Structure of the Psyche." *Collected Works*, vol. 8.

Jung, C. G. "The Transcendent Function." *Collected Works*, vol. 8.

Jung, C. G. "Synchronicity: An Acausal Connecting Principle." *Collected Works*, vol. 8.

Jung, C. G. "Analytical Psychology and Weltanschauung." *Collected Works*, vol. 8.

Jung, C. G. "Archetypes of the Collective Unconscious." *Collected Works*, vol. 9i.

Jung, C. G. "Concerning the Archetypes, With Special Reference to the Anima Concept." *Collected Works*, vol. 9i.

Jung, C. G. "A Study in the Process of Individuation." *Collected Works*, vol. 9i.

Jung, C. G. "Psychological Aspects of the Mother Archetype." *Collected Works*, vol. 9i.

Jung, C. G. "The Psychological Aspects of the Kore." *Collected Works*, vol. 9i.

Jung, C. G. "The Psychology of the Child Archetype." *Collected Works*, vol. 9i.

Jung, C. G. "Aion: Researches Into the Phenomenology of the Self." *Collected Works*, vol. 9ii.

Jung, C. G. "The Role of the Unconscious." *Collected Works*, vol. 10.

Jung, C. G. "A Psychological View of Conscience." *Collected Works*, vol. 10.

Jung, C. G. "Flying Saucers: A Modern Myth of Things Seen in the Skies." *Collected Works*, vol. 10.

Jung, C. G. "The Undiscovered Self." *Collected Works*, vol. 10.

Jung, C. G. "Answer to Job." *Collected Works*, vol. 11.

Jung, C. G. "Transformation Symbolism in the Mass." *Collected Works*, vol. 11.

Jung, C. G. "A Psychological Approach to the Dogma of the Trinity." *Collected Works*, vol. 11.

Jung, C. G. "Psychology and Religion." *Collected Works*, vol. 11.

Jung, C. G. "Psychology and Alchemy." *Collected Works*, vol. 12.

Jung, C. G. "Commentary on 'The Secret of the Golden Flower.'" *Collected Works*, vol. 13.

Jung, C. G. "Alchemical Studies." *Collected Works*, vol. 13.

Jung, C. G. "Mysterium Coniunctionis." *Collected Works*, vol. 14.

Jung, C. G. "Fundamental Questions of Psychotherapy." *Collected Works*, vol. 16.

Jung, C. G. "Problems of Modern Psychotherapy." *Collected Works*, vol. 16.

Jung, C. G. "The Practical Use of Dream-Analysis." *Collected Works*, vol. 16.

Jung, C. G. "The Psychology of the Transference." *Collected Works*, vol. 16.

Jung, C. G. "The Development of Personality." *Collected Works*, vol. 17.

Jung, C. G. "Psychic Conflicts in a Child." *Collected Works*, vol. 17.

Jung, C. G. "Foreword to Jung, 'Phénomènes Occultes'." *Collected Works*, vol. 18.

Jung, C. G. "Foreword to Mehlich: 'J.H. Fichtes Seelenlehre und ihre Beziehung zur Gegenwart'." *Collected Works*, vol. 18.

Jung, C. G. "Foreword to Michael Fordham, 'New Developments in Analytical Psychology.'" *Collected Works*, vol. 18.

Jung, C. G. "Foreword to Perry, 'The Self in Psychotic Process'." *Collected Works*, vol. 18.

Jung, C. G. "Foreword to Von Koenig-Faschenfeld: 'Wandlungen des Traumproblems von der Romantik bis zur Gegenwart'." *Collected Works*, vol. 18.

Jung, C. G. "Jung and Religious Belief." *Collected Works*, vol. 18.

Jung, C. G. "Review of Waldstein: 'Das Unbewusste Ich'." *Collected Works*, vol. 18.

Jung, C. G. "To Markus Fierz." 2 Mar. 1950. *Collected Works*, vol. 18.

Jung, C. G. "The Tavistock Lectures." *Collected Works*, vol. 18.

Kant, I. *Critique of Pure Reason*. Trans. Norman Kemp Smith. London: Macmillan, 1929.

Kant, I. *Critique of Judgment*. 1790. Trans. James Meredith. Rev. ed. Nicholas Walker. Oxford and New York: Oxford UP, 2007.

Keats, J. "Letter to Richard Wodehouse." 27 Oct 1818. *Selected Letters*. Rev. ed. Ed. G. Scott. Cambridge and London: Harvard UP, 2002. 194–196.

Kerr, J. *A Most Dangerous Method: The Story of Jung, Freud, and Sabina Spielrein*. New York: Vintage, 1994.

Kerslake, C. "Rebirth Through Incest: On Deleuze's Early Jungianism." *Angelaki* 9(1); 2004: 135–157.

Kerslake, C. *Deleuze and the Unconscious*. London and New York: Continuum, 2007.

Kerslake, C. "Desire and the Dialectics of Love: Deleuze, Canguilhem, and the Philosophy of Desire." *Deleuze and Psychoanalysis: Philosophical Essays on Deleuze's Debate with Psychoanalysis*. Ed. L. De Bolle. Leuven: Leuven UP, 2010. 51–81.

Kirsch, J. *A Jungian Life*. Carmel, CA: Fisher King Press, 2014.

Kojève, A. *Introduction to the Reading of Hegel: Lectures on the* Phenomenology of Spirit. Trans. James Nichols, Jr. Ithaca and London: Cornell UP, 1980.

Krell, D. *Contagion: Sexuality, Disease, and Death in German Idealism and Romanticism*. Bloomington: Indiana UP, 1998.

Krell, D. "Three Ends of the Absolute: Schelling on Inhibition, Hölderlin on Separation, and Novalis on Density." *Research in Phenomenology* 32; 2002: 60–85.

Krell, D. *The Tragic Absolute: German Idealism and the Languishing of God*. Bloomington and Indianapolis: Indiana UP, 2005.

Lacan, J. "The Mirror Stage as Formative of the *I* Function as Revealed in Psychoanalytic Experience." *Écrits*. Trans. Bruce Fink. New York: Norton, 2002. 75–81.

Lacan, J. "The Situation of Psychoanalysis and the Training of Psychoanalysts in 1956." *Écrits*. Trans. Bruce Fink. New York: Norton, 2002. 384–411.

Lacoue-Labarthe, P. and J-L. Nancy. *The Literary Absolute: The Theory of Literature in German Romanticism*. 1978. Trans. Philip Barnard and Cheryl Lester. Albany: State U of New York P, 1988.

Laplanche, J. and J-B. Pontalis. *The Language of Psycho-Analysis*. Trans. Donald Nicholson-Smith. New York: Norton, 1973.

Levere, T. "Hegel and the Earth Sciences." *Hegels Philosophie der Natur: Beziehungen zwischen empirischer und spekulativer Naturerkenntnis*. Eds. R-P. Horstmann and M. Petry. Stuttgart: Klett-Cotta, 1986. 103–120.

Linafelt, T. "The Undecidability of דרב in the Prologue to Job and Beyond." *Biblical Interpretation* 4(2); 1996: 154–172.

Lyotard, J-F. *Discourse, Figure*. Trans. Antony Hudek and Mary Lydon. Minneapolis: U of Minnesota P, 2011.

Matthews, B. "Translator's Introduction." *The Grounding of Positive Philosophy: The Berlin Lectures*. F. Schelling. Trans. Bruce Matthews. Albany: State U of New York P, 2007. 1–84.

Matthews, B. "The New Mythology: Romanticism Between Religion and Humanism." *The Relevance of Romanticism: Essays on German Romantic Philosophy*. Ed. D. Nassar. New York: Oxford UP, 2014. 202–218.

McGann, J. *The Romantic Ideology: A Critical Investigation*. Chicago: U of Chicago P, 1983.

McGrath, S. "Is Schelling's Nature-Philosophy Freudian?" *Analecta Hermeneutica* 3; 2011: 1–20.

McGrath, S. *The Dark Ground of Spirit: Schelling and the Unconscious*. New York: Routledge, 2012.

McGrath, S. "The Question Concerning Metaphysics: A Schellingian Intervention in Analytical Psychology." *International Journal of Jungian Studies* 6(1); 2014: 23–51.

McGrath, S. "Schelling and the History of the Dissociative Self." *Symposium* 19(1); 2015: 52–66.

Mesmer, F. A. "*Dissertation by F.A. Mesmer, Doctor of Medicine, on his Discoveries*." *Mesmerism: A Translation of the Original Scientific and Medical Writings of F.A. Mesmer*. Trans. George Bloch. Los Altos, CA: William Kaufman, 1980. 87–132.

Mesmer, F. A. "Dissertation on the Discovery of Animal Magnetism." *Mesmerism: A Translation of the Original Scientific and Medical Writings of F.A. Mesmer*. Trans. George Bloch. Los Altos, CA: William Kaufman, 1980. 41–78.

Milton, J. *Paradise Lost*. Introduced by John Pullman. Oxford: Oxford UP, 2005.

Mitchell, R. and R. Broglio. "Introduction." *Romanticism and the New Deleuze* 2008. Romantic Circles Praxis Series (RCPS). https://romantic-circles.org/praxis/deleuze/index.html. Accessed 16 June 2019.

Mitchell, R. *Experimental Life: Vitalism in Romantic Science and Literature*. Baltimore: Johns Hopkins UP, 2013.

Molnár, G. v. *Romantic Vision, Ethical Context: Novalis and Artistic Autonomy*. Minneapolis: U of Minnesota P, 1987.

Monahan, P. "C.G. Jung: Freud's Heir or Janet's? The Influence upon Jung of Janet's Dissociationism." *International Journal of Jungian Studies* 1(1); 2009: 33–49.

Nassar, D. *The Romantic Absolute: Being and Knowing in Early German Romantic Philosophy, 1795-1804*. Chicago and London: U of Chicago P, 2014.

Nauen, F. *Revolution, Idealism and Human Freedom: Schelling Hölderlin and Hegel and the Crisis of Early German Idealism*. The Hague: Martinus Nijhoff, 1971.

Nietzsche, F. "On Truth and Lying in a Non-Moral Sense." *The Birth of Tragedy and Other Writings*. Trans. Ronald Speirs. Cambridge: Cambridge UP, 1999. 139–53.

Nietzsche, F. *The Birth of Tragedy*. *The Birth of Tragedy and Other Writings*. Trans. Ronald Speirs. Cambridge: Cambridge UP, 1999. 1–116.

Noll, R. *The Jung Cult: Origins of a Charismatic Movement*. 1994. New York and London: Free Press, 1997.

Novalis. "Faith and Love or the King and Queen." *Philosophical Writings*. Trans. Margaret Stoljar. Albany: State U of New York P, 1997. 85–100.

Novalis. "Logological Fragments." *Philosophical Writings*. Trans. Margaret Stoljar. Albany: State U of New York P, 1997. 47–81.

Novalis. *The Novices of Sais*. Trans. Ralph Manheim. Brooklyn: Archipelago Books, 2005.

Novalis. *Notes for a Romantic Encyclopedia (Das Allgemeine Brouillon)*. Trans. David Wood. Albany: State U of New York P, 2007.

Onorato, R. *The Character of the Poet: Wordsworth in The Prelude*. Princeton: Princeton UP, 1971.

Pauli W. and C. G. Jung. *Ein Briefwechsel 1932-1958*. Heraus. von C.A. Meier. Berlin: Springer Verlag, 1992.

Peeters, B. *Derrida: A Biography*. Trans. Andrew Brown. Cambridge: Polity, 2013.

Peterson, K. "Translator's Introduction." *First Outline of a System of the Philosophy of Nature*. F. Schelling. Trans. Keith Peterson. Albany: State U of New York P, 2004. xi–xxxv.

Pfau, T. *Romantic Moods: Paranoia, Trauma, and Melancholy 1790-1840*. Baltimore: Johns Hopkins UP, 2005.

Pinkard, T. *German Philosophy 1760-1860: The Legacy of Idealism*. Cambridge: Cambridge UP, 2002.

Pippin, R. "On Not Being a Neostructuralist: Remarks on Manfred Frank and Romantic Subjectivity." *The Persistence of Subjectivity: On the Kantian Aftermath*. Cambridge: Cambridge UP, 2005. 168–185.

Plotnitsky, A. "Conclusion: Without Absolutes." *Idealism Without Absolutes: Philosophy and Romantic Culture*. Eds. T. Rajan and A. Plotnitsky. Albany: State U of New York P, 2004. 241–251.

Plotnitsky, A. "Curvatures: Hegel and the Baroque." *Idealism Without Absolutes: Philosophy and Romantic Culture.* Eds. T. Rajan and A. Plotnitsky. Albany: State U of New York P, 2004. 113–134.

Plotnitsky, A. "The Calculable Law of Tragic Representation and the Unthinkable: Rhythm, Caesura, and Time, from Hölderlin to Deleuze." *At the Edges of Thought: Deleuze and Post-Kantian Philosophy.* Eds. C. Lundy and D. Voss. Edinburgh: Edinburgh UP, 2015. 123–145.

Plug, J. "Romanticism and the Invention of Literature." *Intersections: Nineteenth-Century Philosophy and Contemporary Theory.* Eds. T. Rajan and D. Clark. Albany: State U of New York P, 1995. 15–37.

Rajan, T. *Dark Interpreter: The Discourse of Romanticism.* Ithaca: Cornell UP, 1980.

Rajan, T. "Romanticism and the Death of Lyric Consciousness." *Lyric Poetry: Beyond New Criticism.* Eds. C. Hosek and P. Parker. Ithaca: Cornell UP, 1985. 194–207.

Rajan, T. *The Supplement of Reading: Figures of Understanding in Romantic Theory and Practice.* Ithaca: Cornell UP, 1990.

Rajan, T. "Phenomenology and Romantic Theory: Hegel and the Subversion of Aesthetics." *Questioning Romanticism.* Ed. J. Beer. Baltimore: Johns Hopkins UP, 1995. 155–178.

Rajan, T. *Deconstruction and the Remainders of Phenomenology: Sartre, Derrida, Foucault, Baudrillard.* Stanford: Stanford UP, 2002.

Rajan, T. and A. Plotnitsky Eds. *Idealism Without Absolutes: Philosophy and Romantic Culture.* Albany: State U of New York P, 2004.

Rajan, T. "Introduction." *Idealism Without Absolutes: Philosophy and Romantic Culture.* Eds. T. Rajan and A. Plotnitsky. Albany: State U of New York P, 2004. 1–14.

Rajan, T. "Philosophy as Encyclopedia: Hegel, Schelling and the Organization of Knowledge." *Wordsworth Circle* 35(1); 2004: 6–11.

Rajan, T. "First Outline of a System of Theory: Schelling and the Margins of Philosophy, 1799-1815." *Studies in Romanticism* 46(3); 2007: 311–335.

Rajan, T. "The Encyclopedia and the University of Theory: Idealism and the Organization of Knowledge." *Textual Practice* 21(2); 2007: 335–338.

Rajan, T. "'The Abyss of the Past': Psychoanalysis in Schelling's *Ages of the World* (1815)." *Romantic Psyche and Psychoanalysis.* 2008. Romantic Circles Praxis Series (RCPS). https://romantic-circles.org/category/praxis-series/romantic-psyche-and-psychoanalysis. Accessed 31 May 2009.

Rapp, D. "The Early Discovery of Freud by the British General Educated Public, 1912-1919." *Social History of Medicine* 3(2); 1990: 217–243.

Richards, R. *The Romantic Conception of Life: Science and Philosophy in the Age of Goethe.* Chicago and London: U of Chicago P, 2002.

Ricoeur, P. *Freud and Philosophy: An Essay on Interpretation.* New Haven and London: Yale UP, 1970.

Rowland, S. "Jung and Derrida: The Numinous, Deconstruction, and Myth." *The Idea of the Numinous: Contemporary Jungian and Psychoanalytic Perspectives.*

Eds. A. Casement and D. Tacey. London and New York: Routledge, 2006. 98–116.

Rudwick, M. *Bursting the Limits of Time: The Reconstruction of History in the Age of Revolution.* Chicago and London: U of Chicago P, 2005.

Samuels, A. "Transference/countertransference." *The Handbook of Jungian Psychology: Theory, Practice and Applications.* Ed. R. Papadoupoulos. London and New York: Routledge, 2006. 177–195.

Schelling, F. W. J. *Sämmtliche Werke.* Ed. K. Schelling. 14 vols. Stuttgart/ Augsburg: J.G. Cotta'scher Verlag, 1856–1861.

Schelling, F. W. J. *System of Transcendental Idealism (1800).* Trans. Peter Heath. Charlottesville: UP of Virginia, 1978.

Schelling, F. W. J. *Philosophical Letters on Dogmatism and Criticism. The Unconditional in Human Knowledge: Four Early Essays (1794-1796).* Trans. Fritz Marti. Cranbury, NJ: Associated U Presses, 1980. 151–196.

Schelling, F. W. J. *Ideas for a Philosophy of Nature.* Trans. Errol Harris and Peter Heath. Cambridge: Cambridge UP, 1988.

Schelling, F. W. J. *The Philosophy of Art.* Trans. Douglas Stott. Minneapolis: U of Minnesota P, 1989.

Schelling, F. W. J. *On the History of Modern Philosophy.* Trans. Andrew Bowie. Cambridge: Cambridge UP, 1994.

Schelling, F. W. J. *The Ages of the World [1813]. The Abyss of Freedom/Ages of the World.* Trans. Judith Norman. Ann Arbor, MI: U of Michigan P, 1997. 105–182.

Schelling, F. W. J. "On the Nature of Philosophy as Science." Trans. Marcus Weigelt. *German Idealist Philosophy.* Ed. R. Bubner. London and New York: Penguin, 1997. 210–243.

Schelling, F. W. J. *The Ages of the World (Fragment), From the Handwritten Remains: Third Version (1815).* Trans. Jason Wirth. Albany: State U of New York P, 2000.

Schelling, F. W. J. *First Outline of a System of the Philosophy of Nature.* Trans. Keith Peterson. Albany: State U of New York P, 2004.

Schelling, F. W. J. *Philosophical Investigations into the Essence of Human Freedom.* Trans. Jeff Love and Johannes Schmidt. Albany: State U of New York P, 2006.

Schelling, F. W. J. *Historical-Critical Introduction to the Philosophy of Mythology.* Trans. Mason Richey and Markus Zisselsberger. Albany: State U of New York P, 2007.

Schelling, F. W. J. *The Grounding of Positive Philosophy: The Berlin Lectures.* Trans. Bruce Matthews. Albany: State U of New York P, 2007.

Schelling, F. W. J. *Philosophy and Religion.* Trans. Klaus Ottmann. Putnam, CO: Spring Publications, 2010.

Schelling, F. W. J. *On the World-Soul.* 1798. Trans. Iain Hamilton Grant. Albany: State U of New York P, forthcoming.

Schlegel, F. *Blütenstaub. Philosophical Fragments.* Trans. Peter Firchow. Minneapolis: U of Minnesota P, 1991. 17.

Schlegel, F. *Philosophical Fragments*. Trans. Peter Firchow. Minneapolis: U of Minnesota P, 1991.

Sha, R. *Perverse Romanticism: Aesthetics and Sexuality in Britain, 1750-1832*. Baltimore: Johns Hopkins UP, 2009.

Shamdasani, S. *Jung and the Making of Modern Psychology: The Dream of a Science*. Cambridge: Cambridge UP, 2003.

Shamdasani, S. *Jung Stripped Bare by His Biographers, Even*. London and New York: Karnac, 2005.

Shamdasani, S. "Introduction." *Jung Contra Freud: The 1912 New York Lectures on the Theory of Psychoanalysis*. C. G. Jung. Trans. R.F.C. Hull. Princeton: Princeton UP, 2012. vii–xix.

Shamdasani, S. *C.G. Jung: A Biography in Books*. New York: Norton, 2012.

Shelley, P. B. "To Wordsworth." *The Poems of Shelley, Volume 1: 1804-1817*. Eds. G. Matthews and K. Everest. London and New York: Longman, 1989. 454–455.

Shelley, P. B. *Prometheus Unbound: A Lyrical Drama in Four Acts. The Poems of Shelley, Volume Two: 1817-1819*. Eds. K. Everest and G. Matthews. Harlow: Pearson, 2000. 456–654.

Shelley, P. B. "A Defence of Poetry." *Shelley's Poetry and Prose*. 2nd ed. Eds. D. Reiman and N. Fraistat. New York: Norton, 2002. 509–535.

Shelley, P. B. "On Life." *Shelley's Poetry and Prose*. 2nd ed. Eds. D. Reiman and N. Fraistat. New York: Norton, 2002. 505–509.

Simondon, G. *L'Individuation Psychique et Collective*. 1989. Paris: Editions Aubier, 2007.

Simondon, G. "The Position of the Problem of Ontogenesis." Trans. Gregory Flanders. *Parrhesia* 7; 2009: 4–16.

Simons, T. "Prometheus and the Process of Individuation: A Jungian Reading of Shelley's *Prometheus Unbound*." *Journal of Jungian Scholarly Studies* 2; 2006. http://jungiansociety.org/images/e-journal/Volume-2/Simons-2006.pdf. Accessed 16 June 2019.

Simpson, D. "Romanticism, Criticism and Theory." *The Cambridge Companion to British Romanticism*. Ed. S. Curran. Cambridge: Cambridge UP, 1993. 1–24.

Sitterson, J. "Oedipus in the Stolen Boat: Psychoanalysis and Subjectivity in *The Prelude*." *Studies in Philology* 86(1); 1989: 96–115.

Snow, D. *Schelling and the End of Idealism*. Albany: State U of New York P, 1996.

Somers-Hall, H. *Deleuze's* Difference and Repetition*: An Edinburgh Philosophical Guide*. Edinburgh: Edinburgh UP, 2013.

Steigerwald, J. "Degeneration: Inversions of Teleology." *Marking Time: Romanticism and Evolution*. Ed. J. Faflak. Toronto: University of Toronto Press, 2017. 270–299.

Steinberg, W. "The Evolution of Jung's Ideas on the Transference." *Journal of Analytical Psychology* 33; 1988: 21–37.

Stevens, A. "The Archetypes." *The Handbook of Jungian Psychology: Theory, Practice and Applications*. Ed. R. Papadopoulos. London and New York: Routledge, 2006. 74–93.

Vater, M. "Introduction." *System of Transcendental Idealism (1800)*. F. Schelling. Trans. Peter Heath, Charlottesville: UP of Virginia, 1978. xi–xxxvi.

Vidal, F. *The Sciences of the Soul: The Early Modern Origins of Psychology*. Trans. Saskia Brown. Chicago and London: U of Chicago P, 2011.

Voogd, S de. "C.G. Jung: Psychologist of the Future, 'Philosopher' of the Past." *Spring* 1977: 175–182.

Warnek, P. "Prolegomena to Monstrous Philosophy or Why it is Necessary to Read Schelling Today." *Comparative and Continental Philosophy* 6(1); 2014: 49–67.

Wasserman, E. *Shelley: A Critical Reading*. Baltimore: Johns Hopkins UP, 1971.

Weeks, A. *German Mysticism from Hildegard of Bingen to Ludwig Wittgenstein: A Literary and Intellectual History*. Albany: State U of New York P, 1993.

Weiskel, T. *The Romantic Sublime: Studies in the Structure and Psychology of Transcendence*. Baltimore: Johns Hopkins UP, 1976.

Welchman, A. "Schopenhauer and Deleuze." *At the Edges of Thought: Deleuze and Post-Kantian Philosophy*. Eds. C. Lundy and D. Voss. Edinburgh: Edinburgh UP, 2015. 231–252.

White, A. *Schelling: An Introduction to the System of Freedom*. New Haven and London: Yale UP, 1983.

Whyte, L. *The Unconscious Before Freud*. New York: Anchor Books, 1962.

Williams, J. *Gilles Deleuze's* Difference and Repetition*: A Critical Introduction and Guide*. Edinburgh: Edinburgh UP, 2003.

Wilson, D. *The Romantic Dream: Wordsworth and the Poetics of the Unconscious*. Lincoln and London: U of Nebraska P, 1993.

Wilson, E. *The Spiritual History of Ice: Romanticism, Science, and the Imagination*. New York: Palgrave Macmillan, 2003.

Wirth, J. "Translator's Introduction." *The Ages of the World (Fragment), From the Handwritten Remains: Third Version (1815)*. F. Schelling. Trans. Jason Wirth. Albany: State U of New York P, 2000. vii–xxxii.

Wirth, J. *The Conspiracy of Life: Meditations on Schelling and His Time*. Albany: State U of New York P, 2003.

Wirth, J. *Schelling's Practice of the Wild: Time, Art, Imagination*. Albany: State U of New York P, 2015.

Woodman, R. *Sanity, Madness, Transformation: The Psyche in Romanticism*. Ed. J. Faflak. Toronto: U of Toronto P, 2005.

Wordsworth, W. "Preface to *The Excursion*." *The Prose Works of William Wordsworth*. 3 vols. Eds. W. J. B. Owen and J. Smyser. Vol. 3. London: Oxford UP, 1974. 1–12.

Wordsworth, W. "The Sublime and the Beautiful." *The Prose Works of William Wordsworth*. 3 vols. Eds. W. J. B. Owen and J. Smyser. Vol. 2. London: Oxford UP, 1974. 349–360.

Wordsworth, W. "Introduction: The Growth of the Two-Part *Prelude*." *The Prelude, 1798-1799*. Ed. S. Parrish. Ithaca: Cornell UP, 1977. 3–36.

Wordsworth, W. *The Poems*. 2 vols. Ed. J. Hayden. New Haven and London: Yale UP, 1981.

Wordsworth, W. *The Fourteen-Book Prelude*. Ed. W. J. B. Owen. Ithaca and London: Cornell UP, 1985.

Wordsworth, W. *The Thirteen-Book Prelude*. 2 vols. Ed. M. Reed. Ithaca and London: Cornell UP, 1991.

Wu, D. *Wordsworth's Reading 1770-1799*. Cambridge: Cambridge UP, 1993.

Young, E, Genosko, G. and Watson, J. "Sense." *The Deleuze & Guattari Dictionary*. London and New York: Bloomsbury, 2013. 278–279.

Young-Eisendrath, P. *Subject to Change: Jung, Gender and Subjectivity in Psychoanalysis*. New York: Brunner-Routledge, 2004.

Zabriskie, B. "Jung and Pauli: A Meeting of Rare Minds." *Atom and Archetype: The Pauli-Jung Letters, 1932-1958*. Trans. David Roscoe. Ed. C. A. Meier. London and New York: Routledge, 2001. xxvii-l.

Žižek, S. "The Cartesian Subject Versus the Cartesian Theater." *Cogito and the Unconscious*. Ed. S Žižek. Durham and London: Duke UP, 1998. 247–274.

Žižek, S. "Foreword." *Ethics of the Real: Kant, Lacan*. A Zupančič. London: Verso, 2000. vii–xiii.

Žižek, S. *The Ticklish Subject: The Absent Centre of Political Ontology*. London: Verso, 2008.

Index